FOUNDATIONS FOR ORGANIZATIONAL SCIENCE

A Sage Publications Series

Series Editor

David Whetten, *Brigham Young University*

Editors

Anne S. Huff, *University of Colorado* and *Cranfield University* (UK)
Benjamin Schneider, *University of Maryland*
M. Susan Taylor, *University of Maryland*

The FOUNDATIONS FOR ORGANIZATIONAL SCIENCE series supports the development of students, faculty, and prospective organizational science professionals through the publication of texts authored by leading organizational scientists. Each volume provides a highly personal, hands-on introduction to a core topic or theory and challenges the reader to explore promising avenues for future theory development and empirical application.

Books in This Series

Dennis W. Organ • Philip M. Podsakoff • Scott B. MacKenzie

Organizational Citizenship Behavior

Its Nature, Antecedents, and Consequences

Foundations for
Organizational
Science
A Sage Publications Series

SAGE Publications
Thousand Oaks ■ London ■ New Delhi

For information:

Sage Publications, Inc.
2455 Teller Road
Thousand Oaks, California 91320
E-mail: order@sagepub.com

Sage Publications Ltd.
1 Oliver's Yard
55 City Road
London EC1Y 1SP
United Kingdom

Sage Publications India Pvt. Ltd.
B-42, Panchsheel Enclave
Post Box 4109
New Delhi 110 017 India

Printed in the United States of America

Library of Congress Cataloging-in-Publication Data

Organ, Dennis W.
Organizational citizenship behavior: Its nature, antecedents, and
consequences / Dennis W. Organ, Philip M. Podsakoff, Scott B. MacKenzie.
    p. cm. — (Foundations for organizational science)
Includes bibliographical references and index.
ISBN 0-7619-2995-9 (cloth) — ISBN 0-7619-2996-7 (pbk.)
    1. Organizational behavior. 2. Organizational effectiveness. 3. Psychology,
Industrial. 4. Job satisfaction. I. Podsakoff, Philip M. II. MacKenzie, Scott Bradley,
1954 – III. Title. IV. Series.
HD58.7.O6682 2006
158.7—dc22   2005008598

This book is printed on acid-free paper.

05   06   07   08   09   8   7   6   5   4   3   2   1

Acquisitions Editor:	Al Bruckner
Editorial Assistant:	Maryann Vail
Production Editor:	Diane S. Foster
Copy Editor:	Meredith L. Brittain
Typesetter:	C&M Digitals (P) Ltd.
Proofreader:	Kevin Gleason
Indexer:	Molly Hall
Cover Designer:	Edgar Abarca

Contents

This book is dedicated to:
Ann Smith, a good soldier to the end (DWO)
Vernie and Nathan, who have been good sports throughout this process (PMP)
Jane, Sarah, Karen, Matthew, Katherine, Caroline, and the God we love and serve (SBM)

1 The Good Sam

"Dennis! The paper mill wants you on the phone!" Thus did my mother interrupt a most pleasant Saturday evening in the summer of 1962. I was sitting in my sister's upstairs bedroom watching the movie *People Will Talk* (starring Cary Grant and Jeanne Crain) on her television. An afternoon of tennis and a steak supper had put me in a mellow mood that welcomed passive entertainment. I came downstairs to take the call, and the voice on the other end confirmed my foreboding: I was needed on the third shift in the shipping department, meaning I had to go to work at 11 p.m., or in about two hours. I went back upstairs to finish watching the movie, but the mood just wasn't the same anymore.

The "call board"—the arrangement by which the local paper mill employed college-bound youths in the summer—had struck again. The call board called you when the paper mill needed you, usually on short notice, more often than not on the third shift. You might come in for one night only, or you might fill in for a week or more. Regardless, after the regular worker returned, your name went back to the bottom of the call board, and you waited again to be called when needed. The pay was good, and you really did want the work, but sometimes the call came when you really did not want to be summoned.

I dutifully checked into the shipping department just before the start of the third shift to find out what kind of work I would be doing. The type of job performed by call board workers varied, but it always involved minimal learning time. Or so I thought.

On this particular night, my assignment was to push large rolls of paper off an elevator and fit metal bands around each end of each roll. Pushing the rolls of paper off the elevator toward the loading dock

---

Author's Note: The opening anecdote is based on the first author's personal experience.

was not a problem, although the task was strenuous (each roll was about 8 feet long, 6 feet in diameter, and weighed half a ton or more). The tricky part was attaching the metal bands with a special tool that contained a large, tightly wound spool of banding that enabled its user to simultaneously cut and staple the ends of the band around the paper. Most people probably could have mastered this operation in a few trials, but not me—mechanical aptitude has never been my forte (to this day, I still cannot competently use a tire pressure gauge on either my car or my bicycle, managing only to let air escape through the valve).

I worked fitfully during the first hour or two. I must have wasted a lot of that metal banding, and I suspect that somewhere between North Carolina and Georgia several rolls of paper came unwound on the railroad cars. The elevator hewed to its relentless schedule of greeting me, tauntingly, with a load of paper every 15 or 20 minutes. In my frustration-charged imagination I could imagine all of the regular paper mill workers amusing themselves at the spectacle of a college boy without enough common sense to bind rolls of paper.

Fortunately, the disaster potential in the situation was never realized. One of the regular paper mill employees working nearby could see my struggle and came over to help. Several times he helped tighten a wobbly band, unhook the stapler, or reload or rewind the metal spool. Once he even came over to help push the backed-up rolls of paper farther down the floor so there would be room for unloading the next elevator's load. With his timely aid and totally patient and uncritical manner, I managed to cope. I did not reach the stage of panic that would have induced me to walk off the job and forgo my earnings; the general foreman did not have to order the monstrous paper machines shut down; the shift was not paralyzed by the bottleneck of a klutzy operator. Although I never became a virtuoso with that special tool for binding rolls of paper, to my knowledge none of the paper mill's customers perished for want of brown wrapping paper.

The fellow who helped me out (let us refer to him as Sam, short for the Good *Sam*aritan) has no doubt long since forgotten this episode, having attached little significance to what he did. He, along with many other workers at the paper mill, probably rendered such humble aid hundreds of times over the course of a month's work. I, however, attached enormous significance to the incident at the time, and also later, when I related it to my study of organizations.

Sam's assistance represents what we call organizational citizenship behavior (OCB).

The Anatomy of a Helping Hand

Let us analyze Sam's behavior. First, the assistance that he gave was not part of his job duties; he had his own work to do. We have no idea what his formal job description was, but we are confident that if such a document existed it made no reference to an obligation to assist call board college-bound chaps with ten left thumbs. Second, the assistance was spontaneous, at least as far as I could tell. The shipping foreman, who wasn't around much during the third shift, had not directed him to do this. In fact, the assistance was not preceded even by any overt request. Third, Sam's actions didn't result in any prize from the organization's formal reward system—he received no bonus pay, no brownie points, no citations. (Sam did, of course, earn Dennis's considerable gratitude, a token of which was demonstrated later in the evening when Dennis helped Sam, in the course of which Dennis toppled a 200-pound roll of paper onto his own foot and broke his toe. This ironic epilogue to the story probably explains the durability of Dennis's memory of the evening.)

Fourth, although Sam's assistance was not part of his job and gained him no formal accolades, he undeniably contributed in a small way to the functioning of the group and, by extension, to the plant and the organization as a whole. By itself, his aid to one individual might not have been perceptible in any conventional measures of efficiency, production, or profits. However, if such helping actions were repeated many times over by Sam and others, the aggregate of such actions over time must certainly have made that paper mill a more smoothly functioning organization than would have been the case if such actions were rare.

In essence, then, we have used the example of Sam's behavior and our analysis of its properties to define what we and others in the field now call organizational citizenship behavior (OCB): *Individual behavior that is discretionary, not directly or explicitly recognized by the formal reward system, and in the aggregate promotes the efficient and effective functioning of the organization.*

Is OCB the Same as Altruism?

The reader might justifiably question whether Sam's actions are novel or profound. After all, he simply helped another person. Like the Good Samaritan from the account given in Luke 10:30–37, he saw someone in need and gave assistance. The Good Samaritan in the Bible didn't *have* to do this. In fact, two other persons, including a priest, had earlier noticed the distressed individual and passed by without stopping to assist him. And as far as we know, the Good Samaritan was altruistic (selfless) in that he did not gain anything of substance from his ministration to the stranger. Whether the act of helping made the community more "efficient" or "effective" is debatable. Still, one could certainly argue that a community in which most people freely help those in need would probably offer a greater quality of life for its people, compared to a community in which such helping is infrequent.

In fact, researchers' early thinking about OCB (see Organ, 1988, Chapter 3) was influenced by a substantial body of theory and research in social psychology on prosocial behavior. This type of behavior takes many forms, such as helping someone in the shopping mall pick up dropped parcels, making a phone call on behalf of a stranded motorist, or helping someone find a lost contact lens. The common denominator of such episodes is that *prosocial behavior* is spontaneously directed toward the benefit of a specific individual (usually a stranger), with no apparent prospect of extrinsic reward to the person giving aid.

A review by Krebs (1970) of the considerable empirical literature on prosocial behavior to that point identified mood state as the most strongly supported antecedent of such actions. Experimental studies in naturalistic settings find that if unwary subjects, for whom some good fortune had been contrived to happen, subsequently encountered someone in need of help, they were more likely to offer such help than subjects for whom no such good fortune had been contrived. And in laboratory studies, subjects who received contrived ego-enhancing feedback following some task were more likely than subjects who didn't receive such feedback to offer help later in another contrived situation where such help was ostensibly needed. The inference is that people who are in a good mood, for whatever reason, are more likely to respond constructively to a stranger's plight or a worthy cause.

Conversely, many studies (e.g., Cohen, 1980) have found that subjects are less likely to render prosocial behavior when they are placed under greater than normal stress. Whether the stressor is loud and aversive noise, information overload, a depressing movie, or approaching midterm exams, it seems to inhibit spontaneous helping to needy persons or charitable organizations.

An apparent contradiction to results of this research, however, is the finding that negative mood can actually increase the likelihood of helping (Cialdini & Kenrick, 1976), because in some instances people believe that helping someone will mitigate a bad mood state. For example, students who have just done poorly on an exam might think that a good way to brighten up their outlook would be to visit a friend who is in the infirmary with the flu. Another possible reason for spontaneous helping is that it could offer a temporary distraction from whatever might be causing the negative mood. A former dean of the Indiana University School of Business once remarked that he was much more inclined to help his wife with household chores when the alternative was to work on his income tax returns.

Mood is not the only factor associated with prosocial behavior. Krebs (1970) concluded that to some extent, helping others is a function of how deeply one has internalized a norm or conviction that it is a person's duty to provide help when the costs to the helper are not unreasonable. In addition, some studies (e.g., Macauley, 1970) have found that we are more likely to help when we see that others have done so; in other words, charitable behavior can be modeled. And one should also not overlook more mundane reasons to explain why someone does or does not help. Darley & Batson (1973) conducted a study in which people who were in a hurry because of a prior engagement (in fact, they were rushing to a lecture on the parable of the Good Samaritan!) were less inclined to attend to a moaning derelict than those who were not so rushed.

Although it is unclear whether there is such a thing as a "prosocial personality," some suggestive findings indicate that a somewhat greater tendency toward helping exists among those who are socially well adjusted, generally lacking in neurotic symptoms, and extroverted (Krebs, 1970). Moreover, because positive affect is a key factor in helping, and if—as we now have reason to believe (see Watson & Tellegen, 1985)—individuals differ characteristically in frequency of positive or negative affect, then some dimension of personality appears to be implicated in helping behavior as well.

This brief review of evidence and theory on prosocial behavior shows why it seemed to offer a promising framework in which to study OCB. Prosocial behavior is spontaneous, occurs without prospect of compensation, and can be a function of mood, an internalized norm, the time available, and/or stable individual differences. All of these factors could fit the Sam episode. Maybe Sam was in a good mood the night he helped me at the paper mill, and perhaps he was generally in a good mood at work. He had the time to divert from his own work to help someone. Conceivably he had seen others do this at work. Or possibly he was just one of those people who believe in the obligation to respond as he did.

However, although many of the instances of OCB could fit into the prosocial behavior framework, we feel that the social psychology of prosocial behavior is not fully adequate for our purposes, for several reasons.

First, we have identified other forms of OCB, such as impersonal conscientiousness and involvement in workplace governance, that do not represent forms of immediate help for a specific person. Although OCB probably benefits a number of persons ultimately, to the extent that it contributes to organizational effectiveness, some OCB does not have as its focus an individual needing help in the here and now.

Second, the "organizational" in OCB is important. Much of the work on prosocial behavior has to do with helping strangers in one-shot episodes, with the helper anticipating little if any recurrent interaction with the person helped. Our concern is with cumulative patterns of contributions to people with whom one is involved in some collective enterprise. In other words, OCB occurs in settings that have significant structure, context, and continuity. One could extend altruistic helping to many strangers, but the single episodes of helping are not connected toward some more focused end. That is, helping a homeless person today is independent of assisting a mall shopper tomorrow. On the other hand, tutoring a new hire today and making suggestions today for achieving on-time delivery are related in the sense that they both have constructive effects on organizational functioning.

However, comparing prosocial behavior or altruism with OCB does raise the question of motive.

Is OCB Defined by Its Motivation?

If we attach major significance to a helping action, shouldn't the motive for the action figure into our definition or labeling of the behavior? In the case of paper mill worker Sam, we frankly doubt that any premeditated, conscious motive was at work. Given the spontaneity of the help, we cannot imagine that Sam engaged in any conscious or serious analysis of the pros and cons of stopping his own work and lending a hand. Of course, what we term a "motive" need not be of the consciously calculated variety—motives can silently shape and govern our behavior in the background without calling attention to themselves. If Sam had been asked, "Why are you doing this?" and were given ample time to introspect (while being encouraged to be both explicit and thoroughly honest), he might have answered in one of the following ways:

"If I don't help this dude out, sooner or later we're all going to have a king-sized mess."

"It bothers me to see the kid screwing up. I've been in spots like that myself, and I know how it feels."

"If I do my part, and if I do a little extra when it's needed, in the long run, somehow, I'll get what I deserve. Eventually, the ones who put out get it all back."

"I don't know where they got this kid, or why they put him in here, but I just can't stand by and see a job botched."

"It wouldn't be right to just ignore somebody having trouble, because it won't take much time or effort for me to go over and help him out."

"Anything I do to help keep things running smoothly is going to be noticed by somebody. It all adds up to determine how I stand in the group and what the foreman thinks of me. Sooner or later, I'm pretty sure that it will make a difference in terms of how the boss treats me or what the rest of the crew thinks of me."

Any or all of these reasons might have been given, or maybe none of them. Some of the explanations are more admirable than others. The answer Sam would have given would probably have been different than the answer of someone else who had done the same thing.

Our position is that OCB, like most human behaviors, is caused by multiple and overlapping motives. Sam might have helped, in part, for selfish reasons, but that does not rule out the possibility that other reasons—such as affiliation (the desire to have positive relationships with other people), power (the kind of power that comes about from people being in debt to you for favors), or organization loyalty—also were at play.

Ultimately, if we regard Sam's assistance as representing a theoretically significant phenomenon, we are bound to ask what conditions increase or decrease its likelihood of occurrence. However, our contention is that understanding the proximal motive for OCB is not essential to our appreciation of it, nor to our recognition, definition, or understanding of it. In the definition of OCB, then, that we presented earlier in this chapter, we excluded from it any qualifiers about motive. In Chapter 4, we discuss some motivational issues that pertain to the prediction and explanation of OCB, but our interest in doing so at that point is to identify the antecedents of OCB, not to define it.

Let's look more closely at the definition of OCB that we presented earlier in this chapter: *Individual behavior that is discretionary, not directly or explicitly recognized by the formal reward system, and in the aggregate promotes the efficient and effective functioning of the organization.* By *discretionary,* we mean that the specific behavior in a specific context is not an absolute requirement of the job description (that is, the literal or clearly specifiable terms of the person's employment contract with the organization). Rather, the behavior involves some degree of personal choice, such that the person will not be punished if he or she chooses not to engage in the behavior. Thus, college professors who prep for their courses, teach, do research, and write are not, by our construction, exhibiting OCB, no matter how good their teaching and research are judged by others. Similarly, the mail carrier who reliably courses the route and delivers the letters and magazines safely to the mailboxes does not, on that account, demonstrate OCB. In both instances, the professor and the postal carrier enact their contractual obligations to the employing organization. If each does so with superior performance, that would, of course, be praiseworthy, but not all praiseworthy job performance fits the criterion we wish to use for OCB.

Our definition of OCB requires that it is *not directly or explicitly recognized by the formal reward system* of the employing organization. Consider the case of a department store salesperson. That person must demonstrate some minimal standards of job knowledge, competence, and effort to meet the contractual obligations of the job. Of course, some level of sales is also expected. Some of the staff will exert a level of effort just sufficient to meet that goal. Others will exert effort to attain sales well beyond that goal, and doing so would generally be regarded as discretionary, because a lower level of sales would be sufficient to meet minimal job requirements. However, to the extent that sales beyond the standard level contractually qualifies for higher pay, we would not regard this particular dimension of discretionary performance as OCB—although we probably would regard it as meritorious, even virtuous.

On the other hand, a sales clerk who clearly went beyond the call of duty to assist a customer *after* the successful closure of a transaction would meet the definition of OCB. So would help given to a colleague, such as helping him or her resolve a complaint voiced by a past or prospective customer.

The reader may ask: Do you mean that OCB must be limited to those gestures that are utterly lacking in any tangible return to the individual who demonstrates them? Not necessarily. Over time, a steady stream of OCB of different types (in Chapter 2, we identify several qualitatively different subsets of OCB) could determine the impression of an individual held by a supervisor or coworkers. That impression, in turn, could influence the recommendation by the boss for a salary increase, a job upgrade, a promotion, or incremental job resources (e.g., a new computer, company car, or increased budget). The important distinction is that such rewards must be *not* contractually guaranteed by any formal policies and procedures, at best probabilistic in nature, at most an inference on the part of the individual who contemplates such returns, and their attainment must be uncertain in terms of time and manner. In other words, a person demonstrating OCB may certainly hope that in some rough, vaguely defined manner the behavior eventually brings some returns, but not in any point-for-point, one-to-one correspondence between specific action and specific reward as promised by written or verbal guarantees. Or, worded somewhat differently, a person may render OCB on the assumption that this is a discretionary increment to the person's total contribution to the organization and that in the long run the person's total contribution secures an equitable or just recompense. (We have much more to say about equity and justice in Chapter 4, and we shall see that OCB can and does bear upon eventual rewards received by those whose OCB is regarded as estimable.)

The reader is forgiven for thinking that we have here a rather slippery distinction concerning the reward versus nonreward criterion for OCB. The degree to which contributions are rewarded in an organization is a continuum—at one extreme a contribution is certain not to be rewarded, and at the other extreme it is certain to be rewarded, with varying degrees of probability in between. What we are doing is simplifying the issue, for purposes of argument, by containing OCB within that region of discretionary contributions that are regarded by the person as more uncertain as to whether, when, and how they might be rewarded or are less likely to lead along any clear, fixed path to formal rewards. At the present state of theory development, this seems the best we can do. As we shall see in Chapter 2, researchers have defined a theoretical construct closely related to OCB—contextual performance—such that neither probability of reward nor formal job description is conceptually relevant.

Finally, the last part of the definition of OCB requires that it *in the aggregate promotes the efficient and effective functioning of the organization.*

With the qualifier *in the aggregate,* we refer to summing across time for a single person and also summing across persons in the group, department, or organization. Most OCB actions, taken singly, would not make a dent in the overall performance of an organization. The help that Sam rendered at the paper mill would not by itself change the profit and loss statement of the company. It was a modest, some would even say trivial, occurrence. But that is in the nature of OCB—any single occurrence of it is usually modest or trivial. A good analogy in the broader sphere of citizenship is the act of voting. A single vote by a single person is trivial, except in the most extraordinary and unforeseeable situations. Yet in the aggregate, voting by the electorate sustains the democratic process.

Furthermore, it is precisely the characteristic modesty and mundaneness of most OCB gestures that make the idea of a formal reward system taking account of them on a case-by-case basis almost ludicrous. The tallying of every such action would require an army of scribes and an oppressive intelligence system. Indeed, if such a system called attention to every discretionary helpful act, however small, people (especially those of shy temperament) would probably be discouraged from performing a large proportion of them. Note that we do not intend to rule out heroic, epic contributions from OCB; we simply wish to underscore the point that the manner in which we define OCB—discretionary, not directly rewarded—is such that much of OCB consists of specific actions that in and of themselves do not often invite public scrutiny or official documentation.

We do require of OCB that, in the aggregate, it results in a more effective organization. To make such a requirement as a conceptual statement leads us to the difficult question of defining "organizational effectiveness." Many articles have addressed this problem, and no standardized answer has been formulated. What scholars in organization theory do agree on is that organizational effectiveness is multidimensional, and the dimensions vary according to the different stakeholder groups connected to the organization (Freeman, 1984). If we think in terms of a particular firm, those stakeholder groups include owners or investors, customers, creditors, suppliers, and employees. In the case of a not-for-profit organization, the stakeholder groups include the sources of funding, the clients served, and the paid and volunteer staff of the institution. An organization is effective to the extent that it meets or exceeds the reasonable expectations of these stakeholder groups.

In Chapter 7, we refer to several studies that have found collective OCB to be associated positively with indicators of several dimensions of effectiveness that span two or more stakeholder groups. OCB by the group or department as a whole has been linked to efficiency of operation, customer satisfaction, financial performance, and growth in revenues. Frameworks for studying organizations also generally agree that to be effective over any appreciable period of time, an organization must adapt to changes in the environmental matrix that surrounds it. Markets, technologies, cultures, sources of supply, industry structures, competitive pressures—they all change, sometimes suddenly and unpredictably. To sustain or enhance effectiveness, organizations have to anticipate and monitor such changes and figure out how to deal with them. Moreover, although an organization must use strategic analysis to respond to such changes, it must also implement strategic redirection. The implementation of strategic changes ultimately derives from the many small changes people make in their behavior, including the suggestions they offer for how best to implement a new strategy. Making such suggestions often goes beyond the scope of core job responsibilities. Thus, discretionary behaviors would be quite likely to contribute to organizational effectiveness to the extent that they involve monitoring the organization's environment (for example, finding out from customers how their tastes or buying habits have changed, or querying suppliers about imminent technological breakthroughs), advocating new or different initiatives by the organization to capitalize upon or adapt to changing conditions, and exercising a proactive stance toward making new initiatives practicable and efficient.

A Look Ahead

Having now established what we mean by OCB, in Chapter 2 we flesh out this construct by demonstrating how it is operationally defined—that is, how it can be measured. We describe some qualitatively different forms of OCB and take due account of some other frameworks that inform our thinking about OCB. Finally, we address the issue of how national or societal cultures condition one's thinking about specific forms of OCB.

Chapter 3 attempts to connect OCB to larger frameworks, past and present, of organizational theory. We believe the "organizational" part of OCB is important, and in Chapter 3 we make our case for why we think OCB is different in kind from prosocial or altruistic behavior in nonorganizational settings. We also explore how our thinking about

OCB correlates with well-established classic and modern concepts of organization.

In Chapter 4, we develop a conceptual framework for the prediction of OCB at the level of the individual. We connect this framework to the long-debated issue of whether satisfaction causes performance, concluding that job attitudes and dispositional variables should relate more closely to OCB than to measures of individual task productivity. We review and interpret a large body of the relevant research on correlates of individual OCB.

The thrust of Chapter 5 is management—that is, what managers can do to evoke and sustain OCB. How does OCB relate to leadership, trust, job characteristics, organization culture, and pay systems? We draw from established theoretical frameworks to derive some propositions that address how work environments might affect OCB, and we review relevant research to test these propositions.

Chapter 6 shifts focus to the consequences of OCB. We cover the following important issues: Do managers actually place considerable value on OCB? Is OCB taken into account in evaluations of subordinates' performance (and if so, what are the implicit models in which managers evaluate OCB within their larger estimation of an individual's value to the organization)? Do managers make accurate or valid assessments of individual OCB (and if not, how might their assessments be made more valid)? Are some forms of OCB given higher valuation than others, and is the same form of OCB valued more highly for some individuals than for others?

In Chapter 7, we revisit the definition of OCB, in particular the idea that it pertains to discretionary contributions that sustain and enhance organizational effectiveness. What is the conceptual basis for believing that specific forms of OCB, as operationally defined in terms of specific behaviors, should make organizations more effective? Having developed such a conceptual foundation, we review studies testing the proposition that group- and organization-based levels of OCB, as measured by specific behaviors, should relate to empirical indicators of certain dimensions of organizational performance.

Chapter 8 takes stock of where we stand now in regard to application (for practitioners) as well as conceptualization and measurement (for researchers) of OCB, in light of what has been reported and discussed in the preceding chapters. In retrospect, we can see how the evolution of the OCB construct provides an instructive example of what Donald Schwab (1980) called the "sequential interactive process of construct validation." We offer suggestions about what kind of construct OCB represents, the appropriate model for interpreting measures of OCB, and how the research community should proceed with further development, validation, and evaluation of OCB measures. We offer some plausible statements about how OCB can be affected by reward systems, supervision, performance appraisal, and selection processes, among others.

Finally, in an appendix intended for researchers and serious practitioners who wish to explore the nature of OCB and its measurement in greater detail, we discuss the development of the most frequently used OCB scales and evaluate their content validity and psychometric properties. As part of this discussion, we attempt to clarify the conceptual similarities and differences among the various forms of OCB by briefly reviewing the literature on OCB and other related constructs. We end our discussion with some recommendations for future research in the conceptualization and measurement of OCB.

Before we proceed with the weighty issues addressed in subsequent chapters, we invite you to test for yourself the usefulness of the basic idea of OCB as we have articulated it thus far.

Questions for Discussion

1. Drawing from your experience as a student, develop a list of discretionary undergraduate student behaviors that you think serve to promote effectiveness in the classroom. What enters into your conception of "effectiveness"? Why do the discretionary contributions you cite relate to the criteria (note the plural form of this term) of "classroom effectiveness"? Do you think some or all of these contributions are rewarded by the instructor? If so, how? Why do some students make more of these contributions than others? Why do some classes or courses feature more or fewer of such behaviors?

2. Think of a part-time, full-time, or summer job you have had. What specific behaviors did your supervisor say were rewarded? Which ones, in your opinion, were actually rewarded? How validly do you think your supervisor assessed your contributions? Which behaviors that you or your coworkers exhibited fit our definition?

 **2**

The Study of OCB: Its Roots, Structure, and Frameworks

B e careful what you say. You never know when people might take you seriously.

In 1977, the first author of this book published a paper that was meant only as an exercise in devil's advocacy (Organ, 1977). By that time, academic researchers had spent a quarter century chipping away at the popular belief that worker satisfaction affected productivity. Empirical findings offered little evidence to support such a view. The devil's advocacy piece tried to explain and defend the popular view by making a distinction between quantitative measures of output or productivity and some other, more subtle, forms of worker contribution that often are not reflected in measures of individual output. The author suggested that these subtler contributions might take the form of helping coworkers, following the spirit as well as the literal rules of workplace governance, and accommodating the changes that managers often have to make to improve operations. Sound familiar? However, the essay did not call these subtle contributions OCB nor contemplate further study of such contributions. All the author wanted to do was appeal to professional colleagues so that they wouldn't come down too hard on management practitioners who believed (through personal observation) that job satisfaction was an important factor relating to job performance.

However, to repeat, sometimes people will take you seriously. In this case, two of Dennis Organ's doctoral students at Indiana University, Tom Bateman and C. Ann Smith, read the 1977 paper as part of the material for a doctoral seminar and had the audacity to propose some research to test the ideas in the article.

Bateman's study (Bateman & Organ, 1983) actually took the form of an add-on to a project primarily intended to test the effects of job overload on behavior and attitudes. The researchers measured overload, personality, behavior, and attitudes of a group of nonacademic employees at Indiana University at two different times, about six to eight weeks apart. This study design made it possible to draw some reasonable inferences about directions of causality (for example, whether earlier overload predicted later behavior and attitudes, or the reverse). Bateman proposed adding to the study the supervisors' ratings of subjects' job performance, which would include a rating of productivity but also a measure of those subtler contributions casually described in the 1977 essay. The researchers came up with enough items to constitute at least a crude measure of what was then called *qualitative performance* (as opposed to *quantitative performance*—that is, productivity).

The results of the study (Bateman & Organ, 1983), while of some interest, were mixed and would hardly have presaged the amount of research that has been done on OCB since then. On one hand, the findings did suggest that earlier job satisfaction predicted later OCB. But the correlation between earlier OCB and later job satisfaction was also significant, though not quite as large as the converse. Also, the correlation at both times between qualitative performance (OCB) and quantitative performance (job performance) was higher than desired, probably because of common method variance (that is, the same person rated a specific individual on both kinds of performance). Finally, the qualitative performance measure was a factor analytic mess. Although most of the items loaded on one general factor, they also loaded on one or more other factors that had no obvious or distinctive meaning.

There might not have been much if any further research in this area if Ann Smith hadn't become interested in the interpretation of findings and ideas from the classic Hawthorne studies as discussed in *Management and the Worker* (Roethlisberger & Dickson, 1939). That curiosity led her toward a study (Smith, Organ, & Near, 1983) in which she interviewed several supervisors in manufacturing plants in southern Indiana, asking them, in effect, "What are the things you'd like your employees to do more of, but really can't *make* them do, and for which you can't guarantee any definite rewards, other than your appreciation?" Note that an assumption here is that managers, who are accountable for results (i.e., the effectiveness of their groups or departments), would talk about actions that they believe contribute to effectiveness. Perhaps they would also mention things that make the manager's job easier. We would argue that, even so, we are still talking about organizational effectiveness—making the manager's job easier arguably makes it more likely that the manager can perform distinctly managerial functions, such as planning and thinking about ways to improve and streamline the workflow. The corollary assumption is that managers are reasonably knowledgeable about what makes their departments effective and thus can speak with some confidence about what particular actions by subordinates help to achieve that end.

Varieties of OCB

The actions mentioned most frequently by the managers in the Smith et al. (1983) study are shown in Box 2.1. Such items represent actions that managers appreciate, because such actions either enhance effectiveness and efficiency or make the manager's job easier. However, these items are also tasks they cannot enforce, nor can they promise specific or immediate incentives to employees for performing them.

Box 2.1 Measures of OCB

---

1. Helps other employees with their work when they have been absent.

2. Exhibits punctuality in arriving at work on time in the morning and after lunch and breaks.

3. Volunteers to do things not formally required by the job.

4. Takes undeserved work breaks.*

5. Takes the initiative to orient new employees to the department even though it is not part of his/her job description.

6. Exhibits attendance at work beyond the norm (for example, takes fewer days off than most individuals or fewer than allowed).

7. Helps others when their workload increases (assists others until they get over the hurdles).

8. Coasts toward the end of the day.*

9. Gives advance notice if unable to come to work.

10. Spends a great deal of time in personal telephone conversations.*

(Continued)

Box 2.1 (Continued)

11. Does not take unnecessary time off work.

12. Assists me with my duties.

13. Makes innovative suggestions to improve the overall quality of the department.

14. Does not take extra breaks.

15. Willingly attends functions not required by the organization but that help its overall image.

16. Does not spend a great deal of time in idle conversation.

SOURCE: Smith, C. A., Organ, D. W., & Near, J. P. (1983). Organizational citizenship behavior: Its nature and antecedents. *Journal of Applied Psychology, 68,* 653–663. Copyright © by the American Psychological Association. Reproduced with permission.

* Item is reverse scored.

Smith later constructed a scale containing the items shown in Box 2.1 and asked a group of evening MBA students (most of whom were currently working managers) to think of a specific subordinate or coworker and rate that person in terms of the frequency with which he or she exhibited such behaviors (Smith et al., 1983). Analysis of the responses identified two separate factors. One factor was initially labeled "altruism," but nowadays researchers use the term "**helping,**" because critics have argued that "altruism" implies something about the motive behind the behavior or suggests something like "selflessness" on the part of the actor. Whatever we label it, the items comprising this factor (Smith et al., 1983) clearly denote a type of OCB that is directed at a specific individual— usually a coworker, but sometimes the supervisor or a customer. In other words, the target of the behavior, the immediate beneficiary, is a person. This factor includes items such as helping a new worker learn the job or helping an overloaded worker catch up with the workflow or solve a problem. Of course, this is also the form of OCB that Sam demonstrated (refer to Chapter 1) when he helped with banding the rolls of paper.

The other OCB factor consisted of items that did not have the immediate effect of helping a specific person but rather contributed in a more impersonal and generalized fashion to the group, department, or organization. For example, punctuality in arriving at work or at meetings, exemplary attendance (i.e., very low absenteeism), and refraining from unnecessary breaks and idle conversation do not appear to help any specific individual (although one could make the case that such behavior does, at least indirectly, help the supervisor or manager). What these behaviors exemplify is a particularly high order of compliance with the constraints upon individuals necessary to make a cooperative system. Initially, this factor was called "generalized compliance," and later "conscientiousness." However, as research on OCB eventually delved into personality traits that might predict OCB and looked at a personality factor usually referred to as "conscientiousness," some confusion naturally arose as to whether the term referred to conscientiousness as a behavior or a trait. Therefore, "generalized compliance," or simply "compliance," came back in usage. However, it should be understood that "**compliance**" as a form of OCB does not imply merely strict obedience to an order. It denotes rather the more general adherence to the spirit as well as the letter of the rules or norms that define a cooperative system.

Larry Williams, a doctoral student at Indiana University who came after Bateman and Smith, conducted research to determine whether helping and compliance were really empirically distinguishable from each other and whether both were distinguishable from what people do to carry out their specific job duties. He asked working students in an evening MBA class to respond to some attitudinal measures and then had each subject take three other measures—intended to measure the OCB factors and core job performance—to his or her supervisor, who rated the subject on the three factors. From the resulting data, he used structural equation modeling (SEM) to analyze the results. SEM determines whether the observed raw correlations (actually, covariances) among the set of items comprising compliance, helping, and core job performance could be derived just as well by assuming one, two, or three underlying factors. He found that the best-fitting model was in fact one that assumed three different factors and that the items intended to measure each of the three factors loaded only on the assumed factors. That is, the compliance items fit the model hypothesized as compliance, the helping items fit only the model interpretable as helping, and the core job performance items made up a separate job performance factor (Williams and Anderson, 1991).

We should note that about this same time, Sheila Puffer (1987), drawing her lead from the abundant literature in social psychology on antecedents of helping strangers, fashioned a measure of prosocial behavior in a retailing organization that has much in common with the measures used by Smith and Williams, the major difference being that Puffer's scale was more specific to the retailing environment.

How Do Helping and Compliance Fit the Definition of OCB?

We think it is rather intuitively obvious how helping and compliance qualify as OCB. By helping someone else with a different job, Sam was diverting some productive energy from his own work, but the tradeoff was that his help greatly improved how another worker was doing his job and therefore prevented a bottleneck in the workflow. The sacrifice to Sam's output was miniscule in comparison to the gain in another's productivity.

Helping that is directed toward outsiders, such as customers or suppliers, sometimes improves an organization's ability to import resources. Discretionary kindness toward outsiders positively influences their sentiments about the organization, at the very least. This in turn can facilitate timely delivery or the processing of special orders from suppliers, greater loyalty on the part of customers (who respond with continued inputs of revenues and praise of the organization to other potential customers), and perhaps the recruitment of future employees.

That such wonderful benefits would originate from a single episode of helping an external constituent might seem exaggerated. The point, though, is not to prove or even assert a direct, one-to-one relationship between each and every instance of helping and some specific benefit but to suggest that continuous streams of helping given by many participants will eventually provide such advantages.

How does OCB in the form of the compliance factor contribute to organizational effectiveness? Lower rates of absenteeism result in fewer people needed on the payroll, lower costs in contracting for "temps" needed to fill in for absent workers, and less administrative time consumed in redeploying the people present. When less time is spent in excessive breaks, personal phone calls, and idle chatter, more productive labor can be expended in doing the job. And when more employees adhere to workplace rules regarding the use of organizational resources, the resources can be used more efficiently by all concerned parties.

You might well pose the question: Isn't attendance part of the job description? Aren't employees expected by management to use work hours for doing their jobs and not for personal matters? In other words, how can these behaviors qualify as OCB if they're already part of the job description? Our response to this reasonable question is that there is a discretionary dimension to the *degree* to which individuals comply with the arrangements of workplace governance. Attendance is required, but some degree of absenteeism is both expected and wholly justified (e.g., by illness, family emergencies, extreme weather conditions).

What is discretionary is the extent to which an employee considers sickness or personal contingencies sufficiently compelling to stay home or leave work early. Some individuals feel bound to come to work and do their best as long as they can stand up without passing out, whereas others consider a bit of nausea or a mild headache reason enough to call in sick. When a heavy snowstorm hits overnight, some workers will start out an hour earlier than usual so they can punch in on time, but others will hear the traffic and weather reports and decide that they have a good excuse to cancel work for the day because it's not wise to drive. Some people take care of their personal business on their own time, and indeed plan and arrange their affairs so that personal business isn't likely to intrude on work schedules, whereas others seem to search for reasons to leave work early or come in late. Ultimately, excessive absenteeism and obvious abuse of break time, attending to personal business during work hours, and the like represent delinquencies that violate the employment contract. However, as any supervisor knows, this is a gray area. Some people are consistently in the good part of that gray area— meaning that they are conscientious even though it is difficult for the supervisor to reward them for their conscientiousness—and others are just sufficiently inside that gray area such that they are not likely to invite formal sanctions.

Consider a study by Blau (1994) on lateness among 353 hospital staff and 402 bank employees. His analysis easily discerned four categories of lateness behavior: Increasing and chronic, stable and periodic, unavoidable, and never late. Perhaps some of the increasing and chronic latecomers eventually met with some disciplinary actions by management, because reasonable punctuality in arriving at work is generally understood as an essential condition for continued employment. Nonetheless, the variance in the distribution for coming late to work strongly suggests that between the extremes of "absolutely never late" and "so late, so often as to justify dismissal," there existed a substantial portion of the continuum in which degree and frequency of lateness were at least tolerated, and therefore in some sense a matter of employee discretion and intention. Moreover—and to anticipate what we will show in Chapter 4—the correlations between job satisfaction and chronic lateness were −.45 and −.39 in the bank and the hospital, respectively. The correlations between a measure of affective commitment to the organization and chronic lateness were −.35 and −.38. Correlations at this level would not obtain if the variance in lateness were minimal. The correlation with job attitudes also supports the view that we articulate in Chapter 4 about the linkage between job satisfaction and OCB.

The helping and compliance factors consistently and clearly emerge in many published studies from several different measures of OCB. However, a few other factors can, at least conceptually, be distinguished from helping and compliance, and in one or more studies factors have emerged from the analysis as statistically independent of helping and compliance (see Box 2.2). One such factor is what we call "**sportsmanship**." Often sportsmanship as a form of OCB relates to things people *choose not to do*—such as complaining.

Box 2.2   Items Intended to Measure Forms of OCB Other than Helping and Compliance

---

Sportsmanship:

1. Complains a lot about trivial matters.*

2. Always finds fault with what the organization is doing.*

3. Expresses resentment with any changes introduced by management.*

4. Thinks only about his/her work problems, not others'.*

5. Tries to make the best of the situation, even when there are problems.

6. Is able to tolerate occasional inconveniences when they arise.

7. Does not complain about work assignments.

Courtesy:

8. Tries to avoid creating problems for others.

9. Considers the effects of his/her actions on coworkers.

---

10. Consults with me or other people who might be affected by his/her actions or decisions.

11. Informs me before taking any important actions.

Civic Virtue:

12. Stays informed about developments in the company.

13. Attends and participates in meetings regarding the company.

14. Offers suggestions for ways to improve operations.

SOURCE: Konovsky, M. A. & Organ, D. W. (1996). Dispositional and contextual determinants of organizational citizenship behavior. *Journal of Organizational Behavior, 17,* 253–266. Copyright © by John Wiley & Sons Limited. Reproduced with permission.

*Item is reverse scored.

As we noted earlier, to be effective, organizations have to adapt to environmental forces by making changes—for example, in the physical plant, in how the workforce is deployed, in methods of production, in the services they provide, in hours of operation. Inevitably, the burden of such changes falls more on some members of the organization than on others. To some people, such changes might not seem fair, and they feel that they have a right to complain, to strenuously object, to take their case to every possible level of appeal. In some instances, we would applaud their efforts. But again there are differences in degrees and thresholds for registering one's complaints when change yields impositions, constraints, and inconveniences. Some people roll with the punches; although they might not be happy about the situation, they are willing to gut it out, at least for the time being. And then there are those who would rail against the slightest, most fleeting inconvenience, protesting to anyone who will listen, making a federal case out of small potatoes. The more widespread the generalized willingness to make the best of the situation, the more smoothly the organizational change is likely to unfold, and with less diversion of resources into quasilitigious proceedings.

Sportsmanship conserves the stamina—notably, the stamina of administrators—that can be devoted to constructive purposes. Every grievance, regardless of its disposition, consumes executive resources. Such stamina is then lost from the more productive activities of planning, scheduling, and organizational analysis. When we hear a supervisor say, "Good old _____, he (or she) never gives me a minute's trouble," only the uninitiated would mistake this as damnation with faint praise.

In a paper on the matter of citizenship within organizations, Jill Graham (1986a) drew from Greek philosophical treatises on citizenship and suggested that **civic virtue** is also a worthwhile construct for capturing some of the important discretionary contributions by participants. Civic virtue describes a posture of responsible, constructive involvement in the political or governance process of the organization. This concept has been operationalized in two forms. Konovsky & Organ (1996), as shown in Box 2.2 stressed the more mundane, ongoing activities pertaining to governance, such as reading work-relevant mail, attending meetings, keeping up with what is going on in the firm, discussing with colleagues the issues of the day, and taking part in the various rituals that mark continuity of the organization's traditions and identity. Graham (1989) stressed the less frequent and more dramatic instances of civic virtue, in which someone challenges existing organizational practices or policies, voices critiques or objections to policies proposed by high-level officers, and more generally acts as the conscience of the organization (Graham, 1989). Although both of these definitions of civic virtue appear to qualify as OCB, the more dramatic form is probably less likely to meet with unqualified appreciation by managers, at least to the same extent as other forms of OCB (helping, compliance, sportsmanship, or civic virtue as played out in attendance at meetings and keeping up with the news).

Organ (1988) made a case that **courtesy** is a distinguishable form of OCB. Whereas helping pertains to mitigating or solving a problem confronted by a colleague, courtesy consists of actions that help prevent those problems from occurring. The basic idea is to avoid practices that make other people's work harder and, when you have to add to their load, to give them enough notice that they'll be prepared to deal with it. In the gym, where people work out with weights, a common courtesy is to take the plates off the barbells when you're finished with your routines on the bench so that the next person to use the bench doesn't have to take your plates off before putting on the ones he or she wants to use. There are countless variations of this at work, such as leaving the copier, printer, or company car in as good as (or even better than) the condition in which you found it. Another example would be informing affected coworkers when you realize that you have to make a decision or take some initiative—such as committing to a customer to deliver a special order—that, downstream, could complicate others' tasks if they aren't forewarned.

Organ (1990b) suggested two other variants of OCB—**cheerleading** and **peacemaking**—that have attracted little empirical scrutiny to date. Cheerleading involves the celebration of coworkers' accomplishments (be they grand or humble). The effect is to provide positive reinforcement for positive contributions, which in turn makes such contributions more likely to occur in the future. It's nice when top management or the immediate superior cites one's good works, but it's even better when one or more of your colleagues call attention to them, because then you know the extent to which others recognize, appreciate, and admire what you've done. Peacemaking occurs when someone notices that a conflict (perhaps a conflict that started out as work-related and civil) is on the verge of developing into a personal war between two or more parties. The peacemaker steps into the breach, giving people a chance to cool their heads, helping the antagonists save face, and helps discussants get back to consideration of impersonal issues.

Some researchers have theorized that OCB includes a category they call **loyalty** (George and Brief, 1992; Graham, 1989, 1991). Some members do a lot of discretionary good for their employers when they "talk up" their organization, countering criticisms by outsiders, stressing the positives of where they work as they chat with potential future hires or customers. We can all think of people who seemed to be self-appointed ambassadors of goodwill for the company they worked for (just as we can identify folks who say only bad things about their managers). Surely it has not hurt Southwest Airlines' business that its workforce constantly expresses how proud they are to work there.

Although it didn't use the terminology of OCB, a seminal paper by Katz (1964), pointed to **self-development** and **protecting the organization** as important behaviors that go beyond formal role requirements and that often do not occur in response to formal reward systems for differential individual performance. Self-development, as the term suggests, encompasses the discretionary measures people take to broaden their work-relevant skills and knowledge, including voluntary enrollment in company-sponsored training courses as well as informal study. Protecting the organization involves taking the initiative to notice and correct conditions of impending harm to company resources or reputation—such as halting a shipment of damaged goods to a customer, reporting a potential safety hazard no one else seems to have noticed, even pulling the plug on a project that threatens to consume excess resources without delivering any benefits.

We could go on from here to explore other constructs that might capture some particular form of OCB not obviously apparent in the factors described above, but sometimes our capacity for conceptual distinctions outruns our ability to capture those distinctions empirically. The most robust distinctions that we have seen supported by empirical analysis involve the factors that we have referred to as helping, compliance, sportsmanship, and the more challenging type of civic virtue. As we discuss in Chapter 8, confirmatory factor analyses suggest that altruism, courtesy, peacemaking, and cheerleading fit together under a broader construct that might be called "helping." The more mundane form of civic virtue (such as meeting attendance and reading and answering mail) sometimes seems to be hard to distinguish empirically from the more general measures of compliance. The remaining factors—loyalty, self-development, and organizational protection—have not undergone sufficient empirical analysis to determine whether distinguishing them from the other factors is practicable or profitable. Although 40 measures of OCB dimensions have appeared in the literature (LePine, Erez, and Johnson, 2002), analysis suggests that seven factors capture the distinctions within and among OCB dimensions: helping, compliance, sportsmanship, civic virtue, organizational loyalty, self-development, and individual initiative. (**Individual initiative** is a broad category that seems to capture most forms of going beyond what one is instructed to do when necessary to solve or prevent a problem.) In Chapter 8, we describe the definitional and measurement issues regarding these factors in greater detail.

Cultural Variations on OCB

Although all but a few of the published empirical studies on OCB have occurred in North America, primarily in the United States, we should ponder whether significant OCB takes different forms in varying cultures and economic systems. Hofstede's framework (1984) identifies four major dimensions of differences among societal cultures:

- *Individualism-collectivism* reflects which influences members of a culture use to guide behavior: one's own personal values and interests versus emphasis on the interests and values of one's larger group, such as an extended family, tribe, or comrades. In individualistic cultures, people emphasize the freedom to define one's own personal identity, whereas collectivist cultures assume that identity derives from one's larger group.

• *Power distance* refers to the extent to which members of a society not only recognize, but are comfortable with, an inherent hierarchy that clearly defines power differences among individuals.

• *Uncertainty avoidance* encompasses differences among societal cultures that relate to risk taking, tolerance of ambiguity, and the need for strict rules and procedures.

• *Masculinity-femininity* reflects differences in emphasis on competition versus cooperation, tasks versus relationships, esthetics and quality of life versus material wealth, and, importantly, differences in specialization of gender roles and attributes (for example, masculine cultures make sharper distinctions between the virtues of ideal men and women).

The United States and other English-speaking cultures are the most individualistic societies, and East Asian peoples have the strongest collectivist values. English-speaking societies, along with Latin cultures and Japan, are characterized as more masculine, whereas Scandinavian countries and the Netherlands fall toward the feminine end of the continuum. The United States tends toward greater acceptance of risk and uncertainty, and Germanic-speaking countries and Arab societies try to avoid uncertainty and risk. In the power-distance dimension, Anglo cultures occupy a low-to-medium position, Latin and Asian cultures tend toward a higher degree of social hierarchy, and the Dutch, Scandinavians, and Germanic peoples are more egalitarian.

Two of the many differences in economic systems that we would like to emphasize in discussing OCB are the degree to which firms are disciplined by free, competitive markets and the degree to which legal and regulatory contexts govern economic transactions. North American and Western European economies have a highly developed legal and regulatory context for transacting business so that a level playing field of competition exists. To compete effectively, firms must execute some combination of internal efficiency and innovation. One would expect, then, that OCB—if defined such that it must contribute ultimately to organizational effectiveness—would pertain to matters of efficiency and a quality of involvement that facilitates innovative ideas, whether grand or incremental.

One consequence of an individualistic culture, such as the United States, is that individuals belong to many separate, partially overlapping groups—that is, a person's identity is not defined by inclusion in one extended "in-group." Therefore, conflict that arises in organizations is unlikely to escalate such that one large group closes ranks in a bitter, fight-to-the-end struggle with an opposing group. When contentious issues arise, as they often do when the matter of organizational change is broached, organizations tolerate, even encourage, some degree of conflict over those issues. Oracle CEO Larry Bossidy exemplifies this bias by saying

> Harmony . . . can squelch critical thinking and drive decision making under-ground. When harmony prevails . . . after the key players leave the session, they quietly veto decisions they didn't like but didn't debate. . . . A good motto to observe is "truth over harmony." (Bossidy and Charan, 2002, p. 103)

In contrast, the People's Republic of China (PRC) does not have such a well-developed institutional infrastructure for free-market transactions. To some extent, people do business with those whom they know and can trust. Although price and quality are both important, at the margin some firms will trade off on both of these dimensions for deals based on personal relationships. Thus, internal efficiency and innovation don't have as direct a relationship to effectiveness as would be the case in the Western world. On the other hand, external reputation and goodwill are crucial.

Many firms in the PRC are owned by the state. Such a firm, to be considered effective, must contribute to the larger community, not only in production of marketable goods but also in certain intangible qualities—devotion to the state and the community welfare and spirit. Also, state-owned firms acquire resources from the state at least partly as a function of the reputation of the firm within the larger community. That reputation hinges to some degree on how well firm members are regarded in terms of moral character and devotion to the welfare of the community. One might therefore suppose that OCB could take the form of charitable services to the community, aid to those in need, and public conduct that is considered praiseworthy.

Culturally, China stands at the opposite pole from the United States as strongly collectivist. A person is defined by reference to an extended in-group, which might encompass a family, province, school, or some combination. As we can see from history, especially that of China, highly collectivist cultures are prone to open-ended escalation of conflict to the point that it is bitter, destructive, even bloody. We might expect, therefore, to see less encouragement of open debate and controversial positions in the PRC and less tendency to view challenging or critical comments as OCB.

Farh, Zhong, and Organ (2002) tested these ideas with a group of 166 employees and managers in 75 state-owned, collective (town and village) firms and cooperatives, foreign invested firms, and private enterprises in the PRC. These subjects were given the definition of OCB and asked to provide descriptions of incidents in their experience that illustrated OCB.

The subjects recounted 756 incidents (averaging 4 to 5 per respondent), from which a rigorous content analysis revealed 10 dimensions of OCB. Although several of the dimensions bore obvious familiarity to some of those noted previously, others were unprecedented in research in the United States. One such dimension was "social welfare participation," referring to employee participation in community service, such as planting trees. This dimension emerged particularly strongly among employees and managers in state-owned firms. In addition, members of that group emphasized "interpersonal harmony," which is not surprising given the risks of escalation of conflict. A factor suggestive of the "voice" dimension posited by Van Dyne, Graham, and Dienesch (1994) involved speaking out to discourage activities harmful to the organization as opposed to criticizing the organization or its policies.

Even some of the dimensions that at first glance looked like those found in Western studies reflected some subtle differences. For example, a dimension similar to the "helping" factor accounted for 72 of the items generated, but in the PRC this factor included not just task-relevant helping or helping in the workplace but also personal help rendered away from the job—such as helping a coworker repair a home damaged by water or tending to a sick family member. In other words, "helping" had a more diffuse, unbounded character than when observed in U.S. studies of OCB. This finding is consistent not only with the collectivist tone of Chinese culture but also with the extent to which social roles are "diffuse" (i.e., they cut across sectors of life and experience, as opposed to the more "specific" character of social roles and relationships in the United States, which are circumscribed by specific situations).

We have compared the U.S. and Chinese cultures at some length because we have data to inform this comparison. The researchers undertook this study because they expected that two cultures that feature such marked contrasts in so many respects would exhibit the effect of cultural context on OCB. However, other cultural comparisons easily come to mind. For instance, the Latin culture found in most of Mexico includes a strong awareness of power distance. Managers whose firms include many immigrants from Mexico have noted that Mexicans usually work hard but seldom make any suggestions for improving operations and sometimes "lack initiative." These observations, if accurate, might well derive from cultural differences in sensitivity to power distance. Someone from a high power distance culture would think it an insult to suggest, even obliquely, what a powerful manager should do. And someone influenced by a culture high in uncertainty avoidance might be too worried about the risks of doing something wrong if he or she "takes some initiative"—that is, goes beyond what he or she has been explicitly instructed to do by someone in a powerful office. Thus, taking initiative and making suggestions for improvement might not be regarded as OCB in cultures defined by high uncertainty avoidance and high power distance.

We should keep in mind that the term *culture* is not synonymous with the term *country*. For example, the northernmost areas of Mexico, especially in the business community, have assimilated many of the values and practices dominant in the United States. Perhaps that explains why Konovsky, Elliot, and Pugh (1995) found in a study conducted in Monterrey, Mexico, the same factor structure of OCB that she had previously identified in U.S. locations.

The results of studies such as Farh, Earley, and Lin (1997) and Farh et al. (2002) argue strongly for considering societal culture in the process of operationalizing OCB. One could also argue for consideration of other kinds of contexts, even for studies in the United States. For instance, significant forms of OCB in nonprofit organizations might take a somewhat different form or emphasis—and therefore require variations in operationalization—from what we see in the private sector. Other examples of comparisons we could make include contrasting OCB in health care organizations, academic institutions, or professional partnerships with OCB in manufacturing or retail firms.

Frameworks Related to OCB

Contextual Performance

As we noted earlier in this chapter, the ideas associated with OCB arose from the satisfaction-productivity controversy. Conventional wisdom, dating at least from the so-called "human relations era" of the late 1930s (see Chapter 3), had assumed that a worker's satisfaction would affect productivity. However, beginning in the early 1950s, one empirical review after another could find little basis for this belief. Organ (1977) suggested that one way of resolving the gap between conventional wisdom and the empirical record was to explore the possibility that job satisfaction influences the more discretionary or spontaneous contributions of workers, not their productivity in the more narrow sense of objective task performance.

A related piece of conventional wisdom had long held that personality affected how hard a person worked and therefore influenced the level of productivity that worker achieved. But again, many reviews of empirical evidence over most of the 20th century found little basis for believing that a measure of one or more personality traits could predict a worker's performance. A group of industrial psychologists (e.g., Borman and Motowidlo, 1993; Campbell, 1994; Pulakos, Borman and Hough, 1988) involved in a large-scale human resources project for the U.S. Army (known to many as "Project A") sought to resolve this particular discrepancy by distinguishing between "task performance" and "**contextual performance.**"

The best predictors of individual task performance are knowledge, skills, and abilities (KSAs), with particular emphasis on measures of cognitive abilities and general intelligence. Project A researchers argued that personality or dispositional variables, on the other hand, better predict those contributions that individuals make to the social and psychological context in which technical or task performance occurs. Contextual performance (CP), then, is defined by those contributions that sustain an ethos of cooperation and interpersonal supportiveness of the group. CP can take the form of **interpersonal facilitation** (such as helping and good colleagueship) or **job dedication**, which has much in common with the OCB compliance factor because it encompasses self-disciplined behaviors with respect to rules and use of time.

The measures of CP bear more than a passing resemblance to those used in the helping and compliance measures of OCB, and research using those CP measures does indeed support the idea that established personality measures predict CP better than they predict core task performance or productivity. The latter is better predicted by cognitive ability measures, such as a measure of general intelligence (or g), the common factor that seems to cut across many different measures of specific mental abilities, such as verbal fluency, logical reasoning, skill in using number, among others does. Moreover, ratings by different observers of CP and task performance both contribute independently to ratings of overall performance (Borman, White, & Dorsey, 1995).

We would like to emphasize that even though measures of OCB and CP look much alike, the concepts operationally defined by those measures are different. Recall that OCB specifies contributions that are neither strictly required by the job description nor rewarded by formal incentives. The CP framework makes no reference to what is expected in the job description or the prospect of formal rewards. This is an important distinction, because some have argued that the items in the OCB measures refer to actions that often, perhaps even usually, are expected as part of the job and in fact are often assumed to qualify for formal rewards. The OCB framework is vulnerable on this issue, whereas the CP approach is not affected by it.

Prosocial Organizational Behavior (POB)

Brief and Motowidlo (1986) used the concept of prosocial organizational behavior (POB) to describe any behavior in an organizational setting aimed at improving the welfare of someone to whom the behavior is directed. Note that the definition does not constrain the behavior to have specific or direct organizational relevance. POB could include helping a coworker with a personal issue (e.g., offering advice about how to improve child care or save money while shopping), provided that it occurs in the organizational setting. Nor does the definition rule out prosocial gestures that could be part of the job description (such as a sales clerk arranging timely delivery of a purchase to a customer's residence or vehicle).

Motowidlo's interests soon led him to work with Borman and others (e.g., Borman & Motowidlo, 1993) on contextual performance (which, of course, assumes organizational relevance of the contribution). Brief joined with George (George and Brief, 1992) to develop a theoretical statement about "**organizational spontaneity.**" This term takes its cue from the language used by Katz (1964) in discussing "innovative and spontaneous" behavior that promotes organizational effectiveness. In practice, the term follows the taxonomy offered by Katz, including cooperating with others, protecting the organization, volunteering constructive and creative ideas, self-development, and cultivating a favorable view of the organization by outsiders. The thrust of the

George and Brief discussion was to build a case for the importance of positive affect or mood—in terms of both the individual and the atmosphere of the group—as a determinant of such behaviors. As is the case with CP, the specific behaviors that operationally define organizational spontaneity sound much like those that define OCB. Also like CP, no restrictive assumptions are made about whether or not the particular behaviors go beyond the job description or must not be contractually recompensed.

Extra-Role Behavior

Van Dyne, Cummings, and McLean-Parks (1995) positioned OCB within a larger framework of **extra-role behavior (ERB)**. This term, which has a meaning similar to that of OCB, is defined as behavior that attempts to benefit the organization and that goes beyond existing role expectations. However, this framework would exclude much of what inheres in the OCB dimension of compliance because it generally involves adherence to expectations that are either explicit or implied in the job definition. Van Dyne et al. would, however, place the helping dimension within ERB, characterizing it as an affiliative form of ERB. In other words, OCB/helping is a form of ERB that enhances the affective bonds among organizational members, arises from and generates positive emotional states of members, and promotes consensus rather than conflict.

In contrast to OCB/helping are **whistle-blowing (WB)** (Near and Miceli, 1987) and **principled organizational dissent (POD)** (Graham, 1986b). WB brings to light unethical or illegal practices occurring within the organization and initiates actions by authorities who can terminate such practices. POD voices conscientious objection to existing organizational conditions because of concerns about efficiency, legitimacy, or justice. WB and POD both qualify as ERB in that they aim to establish the greater good of the firm and go beyond routine job expectations. (Admittedly, some forms of WB might be part of formal job responsibilities, as with officers in charge of compliance with federal and state laws regarding treatment of minorities and financial accounting.) However, unlike OCB/helping, WB and POD are challenging forms of ERB because, in the short run, they meet with resistance and invite controversy rather than consensus and positive regard. The distinction between affiliative and challenging forms of ERB is significant because we would expect both the antecedents and the immediate consequences of such behavior to be quite different.

We wish to make clear to the reader that we do not hope or expect to do justice to all of these frameworks within this volume. Pursuing the implications of all of the nuances between and among these concepts, as well as the fine distinctions suggested by writers within each of these frameworks, would take us far afield and probably bog us down in an unwieldy collection of constructs. We strongly encourage the reader to explore these other frameworks. The Van Dyne et al. (1995) selection would be a good place to start, because these researchers have provided an instructive approach to thinking about linkages, overlaps, and contrasts among the concepts we have mentioned.

We note several frameworks here (and at selected points throughout the book) because, together with OCB, they represent dependent variables or criteria that go beyond the more traditional notion of task performance that dominated research on organizational behavior prior to 1983 (Organ & Paine, 1999). Up to that time, researchers justified the study of individual and group psychology in organizations, at least as an applied science, because they hoped it would explain differences in task productivity among individuals in the workplace. Now, the general understanding is that task productivity is determined largely by technology and the design of workflow, with variations that are largely accounted for by an individual's cognitive ability. The more discretionary contributions that go beyond narrowly defined task productivity are more likely to involve either "trait" variables (personality factors) or "state" conditions, such as beliefs, attitudes (notably attitudes about workplace features such as supervision and pay), and emotions.

Our main focus in this volume is what the research community refers to as OCB, because far more empirical research has addressed OCB as originally defined and measured than any of the other variants of extra-role behavior. The continuity or this research stream vastly facilitates the job of providing a narrative of developments in this area.

However, before concluding this chapter, we need to reckon with an issue some scholars have raised regarding the interpretability of OCB research.

Are OCB Measures Consistent With the Construct Definition?

In Chapter 1, we defined OCB as pertaining to discretionary contributions that go beyond the strict description or interpretation of job requirements and that do not lay claim to contractual recompense from the formal reward system. Yet measures used in OCB research refer to specific behaviors that some would argue are generally expected of participants and explicitly agreed to in accepting a position in the organization. Examples include being on time, maintaining regular attendance, giving notice when unable to come to work, keeping a clean workplace, staying informed about developments in the company, attending and participating in meetings, following the rules, not abusing rights or privileges, and respecting the rights and privileges of others. Moreover, these and other items in most OCB scales (such as making suggestions for improvement of operations), to the extent that they describe a "good team player," are apt to be given some credit by their supervisors, even to the extent that they figure in formal appraisal of participants' performance. Some critics reasonably suggest, then, that measures that include these types of behaviors are not entirely consistent with the definition of OCB—although such behaviors are certainly laudable and go beyond what we usually think of as productivity or task performance.

Research by Morrison (1994) indicates that employees themselves tend to describe many if not most of the OCB scale items as "part of their job." Moreover, she found a positive correlation between the extent to which the workers regarded these behaviors as part of the job and how often they performed them. Finally, MacKenzie, Podsakoff, and Fetter (1991, 1993) have documented the assertion that performance ratings—even of salespeople, whose productivity can be measured in unambiguous, objective terms—are strongly correlated with superiors' ratings of the items that comprise OCB scales, and to an extent that cannot be explained by sales volume alone.

Organ (1997a) agreed that these observations need to be addressed. Organ cited a *Fortune* cover story titled "The End of the Job . . ." that suggested that the "job"—as an unambiguous, bounded, explicit, and formal statement of tasks and responsibilities—was on the way out, to be replaced by the more open-ended charge of "doing what one can and what needs to be done." Organ noted as well that few rewards in organizations are absolutely contractual, in any case, and much less so as business firms in the 1990s began to shy away from unequivocal promises of salary increases, bonuses, even steady work.

A tempting means of resolving the apparent contradictions between theoretical specification of OCB and its operational research definition is to buy into the definition of contextual performance (i.e., member contributions that sustain or enhance the social, psychological, and perhaps political context that supports task performance and operations). This approach would seem all the more promising given that the measures of OCB and CP are so similar, and thus the research in the name of both constructs can be merged with considerable coherence and continuity. Thus, Organ (1997a) confessed that he sympathized with the position of defining OCB along the same lines as CP, without reference to job requirements or system rewards.

However, the merging of OCB and CP becomes problematic when you consider frameworks besides OCB and CP, and when you take into account research since 1997, especially in non-U.S. settings. Consider, for example, the finding by Farh et al. (2002) that Chinese managers, when asked to provide examples that fit the original definition of OCB, include various forms of self-training or self-development—a form of contribution also noted by Katz (1964) in calling attention to constructive behaviors not explained by routine role expectations or system rewards. If CP means contributions that support and enhance the social and psychological environment in which task performance occurs, this definition does not encompass quiet study or any forms of self-development that take place in solitude.

Moreover, what would be excluded by the phrase "social and psychological environment"? One important requirement for the heuristic value of a construct is that we can specify with some clarity what it is *not*. CP would appear to exclude only what pertains to the technical, presumably nonsocial and noninteractive, requirements of a task—something like a flowchart of the prescribed operations for performing a unit of the job. Would all other behaviors in the work setting then potentially qualify as CP (or perhaps as "anti-CP"—i.e., behaviors that hurt the social and psychological context)?

Which leads us to another question: What social and psychological environments are optimal for organizational effectiveness? Results of the studies done by Farh et al. (1997) and Farh et al. (2002) in the People's Republic of China suggest that Chinese managers place much emphasis on behaviors that preserve harmony, which is an obvious manifestation of the larger notion of sustaining and enhancing the social environment. But would we generalize this finding to the assumption that more harmonious environments invariably lead to more effective organizations? At least in some cultures and industries, can some organizations be a bit too harmonious, because opinions about important issues that normally provoke heated differences of opinion, even fierce discord, are bottled up?

In truth, the way we should define OCB is not crystal clear. The two common explicit themes in the different frameworks are that OCB (a) focuses on something other than the routine functions of the job or conventional hard measures of individual productivity, and (b) contributes, directly or indirectly, to more effective organizational functioning. The varying frameworks also share two implicit themes: (a) some element of *discretion*—that is, choice, volition, and (b) variance (as should be the case in any construct pertaining to individual behavior in the workplace)—that is, OCB should refer to something that some people or groups in the organization contribute more than others do, and by extension something that is found in greater measure in some organizations than in others.

Now we come to the question of whether existing measures of OCB are consistent with the definition of OCB contained in this book, as well as with the explicit and implicit themes noted in the preceding paragraph. We would first note that such measures derive in large part from the original Smith et al. (1983) study that asked managers, "What are the things you'd like your employees to do more of, but really can't *make* them do, and for which you can't guarantee any definite rewards, other than your appreciation?" Because the managers included in their responses behaviors such as attendance, punctuality, and following the rules of the workplace, we would infer that beyond some baseline level, there was both discretion and variance in how well people exhibited such behaviors. Whatever the prescribed norm for such behaviors, obviously some individuals went well beyond the norm, or else we would have seen no variance on these items in studies of OCB. Indeed, the variance is sufficient such that fairly robust correlations with other variables— measured by different procedures from different sources—result.

We point out findings by Morrison (1994) and others that individual respondents in a work unit include the majority of OCB scale items in what they construe as "the job." We also note that individual respondents within the same unit, doing what was ostensibly the *same job*, differed in how broadly they defined that job—that is, how many of the OCB items they included. Moreover, Morrison found that "breadth of the perceived job" accounted for much of the correlation of certain attitudinal factors with rated OCB. What individuals construe as the job contains a certain degree of what we might call "moral obligations" that are not enforceable or contractual obligations of the job. Some university faculty members, for example, see it as part of the job to don academic robes and participate in commencement proceedings and similar academic ceremonies. Others consider such participation a nice thing to do and would even applaud those who do participate, but they don't feel obliged to take part themselves if pressing personal business makes it inconvenient to do so. Still others would say they have no incentive to do such things, they don't enjoy it, and it was never stipulated as a job requirement.

We believe that what people do because they consider it a moral obligation of the job can be quite consistent with how we define OCB. The point is that they are sensing an obligation that goes beyond the minimum. Indeed, Morrison (1994) noted that a distinction can be made between what is obligated by a transactional as opposed to a relational contract. Transactional contracts specify an explicit set of obligations with a precise time and manner of rendering those obligations, as well as a means of enforcement. Relational constructs are more open-ended, with some discretion as to form and timing of obligations, and depend on trust. (See Rousseau and Parks, 1993, for further discussion of different forms of contracts.)

The blurring between OCB and "the job" causes more problems of interpretation when applied to managers than is the case with hourly or nonmanagerial employees. As a rule, the higher the level of management, the more open-ended, variable, and subjective is the definition of "the job." Most managers don't punch a time clock or get paid for over-time, so much of what we think of in connection with compliance just doesn't pertain there. Managers are seldom held to some specific mini-mum level of conduct on anything. Although their level of authority and responsibility might be well-defined, specific tasks aren't. We should not be surprised, then, that the dimensional clarity of OCB appears stronger in studies of lower-level participants.

However, even studies of managers show substantial variance in how they are rated on certain dimensions of OCB, notably helping and sportsmanship (e.g., MacKenzie, Podsakoff, & Paine, 1999). We might conjecture that much of OCB at the higher ranks bespeaks considera-tion for the less powerful members. For example, a manager who con-sults with a subordinate before making out a work schedule is not necessarily attempting to adopt a participative or democratic style; he or she is probably simply engaging in common courtesy.

We would like less softness in the present definition of OCB and some means of ascertaining which OCB scale items should be modified to minimize the apparent gap between measure and definition. Indeed, what qualified as OCB in the Smith et al. (1983) study, based on managers in a manufacturing shop floor with unionized operators, would probably not be the same in a study of a service business staffed by professionals. Ideally, OCB studies should start from the ground up, as Farh et al. (2002) did when investigating the topic in a different cul-ture, so researchers can couch the measures in site-specific norms of what supervisors and others view as discretionary contributions beyond those functions mandated by consensual definitions of the job. However, to do this is often to reinvent the wheel. A more practical compromise is to work toward the evolution of measures that have substantial face validity and general applicability across a large number of work settings.

In any event, we have to recognize that precise formulation of constructs is a complex and tricky business (St. Clair & Quinn, 1997). Seldom can we say with confidence that a particular definition is, on its face, "right" or "wrong." Because constructs by their nature are abstract, one cannot point to any one concrete referent and say "that's it." We can be more confident and precise, and reach consensus more quickly, when defining lower-level concepts, but these types of ideas do not provide the power and generality we seek in social science theory.

In *The Conduct of Inquiry*, Abraham Kaplan's (1964) classic statement of a philosophy of science for the behavioral sciences, Kaplan warned against the rush for "premature closure" in a scientific construct:

> The demand for exactness of meaning and for precise definition of terms can easily have a pernicious effect, as I believe it often has had in behavioral science . . . [quoting Quine, 1953] "We may prudently let vagueness persist. . . ." That a cognitive situation is not as well structured as we would like does not imply that no inquiry made in that situation is really scientific . . . Tolerance of ambiguity is as important for creativity in science as it is anywhere else. (Kaplan, 1964, pp. 70–71)

In addition, Kaplan (1964) states that one of the criteria by which we evaluate theories and constructs is the "norm of pragmatism," which asks: How useful is the theory for research? The volume of research conducted to date under the framework of present formulation of OCB and its measures would suggest that the construct and its measures have met the norm of pragmatism. However, we should not be surprised if continuation of research and conceptual development lead to some refinements in how we define OCB and how to measure it.

Implications for Future Research

What Do We Mean by "Contributions *Beyond* the Requirements of the Job"?

We have defined OCB as contributions that go beyond the strict terms of the job or what the job is said to actually require. But which or whose job description are we talking about? Does it make a difference whether we're talking about the written job description (assuming there is such a document), the supervisor's definition of the job and what it involves, or the employee's concept of what the job requires? Which definition do you think is most appropriate? If we were to agree that the employee's definition is the most appropriate, what questions arise if employees who do the same job disagree among themselves as to what the job requires of them? For that matter, why *would* employees disagree about what the job definition is?

What Is the Most Useful Criterion for Developing a Parsimonious Taxonomy of Major Forms of OCB?

We noted in this chapter that researchers have proposed as many as 40 different forms of OCB. Some have suggested that one means of collapsing these types into a smaller number of factors is to distinguish between those that are directed toward a specific individual and those that indirectly benefit the group or organization as a whole. Others have argued for categorizing different types of OCB according to the context of time and situation in which it occurs—for example, some OCB takes place within the immediate work unit, and some arises in dealings with people outside the organization. What are the pros and cons of using each of these two particular criteria (that is, the target of the OCB or the context)? What system would you recommend? What factors would you use to determine whether any one system is better or makes more sense than another?

What Sources Should Provide the Basis for Measuring OCB?

A measure developed from interviews with managers (in particular, lower-level managers or supervisors) has been a major influence in OCB research. The assumption on the part of the researchers was that such managers would have a good sense of what behaviors on the part of subordinates are discretionary and contribute to organizational effectiveness. Is this a reasonable assumption? Why or why not? Do manager ratings of OCB contain systematic error in the form of bias? What alternative sources should be used?

Does OCB Have a Different Meaning When Applied to Executive and Professional Employees?

The bulk of research on OCB has pertained to lower-level employees, especially hourly employees in manufacturing, retailing, or health care organizations. From that research, dimensions of OCB have been defined. Do those dimensions, as well as other inferences or conclusions from research on lower-level employees, pertain to professional and/or managerial employees as well? Are there forms of OCB by managers that might be quite different from those more usually found among hourly workers? Would the forms of OCB most valued by supervisors of managerial employees differ from those valued by people who supervise rank-and-file, nonmanagerial employees? Why or why not?

3 OCB in the Context of Organization Theory

The construct that we introduced in the preceding chapters as organizational citizenship behavior (OCB), as well as related frameworks such as contextual performance (CP), are of recent vintage. Attempts to measure these constructs and relate them empirically to other variables date from about 1980. However, this does not mean that OCB was discovered in recent years. Indeed, for 70 years or more, the most important and influential theories of organization have made reference in some form to what we now call OCB.

Our task in this chapter is twofold: (a) To document the precedent set by early theorists for treating OCB (or something similar) as an important form of contribution by organizational participants, noting the continuity of ideas about OCB across eras of manifestly different fashions of managing and organizing; and (b) to sketch linkages between OCB and current perspectives on formal organizations, with particular reference to the contrasting forms of organizing represented by markets, hierarchies, and clans. We begin this task by reviewing some of the concepts articulated by Chester Barnard, author of a classic statement on the nature of organizations and perhaps the first architect of a general theory of collective action. We take note as well of Roethlisberger and Dickson's accounts of the celebrated Hawthorne studies that were conducted in the Western Electric company in the 1920s, because the interpretation of those studies borrowed substantially from the work of Barnard.

Katz and Kahn's *The Social Psychology of Organizations* (1966) provides us with a more contemporary point of departure for thinking about OCB within the context of open systems as a model for organization theory. We then turn to sociologist Peter Blau's masterful analysis of different dynamics of exchange as they occur within groups and organizations. Blau's work quite naturally leads us into the contemplation of the exchange that occurs between managers—that is, leaders—and members of their work group. Dansereau, Graen, and Haga's theory about leader-member exchange is quite instructive regarding the implications of economic and social exchange between supervisors and subordinates. Concepts of exchange further lead us to inquire into the nature of *transactions,* a topic eloquently addressed in more contemporary works by economists (notably Oliver Williamson) and organization theorists (such as William Ouchi).

We have several reasons for including these particular figures— Barnard, Roethlisberger and Dickson, Katz and Kahn, Blau, Dansereau et al., Williamson, and Ouchi. First, they have made signal contributions to the larger field of organization theory. Second, these theorists all articulated concepts, propositions, and assumptions about something that we would now translate as OCB. Finally, they represent diverse backgrounds and perspectives—managerial experience, industrial psychology, sociology, social psychology, and economics, as well as more general organization theory.

Barnard

Nearly 70 years ago, Chester Barnard (1938) undertook what was probably the first thorough analysis of the very nature of the organization as what he called a "cooperative system." He posed some startling, fundamental questions, such as: Why do organizations exist? What sustains their existence? What creates the need for authority (i.e., "the executive")?

Barnard's perspective on organizations was quite different from the views of his contemporaries. The latter put strong emphasis on the importance of formal structure and controls as the essence of organization. Massie (1965) has summarized the basic assumptions of such an approach:

> Members in a cooperative endeavor are unable to work out the relationships of their positions without detailed guidance from their superiors . . . unless clear limits are defined and enforced, members will tend to be confused and to trespass on the domains of others . . . will not cooperate unless a pattern is planned formally for them . . . coordination will not be achieved unless it is planned and directed from above . . . it is possible to predict and establish clear-cut patterns of future activities and the relationships among activities. . . . (Massie, 1965, p. 405)

Barnard realized that although formal structure and controls have their place, they do not define the essential nature of cooperative systems. He argued that "it is clear that the *willingness* of persons to contribute efforts to the cooperative system is indispensable" (Barnard, 1938, p. 84). To Barnard, "willingness" was more than grudging compliance, more than the ability to carry out specific functions in exchange for contractual compensation, more than possession of skills for performing tasks. His "willingness to contribute" went beyond such things to refer to qualities that "are commonly understood to refer to something different from effectiveness, ability or value of personal contributions" but are collectively "vaguely recognized as an essential condition of organization" (p. 84). In other words, collective endeavors require from participants some generalized attitude that we might refer to as "commitment"—a sense of being bound with the larger collective. A necessary condition is the inclination to think in terms of something larger than one's immediate task, a consciousness of the interconnectedness of individuals and their tasks, and an understanding that the quality of that interconnectedness determines the benefits for all.

An accurate rendering of Barnard's work must hew closely to his concept of organizations as "associations of cooperative efforts" (Barnard, 1938, p. 4). Consistent with this notion, Barnard stressed the indispensability of the "*willingness* of persons to contribute efforts to the cooperative system" (p. 83, italics his). Barnard here referred not to the mere willingness to join an organization in a contractual sense; nor did he intend his concept of "willingness" to mean anything like performance in a neatly defined role. He aimed rather at describing that aspect of people that prompts a cooperative stream of endeavors among a group of people. Barnard notes that this quality of "willingness . . . means self-abnegation. . . ." (p. 84). Furthermore, it is a quality noted by "the indefinitely large range of variation in its intensity among individuals" (p. 84) and, within individuals, it "cannot be constant in degree. It is necessarily intermittent and fluctuating" (p. 85).

Barnard, one must remember, does not equate the term "organization" with a formally designated entity, such as Acme, Inc. or the customer service department. Such designations simply summarize the numerous interlacing informal organizations that occur and endure at a smaller level. For Barnard, organizing is a "bottoms up" process; there are many "spontaneous organizations" (Barnard, 1938, p. 102), and "all large formal organizations are constituted of numbers of small organizations" (p. 104). He argues persuasively that conventional thinking is fallacious in imagining that a large corporation or bureau is first conceived into existence and then subdivided into successively smaller spheres; in fact, he states, the process works the other way around, except for the allocation of labels and official charters and descriptions. Cooperative systems begin at a low level and successively accumulate.

Thus, for Barnard, authority is also a "bubble up" process. It arises from, rather than initiates, the process of organizing, or the adjoining of individual actions in a cooperative endeavor. Authority follows a lagged, not a leading, relationship to the actions of individuals. Authority cannot create by fiat a stream of cooperative gestures that do not naturally arise from customs, habits, and routines that define a "willingness to cooperate" by individual actors.

For Barnard, then, the "informal organization" is of vast importance. The informal organization legitimates and stabilizes the emergent system of formal authority. Barnard's discussion (Barnard, 1938, p. 225) goes one step further by arguing that the authority system is best maintained by not overloading it. That is, the greater the extent to which necessary contributions are secured spontaneously from "willingness," the less strain is placed on formal authority, and—perhaps ironically—the more people will accept the authority system as within the bounds of what is reasonable and appropriate.

From various passages in *The Functions of the Executive* (Barnard, 1938), we may piece together some of Barnard's ideas about the determinants of OCB, or, in his terms, the "willingness to cooperate." In one instance, Barnard asserts, without elaboration, that "willingness to cooperate, positive or negative, is the expression of the net satisfactions or dissatisfactions experienced or anticipated through alternative opportunities" (p. 85). We must be careful, however, in interpreting this statement, for elsewhere (p. 140, footnote) Barnard notes that "only occasionally is the determination of satisfactions and dissatisfactions a matter of logical thought." In this regard, Barnard was decades ahead of his time in recognizing, at least implicitly, that satisfaction or dissatisfaction is a function of some uncertain, variable weighting of conscious assessments and nonrational or affective responses.

Discussing the various forms of specialization, Barnard perceptively notes that "every relatively stable or enduring unit of organization is an associational specialization in itself" (Barnard, 1938, p. 131). In other words, some combinations of individuals yield a synergistic contribution because of the way their actions uniquely complement each other. Again, we note that the resultant contribution is not borne of authoritative edict; rather, it is emergent. Such contributions vary with every potential combination of individuals. For our purposes, then, it seems that Barnard is speaking, at least obliquely, of the cohesion of the various informal organizations as a determinant of much of OCB. Barnard, not surprisingly, goes on to note the importance of "associational attractiveness" as a key inducement of cooperative efforts.

Because of the importance of "associational attractiveness" and "associational specialization," Barnard contends that effective organizations practice a "rejection of some of those best able to contribute the material production and acceptance of some less able" (Barnard, 1938, p.155). A premium is placed on compatibility of personnel; people must fit, and "this question of 'fitness' involves such matters as education, experience, age, sex, personal distinctions, prestige, race, nationality, faith, politics, sectional antecedents; and such very specific personal traits as manners, speech, personal appearance, etc." (p. 224). Instinctively, we recoil at Barnard's apparent approval of localized discrimination on the basis of race, sex, age, faith, but in fairness to him he recognized (p. 225) that "excessive compatibility or harmony is deleterious." Also, he was not writing as a moralist—he simply was compelled by intellectual honesty to observe that cohesiveness, even when maintained by exclusions we might consider repugnant, has its advantage in promoting the willingness for spontaneous, cooperative efforts. Aside from the ethical question, there is the additional trade-off that "excessive compatibility" breeds rigidity in thinking and impedes the group's capacity for adapting to sudden changes in its environment.

Barnard was vehement in his contention that "it appears utterly contrary to the nature of men to be sufficiently induced by material or monetary considerations to contribute enough effort to a cooperative system to enable it to be productively efficient to the degree necessary for persistence over an extended period" (Barnard, 1938, p. 93). In other words, the full extent of what he termed "willingness to cooperate" is not purchased in a purely contractual exchange. "Associational attractiveness," sense of purpose, and many other "satisfactions" that, consciously or otherwise, accrue incidentally to the process of cooperative endeavor are vital to the maintenance of the willingness to cooperate.

Remember that the word "executive" in the title of Barnard's book does not refer merely to a single person acting in a formally defined role, and "the functions are not, as so frequently stated, to manage a group of persons" (Barnard, 1938, p. 216). Executive functions, rather, "serve to maintain a system of cooperative effort," and Barnard devotes considerable space to noting how the informal organization renders executive functions.

In sum, then, much in the tone and spirit of Barnard's exposition suggests the importance of spontaneous contributions by individuals that go beyond the content of contractual obligations, obedience to legitimate authority, or calculated striving for remuneration as mediated by the formal organization. In his analysis, the requirement of a generalized "willingness to cooperate" is presented as a fundamental basis of organized activity.

Roethlisberger and Dickson

Historically, Roethlisberger and Dickson's (1939) *Management and the Worker* is regarded as the major chronicle of the Hawthorne studies (conducted at the Hawthorne Western Electric plant outside Chicago), which in turn are thought to have inaugurated the human relations school of management and organization theory. As most readers are aware, the Hawthorne studies began with some inconclusive experiments in 1924 intended to establish the relationship between illumination and productivity. In 1927, at the Western Electric plant in Chicago, a different series of experiments began that investigated the effects of rest pauses and schedules of work. Hoping to avoid some of the distractions and complications attendant to the earlier illumination experiments, researchers separated the experimental group of five female operators from the rest of the plant by setting up a special Relay Assembly Test Room. As the experiments proceeded, the researcher took over more of the supervisory functions of the group. The experimental group showed a general trend toward increased productivity over the next 2 years, and researchers felt that the productivity increases could not be fully explained by the rest pauses, hours of work, or even the special job design and pay system that were in effect for this group. The emergent hypothesis was that such factors interacted with the change in supervisory treatment and the unforeseen development of the operators into a cohesive group with its own structure and its own rules of conduct. To pursue the implications of this form of analysis of work behavior, subsequent studies—including a massive interviewing program and extended observation of one particular work group in action—were undertaken.

Preliminary accounts of findings from the Hawthorne studies soon became available to outsiders through unofficial correspondence and presentations to trade groups, even while the experiments were still going on. However, the reports were generally fragmented in nature and, even in their totality, did not provide an adequate account of the full extent of the studies. *Management and the Worker* was Roethlisberger and Dickson's effort to provide a coherent, chronological account of the various studies and, more importantly, to undergird the findings with serious interpretive commentary. Because Roethlisberger and Dickson repeatedly use concepts from the behavioral sciences (anthropology, sociology, clinical psychology) to interpret the data, their work is regarded by many as adumbrating a "behavioral" or "human relations" perspective on organization.

A voluminous body of literature has developed, and continues to grow, from the interest in reanalyzing the Hawthorne data, ascertaining what really went on, and challenging the motives as well as the intellectual rigor of Hawthorne chroniclers. Let us put aside the issue of what the studies proved. (Actually, it is not clear that Roethlisberger and Dickson thought they had proved anything, other than the difficulty of understanding work behavior within the context of conventional management concepts.) Instead, let us examine the overarching framework by which the authors proposed to better comprehend organizational functioning.

Like Barnard—indeed, borrowing from Barnard, whose book is cited twice in footnotes—Roethlisberger and Dickson (1939) drew a distinction between the formal and the informal organization. The formal organization "includes the systems, policies, rules, and regulations of the plant which express what the relations of one person to another are supposed to be in order to achieve effectively the task of technical production" (p. 558). It includes all the "explicitly stated systems of control introduced by the company in order to achieve the economic purposes of the total enterprise and the effective contribution of the members of the organization to those ends" (p. 558).

However, as demonstrated in the various phases of the Hawthorne studies,

> There is something more to the social organization than what is formally recognized ... the formal organization cannot take account of the sentiments and values residing in the social organization by means of which individuals or groups of individuals are informally differentiated, ordered, and integrated. (Roethlisberger & Dickson, 1939, p. 559)

In other words, patterns of informal organization develop incidental to the explicit relationships and transactions governed by the formal system.

One often reads or hears of credit given to the Hawthorne group for "discovering" the informal organization. This attribution is of doubtful validity for, as we have seen, Barnard made a thorough analysis of informal organization. However, an even more serious misattribution by some present-day writers is the distortion of Roethlisberger and Dickson's view of the function of the informal organization. The researchers did not construe an informal organization as a social device created for the purpose of protecting the interests of workers against the exploitative encroachment by management, nor solely as a means of satisfying powerful social needs neglected by the system. To be sure, "sometimes the informal organization develops in opposition to the formal organization" (Roethlisberger & Dickson, 1939, p. 559). The larger point is that "informal social organization exists in every plant, and can be said to be a necessary prerequisite for effective collaboration. Much collaboration exists at an informal level, and it sometimes facilitates the functioning of the formal organization" (p. 559). Furthermore,

> Informal organization appears at all levels, from the very bottom to the very top of the organization. Informal organization at the executive level, just as at the work level, may either facilitate or impede purposive cooperation and communication. In either case, at all levels of the organization informal organizations exist as a necessary condition for collaboration. (Roethlisberger & Dickson, p. 562)

The key words in the foregoing passages, for our purposes, are "collaboration" and "informal." Together, they contain the essence of what OCB is all about.

But there is another key word in Roethlisberger and Dickson's discussion: "sentiments." Sentiments are the underlying dimensions of attitudes, values, and feelings that shape the informal organization. As the Hawthorne researchers realized in the course of interviewing more than 20,000 plant employees, sentiments may be expressed in what ostensibly are statements of fact, but sentiments have their own logic, which is entirely different from the logic of objective fact. Individually and collectively, the sharing and social validation of sentiments determine both the structure and the consequences of informal organization.

Because the term "sentiments" seems so close to what we think of as attitudes, and because it is commonplace to use the terms "job attitudes" and "job satisfaction" interchangeably, perhaps it is understandable that Roethlisberger and Dickson have been interpreted as suggesting that "job satisfaction determines job performance" or, as it is more baldly put, "a happy worker is a productive worker." Such a rendering does not, however, do justice to the subtlety of their analysis.

They were not addressing the matter of individual productivity as such, but the quality of collaboration that goes beyond such performance. And although they may be rightly criticized for not precisely specifying what is encompassed by the notion of "sentiments," their conception probably could not be adequately contained within the instruments typically used today to measure job satisfaction.

Katz and Kahn

Katz and Kahn's *The Social Psychology of Organizations,* first published in 1966 (a revised edition appeared in 1978), is perhaps the best known and most comprehensive behavioral analysis of organizations based on the open system model. The book represents an approach that incorporated the legitimate contributions of both the classical and human relations schools without the oversimplifications of either of those perspectives.

Katz and Kahn (1966) argued that effective organizations must evoke three different forms of contributions from participants: They must (a) attract and hold people within the system, (b) ensure that members exhibit dependable role performance, meeting and preferably exceeding certain minimal qualitative and quantitative criteria, and (c) evoke "innovative and spontaneous behavior: performance beyond role requirements for accomplishments of organizational functions" (p. 337). The third category includes cooperative activities with fellow members, actions protective of the system, original ideas for improvement of the system, self-training for additional contributions, and gestures that promote a favorable climate for the organization in the external environment.

Commenting at further length on spontaneous, or extra-role, behavior, Katz and Kahn noted that "the patterned activity which makes up an organization is so intrinsically cooperative and interrelated that it tends to resemble habitual behavior of which we are unaware" (Katz & Kahn, 1939, p. 339). In other words, this type of behavior is so mundane and undramatic that we almost never feel compelled to account for it. In fact, we generally take it for granted:

> Within every work group in a factory, within any division in a government bureau, or within any department of a university are countless acts of cooperation without which the system would break down. We take these everyday acts for granted, and few of them are included in the formal role prescriptions for any job. (p. 339)

What is particularly edifying about Katz and Kahn's discussion is the recognition that three types of required behaviors arise from different motivational patterns. System rewards—those that accrue to individuals by virtue of membership in the formal system—aid in the recruitment and attachment of potential contributors but offer no incentive for in-role performance above the minimal standards. Individual instrumental rewards (e.g., merit pay) provide an incentive for in-role performance above the minimally accepted levels but do not create a motivational basis for extra-role behaviors. Intrinsic rewards from task operations may sustain high-quality output but do not necessarily bind an individual to the system nor stimulate actions supportive of others. In other words, although all three classes of behavior are important, they are not evoked by the same conditions, and organizational devices that enhance the level of one form of contribution may even decrease one of the other forms.

Although they argue that system rewards fail to motivate incremental performance within the system, Katz and Kahn do acknowledge that such rewards, to the extent that they foster a generalized attraction to the organization, can lead to a higher incidence of cooperative relations among members. For this outcome to be brought about, the administration of system rewards must be perceived as equitable and creating no invidious distinctions among persons or groups: "In our culture we accept individual differences in income but we do not readily accept differences in classes of citizenship" (p. 357). Here, and especially in the elaborations upon this theme in their 1978 revision, Katz and Kahn seem to imply that something like "sense of citizenship" mediates the effect of system rewards upon OCB. A sense of citizenship translates into a readiness to contribute beyond the literal contractual obligations, just as a good citizen in the civic sense does more than simply not violate the law. A good citizen does not rest upon mere compliance; he or she does something more to promote the community. But to feel like a citizen, one must feel that one is treated like a citizen and accorded rights, privileges, and respect.

In the 1978 edition, Katz and Kahn note a dilemma that often proves agonizing for administrators: Differentials in rewards within the system motivate higher in-role performance by those who have the ability to exceed minimal criteria, but varying rewards run the risk of violating the sense of equity, and thus the sense of citizenship, experienced by those receiving lesser remuneration. Increasingly, "in bureaucratic structures equity has replaced respect for tradition as a guiding principle . . . the morale problem for years to come for organizations in Western countries will be one of equity" (1978, p. 391).

This observation proved prophetic. In the 1990s, the effect of increasingly globalized markets ushered in an era of vastly increased differentials in pay and other perquisites in industry, sports, entertainment, even universities. To meet the market price for attracting and holding outstanding talent in management, the professions, artisans, athletes, the organizations employing them skewed their compensation schemes ever more dramatically in favor of "the best and the brightest." Some evidence suggests that this phenomenon in at least some instances took its toll on some dimensions of organizational effectiveness. In a study of more than 100 manufacturing firms, Cowherd and Levine (1992) found that a higher level of inequality of pay was associated with a diminished level of product quality as perceived by customers. The researchers did not measure OCB, but they speculated that lower levels of spontaneous cooperation constituted the link between steep pay differentials and lower product quality. Pfeffer and Langton (1993) studied salary dispersion in 600 academic departments within 300 institutions and found that increased variance of pay within academic units was negatively related to research productivity, satisfaction, and desire to work collaboratively. Of course, a necessary caveat to interpreting these findings is that the studies were cross-sectional. One can imagine reverse causal relationships at work—for example, it is conceivable that high-priced talent was necessary to improve conditions where product quality was already low, or that premiums were necessary to attract productive scholars to institutions not noted for their productivity.

In short, Katz and Kahn's analysis recognizes a trade-off that is unavoidable in organizations. At one extreme stands pure egalitarianism, with all contributors sharing alike as a condition of membership. Such an arrangement perhaps intensifies among the rank and file the sense of citizenship, thereby evoking a broadly distributed pattern of acts of OCB—but blunting the incentive for higher individual task productivity and making it difficult to attract and retain the highest levels of technical and innovative talent. At the other extreme is a structure maximally geared toward the recognition and differential rewarding of individual productivity, thus encouraging technical excellence but curbing the disposition of the less excellent to contribute in the more humble vein of citizenship. In between, of course, lie the mixes of varying emphases on differential treatment versus equal treatment.

Undoubtedly, we have defined the trade-off in unnecessarily stark terms. We can imagine some threshold of differential rewards below which no basic sense of citizenship is violated for the less rewarded. And maybe there is ample room within that threshold to activate the striving for excellence among the most able. However, the extension of Katz and Kahn's logic suggests that we have here two fundamentally different motivational bases of organizational effectiveness.

Blau

One perspective on social and interpersonal relationships is to think of them as the product of a history of exchange. This is the tack that Peter Blau takes in *Exchange and Power in Social Life* (1964). Exchange can be economic or social. *Economic exchange,* according to Blau, has a marketplace character. Each partner to the exchange specifies in advance exactly what will be exchanged and when the exchanges will occur. Each commodity or service that is exchanged has a value that is independent of the person or group offering that commodity or service. The exchange relationship has a finite duration, and trust between the principals is not important (because if either party reneges on contractual obligations, the other party can seek recourse in enforcement mechanisms, such as the courts or some higher authority or referee).

In contrast, *social exchange* does not make explicit what will be exchanged. A party initiates social exchange by spontaneously giving another party something of value—a tangible product or a service, or a favor or gesture of respect, admiration, or support. The value of what is given is subjective and depends on the identity of the person giving it. For example, praise from a high-status or respected person is valued more than praise from a less-respected source, and the support of politically powerful people is prized more than the support of those with little clout.

Someone who receives such a gift is likely to feel some obligation to reciprocate, or to repay the "debt." However, at the time of receipt of the gift, neither party makes reference to what, when, or how the reciprocation will occur, nor does either party entertain any thoughts about "enforcement" of the reciprocation. If reciprocation is indeed forthcoming, and if both parties place value on what they have exchanged, they are likely to increase their rate of interaction with each other, which in turn will present occasions for more frequent—and probably more significant—social exchanges with each other. At some point, they will no longer think in terms of reciprocating each specific gesture, but instead will harbor a more general feeling that the relationship proves rewarding to both. What matters is not some exact "balancing of the books"; rather, because the relationship is open-ended in terms of duration, both parties simply anticipate that they will continue to give and receive from each other elements of social value.

Of course, some of the exchange that occurs between the organization (or its agents) and a participant is of an economic or transactional character. In the employment relationship, individuals contract to perform certain duties, for specified intervals of time, for an agreed-upon package of basic pay, benefits, and privileges. However, when a participant begins to interact with others, patterns of social exchange develop as well. Interactions with coworkers and customers, and with supervisors and other managers in particular, develop in such a way that the relationship often becomes a mix of economic and social exchange. A participant realizes that certain contributions are mandated in exchange for contractually specified inducements. If the individual assesses some of those inducements as going beyond what was contractually promised, he might also feel bound to "pay back" with contributions in some form beyond those obligated by the employment contract. This could happen if, for example, the supervisor is viewed as the most visible agent of the organization and the one who mediates not only the provision of material benefits from the organization but also the larger sense of supportiveness enacted by organizational policy, practices, and culture.

Alternatively, managers or coworkers who see that an individual, group, or indeed the bulk of the workforce goes well beyond what was contractually required also experience some personal or corporate sentiment of indebtedness, and seek to reciprocate with forms of supportiveness beyond those committed to in the employment contract. That is, the initiative for social exchange might come from either direction—agents of the organization or the workforce—and thereafter continue as long as the respective parties anticipate such exchanges of valued elements.

Leader-Member Exchange (LMX) Theory

During most of the 20th century, the theoretical and empirical literature on leadership focused on the leader's *style*, which encompasses how supportive the leader is, to what extent the leader provides structure and clarity to the roles and expected behaviors by group members, and how much participation the leader provides for subordinate input. The assumption in leadership theory and research was that a leader actually has a specific style vis-à-vis the group as a whole and that leader effectiveness could be explained in terms of that style.

In a major departure from traditional thinking about leadership, Dansereau, Graen, and Haga (1975) challenged the validity of thinking in terms of a general leadership style. Previously, Lowin and Craig (1968) and Greene (1975) had demonstrated that leader behavior is, in fact, a function of subordinate behavior. For example, Lowin and Craig, in a field experiment, systematically manipulated the behavior of a subordinate (who was actually a confederate of the researchers) such that the subordinate ("Charlie") was either competent, organized, and conscientious, or incompetent, sloppy, and lackadaisical. The supervisor (the unwitting subject in the experiment) who dealt with the competent Charlie responded with a friendly, participative style of behavior, whereas the supervisor confronted with the incompetent Charlie remained interpersonally aloof and insisted that Charlie strictly adhere to the supervisor's instructions.

Dansereau et al. (1975) reasoned that if leader behavior is some function of the subordinate's abilities and attitudes, *and* if subordinates vary demonstrably in such abilities and attitudes, then the leader will not really enact one style, but different styles with different subordinates (see Graen & Uhl-Bien, 1995, for a review of theory and research on LMX theory). Furthermore, leaders have good reason to vary those styles with different group members. Leaders can seldom fulfill their responsibilities if all group members do only what is minimally required and enforceable. Leaders need that extra margin of contribution that some members are able and willing to provide. To induce such contributions, the leader has to provide to such members more than he or she is bound by formalities to offer. Therefore, the leader makes a distinction between "hired hands" and "cadres." With hired hands, the leader maintains a contractual relationship: The leader gets the minimum required input from the workers and provides them with what he or she is required as a supervisor to give. On the other hand, with cadres, the leader essentially "negotiates" (perhaps implicitly) what he or she is willing to offer (more discretion in task assignments, more input in workplace decisions, access to additional organizational resources, such as training or sponsorship to conferences) in exchange for the subordinate's contribution beyond the strictest definition of the job.

We call attention here to some straightforward implications of LMX theory. The "extra" contributions by the cadres would likely include much of what we have defined as OCB (although it is clear from LMX theory that those extra contributions also include levels of task performance beyond the norm). In addition, the relationship between the leader and a cadre goes beyond the formal or transactional specifications of the job descriptions to include social exchange that is fluid, subjective, and ambiguous as to precisely what is exchanged for what. Therefore, the exchange depends on trust—trust of the supervisor in the cadre and, especially, trust of the cadre in the supervisor. Indeed, in more recent developments of LMX theory and research, trust looms as a critical variable in the maintenance of the social exchange relationship. Note also that research (e.g., Settoon, Bennett, & Liden, 1996) empirically confirms the view that the quality of LMX is strongly associated with subordinate perceptions of organizational supportiveness and with independent ratings of the subordinate's OCB. Moreover, the correlations of LMX with OCB were somewhat higher than the correlations with task or in-role performance.

Williamson and Transaction Cost Economics

In his classic work, *Markets and Hierarchies* (1975), Oliver Williamson sought to explain why market failures occur under certain conditions and why bureaucracy arises as a substitute for markets when those adverse conditions occur. Central to Williamson's analysis is the idea of the transaction costs of market exchanges, which are prohibitive under certain conditions. Although Williamson's approach allows him to address a stunning variety of economic phenomena (e.g., vertical integration, the multidivisional form of organizational structure, oligopoly and monopoly), his perspective on the employment relation is what pertains to our agenda here.

The essence of market exchange is the contract. Two (or potentially more than two, but always "small numbers" (Williamson, 1975)) enter into a contract specifying a quid pro quo for each principal. ("Small numbers" means too small for an impersonal market to determine price; it is small enough that at least one principal can affect market price by making a bid or withdrawing.) Transaction costs are trivial if the exchange involves a commodity for one-time use or consumption and if a market consisting of many buyers and sellers determines the price for the commodity. Contracts can be extended to cover longer periods of repeated exchanges if both principals can be confident that they can foresee the relevant states of nature that will exist during the period of the contract. If potential disruption of these states of nature can be imagined, the principals can include in the contract some statements of "contingent claims"—that is, how the terms of the contract would be altered by specific changes in the relevant states of nature.

Obviously, the more that one has to think about changes in the state of nature and how those changes would alter the rights and obligations of the principals, the greater the costs of such transactions. Another complicating factor includes the specificity of the assets to be exchanged; the more specific they are to the uses and desires of one of the principals, the more strenuous the process of contracting. In addition, under some conditions, one principal will have more knowledge about the benefits of one of the assets exchanged and/or alternative sources or buyers of that asset. The fact that the other principal has to reckon with the disadvantage of less knowledge will also complicate the formulation of a contract.

When applied to the employment relation, the proprietor (supervisor or manager) finds that transaction costs become intractable. The proprietor cannot foresee all contributions that will be desired of an employee. Even many of those that can be foreseen cannot be assessed in terms of their benefits—that is, what they would be worth to the proprietor. Nor can the proprietor, when hiring an employee, determine in advance how specific the prospective employee's skills (knowledge, aptitude, even aspects of temperament) might prove in terms of matching the contributions needed or desired. Thus, rather than forging a contract with complex contingent claims—because doing so exceeds human-bounded rationality for both the proprietor and the employee— the proprietor offers a wage rate with a premium, something well above the most narrowly defined and immediately foreseeable value of the employee's duties. In exchange, the employee agrees to some degree of ambiguity about what he or she might be asked to do. The idea is much like Barnard's (1938) notion of "zone of indifference"—that is, that the manager's authority over an employee lies within an area in which the employee would otherwise be indifferent about accommodating some direction from the manager.

You might well ask, "Why not agree to pay the employee on something like a piece rate system, such that the employee is paid according to the value of contributions rendered over some finite time period?" Of course, in some instances the employee and manager do agree on such an arrangement. However, what if the proprietor cannot foresee all the contributions the employee will make? Moreover, how would the proprietor (who has other things to do) ascertain the actual occurrence and value of contributions claimed by the employee? How would employee and proprietor come to an agreement on what contributions were made and how they should be evaluated? What if the employee, by virtue of practice and experience in the employ of the proprietor, comes to possess skills specific to the tasks carried for this particular proprietor, making his or her contributions more frequent or of higher quality?

Perhaps most of the contributions to be rendered by the employee can be ascertained by monitoring—or, in Williamson's term, "metering." Some oversight or some form of technology might serve this purpose. However, as Williamson notes, "metering" has side effects on sentiments and attitudes, and such effects could adversely influence other important contributions that cannot be feasibly metered.

Thus, metering has its costs. Once again, the preferred arrangement is to offer compensation, which need not refer strictly to salary or wages, but might include other benefits, perquisites, or conveniences. This compensation would include a premium in excess of the value of immediately realizable contributions from the employee, with the understanding that some unspecified tasks might later arise that the proprietor, because of the premium in the compensation, could reasonably instruct the employee to perform.

Williamson's discussion does not make clear whether he thought the employee would make some of these unspecified contributions without the proprietor's knowledge or awareness that such contributions were needed—that is, contributions that the employee would spontaneously perform because he or she might find it appropriate to perform a task not specified in either the original agreement or even ad hoc by the employer. Nonetheless, it is not too much of a stretch to extend Williamson's thinking to the sorts of things we have now placed under the rubric of OCB. So we can reasonably think in terms of an employee's contributions consisting of, first, the originally agreed upon job definition and obligatory tasks; second, some other contributions not originally specified but well within the tacit bounds of what the proprietor might in the future ask of the employee; and third, contributions made spontaneously by the employee that were neither originally specified nor explicitly ordered by the proprietor. Moreover, we can readily see not only how the employment relation explicitly described by Williamson vastly reduces transaction costs, but we realize as well that spontaneous contributions by the employee virtually eliminate certain transaction costs altogether. The proprietor does not have to monitor the work process to know what ad hoc instructions or orders are necessary, nor does he or she have to engage in any implicit negotiations pertaining to the appropriateness of the order within the employment relation.

Williamson's larger point is that the employment relation is an arrangement intended to circumvent the inordinate transaction costs that a "pure market" approach would present. Ironically, organizations sometimes seem to go to great lengths to "bring the market back in." A graphic example of such efforts occurred at BankAmerica ("Many Companies…" 1985). A program initiated there by Mr. Frank Schultz, a senior vice president, "universally and rigorously" assessed each of the 3,500 employees in the credit-card division on 200 specific criteria of performance. "I measure everything that moves," Mr. Schultz reported. Staff officials listened in on telephone calls made by customer-service representatives, and outsiders were hired to place bogus customer calls. The program required 20 full-time staff people and cost about $1 million a year. Schultz obviously believed that management could foresee and specify any employee action that represented a contribution and that his office could accurately monitor and assess those contributions.

Ouchi

The polar opposite of the employment arrangement at BankAmerica is what William Ouchi (1980) has described as the "clan." Ouchi's analysis extends Williamson's work on markets and hierarchies, beginning, as Williamson does, with consideration of the necessary and sufficient conditions for markets—but also hierarchies (bureaucracies)—to function effectively as mechanisms for mediating transactions. Markets resolve the divergent interests of various parties by competitive bidding, which establishes unequivocal quids for particular quos in the contractual relationships among participants. The bureaucratic mechanism of hierarchy replaces the market when the exact nature of certain contributions cannot be spelled out in advance but can be enacted by employee response to directives based on legitimate authority and, ultimately, fairly and reliably compensated by authoritative assessment. In other words, when the conditions requisite to an efficient market no longer obtain, the hierarchy becomes the alternative mechanism of control.

However, conditions may arise such that even the hierarchy does not suffice to mediate efficiently the transactions among parties. In particular, when the value of the contribution of individual members cannot— even after the fact—be reliably assessed, and when contributors cannot assume commonality of interests, the motivational basis of cooperative endeavors is rent asunder.

The clan becomes the viable form of collective action when individual contributions can neither be specified a priori contractually nor computed after the fact. A *clan* is an association of persons bound together by relationships analogous to those defined by kinship or blood relations. The parties construe their individual interests as similar to each other and concordant with those of the collective as a whole. To promote each other's interests is to promote that of the community and vice versa. In the long run, both types of interests promote the individual's own interest, because each member has faith that ultimately the family looks after its own.

In describing Japanese firms, Ouchi (1980, p. 132) notes that it is not necessary for these organizations to measure performance to control or direct their employees, because the employees' natural (socialized) inclination is to do what is best for the firm. In addition, the organizations do not need to derive explicit, verifiable measures of value added, because rewards are distributed according to criteria that are not related to performance (e.g., seniority, age), which are relatively inexpensive to determine.

Ouchi's reference here is not to the study of a particular firm, but to a general or theoretical alternative organizational form that has been approximated in some cultures (such as many Japanese firms at the time of Ouchi's writing) in the clan, affective bonds among members are sufficiently strong, and their interests are sufficiently concordant, that participants can be presumed to act as needed to render contributions to the collective. With markets, we must specify outcomes, their value, and means of measurement. In hierarchies, we pay a premium above the "spot price" to be able to specify "efforts" (the behavioral means to those outcomes) now and on some *ad hoc* basis in the future, but some degree of monitoring or surveillance is required to ensure that such efforts are made. At some level, the costs of surveillance can approach the transaction costs of markets, and, as Williamson noted, such "metering" has potentially negative fallout upon member sentiments. The clan, by virtue of its cohesion and consensus, obviates concern about "free riders" or opportunism and does not require close monitoring. The clan does not require rigorous assessment of outcomes other than a rudimentary understanding of the kinds of outcomes that further the interest of the collective group.

Because he observed actual employment practices in Japanese organizations in the 1970s, Ouchi seems to have regarded the clan as not just a "pure type" or an abstraction, but rather a viable form of organization that can and does exist. Nonetheless, one would certainly imagine that, at least in the United States and other cultures that have strong individualistic values, the requisite conditions seldom exist except in rather small family-owned firms or in nonprofit organizations. At times in American history, we have seen the proliferation of collectives that Graham and Organ (1993) call "covenantal" organizations, which they describe in terms reminiscent of Ouchi's clan. In such collectives, one might argue that OCB as we have construed it was defined away, because participants were not bound to performing just some finite duties, but rather to contributing in any form possible to the welfare of the larger collective.

With few exceptions, the business organizations that came closest to some "pure" clan or covenantal organization were short-lived, lasting perhaps a generation or two. However, a few contemporary business firms have been described in terms that certainly suggest some degree of clan-like properties. Ouchi (1980) characterized a number of American organizations (such as the U.S. Army and Eli Lilly) as "Theory Z" organizations that adapt some clan-like attributes within the constraints of an individualistic societal culture and public policy framework. Others have noted a covenantal character to features of companies such as Herman Miller, Inc. and Cummins Engine (Graham and Organ, 1993).

What we come down to, then, are contrasting prototypes of collective frameworks in terms of their faith in, and dependence upon, what we call OCB. The heuristic value of such prototypes does not depend upon the existence of any organizations that perfectly embody their attributes. As Ouchi (1980) notes, "markets, bureaucracies and clans are therefore three distinct mechanisms which may be present in differing degrees in any real organization."

We are consistent with the main themes of contemporary theorizing about organizations when we choose to array organizations according to the implicit significance that is accorded OCB. At one extreme, organizations might choose to emulate the properties of markets, and in so doing define away the need for OCB. At the other extreme, the clan or covenantal organization also essentially defines away OCB, because it is already understood that members are bound by the commitment to do whatever furthers collective interests. Between those extremes lie organizations with varying explicit duties and efforts for precise compensation. If we assume that in most contemporary Western organizations—especially those of substantial size in the private sector—neither pure markets nor clans are viable (at least, not for very long), we must conclude that OCB in some form must be accorded some importance.

Conclusions

As the foregoing citations show, the concept of OCB has been incorporated in varied paradigms dating back well over half a century, and a careful parsing of even more ancient writings about organization would almost certainly show evidence of concern about its nurturance. Thus, our intent is not to offer a new theory of organizations, nor to do battle with any particular school of thought. Rather, our aim is to establish a clearinghouse of sorts to consolidate and test the insights of different schools concerning the generally recognized aspects of organizations. We would also like to explore OCB as a phenomenon in its own right, to discover the determinants of its occurrence, to speculate about what conditions would evoke it, and to investigate what the countervailing costs of such conditions might be.

Implications for Future Research

How Does the Phenomenon of "Idiosyncratic Deals" Fit Within the Framework of OCB?

To date, the implications of Williamson's transaction cost economics for thinking about OCB have received scant attention. In particular, we know little about the prevalence of "idiosyncratic deals" (Rousseau, 2001), arrangements by which employees explicitly negotiate with their superiors specific resources or opportunities in exchange for taking on tasks or responsibilities not within the purview of their formal job descriptions. Williamson's framework would suggest that the greater the prevalence of such individualized deal making, the greater the transaction costs associated with the internal labor market of the hierarchy compared to traditional market mechanisms. Rousseau (2001) suggests that idiosyncratic deals provide a measure of flexibility by which a firm can retain valued knowledge workers who are hard to replace. On the other hand, because these deals are ad hoc arrangements, suspicions will arise among employees that some workers are getting better deals than others. Therefore, we would predict that the employees would develop beliefs that the system is not fair. Will idiosyncratic deals actually lead to less OCB on the part of those not inclined toward explicit deal-making? Conversely, does idiosyncratic deal-making arise because of a perception that the organization already has indicated that it is moving toward a more transactional style of managing?

Do the Dynamics of Leader-Member Exchange Present a Threat to the Validity of Managerial Ratings of Subordinate OCB?

We have noted the affinity between OCB concepts and the leader-member exchange (LMX) model. In research on OCB, more often than not, the leader (i.e., supervisor or superior) is the one who provides ratings of the OCB subordinates. Conceivably, the favorable rating that the leader gives one subordinate as compared to another is part and parcel of the exchange itself, and the exchange might have more to do with how well the leader and subordinate get along rather than with more substantive contributions to the effectiveness of the workplace. This, in turn, raises the question of whether much of the OCB that is actually rated consists of highly selective, even contrived, gestures that basically amount to a form of ingratiation. Research addressing this issue—for example, studies using both leader and coworker ratings and looking at variables that might correlate with larger discrepancies between leader and peer OCB ratings—could prove instructive.

Would "360-Degree" Performance Appraisals Offer a Promising Approach to Measuring OCB?

One of the hottest new trends in performance appraisal during the 1990s was the practice of "360-degree" appraisal. In practice, this meant performance appraisal from the perspectives of supervisor, coworkers, internal or external customer/client, and even subordinates (for managers being appraised). Some potentially enlightening findings could come from studies on OCB that make use of these 360-degree appraisals. Which raters appear to emphasize OCB the most? Does implementation of this form of appraisal increase the frequency and prevalence of OCB and, if so, of which forms of OCB?

 **4**   Attitudinal and Dispositional
Antecedents of OCB

In Chapter 3, as we drew parallels between OCB and Barnard's (1938) concept of "willingness to cooperate," we took note of Barnard's observation that willingness to cooperate fluctuates within and among individuals. (Barnard observed this both in his long career as an executive as well as in his shorter one as an organization theorist.) Our task in this chapter is to explain why that fluctuation occurs. Drawing from relevant social psychological and organization theory, we establish the case for why job satisfaction and some personality factors should predict an individual's OCB, and also why they should predict OCB better than they predict core task performance. We then test these hypotheses against a large set of empirical studies that have reported the correlations between job satisfaction and OCB, perceived fairness and OCB, and specific personality dimensions and OCB.

Our conception of OCB, in contrast to core job duties and task performance, emphasizes its discretionary character. (Admittedly, we must think of this difference as a matter of degree rather than kind.) By definition, OCB consists of contributions that are not compelled by the job description nor contractually rewarded. We have also characterized OCB in terms of streams of contributions, many of which are mundane, over some extended period of time. Compared to performance of most core job tasks, OCB is less likely to be constrained by the design of the job, the technology that drives the work process, the ability of the person doing the job, or the instructions and orders of the person's boss. Weiss and Adler (1990) refer to "strong" situations as those that are uniformly encoded, generate uniform expectancies, and offer compelling incentives for performance. In contrast, they note that "weak" situations have the opposite characteristics. Thus, we might well refer to OCB as behavior that occurs in "weak" as opposed to "strong" situations.

The current stance in social psychology is that attitudes and dispositions come to the fore in weak situations (Lee, Ashford, & Bobko, 1990; Mischel, 1973; Monson, Hesley, & Chernick, 1982). Neither attitudes nor personality variables predict behavior well in situations marked by strong incentives, societal norms, or pressures to behave in a particular fashion. Nor do attitudes or individual traits score well in predicting any one specific behavior in a single time and place. They do much better at predicting cumulative patterns or trends of behavior (Epstein, 1980) over time, in situations in which external compulsions on behavior are weak or ambiguous. Thus, we have good reason to focus our accounting for OCB by thinking in terms of both attitudes and personality.

Attitudes

Researchers have invoked numerous attitudinal concepts as plausible explanations for what people do on the job—how hard they work, how much they achieve, whether they vote for a union, how frequently they miss work, whether they look for another job. The attitude that has figured most prominently in this regard is what most of us refer to as *job satisfaction*. Indeed, one often sees instances in which this term is used almost interchangeably with the phrase *job attitudes*, because job satisfaction is usually defined as the weighted aggregation of attitudes toward various aspects of the job domain. Some measures of job satisfaction simply ask the respondent to make a general assessment of how good the job is; others distinguish between satisfaction with the work itself and satisfaction with extrinsic benefits (such as pay, benefits, perquisites) derived from the job; still others have the respondent evaluate such differentiated aspects of the job as the supervision, coworkers, pay, and promotion. The almost invariant finding is that measures of satisfaction with specific elements of the job correlate positively and substantially with each other, so researchers frequently sum the specific satisfactions to construct a measure of "overall satisfaction."

The Satisfaction-Performance Hypothesis

A hypothesis that has long intrigued both the layperson and the organizational psychologist is the "satisfaction causes performance" hypothesis. We do not know just where or how this hypothesis arose. Some have attributed it to the so-called "human relations school of management," which in turn is linked to the influence of the Hawthorne studies and their interpretation by Roethlisberger and Dickson (see Chapter 3). Certainly the Hawthorne studies and the accounts of them had much to say about "sentiments"—perceptions, emotions, attitudes—and the logic of such sentiments as contrasted with the logic of "facts." However, one cannot find in Roethlisberger and Dickson's 1939 work, *Management and the Worker,* any assertion that satisfaction causes performance or that a happy worker is a productive worker. Still, the importance that the Hawthorne researchers attached to sentiments might well have fostered an impression among scholars and practitioners alike that if sentiments were important, they would influence a person's productivity and job performance.

It is reasonable to think that the more positive a person's job attitudes or job satisfaction, the more positive the person's behavior will be with respect to the job. We see many apparently confirming instances of this in everyday life. We behave positively toward people we like and respect. We observe that people are generally pretty good at what they like and vice versa. We vote for candidates who support the goals that we favor, just as we also favor the goals endorsed by candidates whom we respect on other grounds. So we naturally would expect that people who like their jobs will be good at those jobs, and vice versa. We would expect them to behave positively in respect to those jobs and to the employer, and we would expect their actions to support supervisors whom they like and respect. Therefore, it would seem to make sense that the greater the overall job satisfaction (including satisfaction with the work, the pay, the conditions of employment, the treatment by coworkers and the supervisor), the more productive and the better the performance of the individual.

Unfortunately, industrial and organizational psychologists have not found strong empirical support for the satisfaction-productivity hypothesis. The earliest known empirical study of job satisfaction and productivity, by Kornhauser and Sharp in 1932, shows little evidence of such a relationship. In 1955, Brayfield and Crockett reviewed several studies and concluded that "no appreciable relationship" existed between measures of job satisfaction and individual performance. In 1964, Vroom brought the Brayfield and Crockett review up to date and agreed with their conclusion. In Vroom's (1964) review, the median correlation between individual satisfaction and performance was .14.

Although this result is positive, it is not strong enough to justify management focused on employee satisfaction (on the premise that such satisfaction will in turn foster a high level of effort and productivity). In 1985, Iaffaldano and Muchinsky updated the empirical record again, using meta-analysis—a quantitative method of review that weights correlations from studies according to the size of the group in the study and corrects for certain artifacts in the measures used in the study. Iaffaldano and Muchinsky's quantitative approach, covering a much larger set of studies than researchers had previously encompassed, led to much the same conclusions as the more qualitative methods of review that Brayfield and Crockett, and Vroom had used on a smaller set of data. Iaffaldano and Muchinsky (1985) concluded that the relationship between satisfaction and performance is "illusory," an erroneous impression in naturalistic observation that persists because we think satisfaction and performance *should* be related.

Iaffaldano and Muchinsky (1985) apparently are correct in suggesting that laypeople stubbornly continue to believe in the relationship between satisfaction and performance. Gannon and Noon (1971) reported that a strong majority of managers and other practitioners in their survey expressed agreement with the assertion that job satisfaction was related to productivity. In another large-scale mail survey by Katzell and Yankelovich (1975), a large majority of both managers and union leaders agreed with the premise that "if workers were more satisfied with their jobs, there would be greater productivity."

However, by the mid-1960s, industrial and organizational psychologists were already taking to heart the consistent evidence that was at variance with such a belief, and they converged upon a much different picture of how satisfaction and performance related to each other. Their view (e.g., Cherrington, Reitz, & Scott, 1971; Lawler & Porter, 1967) conceived of satisfaction not so much as a cause of anything but as a *result*—the result of the amount and kinds of rewards a person derives from the job experience. The real issue, these researchers proposed, was whether those rewards in turn derived from performance. Only if rewards were proportionate to performance would there be a correspondence between satisfaction and performance—and even then it would be because performance led, indirectly via rewards, to satisfaction, not the other way around. This model stated that the reason we find, overall, little empirical relationship between performance and satisfaction is that rarely are the rewards that people experience at work strongly proportional to their performance. Even in many so-called "merit-pay" programs, many benefits that people obtain are mostly contingent upon membership and tenure, and they are at most weakly influenced by differences in performance levels. In theory, the correlation between performance and satisfaction could be strengthened by strengthening the relationship between performance and rewards.

Some journalistic, impressionistic evidence suggests that, in the late 1970s and early 1980s, some practitioners bought into this revised view of performance and satisfaction. Those years featured double-digit rates of inflation, along with high levels of unemployment. During that time, some tough-minded managers, facing competitive pressures and strapped for resources, disavowed the genial approach of keeping people satisfied and instead embraced the view that employees would get only the satisfaction they deserved. The hue and cry were for merit pay plans "with teeth," with no pay increases for those not meeting rigorous and demanding levels of output. Pay for performance became the order of the day.

On the whole, though, practitioners and the general public hold onto their intuitive faith that job satisfaction or morale does bear upon performance. So the question remains: Assuming that managers and union leaders have a rich and extensive basis of observation for thinking about behavior at work, why do they cling to a belief unsupported by decades of empirical research?

"Productivity" vs. "Contributions"

One way to reconcile the discordant views from practitioners and laypeople on the one hand with the empirical record of industrial and organizational psychologists on the other hand is to make a distinction between two different definitions of the term *performance*. The research psychologists who addressed the satisfaction-performance hypothesis probably thought of performance in terms of either "productivity" or "task performance." Certainly there are strong scientific norms for seeking objective and valid measures of performance. Defining performance in terms of measurable or visible output—such as cords of wood, boxes of shoes, sales orders, published articles—could ensure a high order of objectivity. If performance could not be measured in such dimensions, one would need something like a supervisor's rating of a person's job performance. However, ideally, such a measure should be constructed to minimize the effect of bias, such as the degree of liking for the person or some personal quality not really related to how well a person performs. The effect of operationally defining *performance,* either by reference to quantitative output or rigorously constructed rating scales, would most likely emphasize how well people perform the tasks that define their jobs.

Although such a construal of performance facilitates objectivity, it might not capture the full sense of what the practitioner or layperson has in mind when considering the factors that correlate with performance. In a broader sense, *performance* can be taken to mean what Barnard (1938) referred to as "willingness to cooperate." An organization is more than the sum total of the outputs of individual jobs or the composite of the individual task performances. Organized collective effort is efficacious precisely because the sum is greater than its parts. Therefore, part of what the practitioner includes in the notion of performance involves contributions that sustain the quality of organization— the patterns of cooperation, commitment, interdependence, and gestures of "we thinking" that are the essence of organization. Such contributions go beyond the usual scope of job performance because they are not unique to particular jobs, and they are so diverse that they can seldom be captured in formal directives. And, of course, these are the contributions that inhere in the OCB construct.

Suppose, then, that we think of OCB as a criterion distinct from the measure of productivity or task performance. The next question is: Why should OCB have a better chance of relating to job satisfaction? Our answer is based on the assumption that OCB pertains to contributions that are not constrained by situational or ability requirements. Performance of the essential functions of the job is, to varying degrees, a function of the skills and aptitudes of the person doing the job. Obviously, effort enters into performance as well, but someone with modest abilities will not be able to achieve a quantum increase in productivity just because that person has a positive attitude about the job and the firm.

You might counter this argument with the observation that many jobs do not require a high order of aptitude or skill. Indeed, the flow of the work process is frequently designed such that little variance in individual productivity in a particular job is possible. The amount of work that the person can turn out is limited by how much material is input from "upstream" and by how fast other workers "downstream" can process what the person passes on to coworkers. Also, variations in the technology that drives the work process can easily swamp the effects of variations in effort among individuals and groups (Goodman, Ravlin, & Schminke, 1990).

When neither ability nor technology constrains the output from an individual or group, strong situational incentives or constraints often overshadow the effects of attitudes. If an employee's productivity falls below some threshold level, the supervisor or perhaps some coworkers will exert pressure on that employee to work harder, regardless of how that employee feels about the job or the company. If greater output qualifies for bonus pay, someone with the ability to produce more, whose output is not constrained by workflow or technology, will probably respond to that incentive with substantial effort—even if he or she is not all that enamored with the organization, its management, or the boss.

In sum, a person must perform up to some minimal level to keep the job—which the person might not consider a "good" job, but it might be the best job or even the only job available. Conversely, a person cannot perform beyond the limits set by skill or ability, workflow, and technology. Performance of the essential functions of the job description is largely governed by "strong" situations (as previously defined); there is not much variance left to be explained by job satisfaction.

In contrast, OCB is much less constrained by ability. To be sure, some forms of helping do require some skill or ability. The helping rendered in the paper mill anecdote (see Chapter 1) obviously involved some skill derived from some combination of aptitude and practice. However, virtually anyone has the ability to render some forms of helping. As noted by Williamson (1975), workers inevitably acquire site-specific knowledge, even if only in a tacit form, and can draw upon such knowledge to aid others. Soldierly compliance with, and involvement in, workplace governance does not require a high order of skill. Spontaneous rendering of mundane courtesies and good sportsmanship have little to do with cognitive ability.

The fact that OCB—this generalized "willingness to cooperate"—can take so many varied forms and be suited to a variety of situations, many of which are unexpected and unmonitored, renders it eminently viable as a means of expressing positive job attitudes. Conversely, the minimal external compulsions to render OCB leave the individual the choice to withhold it if keeping the position is necessary but does not provide reasonable job satisfaction.

Job Satisfaction and OCB: A Social Exchange View

The foregoing arguments establish the necessary, but not sufficient, conditions for job satisfaction to influence OCB. What we suggest is basically that OCB has a better chance than core task performance of correlating with attitudes, because attitudes find expression in behavior only to the extent that such behavior is not constrained by ability or external forces. What remains to be examined is the logic for expecting that the *potentially* greater correlation obtains. Our reasoning is grounded in concepts of social exchange, specifically in the frameworks of Blau (1964), Adams (1965), and recent developments in the area of psychological contracts (Rousseau and Parks, 1993).

We submit that a substantial portion of the exchange between employees and organizations, and among individuals within organizations, occurs in the context of what Blau (1964) described as "social exchange." The defining conditions of social exchange, according to Blau, are

• Voluntary actions of individuals that "are motivated by the returns [which Blau elsewhere indicates are a mixture of both intrinsic and extrinsic satisfiers] they are expected to bring and typically do in fact bring from others" (Blau, 1964, p. 91)

• The obligation by a party to reciprocate a benefit voluntarily rendered by some other party. However, the obligation is unspecified as to form, degree, or time of reciprocation (what Blau described as "diffuse future obligations . . . left to the discretion" of the party who incurs the obligation) (Blau, 1964, p. 95), with the consequence that, over time, neither party can ascertain precisely when or if the exchange has attained a state of parity—that is, both parties have exchanged a variety of benefits or contributions, but neither party can reckon whether the net balance is one requiring the receipt or giving of additional contributions.

• It depends on trust—that is, confidence that the other party will, in good time and in some appropriate manner and situation, reciprocate benefits, contributions, or favors; reciprocation cannot be enforced by appeal to third parties.

However, not all employment relationships, or even the full measure of any particular relationships, take the form of social exchange. Some organizations aspire to, and perhaps approach, a pure market form of exchange, in which a full set of specific benefits are explicitly and formally promised for a specific set of explicit performance criteria (Graham & Organ, 1993; Rousseau & Parks, 1995). In such an exchange, the nature and timing of what the parties exchange are not left to discretion; they are operationally defined with some precision. However, no expectation exists for either benefits or contributions beyond those made explicit. Moreover, trust plays a minimal role; either party has recourse to a third party (such as an arbitrator) to enforce the agreements. Finally, the duration of the exchange relationship is finite, and both parties maintain vigilance in search of better alternative relationships when the stipulated period of exchange expires.

Most employment relationships begin with some elements of economic or market exchange, but as noted by Williamson (1975), the employer does not attempt to specify all contributions, and could not do so in any case, and therefore the employer offers some premium above what the worker's immediate contributions are actually worth. Such a premium could secure the contributions that are indeed specified at the outset as well as provide compensation for as-yet-unspecified later contributions. However, the duration of the relationship is left unspecified, and the employer (or, most immediately, the manager or supervisor) provides other, noncontractual, forms of support. In turn, the employee renders contributions not previously made explicit, and much of the exchange thereafter takes on more of a social exchange character.

A precondition for such social exchange in the employment relationship to continue, at least on the employee's part, is a sense that the organization, or at least that portion of the organization most proximal to the employee's work experience, represents something like a microcosm of a "just world" (Lerner, 1980). This is the idea that, within this system, over the long run, somehow things work such that contributions, no matter how humble, do not go unrewarded. Note that, as previously discussed, a specific outcome is not contractually or otherwise contingent on a particular contribution. In addition, the employee does not think that someone will notice and earmark some little recompense for every little contribution. Likewise, this is not to suggest that, at any particular moment, fairness in the exchange has been realized. What is important is a belief on the part of the employee that a dynamic toward fairness exists.

What conditions or rules would constitute "fairness"? Unfortunately, we cannot provide a precise definition. Adams' (1965) rule of proportionality of outcomes to inputs is perhaps a good place to start. We can conceive of *inputs* as including not only core task performance (and all of the requisite abilities and skills that pertain to that) and compliance with explicit, enforceable directives but also those contributions that we now associate with OCB. *Outcomes* certainly include the most tangible and visible rewards in the form of pay and benefits but also the more intangible outcomes derived from recognition, supervisory consideration, status in the group, and informal privileges. If we now imagine an individual who has thus far contributed much in the form of OCB but also has come to believe that fairness—in terms of Adams' proportionality rule—does not reign, we would agree with Adams that such a person would be moved to reduce his or her inputs. However, the circumspect individual would be well advised to exercise some selectivity as to which inputs he or she reduces. To reduce core task performance or compliance with enforceable directives is risky, especially to the individual who needs to hold onto that job, avoid censure or reprimand, or qualify for whatever pay raises are forthcoming. Less risky, and what we believe is more probable, is to reduce OCB.

Conversely, the employee who feels that he or she is overcompensated—whether monetarily or in nonmonetary forms of support, or both—for past and present contributions might see little scope in core task performance or enforced compliance for contributing in such a way as to mitigate the uneasy condition of overpayment. A more direct means of whittling away at such overpayment is to increase contributions in the form of OCB.

However, we shy away from endorsing the proportionality rule as the predominant rule by which employees reckon fairness. Although Adams recognizes that outcomes include far more than just money, and even allows that what is a positive outcome for one person might not be considered such by someone else, his model does not help us understand how individuals value an aggregation of quite different forms of outcomes or how one type of outcome compensates for another. The work of Foa and Foa (1980) demonstrates that this is not a trivial issue. Their "exchange wheel" illustrates that according to the empirical evidence, some forms of exchange are not, and by some social norms should not be, exchanged for each other. For example, we usually do not think it is appropriate to exchange money for affection or respect; on the other hand, a personal courtesy might be deemed appropriate as a means of reciprocating a gesture of respect. Furthermore, assuming realistic computations were feasible, evidence suggests (e.g., Brickman, Folger, Goode, & Schul, 1981) that even when the proportionality rule is consistently and precisely followed at the individual level, there can be acute discomfiture at the shape of the distribution or curve thus obtained. For example, the comparison between the outcomes of the top 10% and the bottom 10% is judged as simply too harsh, even by employees in the top tier.

Some findings (Organ, 1990a) also suggest vast differences among individuals regarding which types of inputs evaluators emphasize in following a policy of fair pay. Some individuals put a premium on rated task productivity, whereas others give greater weights to apparent effort or what the external market would pay for a specific skill. And as we all well know, many evaluators—and not just those in large unions or group-oriented societal cultures—attach a premium to length of tenure.

Finally, studies indicate that in some situations—notably, instances of close, cohesive relationships in small groups, and also in times of extreme hardship—proportionality of tangible rewards to measurable contributions is not the obvious rule by which the group reckons fairness. Instead, equality of outcomes is the endorsed rule.

All in all, the weight of evidence indicates that there is no one rule of fairness to which all employees will subscribe, and neither the organization nor the supervisor can apply any one operational rule of fairness that will actually be perceived as fair by all participants. It seems that the best a company or boss can do is avoid rigid or explicit adherence to any one formula. Different criteria at different times, in different situations, for different people, might be more practicable. What this strategy amounts to, in effect, is a sensitivity to incidents when some threshold of unfairness has obtained for particular individuals and a willingness to correct some portion of that unfairness—that is, what we referred to earlier as a microcosm of a just world that tends toward fairness.

Important to an employee's sense of a just world is that person's assessment of fair procedures (Leventhal, 1980) and respectful interpersonal treatment (Bies, Martin, & Brockner, 1993). Although outcomes might at any time be out of kilter, an employee can take comfort in the belief that procedural fairness will ensure that such things are noticed and that some self-correcting mechanisms are in place. If an employee is treated with dignity and respect, he or she probably becomes confident that others will try to make things right in due time, including properly appreciating the employee's contributions.

Fairness and Satisfaction

To this point, we have explained why we believe that job satisfaction, as a set of attitudes about the job, has more potential for correlating with—that is, causing—OCB than with narrower measures of productivity and core task performance. We have used social exchange theory to explain why there actually should be a relationship between satisfaction and OCB. And we have explored concepts of fairness to specify a necessary condition for social exchange processes to function in an employment relationship. The astute reader perhaps sees here the suggestion of a moderated relationship—that is, the relationship between job satisfaction and OCB is moderated by perceived fairness.

What stops us short of specifying such a moderated relationship is that, empirically, there is a strikingly high correlation between self-reports of satisfaction and similar reports of assessed fairness. Moreover, the magnitude of the relationship (which is in the .60 to .80 range, depending on the specific measures) is such that it cannot be cavalierly dismissed as caused by common method variance. The implication is that perceived fairness has much to do with one's job satisfaction, that level of satisfaction itself suggests a fair system, that the two sentiments are overlapping portions of some even broader concept such as "morale" (Organ, 1997b), or that, conceivably, all three connections exist. In whatever way that these connections are ultimately sorted out, the bottom line from a prediction standpoint is that both satisfaction and fairness should predict OCB, and they should predict it better than they predict narrower measures of productivity and performance.

The Findings

A meta-analytic review by Organ & Ryan (1995) of 28 studies found a raw weighted average correlation of .24 between satisfaction and the OCB helping measure. The predicted population correlation coefficient, correcting for variations in reliability of measures, was .28. The 95% confidence interval for the raw average correlation was .20 to .27, which does not overlap with the .13 to .17 comparable range found by Iaffaldano & Muchinsky (1985) for satisfaction and measures of task performance or productivity. The 95% confidence interval for the population correlation between satisfaction and helping was .26 to .31.

For measures of fairness, the raw weighted correlation with OCB-helping from 20 studies was .19, the corrected estimate of the population coefficient was .24, and the 95% confidence interval for the latter was .20 to .28.

For the OCB measure of generalized compliance or conscientiousness, the raw average correlation with satisfaction, based on 25 studies, was .22, and the estimated population coefficient was .28. Raw and estimated correlations with fairness were, respectively, .22 and .27. Again, these estimates are significantly greater than the meta-analytic correlations reported by Iaffaldano and Muchinsky (1985) for satisfaction and traditional measures of overall job performance.

A smaller group of studies have used either single-factor measures of OCB or dimensions of OCB other than helping and compliance. Correlations with one-factor (i.e., "overall") measures of OCB yield findings virtually identical to those for helping and compliance. Correlations with the specific dimension of sportsmanship also mirror those of helping and compliance, whereas correlations with OCB-courtesy and OCB-civic virtue were slightly lower, with corrected estimates of population coefficients of .24 for courtesy and .21 for civic virtue.

The findings cited thus far, with the exception of those based on measures of overall OCB, are based on specific dimensions of OCB. If one treats these dimensions as separate indicators of a more comprehensive concept of OCB and aggregates them into an overall measure of OCB (taking into account the substantial intercorrelations of the various dimensions of OCB when the OCB ratings come from a single source— e.g., a supervisor), the raw sample-size weighted mean correlation between OCB and satisfaction is .38. Correcting for reliability of measurement, the estimate population coefficient is .44.

The Organ & Ryan (1995) meta-analysis also looked at studies with two other measures that can construed as attitudinal: affective commitment and assessments of leader supportiveness. The strength of association between these measures and OCB was comparable to the results cited previously, with affective commitment correlating slightly lower and leader supportiveness slightly higher than the satisfaction and fairness measures.

A later and more inclusive review by Podsakoff, MacKenzie, Paine, and Bachrach (2000) supports and extends the conclusions reached by Organ & Ryan (1995). Podsakoff et al. found that measures of "trust in leader," "core transformational leadership," perceived organizational support, and leader-member exchange (when corrected for reliability) on average correlated in the range of .24 to .28 with the OCB factors interpreted as helping, courtesy, conscientiousness, and sportsmanship. As in the Organ & Ryan (1995) study, Podsakoff et al. found weaker associations (.09 to .15) with the civic virtue factor.

A more recent meta-analytic study, by Judge, Thoresen, Bono, and Patton (2001), of the relationship between job satisfaction and performance reported a corrected estimate of the population correlation coefficient: .30. This finding led them to suggest that previous meta-analyses (e.g., by Iaffaldano & Muchinsky, 1985) had underestimated the strength of association between satisfaction and performance. More pertinent to the current discussion is Judge et al.'s comparison of the .30 estimate and the findings from the Organ & Ryan (1995) meta-analysis, which led them to conclude that the relationship between satisfaction and performance is actually similar to the relationship between satisfaction and OCB.

However, there is a technical reason why that comparison is misleading. In Judge et al.'s analysis, measures of performance were corrected for *inter-rater reliability*, whereas Organ & Ryan made corrections based on *internal consistency reliability*. The opinion of experts differs as to which of these approaches is more appropriate. Murphy and DeShon (2000) contend that inter-rater reliability deals with differences in criteria of the raters as well as differences in what they can and do actually observe at different times, and thus inter-rater correlations *do not* speak to the reliability of the measures they use. Note that estimates of reliability based on inter-rater agreement are almost always much lower than estimates of reliability defined by internal rater consistency. Thus, when corrections for reliability are made, raw correlations will be adjusted upward to a much greater extent. Had the Organ & Ryan (1995) study corrected correlations for reliability based on inter-rater agreement, their estimated population coefficients would certainly have been substantially greater. Moreover, when one compares the estimated correlation between aggregated OCB and satisfaction (.44) with the .30 reported by Judge et al. (2001), the strong implication remains that job attitudes relate more closely to OCB than to traditional performance measures.

Organ (1997b) reanalyzed data from the Organ & Ryan (1995) meta-analysis to test the viability of a more general hypothesis about the relationship between what Organ termed "morale" and OCB. Organ used estimated population correlation coefficients of the associations among four attitudinal measures (satisfaction, fairness, affective commitment and leader consideration) and two OCB dimensions (helping and compliance). He treated the attitudinal measures as indicators of a general underlying construct that might be regarded as "morale" and the helping and compliance measures as indicators of the more general OCB construct. He found support for a causal model in which morale influences OCB, with an estimated path coefficient of .686. Two goodness-of-fit

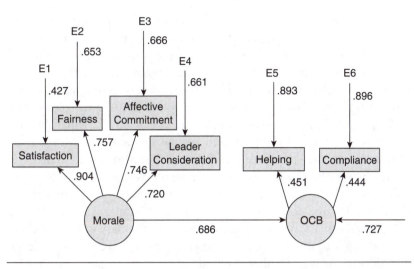

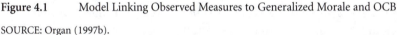

Figure 4.1   Model Linking Observed Measures to Generalized Morale and OCB

SOURCE: Organ (1997b).

measures for this model registered at .94, which suggests a high order of fit between the model and the observed correlations. (See Figure 4.1 for the complete model and coefficients.)

James and James (1989) reported analyses that supported the view that a general factor underlies many measures of emotionally relevant cognitions or evaluations of the work environment. They interpret this general factor as an individual's belief about the extent to which that work environment is personally beneficial to the organizational well-being of the individual. They also think of this factor as analogous to the *g* factor of general intelligence that underlies measures of specific mental abilities. Perhaps this general factor in "emotionally relevant cognitions" also captures what for many years was loosely or informally referred to as "morale"—or, indeed, the *m* factor in work attitudes. If so, then the long-held, but long-contested, notion that morale causes productivity might better be translated to suggest that morale relates more closely to contributions in the form of OCB than it does to traditionally more narrow conceptions of in-role performance or productivity.

In a masterful review of competing models of job motivation, Landy and Becker (1987) concluded that we should not view those approaches as competing; rather, they should be appropriately "nested" according to the dependent variables that each of them best predicts and explains.

Thus, it appears that goal setting best accounts for variance in task productivity; incentives strengthen the motivation for task productivity, to the extent that they either induce commitment to externally imposed difficult and specific goals or elicit covert goal setting. Equity theory—or, more broadly, theories about fairness—best accounts for job satisfaction. Job satisfaction is the single best indicator of the general affective-cognitive assessment of the organization, which in turn has more to do with OCB than with task performance.

Finally, we take note of a compelling laboratory experiment conducted by Wright, George, Farnsworth, and McMahan (1993). It is consistent with Katz and Kahn's (1966) surmise that what motivates one class of employee contributions will not motivate, in fact might well discourage, other kinds of contributions. In this study of the effects of goal setting, incentives, task performance, and OCB, the highest levels of task performance resulted when difficult, specific goals were set for subjects and when the payoffs for subjects were contingent upon reaching those goals. However, this condition also resulted in the least amount of OCB (in the form of helping another subject—actually a confederate of the experimenters—who had arrived late and needed help from other subjects to understand what he or she was supposed to do. Inevitably, strong incentives for particular dimensions of performance pose the potential for some downside in the form of inhibiting effort on other forms of contribution.

The evidence cited here would appear to establish the morale factor, in terms of job satisfaction and the sense of fairness in social exchange, as a major *motivational* condition for much OCB. However, morale is not the only important determinant of OCB. In Chapter 5, we review research on workplace features (such as leadership, job characteristics, the work group, and organizational context) that might serve to evoke and sustain—or conversely, to inhibit—OCB. To the extent that these factors affect job satisfaction, they indirectly determine some variance in OCB because they influence the motivational basis for OCB. However, we must also take into account *means and opportunity* as well as motivation. We can easily imagine instances in which an individual would gladly contribute in forms that go beyond core job requirements but might not understand how to go about doing it, might not have many occasions for doing it, or might not have the resources for doing it. Also, we should take into account the possibility that some workplace characteristics have their own unique and direct motivational effects on OCB beyond their indirect effects on job satisfaction and perceived fairness.

Personality

Like the notion that job satisfaction relates to job performance, the idea that personality traits influence job performance dates from the early 20th century and appears to be just as pervasive among practitioners. As was the case with the satisfaction-causes-productivity hypothesis, the personality-performance proposition did not seem to meet the test of empirical scrutiny by industrial and organizational psychologists. The cumulative empirical record led Guion and Gottier (1965) to conclude that no basis existed for using personality measures as tools for selecting employees.

The same arguments for why job satisfaction should predict OCB better than task performance also apply to personality. Just as attitudes—specifically, job attitudes—do not predict one-shot episodes of behavior very well, neither do measures of personality correlate with discrete actions in a specific time and place. Rather, measures of attitudes and personality both better predict streams of behavior across situations over extended intervals of time and numerous occasions (Epstein, 1980).

Furthermore, just as we would expect attitudes to drive behavior in weak rather than strong situations, we would expect personality traits to be reflected in behavior more frequently in situations in which there are not strong incentives, pressures, threats, or norms to behave in a particular manner. Even extroverts sit quietly in funeral services; even introverts can become vocal and animated at college football games. In contrast, the more usual characteristics of extroverts and introverts would probably surface in situations in which norms are looser, such as a committee meeting or a small dinner party. As we noted before, we think of OCB as behavior that generally occurs in relatively weaker situations—when no one is making explicit demands upon us and when there are no compelling incentives to act one way or another. Much of what constitutes task performance, on the other hand, occurs in response to strong prompts arising from workflow, supervisory directives, explicit peer pressure, and important incentives to perform at a satisfactory or superior level.

The Big Five framework of personality (McCrae and Costa, 1987) includes at least two dimensions of performance that one would expect to pose much relevance for OCB. *Agreeableness* is a Big Five factor that comprises friendliness, likeability, and a general ease of getting along with others in pleasant relationships. People who score high on this factor would presumably be predisposed to think well of customers, coworkers, and colleagues. One could hypothesize that such persons would be inclined to offer help if the appropriate situation presented itself, to anticipate the needs of others, and to not take offense easily. Thus, we might reason that this factor would substantially relate to the OCB dimensions of helping, courtesy, and sportsmanship.

A second Big Five factor, *conscientiousness,* encompasses the personal traits of dependability, planfulness, self-discipline, and perseverance. One might link these characteristics to the more impersonal forms of OCB, such as generalized compliance and possibly what we refer to as civic virtue. Indeed, behaviors that fall into the civic virtue category—for example, punctuality, good attendance, unerringly following the rules of work group governance, and principled conduct—could be considered conscientious behavior.

The Big Five also includes the factors *neuroticism* (sometimes referred to as *emotional stability*) and *extraversion.* (The fifth Big Five factor, *intellectance,* or *openness to experience,* does not have a discernible relationship to OCB.) The case for relating either neuroticism or extraversion to OCB is not as straightforward as for the previous two factors, but some considerations lead us to suppose that there might be connections. For example, because emotionally unstable individuals tend to be preoccupied with their own problems (real or imagined), they might not have the psychic stamina to attend to the problems of others; therefore, they might help coworkers less than their emotionally stable counterparts do. In contrast, extraverts tend to be more responsive to social stimulation and to have wide circles of friends and acquaintances, so they could have more opportunities for providing help than introverts would, and they would derive some gratification from doing so.

Researchers could choose other specific traits to study as possible predictors (either positive or negative) of OCB. For example (to use some trait names from common discourse, some of which have been translated into pencil-and-paper measures), we might think of the following as personal qualities that predispose an individual toward some forms of OCB: empathic sensitivity, need for achievement, need for affiliation, proactivity, passivity, loyalty, and farsightedness. However, the consensus among social psychologists is that the Big Five framework does a good job of capturing many specific traits within a few broad personality factors. If a specific trait has a substantial bearing upon OCB, we should find some evidence of it reflected in measures based on the Big Five scheme.

The Findings

Organ and Ryan's (1995) meta-analysis found that personality measures were weaker predictors of OCB than were job satisfaction and other work-relevant attitudes. Measures that plausibly reflect Big Five dimensions of agreeableness, emotional stability, and extraversion failed to correlate with any dimension of OCB beyond .15 in absolute value. Conscientiousness correlated .22 (estimated population correlation, when corrected for reliability) with the helping dimension of OCB, but the analysis that excluded self-ratings of helping yielded a correlation of only .04.

The one finding that suggests that personality plays a role in determining OCB was an estimated population correlation of .30 between conscientiousness and generalized compliance (Organ & Ryan, 1995). In other words, people who describe themselves in terms of above-average inclinations toward self-discipline, planfulness, and striving for achievement are in fact rated higher by their superiors and peers as more punctual, more regular in attendance, more observant of rules of workplace governance, less likely to fritter away their time at work, and in general as more "workmanlike" in ways that go beyond narrowly defined task performance or productivity.

Researchers following up on the work of Project A, mentioned in Chapter 2 as the basis for distinguishing contextual performance from task performance, have found a stronger link between disposition and OCB. Borman, Penner, Allen, and Motowidlo (2001) reviewed the research conducted on this issue since the studies reviewed by Organ and Ryan (1995). Borman et al.'s findings suggested a more consistent—but still modest—association between various personality measures and various citizenship criteria. Nonetheless, when self-report measures of OCB were excluded, none of the nine weighted mean correlations between personality and OCB exceeded .20. The highest of the nine estimates was .19 for conscientiousness, which supports the conclusion reached by Organ and Ryan (1995). (Curiously, the Borman et al. (2001) paper did not report population correlation estimates adjusted for reliability; otherwise, the estimated correlation for conscientiousness would surely have exceeded .20, and perhaps the estimates for two of the remaining eight coefficients would have reached that level.) Overall, research conducted by various groups (e.g., Van Scotter & Motowidlo, 1996) on personality and OCB suggests that the most robust link is between conscientiousness and the more impersonal forms of OCB (usually dubbed *work dedication*).

Three studies are noteworthy exceptions to the general trend of weak empirical links between disposition and OCB. Kamp and Hough (1988) aggregated the results of several studies that looked at eight personality measures and an index of "delinquency." The delinquency measure included incidents of absence without leave, unfavorable discharges (in military groups), and documented cases of theft and flagrant rule violation (in civilian groups). Relevant dispositional predictors included measures of "adjustment" and "dependability." When corrected for reliability and restriction of range, the two dispositional measures correlated −.43 and −.42 with the index of delinquency. A problem of interpretation, however, is whether delinquency can be considered simply the mirror opposite of OCB. There is little empirical or logical reason to think that those individuals who restrain their contributions in the form of OCB are, on that account only, prone to exhibit extreme misbehaviors (such as theft).

In a study included within Project Alpha, Campbell (1990) found a correlation of .30 between dependability and "personal discipline" (similar to the compliance form of OCB and the work dedication dimension of contextual performance). Motowidlo & Van Scotter (1994) found comparable associations between "work orientation," "dependability," "cooperativeness," and the criterion of contextual performance. In both instances, the measure of "dependability" sounds much like Hogan and Hogan's (1989) "reliability," which they derived by selecting items from various personality domains according to weighted empirical validity evidence. In other words, from a large pool of measurement items, a small number was selected on the basis of demonstrated predictive validity. Although such an approach might provide a good selection instrument in applications to human resource practices and could define a stable syndrome of characteristic work habits, it is not clear how this cocktail of specific traits relates to established frameworks of personality such as the Big Five.

If we take at face value the weaker overall empirical evidence for links between personality and OCB than for ties between attitudes and OCB—excepting the robust connection between conscientiousness and compliance—we might reason as follows: Perhaps the effects of personality are indirect and occur by way of the effect of personality on attitudes. We find abundant evidence to suggest that personal characteristics explain substantial variance in job satisfaction (Arvey, Bouchard, Segal, & Abraham, 1989; Judge, Bono, & Locke, 2000; Staw, Bell, & Clausen, 1986; Steel & Rentsch, 1997). Researchers presume the relevant personal traits to be positive affectivity, anchored in the extraversion Big Five factor, and negative affectivity, based in the neuroticism Big Five factor. Yet we also presume that the tendency of some traits to predispose individuals toward job satisfaction can be overridden by situational issues in the workplace, such as styles of supervision and components of reward systems. In other words, people predisposed to be dissatisfied might find satisfaction because of supportive management and liberal benefits, whereas those prone to satisfaction are driven to dissatisfaction by what they regard as abusive treatment. Thus, both disposition and work situation influence job attitudes (Steel & Rentsch, 1997), and personality relates to OCB only to the extent that personality affects job satisfaction.

Personality might influence *manner* or *motive* more than the substance of OCB (Organ & McFall, 2004). For example, an individual who scores relatively low in agreeableness might be just as likely as a higher-scoring counterpart to help a coworker with a problem, but that worker's reasons for helping might vary. The person low in agreeableness might act to expedite the flow of work, whereas the person high in agreeableness might want to mitigate the discomfort of a friend. In addition, the coworkers' style of helping might differ; the former might have an attitude of cool detachment, maybe even show irritation, whereas the latter might be more cheerful or sympathetic. So perhaps disposition influences the reasons for and styles of helping rather than the frequency, consistency, or efficacy of the OCB itself.

Finally, we should consider the possibility that the workplace suppresses the effects of personality to some extent (Organ & McFall, 2004). People do not give free rein to their spontaneous impulses on the job as compared to the extent they might do so at home or in casual social interaction. At work, one usually thinks more consciously in terms of means and ends, about the cost-benefit trade-offs of what one chooses to do, and what the foreseeable consequences are of alternative behaviors. At a different job, an individual might be dispositionally inclined to help someone, and in a different context would quickly act to render that help, but at work that individual probably is more likely to wonder about the cost in time and effort versus the benefits. Some support for this conjecture comes from Organ & Konovsky (1989), who found that cognitive evaluations of the work environment predicted OCB better than did measures of dispositions in the form of positive or negative affectivity.

Work by Snyder and Cantor (1980) characterizes people as "high self-monitors" versus "low self-monitors." Either type of person might score high or low in, for example, extraversion, agreeableness, or neuroticism. However, high self-monitors attend to cues that might lead them to suppress their more natural selves or put their instincts on hold. In contrast, low self-monitors are less vigilant or sensitive to external cues and act out their prevailing natures. For example, a study (Osborn, Hubert, & Veres, 1998) found that self-monitoring moderated the relationship between extraversion and performance in an interview. Perhaps self-monitoring likewise moderates the link between, say, agreeableness and helping, or negative affectivity and sportsmanship.

Some Qualifying Considerations

We probably should not consider definitive the findings that show weak effects of personality on OCB. Three aspects of the designs of the relevant research might militate against finding real, substantial effects (Organ & McFall, 2004). First, almost all of the studies of predictors of OCB take place in one organization—or, if a study takes place in more than one organization, the organizations are in the same industry (e.g., health care) and geographic area. Second, the measure of OCB is a supervisor's rating, which can be subjective. Third, measures of job attitudes and personality are self-reports gathered in the workplace, and employees might tend to answer in ways that they might like their boss to characterize them, regardless of whether the boss would ever see their answers.

The Unit of Analysis Problem

Studies conducted within one organization or two similar organizations might exhibit reduced variance in some personality measures. If organizations vary substantially in the personality profiles of their participants, then one-site studies tend to attenuate the variance of some personality factors. Schneider, Smith, Taylor, & Fleenor (1998) found that in fact both organization and industry are main effects in some measures of disposition. Their findings support Schneider's (1987) attraction-selection-attrition (ASA) model. The ASA model holds that different personality types are differentially attracted to known or reputed characteristics of organizations, such as the type of work, culture, size, and reward systems. Some organizations also design systems (interviews, assessments, reference checks) to select for certain personality variables—for example, Southwest Airlines is well known for its preference for enthusiastic people who beam with jollity and other expressions of positive affect. Personalities that don't fit the desired profile might experience a discomfort that leads them to find alternative employment.

Now let us see how the ASA model would argue against finding strong statistical relationships between a particular personality dimension and OCB. Many of the studies of antecedents of OCB have been conducted in health care organizations, which might plausibly tend to attract and select individuals whose personalities would be described as high in agreeableness or empathic concern for others. (As an instructive aside, note that the Schneider et al. (1998) study found that organizations varied significantly in mean scores on the Thinking/Feeling dimension of the Myers-Briggs framework, a dimension defined in large measure by concern for impersonal achievement versus concern for other individuals' emotional states.) Furthermore, if the employees in health care organizations are indeed agreeable and empathic, and if in fact such dispositional features were linked to OCB, the organization overall would probably be characterized by a high level of OCB. However, within that organization, we would find diminished variance at the level of the individual in both empathic concern and OCB. With little variance to work with, the correlation between individual empathic concern and OCB would have scant chance of registering in the statistical analysis.

The astute reader might then ask why such attenuation does not characterize single-site studies of job satisfaction and OCB. Most likely it does, but to a lesser extent than in analysis of personality and OCB. Although organizations undoubtedly vary in overall job satisfaction of the collective workforce, job satisfaction is to some degree a function of the cognitive appraisals that occur when individuals compare their lots with the lots of others within the same organization, indeed within the same work unit. Such appraisals virtually guarantee that the degree of job satisfaction will vary within the organization.

In any event, larger units of analysis might be necessary to provide a good test of the personality-OCB connection. Studies of that sort have figured more often in research on the organizational consequences of OCB (e.g., Podsakoff, Ahearne, & MacKenzie, 1997) than in empirical work on antecedents of OCB (exceptions include George, 1990; George & Bettenhausen, 1990).

The Monomethod Problem

Supervisor ratings are procedurally preferable to self-ratings in studies of OCB and personality because of the common method variance issue when both variables come from the same source. However, supervisor ratings have problems of their own. This measure is simply one type of indicator of a diffuse and abstract concept. Because the supervisor's judgment is based on perception or impression, it is vulnerable to certain systematic errors. For example, subordinates sometimes try to ingratiate themselves into the superior's good favor (Bolino, 1999). Subordinates vary in both their inclination to ingratiate themselves and their skill at doing so.

Consider that the one dispositional variable from the Big Five that robustly correlates with OCB is conscientiousness and that the form of OCB that conscientiousness predicts best is the compliance or imper- sonal variety of OCB. That type of OCB probably best catches the supervisor's notice—that is, the boss gets a pretty good idea of which people have the best attendance, are the most punctual, and show the highest respect for rules of workplace governance. On the other hand, supervisors probably have fewer reliable observations about the nature and frequency with which work group members help their peers and exhibit constructive courtesies toward others.

OCB research invariably finds that supervisor ratings of different dimensions of OCB are highly intercorrelated—for example, correla- tions between ratings of helping and compliance commonly range upwards of .50 and beyond. Some of the common method variance that undoubtedly is at work here might arise *not* because supervisors accu- rately rate subordinates on compliance but because they *infer* that the "good employee" who is more reliable in attendance, punctuality, and observance of rules is *also* the kind of good employee who helps others and acts with initiative to solve or prevent work-related problems. Ideally, one would wish for more studies that include both peer and supervisor OCB ratings (e.g., Williams and Anderson, 1991) in research on individual correlates of various forms of OCB.

Self-Ratings of Personality

Although instruments based on self-description of personality traits have attained some degree of predictive validity, perhaps administering such instruments at the workplace compromises some of that validity. Items within the measures of the Big Five are not neutral with respect to what is or is not valued at work; for example, most respondents would immediately intuit that more agreeableness, more conscientious- ness, more emotional stability, and (in many instances) more extraver- sion are somehow "better." Even if researchers proffered guarantees for ensuring anonymity of individual responses, people would probably still feel obliged to pad their self-ratings in the direction of what is "better." To the extent that this happens, the result is once again reduced variance and therefore attenuation of whatever correlations theoretically ought to exist.

Why, you might counter, wouldn't this happen with job satisfaction measures also? We submit that people see their satisfaction as having less to do with their *personal characteristics* and more to do with their *work environments.* To say that one is not very satisfied is not necessarily to say that one is less virtuous; indeed, people who see themselves as quite virtuous might report low satisfaction because they believe their virtue has not been adequately recognized, appreciated, and rewarded.

Interestingly, Mount, Barrick, and Strauss (1994) tested the validity of *observer* ratings of the Big Five dimensions for predicting performance, and they did so in a fashion that broke out of the common method variance bind. They found that coworker ratings of an individual's extraversion correlated .34 with supervisory ratings of performance, and supervisor ratings of extraversion correlated .24 with coworker ratings of the individual's performance. Customer ratings of an individual's agreeableness correlated .30 with coworker ratings of performance and .34 with supervisor performance appraisal. On the other hand, self-ratings of extraversion and agreeableness had hardly any correlation with supervisor and coworker performance ratings. Moreover, a substantial part of the performance rating had to do with factors such as commitment to the job, initiative, customer communications, and interpersonal skills—suggesting that overtones of OCB entered into the performance ratings made by coworkers and boss.

Conclusions

Relevant theory suggests that job satisfaction and related job attitudes should more greatly influence OCB than do measures of core task performance and productivity. Research supports this proposition. Findings also suggest that no single type of job attitude is dominant in terms of predicting OCB. Rather, virtually any measure that plausibly serves as an indicator of morale, including affectively toned descriptions or perceptions of salient workplace characteristics, reliably correlates with independent ratings of a subject's OCB.

Theory also suggests that personality would predict OCB better than it would predict the more objective indicators of productivity or technical excellence of job performance. However, the bulk of the research on this issue does not strongly support the prediction. The most encouraging evidence pertains to the link between individual conscientiousness and impersonal forms of OCB. Surprisingly little support is found for personality predictors of OCB in the forms of helping, courtesy, civic virtue, and sportsmanship. Conceivably, job attitudes mediate any effects of personality—that is, the effects of personality on OCB are mostly indirect. However, research designs set in single organizations, using only supervisor ratings of OCB and self-reports of personality traits, might attenuate the observed correlations.

Implications for Future Research

How Do We Establish Causality in the Association Between Job Attitudes and OCB?

The extant research on individual job satisfaction and OCB is based on cross-sectional correlational research. Although findings from this research confirm an *association* between job attitudes and OCB, they do not indicate causal direction. The evidence is equally supportive of the alternative interpretations that OCB leads to job satisfaction or that OCB and job satisfaction have a common cause. Furthermore, perhaps all three causal effects could exist simultaneously. In principle, controlled experimental research could disentangle the knots of causality. However, such research is not easy to design, particularly if it is done in the laboratory. The experimenter must arrange the opportunity for OCB in a particular place at a specific time, but this restriction would almost certainly constrain the nature or form of OCB. As we have repeatedly stressed, general attitudes best predict patterns of various but related behaviors over substantial periods of time, not specific behaviors at a given moment. Thus, although we would not rule out the potential for laboratory experiments to contribute to our understanding of OCB (Wright et al., 1993, is an exemplary instance of how such studies can provide compelling observations about OCB), we would need an unusually creative experimental design to give the satisfaction-causes-OCB hypothesis a fair test. Perhaps a more realistic strategy is to capitalize upon opportunities in the field for longitudinal observations. Repeated measures of satisfaction and OCB, with proper statistical controls, might provide at least tentative inferences as to how much of the association between the two variables is due to the various causal relationships. Designing such a study for maximum confidence in the findings, however, would require some serious thought about the relevant time lags between variables—that is, how much of an increase in job satisfaction, over what period of time, is necessary to be reflected in an increase in OCB and vice versa?

What Forms of Research Might Provide a Better Test of the Relationship Between Personality and OCB?

Although the evidence to date suggests that the role of personality in determining OCB is mostly limited to the effect of individual conscientiousness on impersonal OCB (compliance with rules and norms, involvement in workplace governance), naturalistic observation still leads many scholars to believe that other aspects of personality are involved with OCB and that the failure to find evidence of that is due to faulty research design. We don't believe the problem is that we haven't discovered the specific trait that is important; the relevant theory and measurement tools are already available and familiar to us. However, more studies along the lines of Mount, Barrick, and Strauss (1994), using independent other-ratings of both OCB and personality, would be a welcome addition to the empirical literature. Also, extant databases containing personality measures from previous contexts, such as those used by Staw, Bell, and Clausen (1986) in their study of personality and job satisfaction, could be valuable resources for addressing the personality-OCB connection.

How Is a Worker's OCB Regarded by Coworkers?

To date, little attention has been given to the potential dynamics between an individual's OCB and other individuals' job attitudes. A recent exception is research by Tepper, Duffy, Hoobler, and Ensley (2004), which found that perceptions of colleagues' OCB were positively associated with job attitudes—unless the supervisor was characterized as "abusive," in which case other workers' OCB was attributed to ingratiation or self-serving motivation and thus was associated with less coworker satisfaction. One might also wonder if the perception of good morale in the group makes an individual more inclined to contribute in the form of OCB—even controlling for the individual's own job satisfaction. Ultimately, questions such as these lead us to wonder if the connections between job satisfaction and OCB at different levels—individual, group, and organization—have different dynamics. In other words, is the social exchange-based perspective on individual job satisfaction and OCB also useful or appropriate for understanding group OCB and satisfaction?

 **5** The Impact of
Leadership and Work
Environments on OCB

The extent to which an employee exhibits organizational citizenship behavior, or any behavior, is a function of the employee's ability, motivation, and opportunity. In part, an employee's motivation and ability are determined by the dispositional factors discussed in Chapter 4. In this chapter, we focus on what a leader can do to influence an employee's motivation, ability, or opportunity to engage in OCB through the leader's own behavior or by shaping the employee's environment. Motivation determines how hard an employee will *try to* engage in the behavior, and the combination of ability and opportunity determine whether the employee *can* successfully exhibit the behavior. We identify the specific conceptual/theoretical mechanisms through which a leader can influence the motivation, ability, or opportunity for employees to exhibit OCB, and we use these mechanisms to explain why different leader behaviors and environmental factors can evoke and sustain OCB. We also discuss possible directions for future research.

Theoretical Mechanisms for Explaining the Determinants of OCB

In our view, an employee's motivation to engage in OCB is determined by how much the employee wants to engage in the behavior and/or how much the employee feels that he or she ought to engage in the behavior. The employee might *want to* engage in the behavior: (a) for the employee's sake, (b) for the sake of others (both his or her leader and coworkers), and/or (c) for the sake of the organization itself. Employees may *want to* engage in citizenship behaviors for several personal reasons. For example, they may find it satisfying to engage in some forms of citizenship behavior, perhaps because it enhances their self-esteem to think that they are the kind of people who would engage in these behaviors (e.g., helping others) or maybe because they like to be listened to by others or to have an impact on what happens in the organization (e.g., voice behaviors). Or, employees may want to engage in the behaviors because they think they may receive recognition or other forms of rewards for it. Other reasons for employees to engage in OCB include a desire to get others to like them or to obligate others to them.

Alternatively (or perhaps in addition to *wanting to* engage in OCB), employees might feel they *ought to* engage in OCB for several reasons. These include the fact that they feel it is their personal responsibility to exhibit OCB, they believe they owe it to others (their leader or coworkers), they believe they owe it to the organization, they feel that they have a moral obligation, and/or they believe it is expected of them based on social norms. As discussed in the next section, a leader can do a number of things to influence the extent to which employees want to or feel they ought to engage in citizenship behaviors.

Leaders can also take other steps to enhance the extent to which their employees *can* engage in OCB. For example, they can select employees who have a greater ability to exhibit OCB because of their dispositional characteristics (e.g., they are naturally conscientious, altruistic, and so on). Or, they can attempt to enhance employees' ability to exhibit OCB through training or modeling forms of the behavior. This is important because even highly motivated employees may not be able to exhibit some forms of OCB if they do not have the skills that enable them to do so.

Finally, leaders can try to shape the work environment to provide greater opportunities for OCB. Indeed, it would be hard for an employee to exhibit altruism if that employee had little contact with coworkers (and therefore no opportunities to observe their need for help) or if the work rules were so inflexible that the employee was prevented from helping coworkers. Similarly, employees would find it difficult to responsibly participate in the governance of the organization or to offer constructive suggestions (i.e., civic virtue) if there were no staff meetings or other forums for doing so. Thus, leaders can potentially enhance OCB by changing the structure of the tasks employees perform, the conditions under which they do their work, and/or human resource practices that govern their behavior.

The Effects of Leadership Behaviors on OCB

Instrumental and Supportive Leader Behaviors

The path-goal theory of leadership is based on the application of the expectancy model of motivation. According to expectancy theory, people choose the levels of effort that they wish to exert at work based on their assessment that increased effort will lead to increased performance, which in turn will lead to increased levels of reward. Within this context,

> The motivational functions of the leader consist of increasing personal payoffs to subordinates for their goal attainment, and making the path to these payoffs easier to travel by clarifying it, reducing roadblocks and pitfalls, and increasing the opportunities for personal satisfaction en route. (House & Dessler, 1974, p. 31)

Thus, effective leaders are ones who motivate subordinates by clarifying the paths by which subordinates can attain their goals and who increase personal outcomes to subordinates when these goals have been reached. These outcomes might include greater pay, promotions, and/or recognition from the leader.

House and his colleagues (House, 1971; House & Dessler, 1974; House & Mitchell, 1974) identified four types of leader behaviors that fit within the path-goal framework, but the research literature has primarily focused on only two of them. The first, instrumental leadership behavior, entails the leader's clarification of what the leader expects of the subordinates and how they should accomplish their work. The second, supportive leadership behavior, encompasses the leader's expressions of concern for the personal well-being of his or her subordinates. Although the relationships between these behaviors and OCB is not a part of the original path-goal framework, Schnake, Cochran, and Dumler (see Schnake, Cochran, & Dumler, 1995; Schnake, Dumler, & Cochran, 1993) have argued that instrumental and supportive leader behaviors may influence OCB because they are likely to be perceived by employees as helping behaviors on the part of the leader that the employees would feel obligated to reciprocate. Supportive leader behavior may be viewed by employees as helpful because it indicates that the leader is concerned and looks out for the employee's welfare. Instrumental leader behavior may be seen as helpful to employees because it reduces their uncertainty about how to do their job. Another possibility is that because these behaviors are beneficial to employees and/or reduce uncertainty, they might cause employees to like their supervisor more, which in turn would make the employees want to help the supervisor in any way that they can (e.g., by being a good sport, making constructive suggestions, etc.). This would be consistent with research on the functional roles of attitudes (e.g., Katz, 1960), which has demonstrated that people develop positive attitudes toward objects that reduce uncertainty and enhance stability. Although this is a subtle distinction, the difference is that in the former case, employees are motivated out of a sense of obligation, and in the latter case, they are motivated because of their liking for the supervisor.

Regardless of the precise mechanism involved, much evidence supports the hypotheses that instrumental and supportive leader behaviors are positively related to employee altruism, courtesy, conscientiousness, civic virtue, and sportsmanship (Podsakoff, MacKenzie, & Bommer, 1996a; Schnake, Cochran, & Dumler, 1995; Schnake, Dumler, & Cochran, 1993). In the work of Schnake et al. (1993) and Schnake et al. (1995), this finding held to be generally true even after controlling for employee perceptions of pay equity, job equity, intrinsic satisfaction, extrinsic satisfaction, self-observation, self-expectation, and self goal-setting, although supportive leadership behavior tended to have stronger relationships with OCB than did instrumental leadership behavior. In the meta-analysis reported by Podsakoff et al. (1996a), this was also generally true even after controlling for a variety of other leader behaviors and subordinate, task and organizational characteristics.

Leader Reward and Punishment Behaviors

Another way that leaders attempt to motivate their subordinates is through the administration of rewards and punishments. Sometimes leaders administer these rewards and punishments contingent upon employee performance in an effort to shape the employee's behavior. However, leaders sometimes allocate rewards and punishments for other reasons. For example, leaders may sometimes reward (or punish) employees depending on if they like (or dislike) them, regardless of how well they have performed on the job. Or, supervisors may reward employees on the basis of other factors, such as the employee's seniority, the educational degree he or she holds, or the performance of the group that the employee belongs to (as opposed to the employee's individual contribution). Thus, a leader's contingent and noncontingent reward and punishment behavior is a key motivator of employee behavior.

However, these behaviors are likely to influence employee performance in different ways. For example, when leaders provide contingent rewards in the form of praise, commendation, and social approval that is based on employee performance, they are likely to be perceived as fair. As a result, the leader may also be more likely to be trusted, because confidence in the fairness and integrity of another person is the essence of trust. In addition, because this leader behavior involves a timely assessment (e.g., through praise) of an employee's performance, it should increase the employee's understanding of his or her role in the organization and lead to reduced role ambiguity. Similar arguments could be made for contingent punishment. This is important because fairness, trust, and role clarity are thought to be key determinants of OCB (Konovsky & Pugh, 1994; MacKenzie, Podsakoff, & Rich, 2001; Organ, 1988; Podsakoff, MacKenzie, Moorman, & Fetter, 1990). Treating employees fairly may motivate them to exhibit OCB because: (a) it produces a sense of unspecified obligation (Pillai, Schriesheim, & Williams, 1999) that is repaid with OCB, (b) it builds trust and enhances employees' confidence that contributions to the organization (perhaps in the form of OCB) will be rewarded in the future, (c) it increases job satisfaction, and (d) employees like managers who are fair and may wish to reward them through OCB for their fairness. The relationship between role clarity and OCB is more complex because role clarity would only be expected to be related to OCB if the manager defines the employee's role broadly enough to include OCB. If the role is narrowly defined, enhanced role clarity might be expected to be negatively related to OCB because the narrow role definition makes it clearer that OCB is not part of the job. However, in Chapter 6 we review evidence that suggests that managers generally define employee performance more broadly to include OCB. Thus, there are a number of reasons why we would expect leader contingent reward and punishment behavior to be positively related to OCB.

Alternatively, when leaders administer punishments on a noncontingent basis, employees will likely perceive that as unfair, causing their liking for and trust in the leader to diminish. It will also decrease employee job satisfaction and will actually increase role ambiguity. Thus, for the reasons mentioned in the discussion of contingent rewards, noncontingent punishment is expected to decrease the motivation to exhibit OCB. When leaders administer rewards on a noncontingent basis, role ambiguity increases, but this action may not necessarily be perceived as unfair and may actually result in greater liking for the leader and greater job satisfaction. Therefore, leader noncontingent reward behavior may increase OCB because it may still (a) engender an unspecified sense of obligation that may be reciprocated through OCB, (b) increase liking for the manager and the probability that employees may wish to reward him or her with OCB, and/or (c) increase job satisfaction.

Consistent with this discussion, empirical research generally shows that contingent reward behavior is positively related to OCB (e.g., MacKenzie et al., 2001; Pillai et al., 1999; Podsakoff et al., 1996a; Podsakoff et al., 1990) and that noncontingent punishment behavior is negatively related to OCB (e.g., Podsakoff, Bommer, Podsakoff, & MacKenzie, 2004; Podsakoff et al., 1996a). However, several studies have failed to find a relationship between leader contingent punishment behavior and OCB and have found only weak evidence of a relationship between noncontingent reward behavior and OCB (e.g., Podsakoff et al., 1996a; Podsakoff et al., 2004).

Transformational Leadership Behaviors

In contrast to the transactional give-and-take exchange process associated with leadership reward and punishment behaviors, transformational leadership involves fundamentally changing the values, goals, and aspirations of employees so that they are intrinsically motivated to perform their work because it is consistent with their values, rather than because it is externally motivated by the expectation that they will be rewarded for their efforts (e.g., Bass, 1985; Bennis & Nanus, 1985; Burns, 1978; Conger & Kanungo, 1988; House, 1977; Kuhnert & Lewis, 1987; Sashkin, 1988; Trice & Beyer, 1986). For example, as noted by Kuhnert and Lewis (1987), transformational leadership "is made possible when a leader's end values (internal standards) are adopted by followers thereby producing changes in the attitudes, beliefs, and goals of followers" (p. 653). Similarly, as Bryman (1992) noted,

> Transforming leadership entails both leaders and followers raising each other's motivation and sense of purpose. This higher purpose is one in which the aims and aspirations of leaders and followers congeal into one . . . Both leaders and followers are changed in pursuit of goals which express aspirations in which they can identify themselves. (p. 95)

A review of the leadership literature by Podsakoff, MacKenzie, Moorman, and Fetter (1990) indicates that transformational leaders get followers to perform above and beyond expectations by articulating a vision, providing an appropriate role model, fostering the acceptance of group goals, providing individualized support and intellectual stimulation, and expressing high performance expectations. These forms of behavior are quite different from the reward and punishment behaviors that are typically associated with transactional leadership. Articulating a vision represents behavior on the part of a leader that identifies and expresses a clear vision of the future of the group/unit/organization. Providing an appropriate model involves setting an example for employees to follow that is consistent with both the values the leader espouses and the goals of the organization. Fostering the acceptance of group goals promotes cooperation among subordinates and encourages them to work together toward a common goal, even at the expense of their personal goals and aspirations. In other words, leaders exhibiting this behavior emphasize collective identities and encourage self-sacrifice for the sake of the group. Providing individualized support represents behavior that indicates that the leader respects subordinates, oversees their individual development, and is concerned with their personal feelings and needs. Intellectual stimulation challenges employees to reexamine assumptions about their work and to find creative ways of improving their performance. High performance expectations represent leadership behavior that demonstrates high expectations for excellence, quality, and/or high performance on the part of employees.

Articulating a vision may influence OCB through a variety of mechanisms. First, it makes action oriented toward the accomplishment of the goals seem more meaningful and important, because it shows how work behavior fits into a bigger picture and/or creates a sense that the organization is moving forward (i.e., evolving) by showing where the organization is going and how it is going to get there. This may increase job satisfaction and an employee's motivation to want to do whatever it takes to achieve the goals articulated. This leader behavior may also motivate action by helping the employee gain a clearer understanding of his or her role and by providing a sense of hope for a better future. In addition, because leaders who exhibit this behavior are likely to be perceived as more competent and predictable, they are more likely to liked and trusted. Liking and trust for the leader should increase an employee's motivation to expend extra effort to achieve the goals articulated.

Leaders who provide an appropriate model may also motivate OCB in different ways. For example, leaders who model the behavior (including OCB) they want their employees to perform may enhance OCB because their modeling serves to establish norms/expectations of appropriate work behavior, thus increasing the likelihood that the employees will feel they ought to exhibit OCB. The leader's modeling of the behaviors he or she thinks are important would also result in greater role clarity and increased job satisfaction for the employees. In addition, if some of the behaviors that the leader models are citizenship behaviors, the demonstration of these behaviors by the leader may enhance the ability of employees to effectively exhibit OCB. Finally, leaders whose behavior is consistent with what they say is important will be liked and trusted more than leaders who "talk the talk but don't walk the walk." Employees are more likely to be willing to expend extra effort for leaders that they like and trust than for ones they don't.

As noted earlier, leaders who foster the acceptance of group goals promote cooperation among subordinates and encourage employees to work together toward a common goal. This behavior enhances employees' sense of a shared identity (i.e., increases the salience of collective identities) and increases the likelihood that pursuits oriented toward self-interest will be voluntarily abandoned for more altruistic or collectivist endeavors in the form of employee OCB. In addition, this behavior on the part of leaders is likely to increase employees' feeling that they ought to exhibit OCB because they are more responsible to the group. Finally, leaders who foster the acceptance of group goals may enhance role clarity by telling employees that they expect them to work together for the collective good. To the extent they are successful, they will encourage employees to exhibit OCB because employees will view OCB as part of their role.

Individualized support behavior on the part of a leader should enhance OCB for the same reasons that supportive leader behavior enhances OCB. Indeed, some have argued that individualized support and supportive leader behavior are indistinguishable (Hunt, 1991), and there is empirical evidence that they are highly correlated with each other (Seltzer & Bass, 1990). Others (Bass & Avolio, 1993) disagree, maintaining that individualized support is subtly different from supportive leader behavior. Regardless of whether they are or are not different, we believe that they encourage employees to engage in OCB in the same way and for the same reasons. For example, an employee is likely to view individualized support as helpful because it is an indication that the leader is concerned for that employee's welfare, which will cause the employee to like his or her supervisor more and make the employee want to help the supervisor in any way possible. Individualized support should also increase employee job satisfaction, especially satisfaction with the supervisor, and cause the employee to want to reciprocate in the form of OCB.

The case for why high performance expectations and intellectual stimulation should be related to OCB is weaker than for the other forms of transformational leadership behavior. High performance expectations may increase OCB if citizenship behavior is an integral part of the leader's performance expectations. Expressing these expectations increases employees' perception that they are obligated to engage in citizenship behavior. In addition, a continual focus on performance expectations could heighten employees' sense of responsibility for work outcomes and motivate them to do whatever it takes (including OCB) to achieve them. Intellectual stimulation may only relate to a few forms of OCB, such as voice behavior. Leaders who encourage employees to think about problems that they otherwise would not have thought about or to think about new ways of solving old problems may also be implicitly encouraging employees to give voice to their suggestions or recommendations. Beyond this, it is not clear why intellectual stimulation should necessarily be related to OCB. Indeed, some reasoning suggests that it would be negatively related to OCB because it may lead to decreased liking for the leader (because she or he is seemingly never satisfied) and/or less trust in the leader (because the leader's behavior increases conflict and job stress and makes the leader seem less predictable).

To date, only a handful of studies have examined the effects of transformational leadership on OCB, and they have modeled the transformational leadership behaviors differently. Two studies (Koh, Steers, & Terborg, 1995; Pillai et al., 1999) used Bass's (1985) MLQ measure to represent the transformational leadership construct and combined all of the leadership dimensions. Two studies (MacKenzie et al., 2001; Podsakoff et al., 1990) combined articulating a vision, providing an appropriate model, and fostering the acceptance of group goals into a "core transformational leadership" construct and left the other dimensions as separate constructs. And one study (Podsakoff, MacKenzie, & Bommer, 1996b) modeled all of the dimensions as separate constructs. All of the studies show effects of transformational leadership on OCB. Moreover, four of the five studies (i.e., all the studies except Podsakoff et al., 1996b) show effects of transformational leadership on OCB, even while controlling for forms of transactional leadership behaviors.

In addition, trust has been identified as a key mediator of the relationships between transformational leadership behaviors and OCB in all three studies in which it was examined (MacKenzie et al., 2001; Pillai et al., 1999; Podsakoff et al., 1990). Podsakoff et al. (1990) found that after controlling for common method variance, trust mediated the positive impact of the core transformational leadership behaviors and individualized support on altruism, courtesy, sportsmanship, and conscientiousness. Pillai et al. (1999) reported that trust (and procedural justice) mediated the effect of the transformational leadership behaviors (as a group) on OCBs (as a group). Finally, MacKenzie et al. (2001) found that trust mediated the positive effects of the core transformational leadership behaviors and individualized support on helping and sportsmanship, and the negative effect of intellectual stimulation on these two forms of OCB.

Podsakoff et al. (1996b) examined the relationships between the transformational leadership behaviors and OCB within the context of a variety of substitutes for leadership, but they did not examine the potential mediating effects of any variables on these relationships. However, because this study contained measures of trust, job satisfaction, and role ambiguity, and because we have suggested that all three of these may serve as potential mechanisms through which transformational leadership behaviors may influence OCB, we reanalyzed the data from this study to explore this issue. In our reanalysis, we modeled articulating a vision, providing an appropriate model, and fostering group goals to represent a "core" transformational leadership construct, and we modeled the other three dimensions of transformational leadership (intellectual stimulation, high performance expectations, and individualized support) as individual constructs. This treatment is consistent with the manner in which both Podsakoff et al. (1990) and MacKenzie et al. (2001) modeled the transformational leadership behaviors.

The results of our analysis (see Figure 5.1) indicated that the core transformational leadership construct was positively related to role clarity, trust in the leader, and job satisfaction, and had: (a) positive indirect effects on sportsmanship, civic virtue, and conscientiousness through job satisfaction and trust; (b) positive indirect effects on altruism and courtesy through job satisfaction; and (c) a positive direct effect on altruism. High performance expectations were positively related to role clarity and had a positive direct effect on courtesy, but no direct or indirect effects on the other OCBs. Individualized support was

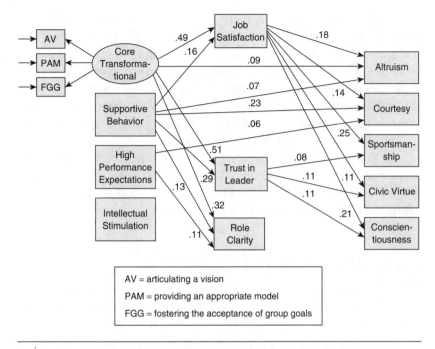

Figure 5.1   Mediators of the Effects of Transformational Leadership Behavior on OCB

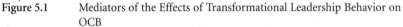

positively related to role clarity, trust in the leader, and job satisfaction, and had: (a) positive indirect effects on sportsmanship, civic virtue, and conscientiousness through job satisfaction and trust; (b) positive indirect effects on altruism and courtesy through job satisfaction; and (c) positive direct effects on altruism and courtesy. Intellectual stimulation was not related to any type of OCB or mediators. Thus, consistent with our expectations, these results indicate that trust in one's leader plays a key role in mediating the effects of the core transformational leadership behaviors and individualized support on OCB. The results also indicate that job satisfaction plays an important role in mediating these same relationships, even when controlling for the mediating effects of trust. This result is consistent with the theoretical statements of Organ (1988) but is inconsistent with the empirical findings of Podsakoff et al. (1990), who found that job satisfaction did not mediate the effects of transformational leadership behaviors on OCB when controlling for the mediating effects of trust. Finally, contrary to our expectations, role clarity was found to be unrelated to OCB.

Therefore, taken together, there is fairly strong evidence that trust mediates the relationship between transformational leadership and OCB, and some evidence that job satisfaction and procedural justice do so as well. However, at present, there is little empirical support for our expectation that role clarity mediates the relationship between these leadership behaviors and OCB. This is somewhat surprising. Because the evidence reviewed in Chapter 6 indicates that managers generally include OCB in their definition of an employee's overall performance, one might expect them to communicate these role expectations to their employees, thus increasing the relationship between role clarity and OCB. Of course, managers might not do a very good job of communicating these expectations to employees.

Leader-Member Exchange (LMX) Relationships

Leader-member exchange theory is based on the assumption that leaders establish a social exchange relationship with their employees and that the nature of this exchange relationship influences the manner in which the leader treats each individual employee. Lower-quality exchange relationships between a leader and his or her employees are characterized by the leader's use of formal authority and average levels of employee performance. In contrast, high-quality exchange relationships involve mutual trust, support, and loyalty between the leader and his or her employees, enhanced levels of interpersonal attraction (i.e., liking), and bidirectional influence. Thus, employees in high-quality exchange relationships are motivated to exhibit higher levels of commitment, conscientiousness, and loyalty to their leaders in return for more favorable performance appraisals, promotions, and other rewards from their leaders. As noted by Wayne, Shore, Bommer, and Tetrick (2002), as the quality of the LMX relationship increases, OCB behavior increases:

> From a social exchange perspective, a high-quality exchange may create a sense of obligation on the part of the subordinate to reciprocate in terms of behaviors valued by the supervisor. Consistent with this perspective, high-quality exchanges tend to be associated with employee behavior that benefits the supervisor and goes beyond the formal job duties (Liden & Graen, 1980). Subordinates may engage in OCB and perform at a high level to reciprocate for rewards and support provided by the supervisor, thus maintaining a balanced or equitable social exchange with the supervisor. (p. 593)

Thus, the quality of the exchange relationship motivates employees to engage in OCB by increasing their sense of obligation, desire to reciprocate, and trust in, liking for, and commitment to the leader. Although a growing body of evidence supports the hypothesized relationship between LMX and OCB (Deluga, 1998; Hui, Law, & Chen, 1999; Settoon, Bennett, & Liden, 1996; Tansky, 1993; Uhl-Bien & Maslyn, 2003; Wayne & Green, 1993; Wayne, Shore, & Liden, 1997; Wayne et al., 2002), surprisingly little research has examined potential mediators of this relationship. One exception is the study by Podsakoff and MacKenzie (1993) that reanalyzed correlational data reported by Tansky (1993) to examine the role of job satisfaction, fairness, and organizational commitment in mediating the effect of LMX on five dimensions of organizational citizenship behavior (altruism, courtesy, civic virtue, sportsmanship, and conscientiousness). They found that LMX was positively related to employee perceptions of fairness, that fairness was positively related to job satisfaction, and that fairness and job satisfaction together completely mediated the effect of LMX on courtesy and civic virtue. In addition, LMX was positively related to altruism, sportsmanship, and conscientiousness, but the relationships were direct and were not mediated by job satisfaction, fairness, or organizational commitment. Thus, there is some evidence that fairness and job satisfaction mediate the relationship between LMX and some forms of OCB. However, it is important to recognize that the results reported by Podsakoff and MacKenzie are based on a reanalysis of data from only one study and that additional empirical research should examine in more detail the mechanisms through which LMX influences OCB.

Servant Leadership

Greenleaf (1970, 1973, 1997) originally developed the concept of servant leadership. For Greenleaf, the essence of leadership is recognizing that leaders have a moral responsibility to serve not only the needs of the organization but also the needs of their followers, customers, and society. With respect to their followers, servant leadership involves three things: nurturing, defending, and empowering. Servant leaders must attend to the needs of followers, help them to develop their capabilities, and help them to become more willing to accept their responsibilities. This requires that leaders must listen to followers, understand their needs and aspirations, and be willing to provide support to them. Rather than using power to control followers, the servant leader must empower followers and encourage them to take responsibility for their actions. Establishing trust is a key element of servant leadership, and servant leaders do this by being honest and open with followers, behaving in a manner consistent with the values they espouse, and demonstrating trust in their followers.

Greenleaf argued that followers of such leaders are inspired by the example set by their leaders to become servant leaders themselves. This style of leadership might encourage OCB on the part of followers for several reasons. First, as noted by Ehrhart (2004),

> The behavior that servant-leaders model includes "serving" their subordinates by forming quality relationships with them and helping them grow and develop. Thus, units with servant-leaders should have members who will emulate this behavior in their interactions with each other and, thus, display higher levels of OCB (pp. 69–70).

This behavior should also help to establish social norms and set expectations of how members of the unit should interact.

Second, because followers observe the leader helping coworkers, they are likely to either be inspired to do the same or believe that they are expected to do the same. Third, because servant leadership involves providing personal support to followers, it would be reasonable to expect that they would be motivated to reciprocate by doing things (such as OCB) that will benefit the leader and help the leader achieve his or her goals and objectives. Finally, because servant leadership demonstrates that the leader has a genuine interest in the well-being of his or her followers, not simply as a means to the end of achieving higher performance but as an end in itself, followers are likely to trust and like servant leaders and feel they have been treated fairly. As a result, they are likely to be motivated to expend extra effort on behalf of the leader.

Despite the apparent relevance of servant leadership to organizational citizenship behavior and its longstanding presence in the literature, to our knowledge, only one study has examined its relationships with OCB. In this study, Ehrhart (2004) examined servant leadership and the procedural justice climate as predictors of OCB at the individual and unit level. He found that servant leadership influenced helping behavior and conscientiousness behavior at the individual level even when common method variance was controlled for and that these effects were partially mediated by perceptions of the procedural justice climate. He obtained similar results at the unit level, except that servant leadership had only a direct effect on conscientiousness and did not have an indirect effect mediated by perceptions of procedural justice climate. Taken together, these results are promising because they show that servant leadership is related to OCB through perceptions of procedural justice climate, but there are several other mechanisms through which this style of leadership may influence citizenship behavior. Indeed, the fact that the mediation was only partial in Ehrhart's (2004) study reinforces this idea and suggests that future research on the mechanisms through which servant leadership influences OCB is warranted.

Leadership Empowerment Behavior

Another leadership behavior that researchers may expect to influence OCB is leadership empowerment. Researchers have conceptualized the empowerment construct in a variety of ways. For example, Spreitzer (1995) refers to empowerment as a psychological state in which individuals feel more able and competent, and Kirkman and Rosen (1997) define empowerment as a multidimensional construct that consists of the "empowered" individual feeling more "potent" and "autonomous," and his or her work having more "meaning" and "impact." Both of these conceptualizations deal with empowerment as an end state. On the other hand, Conger and Kanungo (1988) refer to empowerment not as a feeling or a result, but as a leadership behavior that fosters favorable outcomes such as follower persistence and self-efficacy. In this sense, empowerment is a "motivational construct" (Conger and Kanungo, 1988, p. 473) practiced by management with the intent of moving followers to action.

Considering the work of Conger and Kanungo (1988) and Hui (1994), we posit that leadership empowerment behaviors include enhancing the meaningfulness of the work, fostering participation in decision making, expressing confidence in high performance, and encouraging autonomy. *Enhancing the meaningfulness of work* is defined as behavior on the part of a leader that emphasizes the purpose and meaning of employees' work such that they identify themselves as being important members of the organization. *Fostering participation in decision making* means that a leader solicits inputs from employees in problem situations and invites their active involvement in the decision-making process. This includes creating opportunities for employees to express their job- or project-related opinions and to make joint decisions with their leader. *Expressing confidence in high performance* is behavior on the part of a leader that communicates high expectations and that shows confidence in the employee's ability to meet those expectations. Finally, *encouraging autonomy* is behavior on the part of a leader that encourages employees to perform their jobs in the manner that they feel is most efficient. This is facilitated by giving employees the freedom to decide what needs to be done to perform their jobs with a minimum of managerial and organizational constraints.

Leader empowerment behaviors are expected to be positively related to OCB through a variety of mechanisms, depending on the specific empowerment behaviors. For example, when leaders express confidence in their employees, we expect that employees' perceptions of self-efficacy would increase, which would result in an increased motivation to exert extra effort, perhaps in the form of OCB. On the other hand, when leaders actively encourage employee autonomy and foster their participation in decision making, their sense of ownership and responsibility for work outcomes should increase, which will subsequently increase the likelihood that they will be willing to do whatever it takes (including OCB) to make the organization successful. Finally, enhancing the meaningfulness of work should result in greater job satisfaction, which should lead to more OCB. Thus, to the extent that leader empowerment behaviors cause employees to become more satisfied with their jobs, more confident in their ability to perform, and to have a greater sense of responsibility for their work, employees will be willing to work harder and go beyond job-prescribed roles to make the organization successful.

To our knowledge, only one study (Ahearne, MacKenzie, & Podsakoff, 2004) has examined the effects of leadership empowerment behaviors on OCB, and it was conducted at the group rather than the individual level. Based on reasoning similar to that previously described, these authors hypothesized that leader empowerment behaviors would increase job satisfaction and sales team potency, subsequently resulting in more organizational citizenship behavior. Consistent with these expectations, Ahearne et al. (2004) found that encouraging autonomy, enhancing the meaningfulness of work, and expressing confidence in performance all had significant indirect effects on OCB that accounted for 58% of the variance in group-level citizenship behaviors. The effects on OCB of enhancing the meaningfulness of work and expressing confidence in high performance was mediated by both perceptions of group potency and group job satisfaction. In contrast, the effect of encouraging autonomy on OCB was mediated by group job satisfaction only. Thus, this research suggests that leader empowerment behavior may have important effects on OCB and that it should receive more attention in future research.

The Effects of Task Characteristics on OCB

Although empirical research on the relationships between task characteristics and OCB has shown that task characteristics, like leadership behaviors, influence OCB, there has been little theoretical discussion in the literature of why this is the case. However, models of job and task characteristics (e.g., Dunham, 1979; Griffin, 1982; Hackman & Oldham, 1975; Sims & Szilagyi, 1976) may provide some insights. These models have identified several task characteristics that influence employee motivation to perform the job, including task autonomy, significance, feedback, identity, variety (routinization), task interdependence, goal interdependence, and the intrinsically satisfying nature of the task.

Building on the work of Turner and Lawrence (1965), Hackman and Lawler (1971) defined task autonomy as "the extent to which employees have a major say in scheduling their work, selecting the equipment they will use, and deciding on procedures to be followed" (p. 267). Task autonomy should enhance the employees' sense of ownership and responsibility for work outcomes, thereby increasing their willingness to do whatever it takes (including OCB) to accomplish the task. Another possibility is that because autonomous tasks permit employees to have greater control, they are more satisfying (Langer, 1983). If so, this heightened job satisfaction may increase OCB. On the other hand, low task autonomy may foster learned helplessness (Seligman, 1975), which may decrease some forms of OCB (e.g., helping behavior, civic virtue, and voice).

Task identity, variety (routinization), and significance are likely to influence OCB by increasing employees' perceptions of the meaningfulness of their work (Hackman & Oldham, 1976). According to Griffin (1982), *task identity* is the degree to which the job requires completion of a whole and identifiable piece of work that is done from beginning to end with a visible outcome; *task variety* is the degree to which a job requires a variety of activities in carrying out the work and involves the use of several employee skills; and *task significance* is the degree to which the job has a substantial impact on the lives or work of other people, whether they are inside or outside the organization. Tasks that are high in variety, significance, and identity are likely to be perceived as more valuable and worthwhile than tasks that are highly routine, low in significance, and low in identity (i.e., tasks where the employee does not do the whole job). As a result, employees may be more satisfied and motivated to expend more energy and effort, perhaps in the form of OCB. Thus, task significance, identity, and variety can influence OCB by increasing either employees' perceptions of the meaningfulness of their work or their satisfaction with their work.

Task interdependence is "the extent to which an individual team member needs information, materials, and support from other team members to be able to carry out his or her job" (Van der Vegt, Van de Vliert, & Oosterhof, 2003, p. 717). Smith, Organ, and Near (1983) argued that task interdependence is likely to enhance OCB for a variety of reasons, including the fact that such tasks are likely to foster social norms of cooperation, make the need for collective social responsibility more salient to group members, and enhance group cohesiveness. More specifically, these authors note that

> Reciprocal interdependence . . . requires frequent instances of spontaneous mutual adjustment in order to effect coordination. This requirement presumably fosters social norms of cooperation, helping, and sensitivity to others' needs and makes salient a collective sense of social responsibility (Krebs, 1970). At the same time, it tends to promote . . . higher levels of group cohesion than other task environments (Smith et al., 1983, pp. 655–656).

Building on the previous theoretical work of Smith et al. (1983) and Hackman and Oldham (1976), Pearce and Gregersen (1991) also argued that task interdependence should lead to an enhanced feeling of responsibility among group members toward the group and the organization that should motivate them to exhibit more OCB.

Another important task characteristic is its capacity to produce satisfaction and stimulate task involvement. Tasks with this characteristic (although to some extent this is really a reaction to a task rather than a property of the task itself) are called *intrinsically satisfying tasks* by Kerr and Jermier (1978). Obviously, tasks that possess this property would be expected to influence OCB through their impact on employee job satisfaction. Employees engaged in intrinsically satisfying tasks by definition find the performance of job-related activities to be more rewarding, and as a result, they are motivated to expend greater effort to achieve their task objectives.

Finally, performance feedback provided by the work itself is another property of the task that may affect OCB. Hackman and Oldham

(1976) define *task feedback* as "the degree to which carrying out the work activities required by the job results in the individual obtaining direct and clear information about the effectiveness of his performance" (pp. 257–258). These researchers argued that task feedback has its biggest effect on employee performance through the knowledge it conveys to employees about the results of their effort. According to Kerr and Jermier (1978), task-provided feedback is important because it is often the most immediate, the most accurate, the most self-evaluation evoking, and most intrinsically motivating source of feedback. If a person is committed to task accomplishment, tasks that provide feedback are more self-rewarding and provide greater opportunities for improving performance through trial-and-error learning. These characteristics should enhance job satisfaction, which has been shown to be related to OCB (Organ & Ryan, 1995). We would speculate that task feedback might be more closely related to helping others with work-related problems and the aspect of civic virtue (or voice) that involves making constructive suggestions about how to improve task performance, because these behaviors may require greater knowledge of the factors contributing to task accomplishment than other forms of OCB.

Turning our attention now to the empirical data, the research evidence suggests that task feedback, task variety (routinization), and intrinsically satisfying tasks have significant positive relationships with OCB. Indeed, the meta-analysis reported by Podsakoff et al. (1996a) indicated that these three task characteristics generally explained a larger proportion of the variance in employee altruism, courtesy, sportsmanship, civic virtue, and conscientiousness than leader behaviors did. We previously suggested that job satisfaction should serve as one of the key mediators of the impact of all three of these task characteristics on OCB. Although we are not aware of any previous research addressing this issue, we reanalyzed the meta-analytic data published by Podsakoff et al. (1996a) to examine whether job satisfaction partially or completely mediates the impact of these three task characteristics on OCB.

As indicated in Figure 5.2, our reanalysis showed that task feedback had both direct and indirect effects (mediated by job satisfaction) on all five forms of OCB examined. Job satisfaction completely mediated the effect of task feedback on employee courtesy and partially mediated the effects of task feedback on altruism and sportsmanship. In addition, task feedback had direct effects on civic virtue and conscientiousness. A similar pattern of effects was observed for intrinsically satisfying

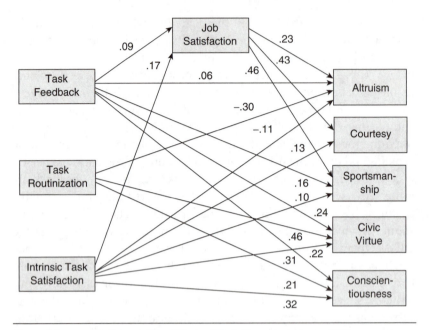

Figure 5.2   Mediators of the Effects of Task Characteristics on OCB

tasks. Job satisfaction partially mediated the effects of intrinsically satisfying tasks on altruism, courtesy, and sportsmanship. Intrinsically satisfying tasks also had significant positive effects on civic virtue and conscientiousness. In contrast, none of the effects of task routinization on OCB were mediated by job satisfaction. Instead, task routinization had a direct negative effect on altruism and positive direct effects on civic virtue and conscientiousness.

Two studies (Pearce & Gregersen, 1991; Smith et al., 1983) examined the impact of task and goal interdependence on OCB. *Goal interdependence* is "the degree to which group members believe that they are assigned group goals or provided with group feedback" (Van der Vegt, Van de Vliert, & Oosterhof, 2003, p. 717). Contrary to their expectations, Smith et al. (1983) found no effect of task independence, either directly or indirectly through employee satisfaction, on either employee altruism or conscientiousness in a sample of bank employees. However, in a follow-up study conducted in a sample of health care and administrative employees in two hospitals, Pearce and Gregersen (1991) reported that felt responsibility completely mediated the relationships between both reciprocal (task) interdependence and work independence and a measure of overall OCB. More specifically, these authors found that task independence increased group members' feeling of responsibility, work independence decreased feelings of felt responsibility, and felt responsibility enhanced OCB.

Pearce and Gregersen (1991) noted that the discrepancy between their findings and those reported by Smith et al. (1983) might be attributable to the fact that the Smith et al. study did not include a measure of felt responsibility. Another possibility is that the task interdependence measure used in the Smith et al. study was unreliable, which would have prevented this variable from being highly correlated with OCB. Indeed, the correlation matrix in the Smith et al. study indicates that the task interdependence measure was not correlated more than .08 with any of the substantive variables in the study, suggesting that low reliability may have been a problem. The reliability of the task interdependence scale may be questionable because it is fairly unusual; it requires respondents to interpret a pictogram and make a judgment of how well it compares to workflows in their unit. This possible problem suggests that additional research is needed on this topic before conclusions regarding the effects of task interdependence can be fully determined.

To our knowledge, no studies have examined the individual effects of task autonomy, task significance, or task identity on organizational citizenship behavior. However, several studies (Blakely, Andrews, & Fuller, 2003; Cardona, Lawrence, & Bentler, 2004; Farh, Podsakoff, & Organ, 1990; Van Dyne, Graham, & Dienesch, 1994) have examined the effect of one or more of these task characteristics, in combination with other task characteristics, on OCB. For example, Farh et al. (1990) examined the effects of these three task characteristics, in combination with task feedback and task variety, on OCB. They found that the combination of these five task characteristics (called *task scope*) had positive effects on both employee altruism and compliance, even after controlling for employees' perceptions of leadership fairness (measured by a combination of contingent reward and supportive leader behavior) and job satisfaction (measured by a combination of satisfaction with supervision and work satisfaction). In addition, their results indicate that neither leader fairness nor job satisfaction had an effect on compliance after controlling for task scope. The combination of these five task variables uniquely accounted for about 4% of the variance in altruism and 4% in compliance.

In a longitudinal study of employees working in a federal research facility, Blakely et al. (2003) examined the effects of self-monitoring behavior on OCB while controlling for the effects of a variety of variables, including measures of task autonomy, variety, significance, feedback, and identity. These researchers reported that the combination of these task characteristics had no significant effects on four measures of OCB in either time 1 or time 2 of the study, when the effects of self-monitoring, job satisfaction, organizational commitment, and perceived organizational support were controlled.

Van Dyne et al. (1994) also examined the combined effects of all five of the task characteristics used in the Farh et al. (1990) and Blakely et al. (2003) studies on five types of OCB. In addition, Van Dyne et al. (1994) also examined the potential mediating effects of the nature of the covenantal relationship between the employee and the organization on the relationships between task characteristics and OCB. Building on Graham's (Graham, 1991; Graham & Organ, 1993) work on organizational covenants, Van Dyne et al. (1994) noted that

> Political philosophy suggests that the nature of the relationship citizens have with their government is critical to their citizenship behavior. The active citizenship syndrome is based on covenantal relationship, which is characterized by open-ended commitment, mutual trust, and shared values (Bromley & Busching, 1988; Elazar, 1980; Graham, 1991; Graham & Organ, 1993; Grover, 1982). Covenants describe relationships of mutual commitment in which specific behaviors required to maintain the relationship or pursue common ends are not specifiable in advance (DePree, 1989). A covenant is "not a bargain but a pledge" (Rowley, 1962: 1515), a mutual promise by individuals to do their best to serve common values for an indefinite period. In contrast to contractual, exchange, or other instrumental relationships (Blau, 1964), covenants are existential; they focus on a state of being and involve intrinsically motivated effort rather than earning something or getting somewhere.... The more strongly a person identifies with the collective entity (such as a particular relationship or community) and feels valued and values the connection, the less that individual will rely on legal sanctions to resolve difficulties (Macneil, 1985) and the more he or she will be an active contributor to the community (Almond & Verba, 1963; Verba & Nie, 1972). Thus, covenant is conceptualized as a reciprocal relationship based on ties that bind individuals to their communities and communities to their members (Kanter, 1968). (Van Dyne et al., 1994, p. 768)

Van Dyne et al. (1994) then went on to argue that several task properties, such as task feedback, autonomy, completion (or identity), and meaningfulness (or significance) could be expected to influence OCB through their effects on employees' perceptions of the covenantal relationship with the organization. For example, the authors argued that jobs that provide feedback to employees or that are made more meaningful to employees by making them aware of how their job contributes to the organization are likely to increase feelings of embeddedness in and accountability toward the organization and that these feelings are characteristic of covenantal relationships.

Consistent with their expectations, Van Dyne et al. (1994) found a positive relationship between jobs that had higher motivating potential scores (i.e., jobs that were rated higher on autonomy, feedback, significance, variety, and identity) and employees' perceptions of their covenantal relationship with the organization. The researchers also found that the covenantal relationship generally served as a complete mediator of the relationships between the job characteristics and OCB. More specifically, they found that employees' perceptions of the covenantal relationship fully mediated the positive relationships between the job characteristics and organizational loyalty (i.e., the employee's tendency to support and defend the organization), functional participation (i.e., the employee's willingness to work beyond the level required by the organization), social participation (i.e., the employee's tendency to interact with others in the work setting), and advocacy participation (i.e., the employee's willingness to advocate change in the organization). However, the findings for advocacy participation should be qualified by the fact that the correlation between the task characteristics and advocacy participation, as well as the correlation between the measure of the employees' perception of the covenantal relationship and advocacy participation, were only marginally significant ($p < .10$) when both were entered in the regression equation at the same time. This finding suggests that neither one of these variables served as significant predictors of advocacy participation when they were both entered into the regression equation and traditional levels of significance (i.e., $p < .05$) were used. Nevertheless, taken together, the findings reported by Van Dyne et al. (1994) do provide some general support for the contention that the effects of task characteristics are mediated by employees' perception of the nature of the covenantal relationship they have with the organization.

Finally, Cardona et al. (2004) examined the relationship between task characteristics and OCB in two samples of physicians working in hospitals in Spain. These authors hypothesized that task feedback and autonomy influences OCB by enhancing affective commitment to the organization. They reported that the relationships between these task characteristics and OCB in both of their samples were completely mediated by affective commitment and that affective commitment had effects on OCB even after controlling for the effects of normative and calculative commitment. However, common method biases (see Podsakoff, MacKenzie, Lee, & Podsakoff, 2003; Podsakoff & Organ, 1986) may have influenced the relationships reported in the Cardona et al. (2004) study, because all of the measures (i.e., task characteristics, organizational commitment, and OCBs) were obtained from the same source.

Although not included in most theories of task characteristics, another aspect of one's job that might influence OCB is role overload. According to Jex and Thomas (2003), *role overload* is the extent to which employees perceive the pace and amount of their work to be consistently demanding. Jex and Thomas (2003) argue that

> When employees perceive that they have a demanding workload, their most likely response to this is to put all of their efforts into meeting the demands that this high level of workload presents. As a result, it is unlikely that employees would have a great deal of discretionary time. And hence there are fewer opportunities to engage in altruistic behavior to other employees. Another likely result of role overload is that employees experiencing this stressor will be less likely to devote themselves to the broader concerns of their work group. (p. 160)

This would suggest that role overload is negatively related to OCB because it reduces the amount of discretionary time available for engaging in OCB and because it reduces the employee's commitment to the group. As expected, Jex and Thomas (2003) found that overload was negatively related to employee altruism. However, they did not examine the potential mediating effects of group commitment on this relationship. Thus, future research directed at this issue may prove beneficial.

The Effects of Group Characteristics on OCB

In addition to leader behaviors and task characteristics, several group characteristics would be expected to influence OCB: group cohesiveness, the quality of the relationship between group members (team-member exchange), group potency, and perceived team support. In this section, we explore the theoretical rationale for why one might expect these group characteristics to be related to OCB and the empirical evidence of the extent to which this is true.

Group Cohesiveness

Group cohesiveness describes the affinity of group members for one another and their desire to remain part of the group. More specifically, George and Bettenhausen (1990) define group cohesiveness as

> a relative property of groups that summarizes the extent to which a group coheres or hangs together (Shaw, 1981). Highly cohesive groups are characterized by heightened member attraction to the group, friendliness, mutual liking, cooperation, and positive feelings about carrying out the group's task (Janis, 1982; Shaw, 1981). Members of highly cohesive groups value their group membership and enjoy being a member of the group. (p. 700)

So, there are several reasons why cohesiveness might be positively related to organizational citizenship behavior. First, members of cohesive groups have stronger feelings of attraction toward each other than members of groups that lack cohesiveness, and therefore they are likely to be more willing to help each other when the need arises. Second, members of cohesive groups have a stronger desire to remain a part of the group, and therefore they are likely to be more careful to exhibit sportsmanship and loyalty toward other members of the group. Third, members of cohesive groups have a stronger sense of group identity than members of groups that lack cohesiveness, and therefore they are more likely to be willing to defend the group from outside threats and criticisms. Finally, members of highly cohesive groups are likely to be more satisfied (at least with their coworkers) and trust each other more than members of groups that lack cohesiveness, and consequently they may be more willing to exert extra effort in the form of OCB on behalf of their fellow group members.

In addition to the potential mediators of the relationship between group cohesiveness and OCB, George and Bettenhausen (1990) suggested that group cohesiveness may interact with group norms to influence OCB. More specifically, they hypothesize that group cohesiveness should be positively related to prosocial behavior more when the group's social norms endorse the importance of this behavior, because the pressure to conform to group norms is greater in highly cohesive groups than in less cohesive groups. Similar hypotheses regarding the potential interaction between group cohesiveness and social norms on OCB have been provided by Kidwell, Mossholder, and Bennett (1997). In addition, Kidwell et al. hypothesize that group cohesiveness may also enhance the impact of affective antecedents of OCB, like job satisfaction and commitment.

Generally speaking, the empirical evidence supports the expectation that group cohesiveness is related to OCB. For example, Podsakoff et al. (1996a) reported that group cohesiveness was significantly correlated with all five forms of OCB that they examined in their meta-analysis (altruism, sportsmanship, courtesy, civic virtue, and conscientiousness). Importantly, this was also true for all of the OCB except for conscientiousness even after controlling for the effects of seven types of leader behavior and 12 other substitutes for leadership variables. Despite this encouraging evidence, virtually no research has examined whether liking for group members, the desire to remain a part of the group, group identity, satisfaction with coworkers, and/or trust in coworkers mediate the relationship between group cohesiveness and OCB.

However, some research has examined whether group cohesiveness moderates some of these variables on OCB. For example, George and Bettenhausen (1990) tested the simple main effect of group cohesiveness on prosocial behavior under conditions where they "had a priori reasons to believe that all of the groups endorsed a norm stressing the importance of the form of prosocial behavior under study" (p. 700). They reported that cohesiveness was related to prosocial behavior under these conditions, thus providing evidence consistent with the hypothesis that cohesiveness moderates the impact of social norms on prosocial behavior. A more direct test of the moderating effects of group cohesiveness was conducted by Kidwell et al. (1997). They found that cohesiveness at the group level influenced the effect of job satisfaction on OCB at the individual level for employee courtesy. However, they did not find support for the interaction of group cohesiveness with organizational commitment on this criterion variable. Taken together, these two studies provide some minimal support for the potential moderating effects of group cohesiveness, but more research examining a greater variety of OCB and a broader range of antecedents is needed.

Team-Member Exchange

Building on the framework of the leader-member exchange model, Seers (1989) noted that the relationships between team members (called *team member exchange*, or *TMX*) may also have an effect on the behavior of team members. According to Liden, Wayne, and Sparrowe (2000),

TMX represents an individual's overall perception of the exchanges with other members of the work group. As with LMXs, TMXs may vary in terms of the content and process of exchange. Low TMXs are limited to exchanges required for the completion of work tasks, whereas high TMXs involve exchange of resources and support that extends beyond what is necessary for task completion. (p. 409)

Team-member exchange would be expected to enhance OCB for several reasons. First, the TMX construct itself is defined in terms of the quality of the relationship between team members, and some of the dimensions on which the quality is judged bear a strong resemblance to OCB. For example, Seers's (1989) TMX scale asks team members to rate "How often I volunteer extra help [to the team]" and "How willing I am to finish work assigned to others." Both of these items capture the extent to which the individual doing the rating is willing to engage in helping behavior. Other items capture aspects of sportsmanship (e.g., "How flexible I am about switching jobs with others"), civic virtue (e.g., "How often I suggest better work methods to others"), and peacekeeping ("Meetings are good for resolving tension and conflict"). Second, TMX would be expected to enhance OCB because it should increase satisfaction with coworkers and perhaps with the work itself. Third, TMX should enhance OCB by increasing trust in coworkers, group cohesiveness, group commitment, and team members' general desire to exert extra effort on behalf of the team (e.g., interpersonal motivation). Finally, TMX should increase the strength of group norms for engaging in behaviors that improve the effectiveness of the group, including OCB.

In view of the many reasons that TMX might be expected to be related to OCB, it is surprising that, to our knowledge, no research has directly tested this relationship. However, one study (Liden et al., 2000) examined the relationship between TMX and a measure of performance that included cooperation and prosocial behaviors (i.e., customer service). They found that TMX predicted performance, even after controlling for (among other variables) LMX and job characteristics. Beyond this, there is empirical evidence that TMX influences some of the mediators previously proposed, such as organizational commitment (Liden et al., 2000), satisfaction with coworkers (Seers, 1989), work satisfaction (Seers, 1989), group cohesiveness (Jordan, Feild, & Armenakis, 2002; Seers, 1989), and interpersonal motivation (Seers, 1989). However, none of these studies included any traditional measures of OCB. Therefore, research examining the effects of TMX on OCB, and the processes that mediate these effects, should be a high priority.

Group Potency

Guzzo, Yost, Campbell, and Shea (1993) define *group potency* as the collective belief of a group that it can be effective, and Kirkman and Rosen (1999) describe it as self-efficacy at the group level. Work in the self-efficacy literature argues that a major hurdle in goal accomplishment is coming to the realization that success is possible and attainable. When group members believe they will be able to achieve their joint objectives if they persevere, they will be more united and more willing to go above and beyond prescribed roles to do whatever it takes to actually reach their goals. Group members will also refuse to be derailed and will be willing to go the extra mile to tolerate less-than-ideal circumstances. They will help each other get through difficult times and support group members who are bogged down with extra work. Belief in the potency of the group will encourage group members to put the interest of the group ahead of individual interests and to do everything necessary to make the group successful, even if it means performing behaviors that are not required.

The relationship between group potency and OCB has been reported in one study (Ahearne et al., 2004), in which the authors examined the effects of group potency on group effort and OCB using data from a sample of 533 pharmaceutical sales teams. The findings indicated that group potency significantly increased OCB, but it did not increase group effort. The latter finding is surprising because one would think that increased perceptions of group potency or group efficacy would translate into greater effort. However, the findings reported by Ahearne et al. (2004) suggest that more potent teams strive to increase sales performance by working better together as a team and making each sales call count rather than by simply exerting greater effort by making more sales calls. These efforts to work together better as a team appear in the form of increased levels of OCB. Although Ahearne et al. did not expect the effects of potency on performance to be completely mediated by OCB, the fact that this was the case does not seem unreasonable, because one of the reasons that companies use sales teams is to create this type of synergy among team members.

Perceived Team Support

The final group variable that researchers have hypothesized to be related to OCB is perceived team support (PTS). According to Bishop,

Scott, and Burroughs (2000), *perceived team support* is the team-level analogue to perceived organizational support (Eisenberger, Huntington, Hutchison, & Sowa, 1986) and is defined as "the degree to which employees believe that the team values their contribution and cares for their well-being" (Bishop et al., 2000, p. 1114). Bishop et al. (2000) argue that when team members perceive that their teammates value their contribution to the team and care about their well-being, they are likely to reciprocate by putting forth greater effort on behalf of the team in the form of OCB. The authors suggest that this greater effort results from team members' enhanced sense of commitment to the team caused by their perception of the team's support for them. Thus, according to Bishop et al. (2000), commitment to the team mediates the effect of perceived team support on OCB.

Bishop et al. (2000) directly tested this hypothesis with a sample of 380 automotive production workers organized into 65 self-directed teams that controlled the pace of their own work, distributed tasks, and scheduled their own work breaks. Bishop et al. reported that team commitment fully mediated the relationship between perceived team support and OCB, and that this was true even after controlling for the effects of organizational commitment on OCB. Two additional studies (Bommer, Miles, & Grover, 2003; Deckop, Cirka, & Andersson, 2003) indirectly tested the effect of team member support on OCB. Deckop et al. (2003) measured team support by asking employees to assess the extent to which they were helped by other members of the team, and the researchers had supervisors rate the extent to which each person provided help to others on the team. The results indicated that the more help an individual received from other team members, the more the person was inclined to exhibit helping behavior toward his or her teammates ($r = .30$). This was true even after controlling for procedural, distributive, and interactional justice, organizational commitment, intrinsic motivation of the task, job level, and job tenure. Bommer et al. (2003) had supervisors rate the extent to which each individual in a group exhibited OCB and then examined the correlation between the rating for an individual and the average of the ratings of the other group members. They found that the average level of OCB exhibited by the group was positively correlated with the individual's level of OCB ($r = .69$). Thus, although these are the only tests of the effect of perceived team support on OCB, they suggest that this group characteristic may be an important one to study in the future.

The Effects of
Organizational Characteristics on OCB

Another major category of factors that may influence OCB is organizational characteristics. In this section, we discuss theoretical reasons why organizational characteristics like formalization, inflexibility, employee-supervisor distance, perceived organizational support, human resource practices, and organizational constraints should be related to OCB and the empirical evidence regarding these expected relationships.

Organizational Formalization and Inflexibility

Organizational formalization is often defined (Hall, 1991) as the extent to which an organization clearly specifies rules and procedures for dealing with various contingencies, whereas *organizational inflexibility* is defined as the extent to which the organization rigidly adheres to those rules and procedures. One would expect organizational formalization and inflexibility to influence a wide variety of factors, some of which may be expected to increase OCB and some of which may be expected to decrease it.

At first glance, one might expect highly formalized and inflexible rules and procedures to be disliked by employees, to reduce their job satisfaction (see Hall, 1991), and to have detrimental effects on OCB because they encourage employees to focus on formalized job procedures and requirements, perhaps to the exclusion of "extra-role" or citizenship behaviors (Organ, 1988). In addition, work rules may be so inflexible that they prevent employees from helping each other on the job or taking the initiative to implement new procedures that would improve performance. However, there may also be some compensating benefits of formalization/inflexibility. For example, organizational formalization and/or inflexibility may enhance perceptions of fairness and procedural justice because formal rules make the organization's expectations clear (i.e., decrease role ambiguity and conflict), and inflexibility may be an indication that everyone is expected to play by the same rules, thereby increasing employee satisfaction, commitment, and trust in the organization. If this is the case, one would expect increased levels of OCB. Thus, there are some reasons to believe that formalization and inflexibility may enhance OCB and some reasons to believe that they may diminish it. Which of these potential mechanisms is stronger is difficult to determine a priori.

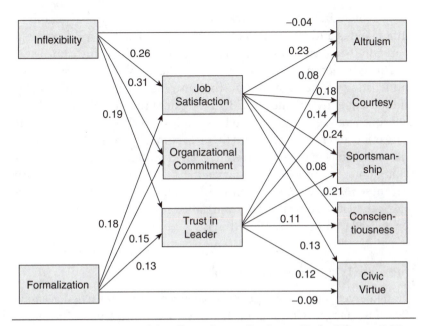

Figure 5.3   Mediators of the Effects of Formalization and Inflexibility on OCB

Unfortunately, to our knowledge, no study has examined the potential mediating effects of satisfaction, commitment, and/or trust on the relationship between organizational formalization/inflexibility and OCB. However, we reanalyzed the data published by Podsakoff et al. (1996a) to examine the potential mediating effects of these variables. We estimated a model in which organizational formalization and organizational inflexibility were hypothesized to indirectly influence OCB through their effects on employee satisfaction, commitment, and trust in the leader. The results of our analysis are reported in Figure 5.3.

As indicated in this figure, both organizational formalization and organizational inflexibility were positively related to employee job satisfaction, commitment, and trust, and they had positive indirect effects on all five types of OCB (altruism, courtesy, sportsmanship, conscientiousness, and civic virtue) through job satisfaction and trust. In addition, organizational inflexibility was also found to have a direct negative effect on employee altruism, and organizational formalization was found to have a direct negative effect on employee civic virtue. These latter findings are interesting because they suggest that the relationship between organizational inflexibility and employee altruism, and the relationship between organizational formalization and civic virtue, are fairly complex. Although it is difficult to account for these complexities, it is possible to speculate that even though making everyone abide by the same set of formalized rules and procedures does make employees more satisfied and trusting of the organization (because everyone is treated equally) and subsequently enhances OCB, to the extent that these rules and procedures encourage employees to focus only on the formal requirements of their job and not deviate from them, they may decrease the employee's willingness to help others with work-related problems (altruism) and/or to play an active role in the organization (civic virtue). However, given that these results were obtained in only one study, additional research on these relationships is clearly warranted before these findings can be generalized to other research settings.

Perceived Organizational Support

Eisenberger and his colleagues (Eisenberger, Fasolo, & Davis-LaMastro, 1990; Eisenberger, Huntington, Hutchison, & Sowa, 1986; Rhoades & Eisenberger, 2002) have noted that employers and employees have different perspectives on the nature of the employment relationship that must be reconciled if either is to achieve their goals. Because employers are generally concerned about productivity and costs, they value employees who are dedicated, loyal to the organization, productive, and less likely to quit their job. On the other hand, employees are generally more concerned about the organization's commitment to them, because being valued by the organization can lead to increased recognition, rewards, and benefits. Rhoades and Eisenberger (2002) suggest that one way to reconcile these different perspectives is through a social exchange process, in which employees trade their effort, loyalty, and commitment to the organization for the tangible benefits and rewards that the organization can provide. This form of social exchange is based on the norm of *reciprocity,* which obliges both the employee and the employer to reciprocate the favorable treatment they receive from each other, leading to beneficial outcomes for both.

According to organizational support theory (e.g., Eisenberger et al., 1986; Rhoades & Eisenberger, 2002), a key element for defining the nature of the relationship between the employer and employee is the employee's perception of the amount of support he or she is likely to receive from the organization (referred to as *perceived organizational support,* or *POS*). The theory assumes that the organization's readiness to provide employees with the necessary aid to perform their jobs effectively, reward and recognize increased work effort, and provide for their socioemotional needs in times of stress determines employees' beliefs about the extent to which their organization values their contributions and is concerned about their well-being. The development of these beliefs results from the tendency of employees to view the treatment they receive by agents of the organization (i.e., supervisors) as an indication of the organization's intent rather than attributing these actions solely to the agent's own personal motives. After these beliefs are developed, they have the potential to influence an employee's behavior toward the organization through a variety of avenues:

> Organizational support theory also addresses the psychological processes underlying consequences of POS. First, on the basis of the reciprocity norm, POS should produce a felt obligation to care about the organization's welfare and to help the organization reach its objectives. Second, the caring, approval, and respect connoted by POS should fulfill socioemotional needs, leading workers to incorporate organizational membership and role status into their social identity. Third, POS should strengthen employees' beliefs that the organization recognizes and rewards increased performance (i.e., performance-reward expectancies). These processes should have favorable outcomes both for employees (e.g., increased job satisfaction and heightened positive mood) and for the organization (e.g., increased affective commitment and performance, and reduced turnover). (Rhoades & Eisenberger, 2002, p. 699)

This suggests that employees' perceptions of organizational support can influence OCB by increasing employees' sense of obligation and desire to reciprocate to the organization, fulfill their socioemotional needs, establish a social identity, and enhance their job satisfaction and commitment to the organization. In addition, Organ and Konovsky (1989) argued that the employees' perceptions of organizational support create a sense of trust that the organization will fulfill its obligation by acknowledging and rewarding efforts they make on its behalf, and we would expect this sense of trust to also increase employee OCB.

There is a fairly substantial amount of empirical support for the hypothesized relationship between POS and OCB (e.g., Bishop et al., 2000; Eisenberger, Armeli, Rexwinkel, Lynch, & Rhoades, 2001; Liden, Wayne, Kraimer, & Sparrowe, 2003; Masterson, Lewis, Goldman, & Taylor, 2000; Moorman, Blakely, & Niehoff, 1998; Rhoades, & Eisenberger, 2002; Settoon et al., 1996; Wayne et al., 2002; Wayne et al., 1997; Witt, 1991). Indeed, the results of the meta-analysis conducted by Rhoades and Eisenberger (2002) suggest that the average corrected correlations between POS and either overall OCB or OCB directed at other individuals is .22, whereas the average corrected correlation between POS and OCB directed at the organization (after removing outliers from the analysis) is .29.

In addition to research on the direct relationship between perceived organizational support and OCB, some studies have examined potential mediators of this relationship. For example, Eisenberger et al. (2001) examined the potential mediating effect that employees' felt obligation toward the organization had on the relationship between perceived organizational support and OCB. Consistent with their expectations, they found that perceived organizational support was positively related to employees' felt obligation toward the organization and that felt obligation served as a complete mediator of the relationship between POS and employees' citizenship behavior. Eisenberger et al. also reported that POS influenced employees' affective commitment to the organization both directly and indirectly through its effects on felt responsibility. However, they did not examine the potential mediating effects of affective commitment on the relationship between POS and OCB.

Bishop et al. (2000) examined the potential mediating effects of organizational commitment on the relationship between perceived organizational support and an overall measure of OCB. They found that perceived organizational support was positively related to organizational commitment and that organizational commitment fully mediated the effects of POS on OCB. Similar results have been reported by both Liden et al. (2003) and Cardona et al. (2004). In a sample of 98 contingent (temporary) employees, Liden et al. (2003) found that organizational commitment mediated the relationship between POS and OCB and that an alternative model that included a direct path from POS to OCB did not fit their data significantly better than their hypothesized model (which did not include this path). Based on these findings, they argued that their hypothesized (fully mediated effects) model should be accepted over the alternative (partially mediated effects) model because it was more parsimonious.

Finally, Cardona et al. (2004) examined the mediating effect of normative commitment on the POS-OCB relationship in two samples of physicians working in Spain. They reported that normative commitment completely mediated the relationship between POS and OCB in both of their samples and that a two-group analysis constraining the relationships between POS and commitment and between commitment and OCB suggested that these relationships were not significantly different across the two samples. These latter findings provide fairly compelling evidence regarding the equivalence of the mediating effects of normative commitment on the POS-OCB relationships in the two physician samples used in the Cardona et al. study. However, because all of the predictor and criterion measures used in this study were obtained from the same sources, it is difficult to know how much these findings were influenced by common method biases (see Podsakoff et al., 2003; Podsakoff & Organ, 1986; Williams & Brown, 1994).

Witt (1991) examined one potential moderator of the POS-OCB relationship. He argued that the relationship between employees' POS and OCB should be moderated by their exchange ideologies (i.e., their perception regarding the appropriateness of basing their concerns for the welfare of the organization on the favorability of the treatment they receive from it). More specifically, he hypothesized that the relationship between employees' perceptions of organizational support and their willingness to engage in OCB should be more positive for employees with a strong exchange ideology than for employees with a weak exchange ideology. Consistent with this expectation, he reported that, although the relationship between POS and OCB was strong and positive for employees in his sample who had a strong exchange ideology, it was weak and negative for employees who had a low-level exchange ideology. However, a word of caution regarding Witt's findings is probably in order, because his sample consisted of only 55 employees working in a small tool and dye company. Thus, the results of this study will have to be replicated in other settings with larger sample sizes before they can be generalized.

Despite the many studies that have found a link between POS and OCB, a few (Blakely et al., 2003; Lambert, 2000) have reported either no relationship or a negative relationship between POS and OCB after controlling for other variables. For example, in a longitudinal study of federal employees working in a government research facility, Blakely et al. (2003) examined the relationship between POS and four OCB dimensions (interpersonal helping, individual initiative, personal industry, and loyal boosterism). They reported that after controlling for the effects of self-monitoring, job satisfaction, and organizational commitment, only the relationship between POS and loyal boosterism was significant.

Lambert's (2000) longitudinal study of 325 employees working in a manufacturing firm in the Midwest also did not support the expected positive relationship between POS and OCB. Lambert (2000) hypothesized that perceived organizational support should serve as a mediator of the relationship between the employees' perceptions of the usefulness of the work-life benefits they received from their organization and the employees' subsequent OCB. Thus, unlike the other studies we have discussed up to this point, in which the authors were interested in the mediators of the POS-OCB relationship, in Lambert's study, POS served as a potential mediator of the relationship between another variable and OCB.

Lambert (2000) used measures of POS gathered from employees in 1991 to predict employees' submission of formal suggestions during the time periods from 1990–1991 and 1993–1994, attendance at quality meetings during a 6-month period in 1994, and self-ratings of employee interpersonal helping behavior in the 1994–1995 time period. She reported that although employees' perceptions of the usefulness of the work-life benefits they received from the organization were directly and positively related to perceived organizational support and all three forms of OCB measured in her study, POS was not related to either attendance at quality meetings or interpersonal usefulness and was negatively related to the number of suggestions submitted. These findings held true after controlling for a variety of factors, including demographic variables such as employee gender, seniority, nature of work; the number of previous suggestion submissions; previous supervisor ratings; perceived supervisor support; and the perceived usefulness of the benefits that the organization provided to the employees. Thus, although POS was found to mediate one of the three relationships between work-life benefits and OCB, the nature of the relationship between POS and the OCB in this case was the opposite of what would have been expected from prior research on the POS-OCB relationship.

Given the fairly consistent positive relationship reported between POS and OCB in previous research, it is somewhat difficult to account for the findings reported by Blakely et al. (2003) and Lambert (2000). However, Blakely et al. (2003) noted that even though the OCB scale used in their study had been used in previous research, its validity had not been established. Indeed, an examination of an initial report of the psychometric properties of the scale used in this study (see Moorman & Blakely, 1995) suggests that almost half (9 of 19) of the items in the scale had more than 50% error variance. Thus, it is possible that their measure of OCB lacked validity. In addition, Lambert (2000) offered several possible explanations for her unexpected findings: (a) organizational support may have caused employees to take the organization for granted and to feel less obligated to take the extra steps of making formal suggestions for improvement and attending quality meetings;

(b) employees who felt supported by the organization may have felt less need for improvement and thus were less likely to submit suggestions; and (c) organizational support may have been reciprocated through behaviors and attitudes not investigated in her study.

Yet another possibility for the general lack of support of the POS-OCB relationship that Lambert (2000) reported is the fairly long delay between the measurement of POS and two of the three citizenship behaviors included in this study. It appears from the description of the Lambert study that the amount of time that transpired between the POS measure and the number of suggestions submitted and attendance at quality meetings ranged from two to three years. These fairly long periods of time may not correspond to the temporal relationships between POS and these variables. Thus, additional longitudinal research on the relationships between POS and these forms of OCB that examines different time lags may be worthwhile.

The results of the Lambert (2000) study notwithstanding, the general pattern of results previously reviewed (Bishop et al., 2000; Eisenberger et al., 2001; Liden et al., 2003; Masterson, Lewis, Goldman, & Taylor, 2000; Moorman, Blakely, & Niehoff, 1998; Rhoades & Eisenberger, 2002; Settoon et al., 1996; Wayne et al., 2002; Wayne et al., 1997; Witt, 1991) indicates that employee perceptions of the support that they receive from their organization are positively related to OCB and that their sense of obligation and their commitment to the organization are mediators of this relationship. This suggests that taking steps to enhance perceptions of organizational support may be an effective way to increase OCB.

Distance Between the Employee and Others in the Organization

Because OCB is often directed at others in the organization, another factor that may have an impact on the frequency of this behavior is the structural, psychological, and functional distance between the employee and others in the organization (Antonakis & Atwater, 2002; Napier & Ferris, 1993). Napier and Ferris (1993) describe these types of distances as follows:

- *Structural distance* is "aspects of distance brought about by physical structure (e.g., actual physical distance between the work spaces of the supervisor and subordinate), as well as organizational structure (e.g., the degree of centralization or span of management control) and supervision structure (e.g., the amount of task and social contact between the supervisor and subordinate). The conceptual link which binds these variables is that they all are associated with the amount of interaction in the dyad which is allowed or encouraged" (p. 333).

- *Psychological distance* refers to the "psychological effects of actual and perceived demographic, cultural, and value differences between the supervisor and subordinate . . . [and] is hypothesized to consist of four logically related facets: demographic similarity, power distance, perceived similarity, and actual value similarity" (Napier and Ferris, 1993, pp. 328–329).

- *Functional distance* is the "degree of closeness and quality of the functional working relationship between the supervisor and the subordinate; in essence, whether the subordinate is a member of the in-group or the out-group of the supervisor. This dimension . . . describes the behavioral manifestations of distance in the functional, working relationship between the supervisor and the subordinate. The four dimensions hypothesized here to comprise functional distance are: affect, perceptual congruence, latitude, and relationship quality" (p. 337).

These types of distance would be expected to influence an individual's motivation, ability, and opportunity to exhibit OCB. For example, when structural distance is high because an employee has infrequent contact with others in the organization and/or because the physical distance between them is great, the opportunity to engage in some forms of OCB (e.g., helping, voice, sportsmanship) may be less than when structural distance is low. Similarly, when psychological distance is high because the employee has little demographic, cultural, or value similarity to others in the organization, the employee may have less motivation or less ability to exhibit OCB than when psychological distance is low. In part, the effects of psychological distance and structural distance on OCB may be mediated by functional distance as predicted by Napier and Ferris (1993). We would expect this to be true especially for the affective (e.g., liking and trust) and relationship quality indicators (e.g., satisfaction with supervisor and satisfaction with the relationship) of functional distance. In addition, we would hypothesize that the effects of distance on OCB would also be mediated by organizational commitment, because the greater the structural, psychological, and functional distance, the less committed employees are likely to be, and commitment has been shown to be related to OCB.

Research that has examined the relationship between structural distance and OCB generally supports the notion that distance is negatively related to OCB. Indeed, Podsakoff et al. (1996a) reported that spatial distance (a form of structural distance) is negatively related to employee altruism, civic virtue, and conscientiousness, even after controlling for the effects of seven forms of leader behavior and 12 task, subordinate, and organizational characteristics. To the extent that certain aspects of functional distance overlap with some of the mediators previously discussed in this chapter (e.g., leader-member exchange relationship quality, and liking, trust, and satisfaction with the leader), we have already described evidence indicating that these variables are positively associated with OCB. However, we are not aware of any studies that have attempted to examine the relationships between psychological distance and OCB. Therefore, this might prove to be a fruitful avenue for future research.

Organizational Constraints

Organizational constraints are conditions that make it more difficult for employees to perform their jobs (Jex, Adams, Bachrach, & Sorenson, 2003; Peters & O'Connor, 1980). Such constraints might include a lack of tools, supplies, equipment, budgetary support, required help from others, training, time, and so on. These same constraints can also potentially limit the ability of employees to engage in OCB. For example, a lack of time, supplies, or training may diminish the ability of employees to help coworkers with work-related problems, responsibly participate in the governance of the organization, make constructive suggestions, and so forth. Organizational constraints may also diminish motivation to exhibit OCB. Jex et al. (2003) argue that although organizational constraints are a source of frustration,

> Employees are typically expected to perform their jobs well despite being faced with constraints. Thus, it is typically in an employee's best interest to try to perform well despite these constraints. To do this, employees will typically focus on in-role behaviors and pay less attention to more discretionary extra-role behaviors. (p. 173)

This would suggest that organizational constraints should be negatively related to OCB because they motivate employees to focus greater attention on in-role behavior. However, Jex et al. qualify this prediction by arguing that they expect this to be true only when affective commitment to the organization is low and that organizational constraints will be unrelated to OCB when affective commitment is high.

As Jex et al. (2003) predicted, organizational constraints were negatively related to altruism when employees had low levels of affective commitment to the organization. They argued that this is due to (a) the negative psychological reactions evoked by the constraints, (b) the tendency of uncommitted employees to respond to stressors by withholding extra-role behaviors rather than more highly monitored in-role behaviors, and (c) the possibility that individuals low in commitment may have narrower role boundaries and may focus more on what they perceive as in-role tasks when faced with organizational constraints.

However, contrary to their predictions, Jex et al. (2003) found that organizational constraints were positively related to altruism among those with high levels of affective commitment to the organization. The researchers speculated that when faced with organizational constraints, highly committed employees may engage in altruistic behavior to achieve their goals in spite of these constraints and/or to circumvent the constraints that they face. These results are interesting because they suggest that organizational commitment may be an important moderator of the effects of some organizational characteristics (e.g., organizational constraints) on OCB at the same time that it serves as a mediator of the effects of other organizational characteristics (e.g., organizational formalization, organizational inflexibility, and perceived organizational support) on OCB.

The Effects of Cultural Context on OCB

The majority of the research on OCB has been conducted in North America. However, given increased globalization researchers have become increasingly interested in the influence that a country's cultural context has on OCB. As noted by Paine and Organ (2000), cultural context may influence the applicability of OCB in a variety of ways:

> It is possible that the cultural context itself may encourage or dissuade OCB-type performance, thus attenuating the effect of established antecedents of OCB as found in North American studies. It is likewise conceivable that national culture might influence those conditions (e.g., organizational commitment) that relate to OCB. Finally, culture might moderate the effects of antecedents (such as perceived fairness or satisfaction) that in the U.S. have been interpreted as having direct effects on OCB. (p. 46)

These authors noted that two dimensions of culture that would be expected to influence the perceptions and expressions of OCB are individualism-collectivism and power distance. Hofstede (1984) observed that individualistic cultures are characterized by loosely knit social structures in which people are responsible for taking care of themselves and their immediate families only. In contrast, collectivist cultures are characterized by tight social structures in which people distinguish between in-groups and out-groups and expect their in-group to be responsible for looking after them in exchange for their absolute loyalty to the in-group. Thus, collectivism does not necessarily imply an abandonment of concern for the individual's well-being or interest; rather, it is based on the assumption that maintaining the group's well-being is the best guarantee for the individual (Hofstede 1984).

According to Hofstede (1984), "The power distance between a boss B and a subordinate S is the difference between the extent to which B can determine the behavior of S and the extent to which S can determine the behavior of B" (p. 72). In cultures that accept a high level of power distance, the leaders have a greater ability to influence their subordinates than subordinates have to influence the leader. In contrast, in cultures where power distance is low, leaders and subordinates are more equal in their ability to influence each other.

Individualism-collectivism and power distance may influence how OCB is perceived as well as whether employees are inclined to demonstrate OCB. In addition, behaviors that appear on the surface to be the same may originate for different reasons or have different consequences. For example, collectivist cultures may be more likely than individualistic cultures to encourage behaviors that benefit the group and to view these behaviors as normative (i.e., expected). To the extent that this is true, one would expect OCB to be more common in collectivist cultures than in individualistic cultures and that OCB would be more likely to be perceived as a required part of the job in collectivist cultures.

Indeed, research by Lam, Hui, and Law (1999) indicates that participants from collectivist cultures like Hong Kong and Japan were significantly more likely to perceive the sportsmanship dimension of OCB to be a required part of the job than participants from individualistic cultures like Australia or the United States. In addition, participants from Hong Kong and Japan were significantly more likely to perceive the courtesy dimension of OCB to be a required part of the job than participants from Australia. However, no significant cultural differences were found in the extent to which the OCB dimensions of altruism, conscientiousness, or civic virtue were seen as a required part of the job. Thus, this research provides partial support for the hypothesis that OCB is more common in collectivist cultures than in individualistic ones.

In addition, Paine and Organ (2000) argued that organizational commitment may be higher in collectivist cultures than in individualistic cultures because of the importance of the in-group in shaping perceptions of self-identity in collectivist societies. We might also speculate that collectivist cultures would have higher levels of trust in their leaders (because in these cultures people trust their leaders to provide for their well-being) and higher levels of group cohesiveness (because the values of these cultures emphasize collaboration, interdependence, and working together). If this is indeed true, these characteristics of collectivist cultures could contribute to a desire on the part of employees to perform OCB. Although this is an interesting possibility, to our knowledge there is no empirical research that has examined the relationship between this aspect of culture and these potential mediators of OCB.

Paine and Organ (2000) also noted that power distance and social stratification may affect perceptions of, and performance of, OCB. They argue that in low power distance cultures, the exchange between leader and subordinate is viewed as a social exchange, and the subordinate's perception of fair treatment in that exchange has a big effect on whether the employee exhibits OCB. Employees who do not perceive a fair exchange are unlikely to exhibit OCB. However, in high power distance cultures, employees are more likely to accept the fact that there will be differences in treatment based on criteria over which they have little control. As a result, employees may continue to exhibit OCB, even when treatment is not fair. Thus, power distance may moderate the relationship between employee perceptions of fairness and OCB.

In addition, employees may feel a greater sense of responsibility for work outcomes in cultures characterized by low levels of power distance (because the employees share power with the leader) than in cultures that are characterized by high levels of power distance (because the leader has all of the power). To the extent that this is true, it would imply that OCB may be higher in low power distance cultures. Furthermore, some forms of OCB may be more (or less) likely to occur in low power distance cultures than in high power distance cultures. For example, civic virtue (in the form of voice behavior), helping behavior, initiative, and self-development may be lower in cultures characterized by high power distance relationships than in cultures with low power distance relationships because these behaviors may be seen as a challenge to leaders. In contrast, compliance and sportsmanship may be more common in high power distance cultures than in low power distance cultures because leaders have greater control over subordinates in these cultures.

Although we are not aware of a direct test of the moderating effects of either individualism-collectivism (IC) or power distance (PD) on the relationships between OCB and its antecedents, two studies (Farh, Earley, & Lin, 1997; Hui, Lee, & Rousseau, 2004) examined the moderating effects of cultural traditionality and modernity (which are related to PD and IC respectively) on the relationships between OCB and its antecedents. Farh et al. (1997) examined the moderating effects of traditionality and modernity on the relationships between procedural, distributive, and interactional justice perceptions and OCB in a sample of Taiwanese electronics employees. According to these authors, in cultures characterized by traditionality, there is an emphasis on social ties between people and respect for authority figures. In addition, individuals occupying higher power positions are expected to have greater amounts of discretion over individuals occupying lower power positions (i.e., high power distance relationships). However, in cultures characterized by modernity, there is an emphasis on egalitarianism, open-mindedness, self-reliance, and the belief that everyone has certain basic human rights regardless of their position (i.e., high individualism-collectivism). Farh et al. (1997) went on to note that traditionality and modernity are not two ends of a continuum, and that cultures may reflect both traditionality (respect for hierarchy) and modernity (emphasis on self-reliance and individuality); in fact, they note that both of these cultural variables would be expected to moderate the relationships between employees' perceptions of fairness and OCB. They reasoned that because employees who endorse traditional values should engage in OCB according to their perceived roles in the organization and are not governed by their perceptions of whether they are treated fairly, there would be a weaker relationship between fairness perceptions and OCB for these employees than for those who endorse less traditional values. In addition, they reasoned that because employees who hold modern values believe that everyone has a right to receive rewards based on their contribution, the relationship between fairness perceptions and OCB should be stronger for those that hold these values than for those who don't.

In their study, Farh et al. (1997) measured five types of OCB, along with employees' perceptions of distributive justice, interactional justice, and two types procedural justice (the amount of participation employees are allowed to have in evaluation and reward decisions, and the presence of formal appeal mechanisms in the organization). They examined the interactive effects of the justice perceptions and traditionality, modernity, and employee gender on OCB. They reported that traditionality moderated 12 of the 20 relationships between justice perceptions and organizational citizenship behaviors, and that modernity moderated 11 of the 20 relationships between justice perceptions and OCB. Consistent with their hypotheses, they found that the relationship between perceptions of justice and OCB was stronger for groups low in traditionality than for groups high in traditionality, whereas the relationship between justice and OCB was stronger for groups high in modernity than for groups low in modernity. However, when all of the interactions between employees' perceptions of justice and traditionality, modernity, and gender were analyzed to determine which of the interactions had the strongest unique effects, they found that the interactions between traditionality and justice perceptions were generally the most potent. Farh et al. (1997) concluded that their findings regarding the moderating effects of traditionality suggest that for less traditional employees, justice perceptions are likely to stimulate OCB through the formation of a covenantal relationship of the employees to the organization, and that for traditionalists, justice perceptions are not critical because these employees establish their expressive tie to the organization through socialization concerning their role in society.

Taken together, the findings of Farh et al. (1997) and Lam et al. (1999) suggest that cultural context may, indeed, have important effects on OCB. However, because only a few studies have empirically examined the relationship between cultural characteristics and OCB, additional research is obviously needed before we can fully understand the impact of cultural variables on OCB.

Implications for Future Research

Need for Additional Research on the Key Mediating Mechanisms That Influence OCB

Throughout this chapter, we have discussed several mediators of the effects of leader behaviors, task characteristics, group characteristics, organizational characteristics, and cultural context on OCB. The most prominent ones include trust (in one's leader or others in the organization), satisfaction (with supervision, coworkers, and the job itself), a sense of obligation or feeling of responsibility (for job outcomes, toward others, and/or toward the organization), the need to reciprocate, social norms/expectations, a sense of commitment (to the work group or organization), perceptions of fairness (procedural, distributive, and interactional), and liking for the supervisor. Although there has been a good deal of research on the relationships between some of these variables (e.g., satisfaction, trust and fairness) and OCB, we need a great deal more on the relationships between other variables (e.g., social norms/expectations, feelings of responsibility/obligation, liking for the supervisor) and OCB. Perhaps more importantly, we need much more empirical research testing which of these potential mediating mechanisms best accounts for the effects of leader behaviors, task characteristics, group characteristics, organizational characteristics, and cultural context on OCB. Beyond these commonly identified mediators, we think that it would also be worthwhile to investigate some of the less frequently studied mediators of the effects of task, group, and organizational characteristics, such as covenantal relationships, efficacy/potency, group identity, and group cohesiveness (as a mediator of the effects of other antecedents).

Are Leadership Behaviors and Group Process Variables the Cause (or the Consequence) of OCB?

In our discussion, we have assumed that leadership behaviors and task, group, and organizational characteristics enhance OCB. That is, we have assumed that these variables *cause* OCB to increase. However, because most of the research that has been reported to date has been cross-sectional in nature, it is possible that OCB may be the causal variable. For example, OCB on the part of employees might cause leaders to provide more support or encouragement to employees who help the leaders or others in the organization than to employees who do not engage in this form of OCB. This would be consistent with research (Farris & Lim, 1969; Lowin & Craig, 1968) demonstrating that subordinate task performance influences the manner in which leaders behave toward their subordinates. Likewise, it would seem logical that groups that engage in OCB directed at other group members will be more cohesive and have higher quality team-member exchange relationships than groups that do not. This suggests that OCB may be a cause, as well as a consequence, of leadership support, team-member exchange, and group cohesiveness. Thus, there may be a reciprocal relationship between OCB and several of the "antecedent" variables discussed in this chapter. Longitudinal and laboratory research designed to examine the causal relationships between these variables would be beneficial.

What Other Implications Does Cultural Context Have for OCB Research?

Our review of the literature suggests that the majority of studies examining the antecedents of OCB have been conducted in the United States, although this has been changing in recent years. This U.S. focus to the literature raises several important questions for future research (Paine & Organ, 2000). For example, does OCB have the same meaning in other cultures, and are there different terms in other languages that describe the same phenomenon? Some evidence (Hui et al., 2004; Lam et al. 1999) suggests that the OCB dimensions of altruism, courtesy, civic virtue, conscientiousness, and sportsmanship captured by Podsakoff et al.'s (1990) scale are generalizable to other cultures, including Australia, Hong Kong, Japan, and China. However, research conducted by Farh et al. (1997) and Farh, Zhong, and Organ (2004) suggests that some culturally specific dimensions may exist as well. Another interesting topic for future research would be to investigate whether the antecedents and mediators of OCB differ across cultures. Indeed, Brockner (2003) has argued that examining these differences in the theoretical (mediating) mechanisms affecting important outcome variables (including OCB) is critical for understanding the effects of culture. We agree and believe that this would be an excellent topic for future research.

 **6**

The Effects of OCB on
Performance Evaluations
and Judgments

The previous chapters focused primarily on the individual and organizational-level antecedents of OCB. However, in this chapter and the next, we turn our attention to the consequences of OCB for both individuals and their organizations. We begin by discussing why OCB might influence evaluations of a person's performance and other consequences that depend upon that judgment. Next, we review the empirical literature on the effects that OCB has on individual-level outcomes, including performance ratings, promotions, and other reward allocation decisions. Finally, we conclude the chapter with a discussion of the implications of the empirical findings for future research.

Theoretical Mechanisms Explaining Why OCB Might Influence Managerial Evaluations

Managers might include OCB in their evaluations of the overall performance of employees for several reasons. As shown in Table 6.1, some of these reasons reflect conscious and/or controlled processes (e.g., managerial beliefs about the importance of OCB, job expectations, OCB as a signal for employee commitment, and notions of reciprocity and fairness), whereas others reflect unconscious and/or uncontrolled processes (e.g., implicit theories, schema-triggered affect, behavioral distinctiveness, attributional processes, and illusory correlations). In this section, we discuss each of these potential mechanisms.

Managerial Beliefs About the Importance of OCB

Managers may value OCBs if they believe that OCBs are related to organizational effectiveness. From the very beginning, Organ's (1988)

Table 6.1 Summary of Reasons That OCBs Might Influence Managerial Evaluations of Performance

Potential Reason	Explanation
Managerial beliefs about the importance of OCB to the organization's success	Organ (1988, 1990c) and Borman and Motowidlo (1993) argued that citizenshiplike behaviors promote the effective functioning of the organization. To the extent that managers believe that these behaviors are important for organizational success, they may acknowledge these contributions in their evaluations of employee performance.
Job expectations	Research by Morrison (1994); Pond, Nacoste, Mohr, and Rodriguez (1997); and Lam, Hui, and Law (1999) suggests that at least some managers and employees believe that OCBs are an integral part of an employee's role responsibilities. Thus, managers may include OCBs in their evaluation of employee performance because they do not distinguish these behaviors from other aspects of the employees' job responsibilities.
OCB as a signal of an employee's commitment	Because OCB is volitional in nature, it may serve as an indicator of how motivated an employee is to work hard and to put the interest of the organization ahead of his or her own self-interest, if necessary. Consequently, employee acts of OCB may serve as behavioral cues on which managerial presumptions of employee commitment to the organization are based.
Norm of reciprocity/fairness	Gouldner (1960), Homans (1961), and Blau (1964) noted that people try to reciprocate when others help them, do them a favor, or treat them fairly. Therefore, if OCBs have positive effects for both the manager and the organization, managers might repay employees who exhibit OCBs (perhaps out of a sense of fairness) by giving them higher performance evaluations.
Attributional processes and informational distinctiveness and accessibility	DeNisi, Cafferty, and Meglino (1984) proposed that managers search for distinctiveness information when they are asked to make evaluations of employees. Because OCBs are generally not considered to be formally required by the organization, they may be particularly distinctive forms of behavior that the managers may seek out and remember during the evaluation process.
Attributional processes (stable vs. unstable/internal vs. external)	DeNisi, Cafferty, and Meglino (1984) noted that "incidents of performance that are attributed to stable, internal causes are most likely to be retained in memory, recalled, and considered in the [manager's] final evaluation" (p. 376). Because OCBs are less likely to be considered a required part of an employee's job, managers are more likely to attribute these behaviors to internal, stable characteristics of the subordinate—which would make these behaviors more accessible and exert a bigger impact on managers' evaluations of performance.

Potential Reason	Explanation
Illusory correlations	Chapman (1967) and Chapman and Chapman (1967) argued that illusory correlations result from the tendency of people to see two things or events as occurring together more often than they actually do. In addition, Cooper (1981) noted that several sources of illusory correlations may occur in rating tasks, including: (a) the rater may have an insufficient sample of either in-role or citizenship behavior (undersampling), (b) the rater may be influenced by a single, salient incident of behavior (engulfing), (c) the rating scales may be abstract and insufficiently defined (insufficient concreteness), (d) the rater may not be sufficiently motivated or have sufficient knowledge to do a good job, and (e) the rater's recall of the subordinate's performance may be distorted—all of which may lead the rater to give greater weight to the OCBs in forming their evaluations (cf. Podsakoff, MacKenzie, & Hui, 1993).
Inferences based on implicit theories	Berman and Kenny (1976) and Bruner and Tagiuri (1954) noted that raters often possess implicit theories about the co-occurrence of events or behaviors. Thus, if a manager implicitly believes that OCB and overall performance are related, and the manager frequently observes an employee engaging in OCB, the manager's "implicit performance theory" might cause him or her to infer that an employee is a high performer.
Schema-triggered affect	Fiske (1981, 1982) and Fiske and Pavelchak (1986) argued that when an object is identified by a person as an example of a previously defined, affectively laden category, the affect associated with the category is quickly retrieved and applied to the stimulus object. Thus, if managers include OCBs, along with high levels of task performance, in their definition of "good employees," employees who exhibit OCBs trigger positive affect and subsequently are evaluated more favorably than those that do not exhibit these behaviors.
Liking	Lefkowitz (2000) argued that OCB increases managers' liking for subordinates and that liking subsequently influences a rater's evaluation of a subordinate's performance. Consistent with these expectations, Allen and Rush (1998) demonstrated that supervisor's liking is related to employee OCB, and Cardy and Dobbins (1986) and Allen and Rush (1998) provided a substantial amount of empirical evidence that suggests that performance evaluations are influenced by a rater's liking for the subordinate.

SOURCE: Adapted from Podsakoff, P. M., MacKenzie, S. B., & Hui, C. (1993). Organizational citizenship behaviors and managerial evaluations of employee performance: A review and suggestions for future research. In G. R. Ferris & K. M. Rowland (Eds.), *Research in Personnel and Human Resources Management, Vol. 11* (pp. 1–40). Mahwah, NJ: Lawrence Erlbaum Associates.

conceptualization of OCB explicitly included the assumption that these behaviors enhance organizational effectiveness. Podsakoff and MacKenzie (1997) and Podsakoff, MacKenzie, Paine, & Bachrach (2000) identified several ways this might happen, including the fact that OCBs may enhance co-worker or manager productivity, free up resources, help to improve the coordination of activities between team members, enhance the organization's ability to attract and retain the best people, increase the organization's ability to adapt to environmental changes, and so forth. (We return to a discussion of the relationship between OCB and organizational effectiveness in Chapter 7.) In addition, Borman and Motowidlo (1993) reasoned that OCB (and contextual performance) enhances organizational effectiveness because it shapes "the organizational, social, and psychological context that serves as the critical catalyst for task activities and processes" (p. 71). Therefore, to the extent that managers believe that OCB enhances the efficiency and/or effectiveness of the organization, they will evaluate more favorably those employees who exhibit OCB.

Job Expectations

Another reason that managers include OCBs in their evaluations is that they may believe that these behaviors are an integral part of an employee's job responsibilities. This idea is consistent with research showing that some employees (Morrison, 1994; Pond, et al., 1997) and some managers (Lam, Hui & Law, 1999) believe that OCBs are part of the employees' role responsibilities. Indeed, Morrison (1994) found that the percentage of employees who viewed specific types of OCB as being "an expected part of the job" ranged from a low of 32% to a high of 88%, and Pond et al. (1997) found that the percentage of employees who viewed OCBs as "not formally evaluated" ranged from a low of 40% to a high of 81%. Moreover, research by Lam et al. (1999) indicates that although this is a fairly general phenomenon across cultures (such as Hong Kong, Japan, Australia, and the United States), employees and their managers can sometimes have different views about the extent to which OCBs are "an expected part of the employee's job." Interestingly, Lam et al. found that supervisors in Hong Kong and Japan were far more likely to view OCBs as "an expected part of the employee's job" than their employees, whereas supervisors in Australia and United States did not differ significantly from their employees in their perspectives of the extent to which these behaviors are an expected part of the job. Thus, taken together, this research suggests that OCBs are often considered to be part of an employee's role expectations.

However, as noted by Podsakoff et al. (2000), these findings may be an artifact of the global manner in which respondents in these studies were asked to define their in-role requirements. In Morrison's (1994) and Lam et al.'s (1999) studies, employees were asked to judge whether a particular behavior was an "expected" part of the job, and in Pond et al.'s (1997) research, the participants were asked to judge whether the behaviors were "formally evaluated" or not. Podsakoff et al. (2000) noted that the potential difficulty with the wording of the questions used to solicit these judgments is that people may feel that certain behaviors are "expected" as part of the job even though they may believe that the behaviors are discretionary and not formally rewarded by the organization. According to Podsakoff et al.,

> To test whether a behavior is an organizational citizenship behavior according to Organ's definition, it would have been better to ask if the behavior was: (a) an explicit part of [the employee's] job description, (b) something [employees] were trained by the organization to do, and (c) formally (and explicitly) rewarded when exhibited, and punished when it was not exhibited." (Podsakoff et al., 2000, pp. 548–549).

Thus, in our view, this issue warrants further research before firm conclusions can be made.

OCB as a Signal of Employee Commitment

Shore, Barksdale, and Shore (1995) argued that managers use OCB as a sign of an employee's level of commitment to the organization. They reason that because OCB consists of constructive or cooperative gestures that are neither required nor contractually compensated by the formal reward system of the organization, they are particularly valuable signals of an employee's commitment to the organization. More specifically, they speculated,

> Logically, a manager may infer that an employee who performs the job well and also goes above and beyond its requirements, thus demonstrating OCB, has a high level of affective commitment, or emotional attachment, to the organization. In contrast, low levels of job performance and OCB may signify to the manager that the employee remains with the organization only because he or she has little or no choice in the matter (continuance commitment). (Shore et al., 1995, p. 1596)

Consistent with these expectations, Shore et al. (1995) found that (a) OCBs predicted managerial ratings of employees' perceived affective commitment, and (b) these perceptions of commitment were positively related to both the supervisors' ratings of the employees' managerial potential and promotability and the supervisors' responsiveness to employee requests for salary increases, training and performance feedback. Allen and Rush (1998) reported similar results in both laboratory and field studies. In their field study, they found that OCBs were positively related to managers' perceptions of employee commitment and that these perceptions of commitment mediated the relationships between the OCBs and the managers' overall evaluations and reward recommendations for the employees. In their lab study, they found that OCBs were positively related to students' perceptions of teacher commitment and that these perceptions of commitment mediated the relationships between the OCBs and the students' overall evaluations and reward recommendations for the teachers. Thus, the available evidence suggests that OCBs may influence a manager's evaluation of an employee, at least in part, because they signal the employee's level of commitment to the organization.

The Norms of Reciprocity and Fairness

Another possible reason that managers may evaluate subordinates who perform OCBs more favorably relates to the norms of reciprocity (Gouldner, 1960; Homans, 1961; Organ, 1977) and fairness (Blau, 1964; Organ, 1988). In their classic article on the impact of subordinate performance on leader behavior, Lowin and Craig (1968) argued that "a person (manager) who perceives that another (subordinate) is contributing a great deal to some situation (the organization) will try to increase the number of desirable outcomes that person equitably receives from the situation" (p. 443). As noted by Organ (1988), because OCBs may have positive effects for both the manager and the organization, one might expect managers to reciprocate (perhaps out of a sense of fairness) by giving higher performance evaluations to employees who exhibit OCBs. For example, an experienced employee who exhibits altruism by showing a newly hired employee how to perform his or her job more effectively not only helps the supervisor's department and the organization become more efficient but also may permit the supervisor to devote his or her time to more important functions. Similarly, employees who exhibit sportsmanship by not complaining to their manager about every little aspect of the job that they dislike permit the manager to conserve energy and direct his or her attention to those aspects of the job that are important to the success of the manager's unit.

Attributional Processes and Informational Distinctiveness

DeNisi, Cafferty, and Meglino's (1984) discussion of the cognitive processes underlying performance appraisals suggests some additional reasons that OCBs may influence a manager's ratings of a subordinate's performance. On the basis of previous research, they propose that appraisal decisions "requiring relatively absolute judgments (e.g., how large a raise to give a worker) will result in a search for distinctiveness information" (p. 374). Because OCBs are not formally required by the organization, they may be seen by the manager as especially distinctive forms of subordinate behavior and thus may be specifically sought by managers for use in forming performance evaluations.

In addition, DeNisi et al. (1984) noted that "incidents of performance attributed to stable, internal causes are most likely to be retained in memory, recalled, and considered in the final evaluation" (p. 376), and that "raters will give the greatest weight to information most easily retrievable from memory" (p. 385). These two propositions suggest another reason that OCBs might be considered in performance evaluations. Because OCBs are not required in a formal organizational sense, the manager may be likely to attribute their occurrence to internal, stable characteristics of the subordinate rather than to external causes. According to DeNisi et al., this would cause incidents of OCB performance to be more accessible in memory and to exert a greater impact on managers' judgments. (See DeNisi & Williams, 1988, for an expanded discussion of the role that cognitive processes play in performance appraisals.)

Illusory Correlations

Another possible explanation for why managers include OCBs in their evaluations may be the forming of an illusory correlation between OCBs and good overall performance. According to Chapman (Chapman, 1967; Chapman & Chapman, 1967, 1969, 1971), *illusory correlations* result from the tendency of people to see two things or events as occurring together more often than they actually do. In more general terms, Hamilton (1981) defined illusory correlations as the erroneous perception of association between two variables or events.

Implicit Personality Theories

According to Tedeschi and Lindskold (1976), implicit personality theories result from the fact that

> The traits assigned by an observer to an actor are tied together in implicative form. Certain traits are seen as rather inevitably going together. Therefore if an actor is perceived to possess a particular trait, the observer will immediately infer that the actor also has all of the associated traits. (p. 162)

Because much of the early research on this topic came from the literature on person-perception, these assumed correlations were often referred to as "implicit personality theories" (Bruner & Tagiuri, 1954).

In the context of the performance evaluation process, Krzystofiak et al. (1988) hypothesize that a manager's schema of an employee contains not only specific and general job-related behaviors but also trait information. In their view, the trait information is superordinate to the behavioral information. Thus, even though specific behavioral information can be accessed from the schema, this lower-level information is subordinate to, and likely influenced by, the trait information. This hierarchy suggests that managers organize employee behavior according to the personality traits implied by an employee's behavior. This tendency toward trait categorization has significant implications for performance evaluation. According to Krzystofiak et al.,

> What is being suggested is that behavioral observations, as well as other information, may influence the initial . . . categorization of a ratee. Once the initial categorization or the implicit theory is formulated, it will direct any additional information processing. Thus, the personality implied by observed behaviors should have an effect on ratings, which goes beyond the direct influence of the behaviors themselves. (Krzystofiak et al., 1988, p. 516)

Thus, if a manager observes that an employee often engages in specific types of helping behavior, the manager may infer that the employee possesses the altruism trait. Moreover, if the manager's implicit personality theory suggests that altruism is linked with the trait of empathy, then the manager, when forming an overall evaluation of the employee, may base that evaluation on the perception that the employee is both altruistic and empathetic. More generally, if a behavior implies a particular trait, and that trait is associated with other traits, the employee's evaluation will be based not only on the employee's behaviors but also the traits directly implied by the behaviors and the other traits that are associated with the implied traits. Consistent with this perspective, Krzytofiak et al. (1988)

found that when they regressed managerial performance evaluations on specific employee behaviors as well as the traits implied by them, the traits accounted for variance in the evaluations over and above that accounted for by the specific behaviors. A study by Kishor (1995) also lends support to the effect of schematic processing on performance evaluations. Kishor found that student raters' evaluations of teacher performance were influenced by their implicit theories of a good instructor. More specifically, the results showed that student raters inferred traits based on vignettes describing an instructor's behavior and subsequently used those traits to infer other behaviors that were not included in the vignettes and to evaluate the instructor's overall performance.

Implicit Performance Theories

Another type of schema that may influence performance evaluations is implicit theories about what constitutes "good performance" at work (Borman, 1983, 1987; MacKenzie et al., 1991, 1993; Podsakoff, MacKenzie, & Hui, 1993). According to Borman (1987):

> Interviews with persons about work on jobs sometimes reveal what appear to be deeply felt and sometimes idiosyncratic "theories" of job performance. Consider these statements: A sales manager says with conviction, "You know what the key to this (sales) job is? Thinking on your feet with customers." And, a first-line supervisor speaks, "Show me a person who comes to work on time and I'll show you a good employee." Concepts such as these can be viewed as elements of folk theories. Folk theories of performance are viewed as reflecting primarily the *content* of a performance category system, just as the focus of personal construct theory is on the content of these constructs. Folk theories may then help shape judgments about the effectiveness of individual employees. (p. 310)

The notion that managers have implicit "folk theories" of performance is also consistent with the research of Jackson, Keith, and Schlacter (1983), who found that almost one quarter of the sales managers they surveyed said that they included "good citizenship" in their evaluations of their sales personnel.

Schema-Triggered Affect

Another way in which OCB may influence supervisory evaluations has to do with the manner in which these evaluations are formed and is closely related to the schema-driven processing strategies just described. Allport (1954), among others, noted that people have a natural tendency to divide objects in the world around them into categories to more efficiently make sense of their environment. This tendency may be particularly strong in managers when they face the task of making judgments about the performance of their subordinates. One of the ways they do this is by trying to determine the extent to which the subordinate matches their idea of a prototypical "good employee" or "bad employee" (and/or by trying to determine how similar the employee is to a specific exemplar of a "good employee" or "bad employee"). Obviously, a prototypically good employee differs from a prototypically bad employee in terms of objective performance levels. However, in the minds of many managers, they may also differ in terms of their OCBs. Managers may expect the prototypical good employee to not only perform at higher levels but to be a good sport, help others on the job, be conscientious, and so forth. According to models of schema-triggered affect (Fiske, 1981, 1982; Fiske & Pavelchak, 1986; Park, 1986), when an object is identified as an example of a previously defined, affectively laden category, the affect associated with the category is quickly, perhaps automatically, retrieved and applied to the stimulus object. Because of this phenomenon, the more the individual employee matches the manager's concept of a good employee, the more likely the positive affect associated with this category will be triggered and used to evaluate the employee. On the other hand, the less often an employee exhibits OCBs, the more likely that the manager will categorize him or her as a bad employee and evaluate him or her negatively because negative affect will be triggered. Thus, the evaluation an individual employee receives depends on the extent to which the employee manifests the in-role and extra-role behaviors the supervisor associates with prototypical good or bad employees.

Liking

Lefkowitz (2000) argued that OCBs increase a manager's liking for subordinates and that liking subsequently influences the manager's evaluation of a subordinate's performance. Most theories of interpersonal attraction (cf. Byrne, 1971; Byrne & Clore, 1970; Lott & Lott, 1974) argue that we like people who are associated with rewards we receive and dislike people who are associated with punishing events. According to Berscheid and Walster (1978),

> Rewarding stimuli arouse positive feelings, while punishing stimuli arouse negative feelings . . . Through the process of simple conditioning, any neutral stimulus that is associated with a reward or with a punishment will acquire the capacity to arouse positive or negative feelings, respectively, and therefore will be liked or disliked as a consequence. If the neutral stimulus is a person, he or she will be liked if associated with rewards, and disliked if associated with punishments" (p. 23).

To the extent that OCBs like sportsmanship, civic virtue, conscientiousness, and so forth are rewarding to the manager, employees who engage in these behaviors will be better liked by the manager—and employees who are liked are more likely to be positively evaluated and receive rewards.

Consistent with these expectations, Allen and Rush (1998) reported that OCB influenced the extent to which employees were liked by their supervisors and that liking influenced the evaluations and rewards they received from their supervisors. Indeed, the researchers found that liking completely mediated the relationship between OCB and evaluations and the relationship between OCB and reward recommendations. Similar results have been reported by Johnson, Erez, Kiker, and Motowidlo (2002), who found that liking partially mediated the effect of helping behavior on raters' reward allocation decisions. Thus, the available empirical evidence suggests that liking may be one of the mechanisms through which OCBs influence managerial evaluations of employee performance.

Empirical Evidence of the Effects of OCB on Performance Evaluations and Other Managerial Decisions

In the previous section, we identified several reasons that managers may value OCBs and take them into account when evaluating employee performance. In this section, we review the empirical research that has been reported on the effects that OCBs and in-role behaviors have on managerial evaluations and decisions. Interestingly, with a few notable exceptions (Allen & Rush, 1998; Johnson et al., 2002; Park, 1986), the majority of studies that have been conducted in this domain have not attempted to examine the reasons that managers include OCBs in their evaluations or reward allocation decisions. However, regardless of the underlying mechanism, the available empirical evidence summarized in this section suggests that OCBs do, in fact, influence managers' evaluations of performance and other related decisions.

Effects of OCB and Objective Measures of Task Performance on Managerial Evaluations

Table 6.2 summarizes the results of studies conducted in field settings that have examined the relative effects of OCBs and *objective* performance on performance evaluations. The first row in the table identifies the researchers who conducted the study, the second row provides the sample characteristics, and the third row specifies the nature of the objective measures of performance used in each study. The next four rows report the proportion of variance in the managers' evaluations that is attributable to in-role behaviors and OCBs. The first of these rows reports the unique contribution of objective task performance to the managers' evaluations, and the next row reports the unique contribution of OCBs to this evaluation. The next two rows report the proportion of variance shared by the objective performance measures and the OCBs, and the total variance explained, respectively. For example, in Avila, Fern, and Mann's (1988) second study of 198 computer insurance sales agents, 19% of the variance in the agents' performance evaluations was uniquely attributable to objective sales performance, 21% was uniquely attributable to OCBs, 19% of the variance was shared between objective sales performance and the OCBs, and the total variance explained was 59%.

The row titled "Common method biases controlled?" indicates whether the authors statistically controlled for the fact that the measures of OCBs and managerial performance evaluations were obtained from the same source. Typically, this was done by adding to the hypothesized model a first-order common-method latent factor, which had each measure obtained from the same source as an indicator. For the studies that controlled for method biases, the adjusted proportion of variance attributable to objective performance and OCBs is shown in brackets [ ]. Thus, in the MacKenzie et al. (1993) sample of 261 insurance agents, objective performance accounted for 13% of the variance in overall evaluations when common method variance was not controlled and 24% of the variance when this bias was controlled. Similarly, whereas OCBs accounted for 44% of the variance in performance evaluations when common method variance was not controlled, they accounted for only 9% when this factor was controlled. Whereas the percent of variance shared between the objective measures and OCBs was 8% before common method variance was controlled, it was 13% after this bias was controlled. Finally, the total variance accounted for by the combination of objective performance and OCBs was 65% before controlling for method effects and 46% afterward.

The bottom five rows of the table identify which of the individual OCBs had significant effects on the overall performance evaluations. In these rows, (+) indicates that the OCB dimension had a significant positive relationship with the performance evaluation, NA indicates that

Table 6.2   Summary of the Percentage of Variance Accounted for in Managerial Evaluations by Objective Performance and OCBs

Researchers	Avila, Fern, & Mann (1988)[†]		Lowery & Krilowicz (1994)[†]	MacKenzie, Podsakoff, & Fetter (1991)	
Sample being rated	Computer salespeople (N = 70)	Computer salespeople (N = 198)	Sewing machine operators (N = 73)	Insurance agents (N = 259)	Insurance agents (N = 113)
Measures of objective performance	Annual % quota Annual net gain in accounts	Annual % quota Annual net gain in accounts	Piece-rate pay	Commission $ # of applications Annual % quota	Commission $ # of applications Annual % quota
Unique contribution of objective task performance → Overall evaluation	.12	.19	.06	.12 [.09]	.25 [.10]
Unique contribution of OCBs → Overall evaluation	.48	.21	.50	.23 [.19]	.27 [.20]
Variance in overall evaluation shared by objective task performance and OCBs	.03	.19	.17	.09 [.17]	.09 [.30]
Total R²	.63	.59	.73	.44 [.45]	.61 [.60]
Common method biases controlled?	Not controlled	Not controlled	Not controlled	Statistically controlled	Statistically controlled
Helping/altruism → Overall evaluation	(+)[a]	(+)[a]	NA	(+)	(+)
Sportsmanship → Overall evaluation	NA	NA	NA	ns	ns
Conscientiousness → Overall evaluation	NA	NA	NA	NA	NA
Civic Virtue → Overall evaluation	NA	NA	NA	(+)	(+)
Composite OCB → Overall evaluation	NA	NA	(+)	NA	NA

(Continued)

Table 6.2 (Continued)

Researchers	MacKenzie, Podsakoff, & Fetter (1993)		Pharmaceutical sales managers (N = 108)	MacKenzie, Podsakoff, & Paine (1999)	Podsakoff & MacKenzie (1994)	Podsakoff & MacKenzie (1994)/ MacKenzie, Podsakoff, & Paine (1999)
Sample being rated	Insurance agents (N = 261)	Petrochemical salespeople (N = 204)	Pharmaceutical sales managers (N = 108)	Insurane agents (N = 987)	Office firnitures makers (N = 379)	Insurance sales managers (N = 161)
Measures of objective task performance	Commission $ # of applications Annual % quota	Commission $	Annual % quota	# Policies sold Commission $	Police-rate pay	Unit-level performace Personal sales performance
Unique contribution of objective task performance → Overall evaluation	.13 [.24]	.03 [-.01]	.03 [.05]	.09 [.22]	.00	.03 [.10]
Unique contribution of OCBs → Overall evaluation	.44 [.09]	.43 [.08]	.54 [.37]	.43 [.13]	.72	.47 [.29]
Variance in overall evaluation shared by objective performance and OCBs	.08 [.13]	-.02 [.30]	.04 [.09]	.06 [-.02]	.08	.15 [.11]
Total R²	.65 [.46]	.44 [.37]	.61 [.51]	.58 [.33]	.80	.65 [.50]
Common method biases controlled?	Statistically controlled	Statistically controlled	Statistically controlled	Statistically controlled	Not controlled	Statistically controlled
Helping/altruism → Overall evaluation	(+)	ns	ns	(+)[b]	(+)	(+)[b]

Researchers	MacKenzie, Podsakoff, & Fetter (1993)	MacKenzie, Podsakoff, & Paine (1999)	Podsakoff & MacKenzie (1994)	Podsakoff & MacKenzie (1994)/ MacKenzie, Podsakoff, & Paine (1999)
Sportsmanship → Overall evaluation	(+)	(+)	(+)	ns
Conscientiousness → Overall evaluation	NA	NA	(+)	NA
Civic Virtue → Overall evaluation	(+)	(+)	ns	(+)
Composite OCB → Overall evaluation	NA	NA	NA	NA

NOTE: The results for studies marked with a † were calculated by the present authors from data reported in the original study. In the bottom half of the table, (+) indicates that the variable of interest was significantly (positively) related to the managers' overall evaluation when controlling for the other predictors, *ns* indicates that the variable of interest was included in the study but was *not* significantly related to the manager's overall evaluation after controlling for the other predictors, and NA (not applicable) indicates that the variable of interest was *not* included in the study. The row labeled "Common method biases controlled?" indicates whether the researchers examined the potentially biasing effects of the fact that the OCB measures and the measure of overall performance were obtained from the same source. In this row, "statistically controlled" indicates that the authors statistically partialled out the effects of a common methods factor to determine whether it had any effect on the conclusions of the study. In the studies that did control for common methods variance, the percentage of variance accounted for *before* methods variance was controlled for is reported outside the brackets, whereas the percentage of variance accounted for *after* method variance was controlled for is reported inside the brackets.

a. For the purposes of our analysis, in this study, the single item measure of "citizenship" behavior ("contributions to cooperating and working with others in the company"") was used to represent "altruism," the two measures of goal achievement were used to represent objective performance, and the two measures of the sales manager's overall assessment were used to represent the manager's overall evaluation.

b. In this study, aspects of altruism and courtesy were combined into an overall "helping" behavior construct. The coefficient for the effect of helping behavior on overall evaluations is shown in the "altruism" row in the table.

SOURCE: Adapted from Podsakoff, P. M., MacKenzie, S. B., Paine, J. B., & Bachrach, D. G. ( ). Organizational citizenship behaviors: A critical review of the theoretical and empirical literature and suggestions for future research. *Journal of Management, 26,* 513–563. Reprinted with permission.

this dimension was not available in the study, and *ns* indicates that although the OCB dimension was included, it did not have a significant relationship with the overall evaluation.

On average, across the eleven samples reported in Table 6.2, objective performance uniquely accounted for 9.5% of the variance in performance evaluations, OCBs uniquely accounted for 42.9% of the variance in performance evaluations, and the combination of OCBs and objective performance accounted for a total of 61.2% of the variance in overall performance evaluations. This suggests that OCBs accounted for substantially more variance in managerial evaluations than objective performance did. The bottom half of the table indicates that helping/altruism behavior was significantly related to performance evaluations in 8 out of 10 studies in which it was included; sportsmanship was significant in 5 out of the 8 studies in which it was included; conscientiousness was significant in all 3 of the studies in which it was included; civic virtue was significant in 6 out of the 8 studies in which it was included; and the composite OCB measure was significant in the one study in which it was included. Thus, each of the citizenship behavior dimensions had a significant effect on performance evaluations in the majority of the studies in which it was included.

In addition to the general pattern of results just discussed, note that the total amount of variance accounted for in managerial evaluations by objective performance and OCBs is substantially greater in the two piece-rate pay samples (sewing machine operators and furniture makers). Indeed, the average total amount of variance accounted for in these samples (73% and 80%) is almost 20 points higher than the average amount of variance accounted for in the other samples. One possible explanation is that in these studies, the managers had greater access to and ability to monitor the behavior of their employees in the workplace. This would make sense in both the office furniture manufacturing and the sewing operations environments, where the employees' supervisors' frequently monitor their behavior.

Turning our attention now to the effects of common method variance, an examination of the findings summarized in Table 6.2 indicates that controlling for common method biases: (a) reduced the proportion of overall variance explained, (b) generally reduced the proportion of variance uniquely accounted for by the OCBs, but (c) generally did *not* eliminate the effects of the individual OCB dimensions on performance evaluations. Across all of the 11 studies reported in Table 6.2, the overall proportion of variance explained by in-role and citizenship behaviors averaged 61.2%, as noted earlier, when common method variance was not controlled but averaged only 46% when this form of bias was controlled. In addition, the table indicates that when common method variance was not controlled, the proportion of variance accounted for in overall evaluations by the OCBs averaged 42.9%, and the amount of variance accounted for by objective performance averaged 9.5% In the seven studies in which common method variance was controlled, the percent of variance accounted for by the OCBs averaged 19.3%, and the amount of variance accounted for by objective performance averaged 11.3%. Thus, these findings suggest that common method variance may have enhanced the impact of OCBs on overall evaluations in those studies in which it was not controlled.

Effects of OCB/Contextual Performance and Subjective Measures of Task Performance on Managerial Evaluations

Table 6.3 summarizes the results of those field studies that have examined the relative effects of subjective measures of in-role and extra-role behavior on performance evaluations. The studies reported in this table differ from those reported in Table 6.2 in that they include *subjective*, rather than *objective*, measures of in-role behavior or task performance. With the exception of Allen and Rush (1998), Van Dyne and LePine (1998), Lovell et al. (1999), and Findlay, McKinlay, Marks, and Thompson (2000), all of the studies reported in this table used contextual performance dimensions, rather than OCB, to represent extra-role behavior.

The first row in the table identifies the researchers who conducted the study, and the second row relates the sample characteristics. The next three rows indicate the sources from which the data were obtained. When both predictor and criterion variables were obtained from the same source, the possibility exists that common method variance may bias the estimated relationships. The row titled "Common method biases controlled?" indicates whether this form of bias was controlled in the study. For example, in Motowidlo and Van Scotter's (1994) study of 421 Air Force mechanics, the in-role measure was obtained from one supervisor, the contextual performance measure was obtained from a second supervisor, and the overall performance evaluation was obtained from a third supervisor. Therefore, because all three measures were obtained from different sources, this study controlled for common method variance. In contrast, common method variance was not controlled in the study reported by Allen and Rush (1998), because they asked the same supervisors to evaluate the employees' in-role and extra-role behavior, as well as to provide the overall evaluation.

Rows six through nine in the table report the proportion of variance attributable to in-role and extra-role performance. For example, the first of these rows reports the unique contribution of in-role perfor-mance to the managers' evaluations, and the next row reports the unique contribution of contextual performance (or OCBs) to this eval-uation. The next two rows report the proportion of variance shared by the in-role performance measures and contextual performance, and the total variance explained, respectively. Thus, in the Motowidlo and Van Scotter (1994) study, 13% of the variance in performance evaluations was uniquely attributable to in-role performance, 11% was uniquely attributable to contextual performance, 5% of the variance in the eval-uations was shared between in-role and contextual performance, and the total amount of variance accounted for was 29%.

The bottom four rows of the table identify which of the individual OCB/contextual performance dimensions had significant effects on the overall performance evaluations. As in Table 6.2, the symbol (+) indi-cates that the dimension had a significant positive relationship with the performance evaluation, NA indicates that this dimension was not available in the study, and ns indicates that although the contextual performance/OCB dimension was included, it did not have a significant relationship with the overall evaluation.

On average, across the 28 samples reported in Table 6.3, in-role perfor-mance uniquely accounted for 10% of the variance in performance eval-uations, OCB/contextual performance uniquely accounted for 13% of the variance in performance evaluations, and the combination of contex-tual performance/OCBs and in-role performance accounted for a total of 56% of the variance in overall performance evaluations. This suggests that contextual performance accounted for as much variance in perfor-mance evaluations as did in-role/task performance. The bottom half of the table indicates that job dedication was positively and significantly related to performance evaluations in 14 of the 15 samples in which it was included, helping/interpersonal facilitation had significant positive effects in 11 of the 14 in which it was examined, the "other" contextual performance dimension was significant in all 11 samples in which it was examined, and the composite OCB/contextual performance measure was significant in all 12 of the samples in which they were tested.

Table 6.3 Summary of the Percentage of Variance Accounted for in Managerial Evaluations by Subjective Measures of Task Performance and OCB/Contextual Performance

Researchers	Motowidlo & Van Scotter (1994)	Borman, White, & Dorsey (1995)		Van Scotter & Motowidlo (1996)	Wayne, Shore & Liden (1997)[†]	Allen & Rush (1998)[†]
Sample being rated	U.S. Air Force mechanics (N = 421)	First-tour U.S. Army soldiers (N = 493)	First-tour U.S. Army soldiers (N = 631)	U.S. Air Force mechanics (N = 760)	Salaried employees in a large U.S. corporation (N = 252)	Employees from multiple organizations (N = 148)
Task performance measure obtained from:	1st supervisor	Scores from rate tests	Scores from rate tests	Scores from rate tests	—	Supervisors
OCB/contextual performance measure obtained from:	2nd supervisor	1st supervisor	1st peer	1st set of supervisors	Supervisors	Same supervisors
Overall evaluation obtained from:	3rd supervisor	2nd supervisor	2nd peer	2nd set of supervisors	Same supervisors	Same supervisors
Unique contribution of task performance → Overall evaluation	.13	.10	.02	.09	NA	.09
Unique contribution of OCB/contextual performance → Overall evaluation	.11	.17	.12	.14	.31	.07

(Continued)

Table 6.3 (Continued)

Researchers	Motowidlo & Van Scotter (1994)	Borman, White, & Dorsey (1995)	Van Scotter & Motowidlo (1996)	Wayne, Shore & Liden (1997)[†]	Allen & Rush (1998)[†]
Variance in overall evaluation shared by task performance and OCB/contextual performance	.05	.02	.22	NA	.33
Total R^2	.29	.29	.45	.31	.49
Common method biases controlled?	Controlled	Controlled	Controlled	Not controlled	Not controlled
Job dedication → Overall evaluation	NA	NA	(+)	NA	NA
Helping/Interpersonal facilitation → Overall evaluation	NA	NA	(+)	NA	NA
"Other" contextual performance dimension → Overall evaluation	(+)	(+)	NA	NA	NA
Composite OCB/ contextual performance → Overall evaluation	NA	NA	NA	(+)	(+)

Researchers	Van Dyne & LePine (1998)[†]					
Sample being rated	Employees from 21 manufacturing and nonmanufacturing organizations (N = 479)	Employees from 21 manufacturing and nonmanufacturing organizations (N = 479)	Employees from 21 manufacturing and nonmanufacturing organizations (N = 479)	Employees from 21 manufacturing and nonmanufacturing organizations (N = 479)	Employees from 21 manufacturing and nonmanufacturing organizations (N = 479)	Employees from 21 manufacturing and nonmanufacturing organizations (N = 479)
Task performance measure obtained from:	Employee self-report (Time 1)	Peer reported (Time 1)	Supervisor (Time 1)	Employee self-report (Time 2)	Peer reported (Time 2)	Supervisor (Time 2)
OCB/contextual performance measure obtained from:	Employee self-report (Time 1)	Peer reported (Time 1)	Same supervisor (Time 1)	Employee self-report (Time 2)	Peer reported (Time 2)	Same supervisor (Time 2)
Overall evaluation obtained from:	Supervisor (Time 2)	Supervisor (Time 2)	Same supervisor (Time 2)	Supervisor (Time 2)	Supervisor (Time 2)	Same supervisor (Time 2)
Unique contribution of task performance → Overall evaluation	.01	.04	.09	.03	.05	.14
Unique contribution of OCB/contextual performance → Overall evaluation	.01	.02	.04	.00	.01	.10
Variance in overall evaluation shared by task performance and OCB/contextual performance	.01	.13	.23	.01	.13	.48

(Continued)

Table 6.3 (Continued)

Researchers

	Van Dyne & LePine (1998)[†]					
Total R²	.03	.19	.36	.04	.18	.72
Common method biases controlled?	Partially controlled by use of supervisors for overall evaluation and obtaining measures at different points in time	Partially controlled by use of supervisors for overall evaluation and obtaining measures at different points in time	Not controlled	Partially controlled by use of supervisors for overall evaluation	Partially controlled by use of supervisors for overall evaluation	Not controlled
Job dedication → Overall evaluation	NA	NA	NA	NA	NA	NA
Helping/ interpersonal facilitation → Overall evaluation	(+)	ns	(+)	ns	ns	(+)
"Other" contextual performance dimension → Overall evaluation	NA	ns	ns	ns	ns	(+)
Composite OCB/contextual performance → Overall evaluation	NA	NA	NA	NA	NA	NA

Researchers		Conway (1999)b		Lovell et al. (1999)	Findley, Giles, & Mossholder (2000)[†]	Barksdale & Werner (2001)[†]
Sample being rated	Meta-analytic data from several studies	Meta-analytic data from several studies	Meta-analytic data from several studies	University residence hall advisors from an East Coast university (N = 109)	Teachers employed in two school systems in the southeastern United States (N = 199)	MBA and MS students attending a Southeastern university (N = 101)
Task performance measure obtained from:	Supervisors	Peers	Self	—	—	Supervisors
OCB/contextual performance measure obtained from:	Same supervisors	Same peers	Self	Peers	Supervisors	Same supervisors
Overall evaluation obtained from:	Same supervisors	Same peers	Self	Supervisors	Supervisors	Same supervisors
Unique contribution of task performance → Overall evaluation	.15	.08	.08	NA	NA	.16
Unique contribution of OCB/contextual performance → Overall evaluation	.08	.16	.11	.15	.11[d]	.07[e]
Variance in overall evaluation shared by task performance and OCB/contextual performance	.38	.41	.20	NA	NA	.51

(*Continued*)

Table 6.3 (Continued)

Researchers	Conway (1999)[c]			Lovell et al. (1999)	Findley, Giles, & Mossholder (2000)[†]	Barksdale & Werner (2001)[†]
Total R^2	.61	.65	.39	.15	.11	.74
Common method biases controlled?	Not controlled[d]	Not controlled[d]	Not controlled[d]	Controlled	Partially controlled by separation of time of measures	Not controlled
Job dedication/ conscientiousness → Overall evaluation	(+)	(+)	ns	NA	(+)	(+)
Helping/interpersonal facilitation → Overall evaluation	ns	(+)	ns	NA	NA	(+)
"Other" contextual performance dimension → Overall evaluation	NA	NA	NA	NA	NA	NA
Composite OCB/contextual performance → Overall evaluation	NA	NA	NA	(+)	NA	NA

Table 6.3 (Continued)

Researchers	Ferris, Witt & Hochwarter (2001)[†]	Johnson (2001)								Wayne, Shore, Bommer, & Tetrick (2002)[†]
Sample being rated	Computer programmers (N = 106)	Secretaries and staff support personnel (N = 298)	Technical support personnel (N = 310)	Customer service and sales personnel (N = 315)	Phone operators (N = 324)	Craft A jobs (N = 153)	Craft B jobs (N = 261)	Engineering support personnel (N = 184)	Warehouse, transportation, and other services (N = 205)	Employees from two metal fabricating plants (N = 211)
Task performance measure obtained from:	Supervisors	Supervisors	Supervisors	Supervisors	Supervisors	Supervisors	Supervisors	Supervisors	Supervisors	—
OCB/ contextual performance measure obtained from:	Same supervisors	Same supervisors	Same supervisors	Same supervisors	Same supervisors	Same supervisors	Same supervisors	Same supervisors	Same supervisors	Supervisors

(Continued)

Table 6.3 (Continued)

Researchers	Ferris, Witt & Hochwarter (2001)†	Johnson (2001)							Wayne, Shore, Bommer, & Tetrick (2002)†
Overall evaluation obtained from:	Same supervisors	Same supervisors	Same supervisors	Same supervisors	Same supervisors	Same supervisors	Same supervisors	Same supervisors	Same supervisors
Unique contribution of task performance → Overall evaluation	08	.09	.12	.09	.15	.08	.09	.10	NA
Unique contribution of OCB/contextual performance → Overall Evaluation	12	.08	.10	.05	.07	.11	.08	.08	.50[e]
Variance in overall evaluation shared by task performance and OCB/contextual performance	.61	.59	.49	.70	.57	.56	.64	.65	NA
Total R^2	.81	.76	.71	.84	.79	.75	.81	.83	.50
Common method biases controlled?	Not controlled	Not controlled	Not controlled	Not controlled	Not controlled	Not controlled	Not controlled	Not controlled	Not controlled
Job dedication → Overall evaluation	(+)	(+)	(+)	(+)	(+)	(+)	(+)	(+)	NA

Researchers	Ferris, Witt & Hochwarter (2001)[†]	Johnson (2001)								Wayne, Shore, Bommer, & Tetrick (2002)[†]
Helping/interpersonal facilitation → Overall evaluation	ns	(+)	(+)	(+)	(+)	(+)	(+)	(+)	(+)	NA
"Other" contextual performance dimension → Overall evaluation	NA	(+)	(+)	(+)	(+)	(+)	(+)	(+)	(+)	NA
Composite OCB/Contextual performance → Overall evaluation	NA	(+)	(+)	(+)	(+)	(+)	(+)	(+)	(+)	(+)

NOTE: The results for studies marked with a † were calculated by the present authors from data reported in the original study.

a. For the purposes of this analysis, the OCB measure consisted of a combination of altruism, conscientiousness, and courtesy.

b. For the purposes of this analysis, the OCB measure consisted of a combination of altruism and conscientiousness.

c. Only managerial samples were included in this meta-analysis.

d. Conway (1999) recognized the potential biasing effects of common method variance and did provide an estimate of the proportion of variance in managerial evaluations that was attributable to trait as well as method variance for each source (supervisors, peers, and self-reports) from which he obtained data. However, the meta-analytic data reported in his tables did not control for method variance.

e. For the purposes of this analysis, the OCB measure consisted of a measure of altruism.

SOURCE: Adapted from Podsakoff, P. M., MacKenzie, S. B., Paine, J. B., & Bachrach, D. G. Organizational citizenship behaviors: A critical review of the theoretical and empirical literature and suggestions for future research. *Journal of Management, 26,* 513–563. Reprinted with permission.

As was the case in Table 6.2, common method variance also was found to have a significant effect on the findings. More specifically, in the 14 samples in which both task performance and OCB/contextual performance were included and common method variance was not controlled, the overall proportion of variance explained by in-role and contextual performance averaged 72%, whereas in the four studies in which this bias was controlled, the overall proportion of variance averaged 31%. In addition, the table indicates that when common method variance was not controlled in those 14 studies that included both task performance and OCB/contextual performance, the proportion of variance accounted for by in-role (task) performance averaged 10%, the proportion of variance accounted for by OCB/contextual performance averaged 9%, and the proportion of total variance shared by task performance and OCB/contextual performance was 52%. However, in those four studies in which both task performance and OCB/contextual performance was included and this form of bias was controlled, the proportion of variance accounted for by task performance averaged 9%, the proportion of variance accounted for by OCB/contextual performance averaged 13.5%, and the proportion of total variance shared by task performance and OCB/contextual performance was only 8.5%.

These findings suggest two things. First, when common method variance is not controlled, the total proportion of variance accounted in overall performance evaluations is dramatically higher (72%) and, importantly, most of the variance in this criterion variable (52%) can be accounted for by either OCB/contextual performance or in-role performance. This substantial proportion of the explained variance in overall evaluations that cannot be uniquely attributed to either OCB/contextual performance or task performance alone may result from halo effects, implicit performance theories about the relationship between in-role performance and OCB, schema-triggered affect, and so on. Second, the findings indicate that when common method variance is controlled, the unique effects of OCBs/contextual performance on overall evaluations are greater (from 13.5%) than when common method variance is not controlled (9%). This suggests that common method variance actually decreases the effect of OCB/contextual performance on overall evaluations. This is a good illustration of the fact that common method biases can sometimes increase and sometimes decrease the strength of the relationships between variables (cf. Cote & Buckley, 1988; Podsakoff, MacKenzie, Lee, & Podsakoff, 2003).

One other finding of note in Table 6.3 relates to the overall percentage of managerial evaluations accounted for by Johnson (2001) across the eight job families that he examined. The average percentage of total variance accounted for in the managers' evaluations in this study was 79%, which is substantially greater than the average of 49% in the other samples that included both in-role and OCB/contextual performance measures. One reason for the dramatically higher proportion of variance accounted for may be attributable to the scales used in this study. Each of the scales had detailed behavioral descriptions of what constituted high, medium, and low levels of performance on the dimension. The example provided in the article suggests that these descriptions may have been confounded with or overlapped with other rating dimensions. This would explain the high proportion of shared variance in these samples (61%) compared to the other samples included in our table (28%). It is also possible that the overall evaluation scale contained behavioral descriptions that explicitly mentioned many of the rating subdimensions. To the extent that this is true, it would help to explain why the rating subdimensions accounted for such a large proportion of the variance in the overall performance evaluation.

Effects of OCB/Contextual Performance and Task Performance on Managerial Decisions

In addition to examining in-role and extra-role behaviors as predictors of managerial evaluations, a few field studies have examined the effect of these behaviors as predictors of managerial decisions. The results of these studies are reported in Table 6.4. This table is similar to Table 6.3, but it omits information on the shared and total variance accounted for in managerial decisions and details on the specific OCB/contextual performance dimensions that had an effect on the criterion variables. The reason for these omissions is that this information was not included in these studies.

As indicated in this table, five samples examined the effects of task performance and OCB/contextual performance on reward allocation decisions, and eight samples examined the effects of these predictors on promotion decisions. Generally speaking, the results suggest that both task performance and OCB/contextual performance accounted for a unique proportion of the variance in these criterion variables. This was true for task performance in seven of the 11 samples and for OCB/contextual performance in eight of the 11 samples. The relative magnitudes of these unique effects were fairly comparable, with OCB/contextual performance having a slightly stronger impact (4% versus 3%, on average). Unfortunately, because these studies did not

Table 6.4 Summary of the Unique Variance Accounted for in Managerial Decisions by Subjective Measures of Task Performance and OCB/Contextual Performance

	Reward Recommendation	Rewards		Medals		Promotability Ratings or Ratings of Management Potential				Rank 1 Year Later		Rank 2 Years Later	
Researchers	Allen & Rush (1998)†	Van Scotter, Motowidlo, & Cross (2000)		Van Scotter, Motowidlo, & Cross (2000)		Shore, Barksdale, & Shore (1995)† [Promotability Rating]	Shore, Barksdale, & Shore (1995)† [Management Potential Rating]	Van Scotter, Motowidlo, & Cross (2000)		Van Scotter, Motowidlo, & Cross (2000)		Van Scotter, Motowidlo, &Cross (2000)	
Sample being rated	Employees from multiple organizations (N = 148)	U.S Air Force mechanics (N = 223)	U.S. Air Force mechanics (N = 282)	U.S. Air Force mechanics (N = 234)	U.S. Air Force mechanics (N = 650)	Managers and their subordinates in a large multinational company (N = 231)	Managers and their subordinates in a large multinational company (N = 231)	U.S. Air Force Mechanics (N = 227)	U.S. Air Force Mechanics (N = 645)	U.S. Air Force mechanics (N = 258)	U.S. Air Force mechanics (N = 761)	U.S. Air Force mechanics (N = 234)	U.S. Air Force mechanics (N = 650)
Task performance measure obtained from:	1st supervisor	1st supervisor	1st supervisor	1st supervisor	1st supervisor	Same supervisors	Same supervisors	1st supervisor	1st supervisor	1st supervisor	1st supervisor	1st supervisor	1st supervisor
OCB/contextual performance measure obtained from:	2nd supervisor	2nd supervisor	2nd supervisor	2nd supervisor	2nd supervisor	Same supervisors	Same supervisors	2nd supervisor	2nd supervisor	2nd supervisor	2nd supervisor	2nd supervisor	2nd supervisor
Managerial decision obtained from:	3rd supervisor	3rd supervisor	3rd supervisor	3rd supervisor	3rd supervisor	Same supervisors	Same supervisors	3rd supervisor	3rd supervisor	3rd supervisor	3rd supervisor	3rd supervisor	3rd supervisor

Researchers	Reward Recommendation	Rewards	Medals	Promotability Ratings or Ratings of Management Potential			Rank 1 Year Later	Rank 2 Years Later
	Allen & Rush (1998)†	Van Scotter, Motowidlo, & Cross (2000)	Van Scotter, Motowidlo, & Cross (2000)	Shore, Barksdale, & Shore (1995)† [Promotability Rating]	Shore, Barksdale, & Shore (1995)† [Management Potential Rating]	Van Scotter, Motowidlo, & Cross (2000)	Van Scotter, Motowidlo, & Cross (2000)	Van Scotter, Motowidlo, & Cross (2000)
Incremental contribution of task performance → Managerial decision	.15**	.01	.01	.14**	.15**	.02*	.03**	.00
Incremental contribution of OCB/contextual performance → Managerial decision	.09**	.06**	.05**	.01**	.01**	.12**	.01**	.02**
Variance in managerial decision shared by task performance and OCB/contextual performance	.44	NR	NR	.05**	.21**	NR	NR	NR

(Continued)

Table 6.4 (Continued)

	Reward Recommendation	Rewards	Medals	Promotability Ratings or Ratings of Management Potential			Rank 1 Year Later	Rank 2 Years Later
Researchers	Allen & Rush (1998)†	Van Scotter, Motowidlo, & Cross (2000)	Van Scotter, Motowidlo, & Cross (2000)	Shore, Barksdale, & Shore (1995)† [Promotability Rating]	Shore, Barksdale, & Shore (1995)† [Management Potential Rating]	Van Scotter, Motowidlo, & Cross (2000)	Van Scotter, Motowidlo, & Cross (2000)	Van Scotter, Motowidlo, & Cross (2000)
Total R^2	.68	NR	NR	.20	.37	NR	NR	NR
Common methods biases controlled?	Not controlled	Controlled	Controlled	Not controlled	Not controlled	Controlled	Controlled	Controlled

NOTE: The results for studies marked with a † were calculated by the present authors from data reported in the original study. In the table, NR indicates that the researchers did not report this information. Asterisks (**) indicate that the percentage of variance accounted for in managers' decisions by the variable(s) of interest is significant at $p < .05$.

provide information on either the shared or total variance accounted for by the combination of task performance and OCB/contextual performance, it is impossible to determine how influential the combination of these factors was in an absolute sense.

Experimental Research on the Effects of OCB/Contextual Performance on Evaluations and Reward Allocation Decisions

All of the studies that we have discussed up to this point have been conducted in field settings using cross-sectional, correlational designs. Thus, no causal relationships between OCB and task performance and managerial evaluations and decisions could be firmly established. Table 6.5 provides a summary of those *experimental* and *quasi-experimental* studies that have examined the effects of OCBs or contextual performance on performance evaluations and rater decisions. The distinction between these studies and those in Tables 6.2, 6.3, and 6.4 is that in these studies, the independent variables of interest (e.g., task performance and OCB/contextual performance) were manipulated, and the effects on the dependent variables (performance evaluations, reward allocation decisions, and so forth) were observed and recorded. Thus, these studies provide stronger evidence than the cross-sectional (correlational) field studies of the direction of causality between OCB/contextual performance and the criterion variables.

As indicated in Table 6.5, the manipulation of both task performance and OCB/contextual performance influenced overall performance evaluations, salary recommendations, promotion recommendations, recommendations for training, and managers' estimates of the standard deviation of performance in terms of dollars (SD_y). Indeed, in every one of the samples in which the effects of OCB/contextual performance and task performance were tested, they were found to have a significant positive effect. These results are consistent with the results of the field studies reported in Tables 6.3 and 6.4 and provide much stronger evidence of the direction of causality.

Interactive Effects of OCB/Contextual Performance on Evaluations and Reward Allocation Decisions

Although the majority of the research that has been reported to date has focused on the main effects that OCB/contextual performance and

Table 6.5   Summary of Experimental and Quasi-Experimental Studies Designed to Examine the Effects of Task Performance and OCB/Contextual Performance on Performance Evaluations, Reward Allocation Decisions, and Estimates of the Standard Deviation of Performance in Dollars

Researcher(s)	Overall Performance Evaluations					Promotion Recommendations	Training Recommendations	SD_y Estimates
	Park (1986)	Werner (1994) [Quasi-Experimental Study]	Allen & Rush (1998) [Lab Study]	Allen & Rush (2001) Study 2	Rotundo & Sackett (2002) [Policy Capturing Study]	Park (1986)	Park (1986)	Orr, Sackett, & Mercer (1989) [Policy Capturing Study]
Subjects of study	137 working professionals and managers	116 supervisors from a large state university	136 business and psychology students	136 business and psychology students at a Southeastern university	504 managers, administrators, and supervisors from a variety of organizations	137 working professionals and managers	137 working professionals and managers	17 managers/supervisors of programmer analysts
Task performance manipulation	(+)	(+)	(+)	NR	(+)	(+)	(+)	(+)
OCB/contextual performance manipulation	(+)	(+)	(+)	(+)	(+)	(+)	(+)	(+)
Total R^2	NR	.43	.40	.07	.67[a]	NR	NR	.84[b]

Salary and Reward Recommendations

Researcher(s)	Park (1986)	Allen & Rush (1998) [Lab Study]	Kiker & Motowidlo (1999)	Allen & Rush (2001) [Lab study]	Johnson, Erez, Kiker, & Motowidlo (2002)[†] Study 1	Johnson, Erez, Kiker, & Motowidlo (2002)[†] Study 2
Subjects of study	137 working professionals and managers	136 business and psychology students	494 undergraduate business students	136 business and psychology students at a Southeastern university	106 undergraduate management students at a Southeastern university	207 undergraduate management students at a Southeastern university
Task performance manipulation	(+)	(+)	(+)	NR	NR	NR
OCB/ contextual performance manipulation	(+)	(+)	(+)	(+)	(+)	(+)
Total R^2	NR	.51	.61	.14	.62	.37

NOTE: The results for studies marked with a † were calculated by the present authors from data reported in the original study. In the table, NR indicates that the researchers either: (a) did not include a task performance manipulation in their study, or (b) did not report the results for this manipulation.

a. The total amount of variance explained included rater differences, counterproductive behavior, and all of the possible interactions between in-role performance, OCB, and counterproductive behavior as predictors in the regression equation.

b. For the purposes of these studies, the percentage of variance reported represents the average total variance accounted for in the study across all of the raters.

task performance have on managerial evaluations and decisions, some studies (Allen & Rush, 1998; Kiker & Motowidlo, 1999; Park, 1986; Rotundo & Sackett, 2002; Werner, 1994) have also examined the interactive effects of these variables. In addition, we reanalyzed the data from some previous studies (MacKenzie et al., 1991, 1993; MacKenzie, Podsakoff, & Paine, 1999; Podsakoff & MacKenzie, 1994) that did not originally explore interactive effects to test whether OCBs interacted with task performance to influence managerial evaluations and judgments. Table 6.6 reports the results of these studies, and Figures 6.1 through 6.17 illustrate the form of the interactions.

As indicated in Table 6.6, 9 of the 20 interaction effects were significant ($p < .05$). An examination of the overall pattern of these significant interaction effects across all of the criterion measures indicates that, generally speaking, higher performers (high or medium) benefit more from engaging in OCB than lower performers (Figures 6.6, 6.7, 6.11, 6.13, 6.15, and 6.16). This general pattern of findings suggests that individuals must perform at some minimum level before OCBs have an impact on their overall performance evaluations and/or reward allocations.

However, note that all of the studies in which this pattern was observed were conducted in experimental settings that permitted a perhaps artificially wide range of performance levels to be manipulated. Perhaps in field settings the very lowest performers are either fired or seek employment elsewhere, which naturally censors the distribution of scores on performance from below. This would be consistent with the fact that a significant task performance by OCB interaction effect was not observed in any of the field studies included in Table 6.6, and the majority of the samples used in these studies came from sales settings in which very poor performers are unlikely to survive for long. Thus, we recommend that researchers attempt to replicate these findings in other nonsales field settings in the future.

Conclusions

The findings summarized in Tables 6.2 through 6.6 indicate that: (a) OCB/contextual performance has a positive impact on several important personnel decisions made by managers, (b) the weight of this evidence suggests that the effect of this form of performance is at least as great as the effect of in-role performance, (c) common method variance has a substantial impact on the relationships between OCB/contextual performance and managerial judgments (although this bias generally

Table 6.6   Summary of Interactions between Task Performance and OCB/Contextual Performance on Performance Evaluations and Managerial Reward Allocation Decisions

	Performance Evaluation								
Researcher(s)	*Park (1986)*		*MacKenzie, Podsakoff, & Fetter (1991)*		*MacKenzie, Podsakoff, & Fetter (1993)*			*Werner (1994)*	*Allen & Rush (1998) [Lab Study]*
Sample/ subjects of study	137 working professionals and managers	137 working professionals and managers	Insurance agents (N = 259)	Insurance agents (N = 113)	Insurance agents (N =261)	Petrochemical salespeople (N= 204)	Pharmaceutical sales managers (N = 108)	116 supervisors from a large state university	136 business and psychology students
Dependent variable	Evaluation of sales performance	Evaluation of interpersonal performance	Overall evaluation	Overall evaluation	Overall evaluation	Overall evaluation	Overall evaluation	Overall evaluation	Overall evaluation
Interaction between task performance and OCB/ Contextual performance	Significant	Non-significant	Non-significant	Non-significant	Significant	Nonsignificant	Nonsignificant	Significant	Significant
Nature of interaction			See Figure 6.1	See Figure 6.2	See Figure 6.3	See Figure 6.4	See Figure 6.5	See Figure 6.6	See Figure 6.7

(Continued)

Table 6.6 (Continued)

| Researcher(s) | Performance Evaluation | | | | Salary and Reward Recommendations | | | | Promotion Recommendation | Training Recommendation |
	Allen & Rush (1998) [Field Study]	Podsakoff & MacKenzie (1994)/ MacKenzie et al. (1999)	MacKenzie et al. (1999)	Rotundo & Sackett (2002)	Park (1986)	Allen & Rush (1998) [Lab Study]	Allen & Rush (1998) [Field Study]	Kiker & Motowidlo (1999)	Park (1986)	Park (1986)
Sample/ subjects of study	Employees from multiple organizations (N = 148)	Insurance agents (N = 987)	Insurance sales managers (N= 161)	504 managers, administrators, and supervisors from a variety of organizations	137 working professionals and managers	136 business and psychology students	Employees from multiple organizations (N = 148)	494 undergraduate business students	137 working professionals and managers	137 working professionals and managers
Dependent variable	Overall evaluation	Overall evaluation	Overall evaluation	Overall evaluation	% raise recommended	Reward recommended	Reward recommended	Reward recommended	Promotion recommended	Training recommended
Interaction between task performance and OCB/ contextual performance	Non-significant	Non-significant	Non-significant	Significant	Non-significant	Significant	Non-significant	Significant	Significant	Non-significant
Nature of interaction	See Figure 6.8	See Figure 6.9	See Figure 6.10	See Figure 6.11	See Figure 6.12	See Figure 6.13	See Figure 6.14	See Figure 6.15	See Figure 6.16	See Figure 6.17

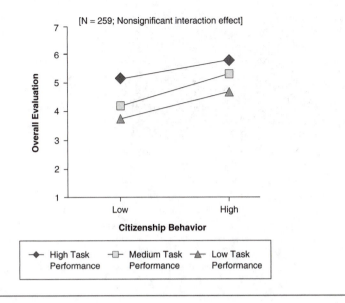

Figure 6.1

SOURCE: Based on re-analysis of data from MacKenzie, S. B., Podsakoff, P. M. & Fetter, R. (1993). Organizational citizenship behaviors and sales unit effectiveness. *Journal of Marketing Research, 31,* 351–363. Used with permission of the authors.

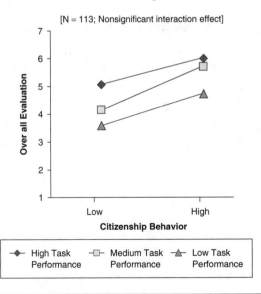

Figure 6.2

SOURCE: Based on re-analysis of data from MacKenzie, S. B., Podsakoff, P. M. & Fetter, R. (1993). Organizational citizenship behaviors and sales unit effectiveness. *Journal of Marketing Research, 31,* 351–363. Used with permission of the authors.

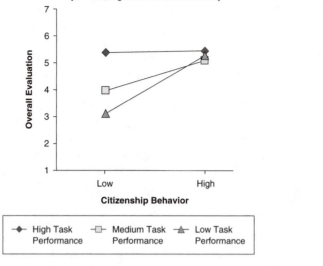

Figure 6.3

SOURCE: Based on re-analysis of data from MacKenzie, S. B., Podsakoff, P. M. & Fetter, R. (1993), Organizational citizenship behaviors and sales unit effectiveness. *Journal of Marketing Research, 31,* 351–363. Used with permission of the authors.

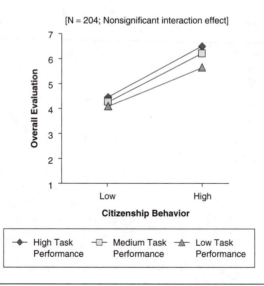

Figure 6.4

SOURCE: Based on re-analysis of data from MacKenzie, S. B., Podsakoff, P. M. & Fetter, R. (1993), Organizational citizenship behaviors and sales unit effectiveness. *Journal of Marketing Research, 31,* 351–363. Used with permission of the authors.

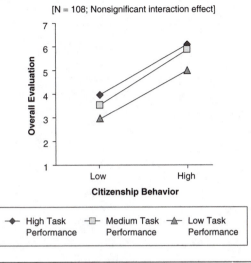

Figure 6.5

SOURCE: Based on re-analysis of data from MacKenzie, S. B., Podsakoff, P. M. & Fetter, R. (1993), Organizational citizenship behaviors and sales unit effectiveness. *Journal of Marketing Research, 31,* 351–363. Used with permission of the authors.

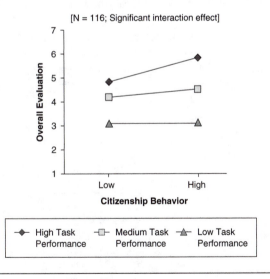

Figure 6.6

SOURCE: Based on research reported in Werner, J. M. (1994), Dimensions that make a difference. *Journal of Applied Psychology, 79,* 98–107. Figure originally published in Werner, J. M. (2001). *Attracting and retraining high-quality employees: New strategies for credit unions.* Session 2 Building employee commitment to the organization, 21–37. Figure 2-2, pg. 28. Copyright © Filene Research Institute P.O. Box 2998 Madison, WI 53701-2998 (608) 231-8550. Copyright © 2001 ISBN 1-880572053-2.

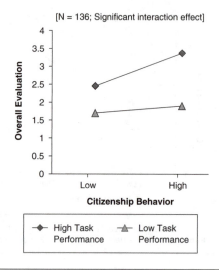

Figure 6.7

SOURCE: Based on research reported in Allen, T. D., & Rush, M. C. (1998). The effects of organizational citizenship behavior on performance judgments: A field study and laboratory experiment. *Journal of Applied Psychology, 83,* 247–260. Data provided directly by T. D. Allen and used with permission of the author.

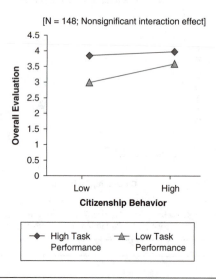

Figure 6.8

SOURCE: Based on research reported in Allen, T. D., & Rush, M. C. (1998). The effects of organizational citizenship behavior on performance judgments: A field study and laboratory experiment. *Journal of Applied Psychology, 83,* 247–260. Data provided directly by T. D. Allen and used with permission of the author.

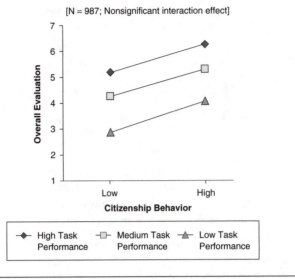

Figure 6.9

SOURCE: Based on re-analysis of data from Podsakoff, P. M. & MacKenzie, S. B. (1994). The impact of organizational citizenship behavior on evaluations of salesperson performance. *Journal of Marketing, 57,* 70–80. Used with permission of the authors.

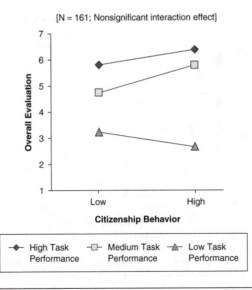

Figure 6.10

SOURCE: Based on re-analysis of data from MacKenzie, S. B., Podsakoff, P. M., & Paine, J. E. (1999). Do citizenship behaviors matter more for managers than for sales people? *Journal of the Academy of Marketing Science, 27,* 396–410. Used with permission of the authors.

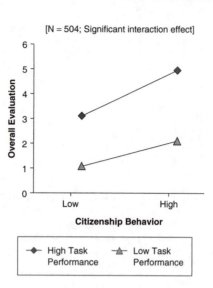

Figure 6.11

SOURCE: Rotundo, M., & Sackett, P. R. (2002). The relative importance of task, citizenship, and counterproductive performance to global ratings of job performance: A policy-capturing approach. *Journal of Applied Psychology, 87,* 66–80. Figure 1a. Copyright © by the American Psychological Association. Reprinted with permission.

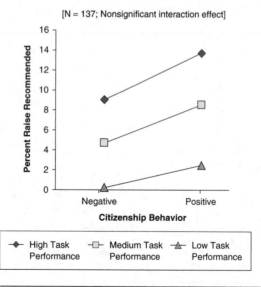

Figure 6.12

SOURCE: Based on data reported by Park, O. S. (1986). *Beyond cognition in leadership: On prosocial behavior and affect in managerial judgment.* Unpublished doctoral dissertation, Pennsylvania State University, State College.

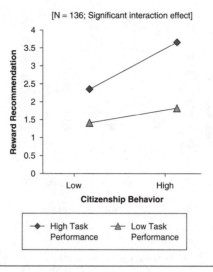

Figure 6.13

SOURCE: Based on research reported in Allen, T. D., & Rush, M. C. (1998). The effects of organizational citizenship behavior on performance judgments: A field study and laboratory experiment. *Journal of Applied Psychology, 83,* 247–260. Data provided directly by T. D. Allen and used with permission of the author.

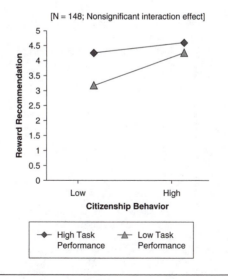

Figure 6.14

SOURCE: Based on research reported in Allen, T. D., & Rush, M. C. (1998). The effects of organizational citizenship behavior on performance judgments: A field study and laboratory experiment. *Journal of Applied Psychology, 83,* 247–260. Data provided directly by T. D. Allen and used with permission of the author.

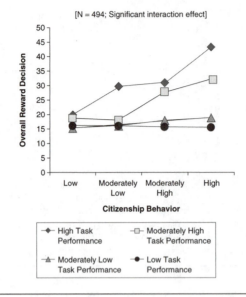

Figure 6.15

SOURCE: Kiker, D. S., & Motowidlo, S. J. (1999). Main and interactive effects of task and contextual performance on supervisory reward decisions. *Journal of Applied Psychology, 84,* 602–609. Figure 1a. Copyright © by the American Psychological Association. Reprinted with permission.

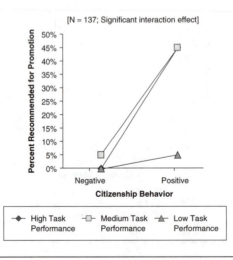

Figure 6.16

SOURCE: Based on data reported by Park, O. S. (1986). *Beyond cognition in leadership: On prosocial behavior and affect in managerial judgment.* Unpublished doctoral dissertation, Pennsylvania State University, State College.

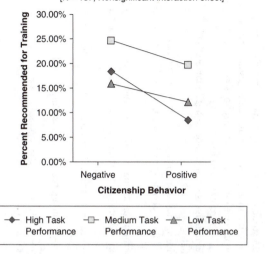

Figure 6.17

SOURCE: Based on data reported by Park, O. S. (1986). *Beyond cognition in leadership: On prosocial behavior and affect in managerial judgment.* Unpublished doctoral dissertation, Pennsylvania State University, State College.

weakens these relationships, it does not eliminate them), and (d) evidence suggests that in-role and extra-role performance may interact when influencing managerial judgments and decisions. Moreover, this pattern of effects is fairly robust across a wide variety of organizational contexts and raters. Table 6.7 provides a summary of the studies that examine the effects of task performance and OCB/contextual performance on managerial evaluations and decisions, organized by the person being rated and the person doing the rating (nonmanager versus manager in both cases). As indicated in this table, only a few studies have focused on ratings of a non-manager by a nonmanagerial rater (e.g., self or peer).

Implications for Future Research

Controlling for Common Method Biases

The evidence reviewed in this chapter suggests that when ratings of OCB and overall evaluations are obtained from the same source, common method biases influence the relationship between these variables. Although an examination of Table 6.2 indicates that method biases

Table 6.7 Summary of Studies Examining Effects of Task performance and OCB/Contextual Performance Managerial Evaluations and Decisions

	Person Being Rated Is a Nonmanager	*Person Being Rated Is a Manager*
Rater is a Nonmanager	Army soldiers (peers)	Manufacturing managers (peer, self)
	Residence hall advisors (students)	Former MBA students in a variety of managerial roles (self)
	Graduate student teachers (students)	District marketing managers (peer and consultants' ratings)
	Hypothetical secretaries, automobile mechanics, and fast-food service employees (students)	Managers in diverse industries, organizations and levels (self, peer, subordinate ratings)
		Middle level managers from corporate headquarters (self, subordinate)
		Social service agency administrators (self, subordinate)
		Top and middle level managers in a manufacturing organization (self, peer)
		First and second-line managers of eight functional divisions of field, plant, laboratory, and headquarters positions of a large company (self)
		Supervisors and leaders from four organizations (self, peer and subordinate)
		Branch managers at a large lending institution (self)
Rater is a Manager	Insurance salespeople	Pharmaceutical district sales managers
	Computer salespeople	Insurance sales managers
	Hypothetical salespeople	Manufacturing managers
	Air Force mechanics	Former MBA students in a variety of managerial roles
	Army soldiers	District marketing managers (former supervisor, regional general manager, regional marketing manager)
	Sewing machine operators	Managers in diverse industries, organizations and levels
	Office furniture manufacturing employees	Middle-level managers from corporate headquarters
	Employees in unspecified jobs in multiple organizations	Social service agency administrators (self, subordinate)

Person Being Rated is a Nonmanager	Person Being Rated Is a Manager
Mechanics and maintenance employees of a multinational company	Top- and middle-level managers in a manufacturing organization
Teachers	First- and second-line managers of eight functional divisions of field, plant, laboratory, and headquarters positions of a large company
Working MBA/MS students	
Computer programmers	Branch managers at a large lending institution
Secretaries and support staff	
Technical support personnel	
Customer service and sales personnel	
Phone operators	
Craft jobs	
Engineering support personnel	
Warehouse, transportation, and other	
Bank tellers	
Hypothetical secretaries at a university	
Hypothetical accountants, nurses, administrative assistants, retail cashiers, and machine operators	
Hypothetical subordinates	
Hypothetical programmer analysts	
Salaried employees in a large U.S. firm	
Employees in metal fabricating plants	

NOTE: Type of rating (by self, by peer, and so on) is shown in parentheses. Item being rating (CP or OCB) is shown in square brackets.

SOURCE: Podsakoff, P. M., & MacKenzie, S. B. (1997). Impact of organizational citizenship behavior on organizational performance: A review and suggestions for future research. *Human Performance, 10*(2), 133–151. Lawrence Erlbaum.

generally increase the strength of the relationships between the OCBs and the ratings of overall performance, it is important to recognize that these biases can also decrease the strengths of these relationships (Cote & Buckley, 1988; Podsakoff et al., 2003). Indeed, Cote and Buckley (1988) demonstrated that common method biases inflate or deflate the observed correlation between the measures depending upon the correlation between the methods. In the case of the relationships between OCB and a person's overall performance evaluation, their research implies that method effects (a) inflate the observed relationship when the correlation between the methods used to measure these constructs is higher than the observed correlation between the measures of these constructs with method effects removed, and (b) deflate the relationship when the correlation between the methods is lower than the observed correlation between the measures with method effects removed (cf. Podsakoff et al., 2003). Therefore, it is important to control for this potential methodological bias in future research.

As recommended by Podsakoff et al. (2003), method biases can be controlled through: (a) the design of the study's procedures, and/or (b) statistical controls. The most commonly used procedural remedy is to obtain the measures of OCB from one source and the evaluation of overall performance from another source (cf. Borman, White, & Dorsey, 1995; Van Scotter & Motowidlo, 1996). The most commonly used statistical remedy is to control for method biases through the addition of a common method factor (cf. MacKenzie et al., 1991, 1993; MacKenzie et al., 1999; Podsakoff & MacKenzie, 1994). Although it is perhaps best to control for method biases through the design of the study whenever possible, the most popular method of doing this raises some interesting questions about informational differences across the different sources of the ratings. These differences are discussed in greater detail in the following subsection. For now, it is sufficient to point out that there are other ways of controlling for method biases through the design of the study that may be preferable (e.g., introducing a temporal, psychological, or proximal separation between the measures of the OCBs and the overall performance rating).

Self- vs. Other-agreement and the Observer's Perspective

Research on performance ratings has found that raters often disagree with each other (Landy & Farr, 1980; Mabe & West, 1982; Thornton, 1980). For example, in a recent meta-analysis on self-supervisor, self-peer, and peer-supervisor performance ratings, Harris and

Schaubroeck (1988) found that peer and supervisor ratings agreed more with each other (corrected r = .62) than either self-supervisor (corrected r = .35) or self-peer ratings (corrected r = .36). These differences are mirrored in studies that have examined the relationships between self, supervisory, and peer evaluations of OCB/contextual performance. For example, based on a meta-analysis of 14 studies in which managers were the focus of the ratings, Conway (1999) reported that, on average, peer and supervisor ratings were correlated .35 (uncorrected), whereas the self-supervisor ratings were correlated .23 (uncorrected), and the self-peer ratings were correlated .18 (uncorrected). Moreover, the reanalysis of Conway's data presented in Table 6.3 demonstrates that the impact of OCB/contextual performance on overall evaluations is greater when peer ratings or self-ratings are used than when supervisory ratings are used. Conversely, the impact of task performance on overall evaluations is greater when supervisory ratings are used than when either peer ratings or self-ratings are used.

The two main reasons why the impact of OCBs on overall performance evaluations may vary across different raters are: (a) because of differences in the raters' perceptions of the extent to which the OCBs occur, and/or (b) because of the weight the raters assign to OCBs when they make their evaluations. Harris and Schaubroeck (1988) and MacKenzie et al. (1991, 1993), among others, have suggested that different raters may have different opportunities to observe the performance of a given employee. For example, when an employee helps a peer (e.g., by lending a helping hand when the peer falls behind in his or her work, by informing the peer before taking actions that might affect him or her, and/or by encouraging the peer when he or she is discouraged about work), the coworker being helped will certainly observe the behavior, but the supervisor may not. This could account for differences in supervisors' and peers' overall ratings of the employee because, in this example, supervisor and peers may have different perceptions of the extent to which the employee exhibits helping behavior.

A similar argument could be used to explain why an employee's evaluation of his or her own performance may differ from his or her supervisor's and peers' evaluations. For example, if an employee helps a number of coworkers, neither the employee's supervisor nor any one of his or her peers may have a complete appreciation of the extent to which the employee engages in helping behavior. In this situation, it would not be surprising if an employee's self-rating on helping is higher than the ratings he or she receives from his or her supervisor or any individual peer. This difference in an actor's and an observer's knowledge of an actor's behavior has been noted by Jones and Nisbett (1972), Nisbett and Ross (1980), and Harvey and Weary (1981), among others.

However, mean level differences in the perceived extent to which a person engages in a particular form of behavior are not the only reasons that raters may disagree about the overall performance of an individual. MacKenzie et al. (1993), MacKenzie et al. (1999), and Orr, Sackett, and Mercer (1989), have noted that the weight or importance given to OCBs when evaluating overall performance, and the dollar value of performance, may also vary across raters. This, too, could explain differences in self, peer, and manager ratings of a given employee. For example, an employee's helping behavior may be a very important factor in influencing a peer's evaluation of the employee, but this behavior may not be appreciated as much by the manager. Or, an employee who exhibits sportsmanship by never complaining about changes the manager makes or about problems that arise at work may be appreciated much more by the manager than by his or her peers. This would be consistent with research by Morrison (1994) indicating that supervisors and employees differ greatly in their beliefs about the extent to which OCBs are a required part of the job.

Thus, differences in self, peer, and supervisory ratings of performance may be accounted for by either differences in perceptions of the extent to which OCBs occur and/or differences in the weight given to OCBs in forming overall evaluations. These reasons would suggest that we might benefit from future research that tries to determine the effects that each of these factors has on managerial evaluations. If the difference in impact is due to differences in perceptions of the mean level of the OCBs, it would be interesting to know whether this results from differences in the ability to observe the behavior or in differences in the salience of the behavior to the rater. On the other hand, if the difference in impact is due to the weight given to OCBs in forming overall evaluations, future research could investigate whether this is due to differences in the rater's implicit theories about the importance of OCBs or to organizational policies or cultures. Thus, designing research that might distinguish between these two mechanisms should be a priority for future research.

The Effects of Prior Performance on Future Job Success

Aside from issues relating to performance appraisals, understanding the role of OCBs in employee performance may also help explain why an employee's performance in one job may not be a very good predictor of his or her success in other jobs. Many managers lament the fact that when they promote their best sales representative (or engineer, research scientist, clerical worker, etc.), they lose their best sales representative and gain their worst manager. One of several factors contributing to this phenomenon may be that the relative importance of extra-role and in-role behaviors varies as one moves up the organizational ladder. For example, Organ (1988) suggested that OCBs increase in importance for upper-level managers because "the higher the rank of an organizational member, the more diffuse are the expected, role related obligations of that member" (p. 13). In a similar manner, Borman and Motowidlo (1993) argued that "because management positions do not contribute directly to the technical core of an organization, differences between their task and contextual components are not as straightforward as in other jobs that do contribute directly to the technical core" (p. 85). This implies that evaluations of higher-level managers are less concrete and rely more heavily on distinctive, organization-enhancing behaviors such as OCBs.

MacKenzie et al. (1999) conducted a study that examined this hypothesis. Their research examined the relative contribution of OCBs and task performance to the overall evaluations of 987 multiline insurance sales agents and 161 of their managers. They hypothesized that the impact of OCBs on overall evaluations would be stronger at managerial levels than at the agent level. Consistent with this hypothesis, they reported that after controlling for common method variance, OCBs uniquely accounted for only 4% of the variance in the sales agents' evaluations and 29% of the variance in the sales manager's evaluations. This difference was significant.

These findings suggest that OCBs may be relatively more important in managerial jobs than in lower-level positions, possibly because the role expectations for managerial jobs are more ambiguous, thus making it more difficult to assess a manager's task performance. On the other hand, perhaps because managerial jobs require people to interact more with others, OCBs are more important in determining managers' effectiveness. The latter would suggest that OCBs would be more important in jobs where people work in teams, need to coordinate their activities, or are interdependent with each other than in jobs where people work independently or as individual contributors. Therefore, job/task characteristics may be an important moderator of the impact of OCBs on overall evaluations of employee performance.

The Dynamic Nature of Performance Criteria

The inclusion of OCBs in the performance evaluation process by managers may also help explain why some investigators have observed instability of performance ratings over time (e.g., Austin, Humphreys, & Hulin, 1989; Bass, 1962; Dennis, 1954, 1956; Fleishman & Fruchter, 1960; Ghiselli, 1956; Ghiselli & Haire, 1960; Henry & Hulin, 1987; Lin & Humphreys, 1977). Although there is a great deal of debate as to whether performance ratings really are unstable over time, Deadrick and Madigan (1990) have suggested that in those cases in which instability occurs, it can be attributed to either changes in the individual employee (performance inconsistency), the organizational context (evaluation inconsistency), or the method of measuring performance (measurement unreliability). Performance inconsistencies and evaluation inconsistencies may be produced by changes in an employee's desire to engage in OCBs or by changes in the importance of those behaviors to the organization.

For example, many managers believe that the criteria used to evaluate performance should change as an employee progresses through his or her career, and these changes may produce evaluation inconsistencies in the managers' judgments over time. This may be particularly true in an academic setting; publication record is often the most important performance criterion at the beginning of a person's career, but after tenure, OCB-type performance appears to increase in importance as the faculty member is expected to shoulder more and more service and/or administrative responsibilities. Similarly, a number of trends in the business environment may have caused organizations to change their evaluation criteria in recent years. Under the rubrics of total quality management (TQM), doing more with less, and doing it right the first time, many companies have begun to emphasize the importance of teamwork, cooperation, and internal and external customer satisfaction. In addition, to counter the increased buying power of many organizations in the public and private sector, many sales organizations are moving toward a selling-center concept, which emphasizes team selling (Spiro, Stanton, & Rich, 2002). Any of these trends might cause organizations to give greater weight to OCBs when evaluating performance, which could account for the instability of performance ratings over time that has been observed by some investigators.

However, instabilities in ratings may sometimes be due to performance inconsistencies rather than evaluation inconsistencies. For example, in the academic example previously mentioned, perhaps after faculty members are tenured, they decide that they want to get into more service or administrative activities and move away from a strong research orientation. If this shift in effort is intrinsically motivated and occurs solely as a result of the desire to pursue personal career objectives, it may lead to the kinds of performance inconsistencies that would cause instability in performance ratings. In general, maybe the longer people are employed by a company, the more committed to the organization they become and the more willing they are to do whatever they can to contribute to its success. Often, this may involve concentrating more of their efforts on various types of extra-role behaviors, including OCBs. However, this may be true only up to a point; the relationship between organizational tenure and citizenship behaviors may be curvilinear (i.e., an inverted V-shape), due to the fact that employees that have been with an organization for an extremely long time might tend to coast along and become less likely to engage in OCBs.

The Role of OCB in Selection-Validation Research

Understanding the impact of OCBs on performance evaluations also may help explain why the performance of prospective employees in job interviews is not always a valid predictor of their future job success. According to Arvey and Faley (1988), "several reviews of research on the interview (Arvey & Campion, 1982; Mayfield, 1964; Ulrich & Trumbo, 1965; Wagner, 1949; Wright, 1969) cast serious doubt on the interview as a process yielding reliable decisions to forecast job behavior and performance" (p. 214). Some researchers have suggested that interviews have low predictive validities because of interviewer differences (Dougherty, Ebert, & Callender, 1986; Dreher, Ash, & Hancock, 1988; Ghiselli, 1966; Zedeck, Tziner, & Middlestadt, 1983) and that if a company had the same interviewer(s) conduct all interviews, the validity coefficient for the interview as a selection device might be higher. This is consistent with Ghiselli (1966), who reported that when the same person (in this case, Ghiselli himself) served as the interviewer over a 17-year period, the validity coefficient was much higher than those found in other validity studies (cf. Arvey & Campion, 1982; Dunnette, Arvey, & Arnold, 1971; Hunter & Hunter, 1984; Mayfield, 1964; Schmitt, 1976; Ulrich & Trumbo, 1965; Wagner, 1949; Wright, 1969).

One individual difference that might be responsible for the low validity coefficients typically observed for interviews is the importance attached to OCBs by different interviewers when forming their overall evaluations of a job candidate. For example, if information about the degree to which a candidate has helped coworkers in his or her previous job surfaces in the interview, one interviewer may be heavily influenced by this information, whereas another may discount it entirely. Another reason that interviews may not be valid predictors of a candidate's job success has to do with the match between the criteria used to judge interview success and the criteria used to judge subsequent job success. If an interviewer gives relatively little weight to OCBs when evaluating a job candidate and the person evaluating the candidate's subsequent job performance gives a lot of weight to OCBs, the validity coefficient for the interview will be lower than if the two agree in their perceptions of the relative importance of OCBs. As depicted in Figure 6.18, the highest predictive validities should be found in situations in which the weight given to OCBs on the predictor variable side matches the weight given to OCBs on the criterion variable side.

In situations in which job success is heavily dependent on an employee's task performance and not very dependent on his or her extra-role contributions, interview procedures that focus on predicting task performance, rather than extra-role aspects of performance, may have greater validity. For example, when interviewing a heating and air-conditioning repairperson for a job, interview procedures that focus on mechanical abilities and aptitudes relevant to the task would have greater validity than questions that ask about the applicant's previous OCBs. Conversely, in situations in which job success is heavily dependent on an employee's extra-role behaviors and not as dependent on his or her task performance, interview procedures that focus on extra-role rather than task performance may have greater validity. For example, when interviewing an employee being considered for membership in a self-managed work team, interviewer procedures that emphasize people-related skills, cooperation, and teamwork would have greater validity. Latham and Skarlicki (1995) examined several types of interview formats to determine which were the most accurate predictors of organizational citizenship behavior and concluded that

> the interview format should focus on interviewee intentions, it should be highly structured in that everyone is asked the same questions, probing interviewee's should not be allowed, and a scoring guide should be provided for interviewers to use when evaluating interviewee responses. (p. 77)

Additional Consequences of OCB for Individuals

The research reviewed in this chapter indicates that OCBs have a number of important consequences for individuals, including the fact that they enhance managerial evaluations of overall performance, reward

Criteria for Job Success

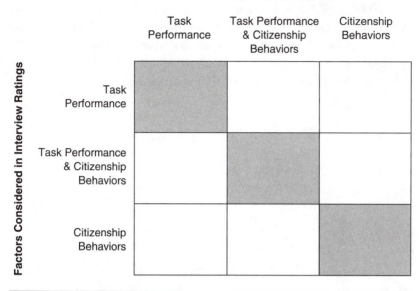

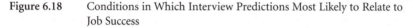

Figure 6.18   Conditions in Which Interview Predictions Most Likely to Relate to Job Success

SOURCE: Podsakoff, P. M., MacKenzie, S. B., & Hui, C. (1993). Organizational citizenship behaviors and managerial evaluations of employee performance: A review and suggestions for future research. In G. R. Ferris & K. M. Rowland (Eds.), *Research in Personnel and Human Resources Management, Vol. 11* (pp. 1–40). Mahwah, NJ: Lawrence Erlbaum Associates.

recommendations, awards, and promotions. However, the consequences of OCBs for individuals may not be limited to these factors. For example, if OCBs increase the probability of getting a promotion, they might also decrease the probability of being laid off or terminated in the case of an organizational downsizing. Employees who exhibit OCBs may also be more likely to be assigned to high-profile or special projects or task force teams, perhaps because OCBs signal a higher level of commitment and/or because OCBs enhance group interactions. Similarly, because employees who exhibit OCBs are more likely to share their experiences with other employees (e.g., in the form of helping behavior), they may be given more opportunities for advanced training. OCBs may also influence the nature of the employee's relationship with his or her supervisor by increasing the likelihood that the leader would be willing to: (a) establish closer leader-member exchange relationships with the employee, (b) serve as a mentor to the employee, (c) recommend the employee for important and/or highly visible assignments, and (d) permit the employee to have more autonomy in deciding how to perform his or her job. Finally, because OCBs can involve helping others, the feedback the employee receives from the people he or she helps may enhance an employee's perceptions of his or her own self-efficacy or self-worth.

 **7** The Effects of OCB on
Organizational Performance
and Success

The empirical evidence reviewed in Chapter 6 indicates that OCBs influence managerial evaluations and decisions for several reasons, including the fact that managers believe that OCBs enhance organizational effectiveness. Indeed, a key tenet of Organ's (1988) original definition of OCB is that when aggregated over time and people, such behavior enhances organizational effectiveness. However, for many years, this assumption went untested, and its acceptance was based more on its conceptual plausibility than on direct empirical evidence (cf. Borman & Motowidlo, 1993; Organ & Konovsky, 1989; Podsakoff & MacKenzie, 1994). Some scholars have argued (cf. Borman & Motowidlo, 1993; Organ, 1988; Smith, Organ, & Near, 1983) that OCBs may enhance performance by "lubricating" the social machinery of the organization, reducing friction, and/or increasing efficiency. In recent years, researchers have identified a number of more specific theoretical mechanisms (cf. Bolino, Turnley, & Bloodgood, 2002; George & Bettenhausen, 1990; Karambayya, 1990; Organ, 1988, 1990c; Podsakoff, Ahearne, & MacKenzie, 1997; Podsakoff & MacKenzie, 1994, 1997; Podsakoff, MacKenzie, Paine, & Bachrach, 2000). A summary of the potential reasons that OCBs might influence organizational effectiveness is provided in Table 7.1.

As indicated in the table, one way that OCBs might increase the efficiency of an organization is by enhancing coworker or managerial productivity (cf. MacKenzie, Podsakoff, & Fetter, 1991, 1993; Organ, 1988; Podsakoff & MacKenzie, 1994). For example, experienced employees voluntarily helping new coworkers learn the ropes enable the new workers to become productive employees faster, thus enhancing the efficiency of the work group or unit. Similarly, over time, helping

Table 7.1 Summary of Reasons That OCBs Might Influence Organizational Effectiveness

Potential Reason	Examples
OCBs may enhance coworker productivity.	• Employees who help another coworker learn the ropes may help the coworker become a more productive employee faster. • Over time, helping behavior can help to spread best practices throughout the work unit or group. • Employees who engage in self-development activities should become more efficient in performing their jobs, and, if the development activities involve cross-training, they may become more versatile in the types of tasks they can perform.
OCBs may enhance managerial productivity.	• If employees engage in civic virtue, the manager may receive valuable suggestions and/or feedback on his or her ideas for improving unit effectiveness. • Courteous employees (i.e., those who avoid creating problems for coworkers) allow the manager to avoid falling into a pattern of crisis management. • Employees who exhibit sportsmanship free the manager from having to deal with small problems and petty complaints.
OCBs may free up resources for more productive purposes.	• If employees help each other with work-related problems, the manager doesn't have to provide assistance; consequently, the manager can spend more time on productive tasks, such as planning. • Employees that exhibit conscientiousness require less managerial supervision and permit the manager to delegate more responsibility to them; thus, they free up more of the manager's time. • To the extent that experienced employees help in the training and orienting of new employees, they reduce the need to devote organizational resources to these activities. • If employees enhance their ability to do their jobs through self-development, they may reduce the need for managerial supervision.

Potential Reason	Examples
OCBs may reduce the need to devote scarce resources to purely maintenance functions.	• A natural by-product of helping behavior is that it enhances team spirit, morale, and cohesiveness, thus reducing the need for group members (or managers) to spend energy and time on group-maintenance functions. • Employees that exhibit courtesy toward others and sportsmanship reduce intergroup conflict, thereby diminishing the time spent on conflict-management activities.
OCBs may serve as an effective means of coordinating activities between team members and across work groups.	• Exhibiting civic virtue by voluntarily attending and actively participating in work unit meetings aids in the coordination of effort among team members, which potentially increases the group's effectiveness and efficiency. • Exhibiting courtesy by touching base with team members or members of other functional groups in the organization reduces the likelihood of the occurrence of problems that would otherwise take time and effort to resolve.
OCBs may enhance the organization's ability to attract and retain the best people by making it a more attractive place to work.	• When employees endorse and promote the organization to outsiders and contribute to its good reputation (organizational loyalty), the organization will seem more attractive to good job candidates. • Helping behaviors may enhance morale, group cohesiveness, and the sense of belonging to a team, all of which may enhance performance and help the organization to attract and retain better employees. • Demonstrating sportsmanship by being willing to roll with the punches and not complaining about trivial matters sets an example for others and contributes to a sense of loyalty and commitment to the organization that may enhance employee retention.
OCBs may enhance the stability of organizational performance.	• Picking up the slack for workers who are absent or who have heavy workloads can help to enhance the stability (reduce the variability) of the work unit's performance. • Conscientious employees are more likely to maintain a consistently high level of output, thus reducing variability in a work unit's performance.

(Continued)

Table 7.1 (Continued)

Potential Reason	Examples
OCBs may enhance an organization's ability to adapt to environmental changes.	• Employees who are in close contact with the marketplace who volunteer information about changes in the environment and make suggestions about how to respond to them help an organization to adapt. • Employees who attend and actively participate in meetings may aid the dissemination of information in an organization, thus enhancing its responsiveness. • Employees who exhibit sportsmanship by demonstrating a willingness to take on new responsibilities or engage in self-development by learning new skills enhance the organization's ability to adapt to changes in its environment.
OCBs may enhance organizational effectiveness by creating social capital.	• Employees who exhibit helping to other employees enhance structural social capital by strengthening network ties, thereby improving information transfer, organizational learning, and the execution of organizational activities. • Employees who attend meetings that are not required but that convey useful information about the organization enhance cognitive social capital by acquiring useful knowledge about organizational activities and developments, and by gaining a better understanding of the organization, its mission, and its culture. • Employees who present their ideas and openly share their opinions with their coworkers enhance cognitive social capital by facilitating the creation of shared language and narratives within the organization. • Employees who exhibit helping behavior to other employees enhance relational social capital by building trust.

SOURCE: Adapted from Podsakoff & MacKenzie (1997). Used with permission.

behavior can be the mechanism through which best practices are spread throughout a work unit or group. Likewise, employees who engage in self-development activities should become more efficient in performing their jobs—and, if the development activities involve cross training, the workers may become more versatile in the types of tasks they can perform. Managerial productivity may also increase when employees: (a) provide valuable suggestions for improving unit performance (civic virtue or voice); (b) avoid creating problems for coworkers (courtesy), which allows the manager to avoid falling into a pattern of crisis management; and/or (c) don't consume the manager's time by complaining about small problems and making petty complaints (sportsmanship).

Another way that OCBs may enhance the efficiency of an organization is by freeing up various types of resources for more productive purposes (cf. Borman & Motowidlo, 1993; MacKenzie et al., 1991, 1993; Organ, 1988; Podsakoff, MacKenzie, & Hui, 1993). For example, employees who help each other with work-related problems enable the manager to spend more time on productive tasks (e.g., strategic planning, improving business processes, securing valuable resources, and so on). Likewise, when employees are conscientious they free up a manager's time, because the manager can delegate more responsibility to them, and they require less supervision. Finally, when employees engage in self-development activities that enhance their ability to do their jobs, they may reduce the need for managerial supervision.

OCBs may also improve organizational performance by: (a) reducing the need to devote scarce resources to purely maintenance functions (Organ, 1988), and (b) helping to coordinate the activities of work groups (cf. Karambayya, 1990; Smith et al., 1983). A natural by-product of helping behaviors like cheerleading and peacekeeping is that they enhance team spirit, morale, and cohesiveness, thus reducing the need for group members (or managers) to spend energy and time on group-maintenance functions. Likewise, not creating problems for others (courtesy) and exhibiting sportsmanship reduces intergroup conflict and diminishes the need to spend time on conflict-management activities. The coordination of activities among group members and between work groups may also improve when employees voluntarily attend and actively participate in work unit meetings (civic virtue or voice), and/or when they touch base with members of their team or members of other groups to avoid creating problems for those workers (courtesy).

OCB may also improve performance by enabling the organization to attract and to retain the best people (cf. George & Bettenhausen, 1990;

Organ, 1988). Many of the best employees and job candidates enjoy working in a positive environment with a closely knit group of coworkers. Obviously, when employees endorse and promote the organization to outsiders and contribute to its good reputation (organizational loyalty), the organization will seem more attractive to good job candidates. Similarly, helping behaviors may directly contribute to such an environment by enhancing morale and fostering group cohesiveness and a sense of belonging to a team), thus making the organization a more attractive place to work. Moreover, when employees exhibit sportsmanship by being willing to roll with the punches and refrain from complaining about trivial matters, they set an example of putting the interests of the work unit or group ahead of their own interests, thus strengthening a sense of loyalty and commitment to the organization.

OCBs might also benefit an organization by reducing the variability in its performance. Minimizing variability is important because it allows managers to more easily plan and allocate scarce resources. Employees may voluntarily do several things to reduce the variability in a work unit's performance, including: (a) picking up the slack for workers who are absent or who have heavy workloads (helping), (b) cross training (self-development) so that workers can fill in for each other, and (c) going above and beyond the call of duty in performing one's work responsibilities (conscientiousness). Individually, these behaviors may be trivial, but collectively they may significantly enhance the performance of an organization.

OCBs may also help to enhance an organization's ability to adapt to changing environments. For example, when employees who are in close contact with the marketplace volunteer information about changes in the environment and make suggestions about how to respond, they help an organization to adapt. Similarly, when workers voluntarily attend and actively participate in meetings (civic virtue or voice), they may enhance an organization's responsiveness by aiding the dissemination of valuable information. And when employees demonstrate a willingness to take on new responsibilities (sportsmanship) or learn new skills (self-development), they may improve an organization's ability to adapt to changes in its environment.

Finally, OCBs may enhance organizational performance by creating structural, cognitive, and relational forms of social capital (cf. Bolino, Turnley, & Bloodgood, 2002). For example, employees who exhibit helping to others enhance structural social capital by strengthening network ties, thereby improving information transfer, organizational learning, and the execution of organizational activities. Cognitive social capital may increase when employees attend meetings that are not required (civic virtue), thus acquiring useful knowledge about organizational activities and developments, and gaining a better understanding of the organization, its mission, and its culture. Similarly, employees who present their ideas and openly share their opinions with their coworkers (voice) enhance cognitive social capital by facilitating the creation of shared language and narratives within the organization. Finally, relational social capital is enhanced when employees build trust by helping coworkers with work-related problems.

To the extent that OCBs do the following, they can become a competitive advantage for the company: (a) enhance coworker or manager productivity, (b) free up resources, (c) help coordinate activities between coworkers, (d) help attract and retain the best employees, (e) enhance the organization's ability to adapt to environmental changes, and (f) create social capital.

Empirical Evidence of the Relationships Between OCB and Organizational Effectiveness

Although the previous discussion suggests that there are a number of plausible reasons that OCBs might be related to organizational effectiveness, when we first started our work on this topic in the early 1990s, only one study had examined this issue. To our knowledge, the first study to explore whether OCBs are related to group or organizational effectiveness was Karambayya (1990). She examined the relationship between work unit performance and satisfaction, and unit members' OCBs, in a sample of 18 intact work groups, composed primarily of white-collar and professional employees from 12 organizations. In her study, she obtained performance ratings for the work units from key division and department heads, employee OCB ratings from supervisors, and self-reports of satisfaction from employees. Consistent with her expectation, she found that employees in high-performing work units were more satisfied and exhibited more OCBs than employees in low-performing work units.

However, Karambayya's (1990) study had some limitations. First, Karambayya's measures of work group performance were subjective ratings provided by key informants in each of 12 organizations rather than quantitative indices of work unit or organizational success. Thus, although she observed a relationship between OCBs and subjective ratings of unit performance, the question of whether OCBs influence *objective* unit performance remained unanswered. For example, the strength of the relationship between OCBs and performance in Karambayya's study may have been influenced by the key informants' implicit theories (cf. Berman & Kenny, 1976; Bruner & Tagiuri, 1954) of the relationship between these two constructs. Second, we believe that there is some question about the construct validity of the measures Karambayya used. For example, although one of her OCB dimensions was labeled "interpersonal helping," the items used to measure this construct (e.g., "keeps quiet about doubts," "honestly expresses opinions," and so on) do not involve traditionally recognized forms of helping behavior. Third, because Karambayya had different raters evaluating performance in each of the 12 organizations in her sample, we do not know whether the measurement metric used by all of the raters was the same. Because the organizations probably differed in their products, services, corporate cultures, and standards, all the raters would probably not have used the same measurement metric. Fourth, as noted by Bagozzi, Yi, and Phillips (1991), measurement error can sometimes be quite high in key informant reports. Finally, although Karambayya identified 2 groups of work units and labeled 11 of them as "high" performing and seven of them as "low" performing, the two groups may have differed on other factors as well. Thus, although Karambayya's results were promising, they were far from conclusive.

Therefore, in the early 1990s, we began a series of studies (Ahearne, MacKenzie, & Podsakoff, 2004; MacKenzie, Podsakoff, & Ahearne, 1996; Podsakoff et al., 1997; Podsakoff & MacKenzie, 1994) that examined the relationships between OCBs and organizational effectiveness in a manner that avoided many of the limitations of Karambayya's research. Table 7.2 summarizes the results of our research along with the findings of other recent studies. The table reports the sample size, the nature of the objective measure of organizational performance used in the study, the types of OCBs influencing organizational effectiveness, and the percentage of variance in organizational effectiveness accounted for by the OCBs.

As indicated in the table, the majority of these studies used objective measures of unit performance, controlled for variations due to industry factors by sampling multiple units within the same organization, and used relatively traditional measures of OCBs. The researchers examined aspects of both the quantity and quality of performance, and they

Table 7.2   Summary of the Effects of OCBs on Group and/or Organizational Effectiveness

Researchers	Karambayya (1990)	Podsakoff & MacKenzie (1994)	Podsakoff, Ahearne, & MacKenzie (1997)	
			Paper mill work crews (N = 40)	
Sample	Work units from a variety of organizations (N = 18)	Insurance agency units (N = 116)	Quantity produced (% of maximum production)	Product quality (% of paper accepted)
Description of effectiveness measure	Key informant's evaluations of work unit's performance	Index of sales performance		
Helping behavior → Organizational performance	(+)	(−)	(+)	(+)
Civic virtue → Organizational performance	NA	(+)	ns	ns
Sportsmanship → Organizational performance	NA	(+)	(+)	ns
"Other" OCBs → Organizational performance	(+)	NA	NA	NA
Anti-citizenship behaviors → Organizational performance	NA	NA	NA	NA
R^2	46%	17%	26%	17%

(Continued)

Table 7.2 (Continued)

Researchers	MacKenzie, Podsakoff, & Ahearne (1996)	Koh, Steers, & Terborg (1995)	Walz & Niehoff (2000)					
Sample	Pharmaceutical sales teams (N = 306)		Limited-menu restaurants (N = 30)					
Description	(% of team sales quota)	School performance	Food cost % (waste)	Revenue FTE	Operating efficiency	Customer complaints	Customer satisfaction	Quality of performance
Helping behavior → Organizational performance	(+)	(+)	(−)	(+)	(+)	ns	(+)	(+)
Civic virtue → Organizational performance	(+)	NA	ns	ns	ns	(−)	ns	ns
Sportsmanship → Organizational performance	ns	NA	(−)	ns	ns	(−)	ns	ns
"Other" OCBs → Organizational performance	NA	ns	NA	NA	NA	NA	NA	NA
Anti-citizenship behaviors → Organizational performance	NA	(−)	NA	NA	NA	NA	NA	NA
R^2	16%	17%	43%	18%	15%	37%	39%	20%

Researchers	Koys (2001)				Dunlop & Lee (2004)			Ahearne, MacKenzie, & Podsakoff (2004)
Sample	Stores from a regional restaurant chain (N = 28)				Fast-food restaurants (N = 36)			Pharmaceutical sales teams (N = 533)
Description	Profit	Profit as a Percentage of sales	Customer satisfaction	Supervisors' ratings of performance	Drive–through service time	Counter service time	Unexplained food figures	% of Team Sales Quota
Helping behavior → Organizational performance	NA	NA	NA	NA	NA	NA	NA.	NA
Civic Virtue → Organizational Performance	NA	NA	NA	NA	NA	NA	NA.	NA
Sportsmanship → Organizational performance	NA	NA	NA	NA	NA	NA	NA.	NA
"Other" OCBs → Organizational performance	(+)	(+)	ns	ns	ns	ns	ns	(+)
Anti-citizenship behaviors → Organizational performance	NA	NA	NA	(−)	(+)	ns	(+)	NA
R^2	19%	21%	—	17%	39%	11%	15%	8%

NOTE: In the table, (+) indicates that the OCB of interest was significantly (positively) related to the criterion variable at the top of the column, (−) indicates that the OCB of interest was significantly (negatively) related to the criterion variable at the top of the column, ns indicates that the OCB of interest was included in the study but was *not* significantly related to the criterion variable at the top of the column after controlling for the other predictors, and NA (not applicable) indicates that the OCB of interest was *not* included in the study. The anti-citizenship behavior measures in the Koh et al. (1995) study were based on negatively worded compliance behaviors (e.g., takes undeserved breaks). In contrast, the anti-citizenship behavior measures in the Dunlop and Lee (2004) study included workplace deviance behaviors (e.g., falsifying receipts on reimbursement reports, discussing confidential company information with unauthorized persons, and so on).

conducted their studies in five distinct organizational contexts: insurance agency units, paper mill work crews, pharmaceutical sales teams, restaurants, and secondary schools.

Four of the studies reported in Table 7.2 (i.e., MacKenzie et al., 1996; Podsakoff et al., 1997; Podsakoff & MacKenzie, 1994; Walz & Niehoff, 2000) used variations of the scales developed by Podsakoff and MacKenzie (1994) to measure three OCB dimensions: helping behavior, sportsmanship, and civic virtue. The overall pattern of results for these studies provides general support for the hypothesis that OCBs are related to organizational effectiveness. On average, OCBs accounted for about 20% of the variance in performance quantity, more than 19% of the variance in performance quality, about 25% of the variance in financial efficiency indicators (operating efficiency, food cost percentage, and revenue full-time-equivalent), and about 38% of the variance in customer service indicators (customer satisfaction and customer complaints). Helping behavior was significantly related to every indicator of performance except customer complaints in the Walz and Niehoff (2000) study. Generally speaking, helping behavior was found to enhance performance. The only exception was that helping behavior had a negative impact on the quantity of performance in Podsakoff and MacKenzie's (1994) study, a result that they attributed to the unusually high level of turnover and other reasons unique to their insurance agency sample.

Sportsmanship had more limited effects; it enhanced the quantity of performance in two of the four samples in which it was studied (insurance agency units and paper mill work crews), and it increased some aspects of financial efficiency and customer service in the limited-menu restaurant sample. However, sportsmanship did not have any effect on performance in MacKenzie et al.'s (1996) sample of pharmaceutical sales teams. Finally, civic virtue was found to enhance the quantity of performance in Podsakoff and MacKenzie's (1994) insurance sales sample and MacKenzie et al.'s (1996) pharmaceutical sales sample and to reduce customer complaints in Walz and Niehoff's (2000) sample of limited-menu restaurants.

Two of the remaining samples (Ahearne et al., 2004; Koys, 2001) reported in Table 7.2 used a single composite measure of OCB based on the measures developed by Podsakoff and MacKenzie (1994). Koys reported that his composite measure of OCBs was positively related to restaurant profits ($R^2 = 19\%$) and profit as a percentage of sales ($R^2 = 21\%$) but not to customer satisfaction. Ahearne et al. (2004) reported that their composite measure of OCBs was positively related to the percentage of quota attained by pharmaceutical sales teams ($R^2 = 8\%$).

Koh, Steers, & Terborg's (1995) study used Smith et al.'s (1983) OCB scales. Koh et al. reported that Smith et al.'s scale factored into three dimensions that Koh et al. labeled altruism, positively worded compliance, and negatively worded compliance. Their negatively worded compliance measure included items such as "takes undeserved breaks." Koh et al. reported that although positively worded compliance did not have any effect on secondary school performance, altruism had a positive relationship, and negatively worded compliance had a negative relationship with this criterion variable ($R^2 = 17\%$). In addition to measuring OCBs directed at the organization.

Dunlop and Lee's (2004) study used items selected from previous OCB scales. Their scale explicitly included measures of workplace deviance behaviors. These behaviors, which are discussed more later in this chapter, include various discretionary forms of "anticitizenship" behaviors that are dysfunctional to the organization (e.g., discussing confidential company information with unauthorized people, falsifying expense reports, and so forth). Dunlop and Lee observed that OCBs directed at the organization had no effect on supervisory ratings of restaurant performance, drive-through service time, counter service time, or food wastage, but workplace deviance behaviors significantly decreased ratings of restaurant performance and significantly increased drive-through service time and food wastage. Together, the OCBs and workplace deviance behaviors accounted for 17% of the variance in supervisory ratings of restaurant performance, 39% of the variance in drive-through service time, 11% of the variance in counter service time (even though neither predictor was significant), and 15% of the variance in food wastage.

Thus, generally speaking, the empirical research clearly supports Organ's (1988) fundamental assumption that OCB is related to performance, although the evidence is stronger for some forms of OCB (e.g., helping) than for others (e.g., sportsmanship and civic virtue). In addition, after controlling for the effects of anticitizenship behavior, there is some question as to whether OCBs influence performance.

Conclusions

In this chapter, we focused on the potential effects of OCBs on organizational effectiveness and success. We provided several explanations for why OCBs would be expected to enhance organizational effectiveness.

Consistent with these hypotheses, the empirical evidence suggests that citizenship behaviors are, indeed, positively related to a variety of important organizational outcomes, such as the quantity and quality of work group productivity, sales team performance, customer satisfaction and complaints, sales revenue, profitability, and operating efficiency. Moreover, as we discuss in the next section, this pattern of findings is inconsistent with the idea that employees engage in OCBs simply for impression-management purposes. In our view, future research should give priority to examining the specific mechanisms that are responsible for the links between OCBs and organizational outcomes, the potential moderators of these relationships, and other types of extra-role behaviors that might have important organizational consequences.

Implications for Future Research

What Is the Direction of Causality Between OCB and Organizational Performance?

In our review of the empirical evidence, we interpreted the correlation found between OCBs and group or unit performance as an indication that OCBs *cause* performance to increase. However, because the vast majority of research in this domain is cross-sectional in nature, one cannot be completely certain whether OCB is the cause or the effect in the observed relationships. Indeed, it is also possible that units that perform well are more willing to engage in extra-role behaviors (e.g., helping, sportsmanship, and civic virtue) because high-performing units have more time, are under less pressure, and/or have members who are more satisfied than units that are not performing well. This argument suggests that a unit's level of performance *causes* OCBs rather than vice versa. Alternatively, the positive relationship between OCBs and unit effectiveness might be spurious. For example, high-performing groups might report that they engage in a great deal of OCBs not because they actually do, but because their implicit theories of performance suggest that high-performing groups help each other, are good sports, and exhibit civic virtue.

Indeed, Staw (1975) observed that group members may have implicit theories regarding the characteristics of effective groups and that these implicit theories may be used to infer the group's characteristics when the group receives feedback regarding their effectiveness. Bachrach et al. (2001) built upon the work of Staw when they examined the effects of positive and negative feedback on group members' ratings of OCBs exhibited in the group. They found that groups that were told that their performance was high rated themselves as exhibiting more OCBs than groups who were told that their performance was low—even though the feedback was *unrelated* to the groups' actual performance. These results suggest that the direction of causality may flow from performance to OCB, rather than vice versa, because the subjects in this study inferred their level of OCB based on the false feedback about their performance that they received. Bachrach et al. reasoned that the subjects in their study did this because they held an implicit theory that performance and OCB are related.

However, the findings of the Bachrach et al. (2001) study cannot explain all of the relationships between OCBs and unit performance reported in the literature, including the results of the study reported by Koys (2001). This researcher examined the relationships between OCBs and unit-level performance in a sample of limited-menu restaurants using a longitudinal design. He reported that the time-lagged OCB → performance correlation was stronger than the time-lagged performance → OCB correlation. More specifically, Koys found that although OCBs measured in year 1 in his sample of restaurants predicted both profit and profit as a percentage of sales in year 2 in the restaurants, neither of the measures of effectiveness measured in year 1 predicted OCBs in year 2. Therefore, these findings suggest that the OCBs exhibited causal priority over the measures of effectiveness in this study.

The findings of the Bachrach et al. (2001) and Koys (2001) studies help us understand the causal relationships between OCBs and organizational effectiveness as well as the potential mechanisms through which these variables are related. Nevertheless, additional research designed to more clearly establish the causal direction of relationships between these variables is needed, preferably through the use of experimental manipulations in laboratory settings. However, when that is not possible, longitudinal designs might be used. Although these designs are obviously not as good as experiments at establishing temporal priority and controlling for confounding factors, they provide better evidence than purely cross-sectional designs.

Moderators of the Relationship Between OCB and Organizational Effectiveness

Because OCBs have been linked to group and organizational effectiveness, researchers need to address several issues. One concern is that the pattern of effects across studies was not completely consistent. Indeed, as indicated in Table 7.2, helping behavior sometimes increased and sometimes decreased the quantity of performance, whereas sportsmanship and civic virtue seem to have affected this criterion variable in some samples but not in others. This finding suggests that there may be factors that moderate the impact of OCBs on the quantity of performance.

Podsakoff and MacKenzie (1997) identified several potential reasons that the relationship between helping behavior and the quantity of performance was negative in one sample (Podsakoff & MacKenzie, 1994) and positive in others (MacKenzie et al., 1996; Podsakoff et al., 1997). One reason for the differences in the findings involves the compensation systems in the three samples. In the insurance sales sample (Podsakoff & MacKenzie, 1994), the agents were compensated on the basis of their individual sales performance. Under such individualistic compensation systems, agents might be less willing to provide help to their peers, or they might be less concerned with the quality of their suggestions because helping their peers results in no personal benefits for them. On the other hand, in the pharmaceutical sales sample (MacKenzie et al., 1996), compensation was completely determined by team performance, and in the sample of paper mill work crews (Podsakoff et al., 1997), compensation was based partially on team performance and partially on the basis of job responsibilities and tenure. Thus, one could argue that when a portion of one's pay is determined by group effort, OCBs might be expected to be directed at helping and supporting one's peers.

Another potential reason the findings differ relates to the nature of the samples in the three studies. In the life insurance sample studied by Podsakoff and MacKenzie (1994), turnover was extremely high (45% in the first year of employment and more than 80% within the first five years), and the agents' average tenure with the company was only 5.29 years. This led Podsakoff and MacKenzie to speculate that although inexperienced agents may sell more with the help of experienced agents, many of the inexperienced agents may not stay with the company very long. Thus, the increase in the sales productivity of the inexperienced agents that results from the help they receive from the experienced agents may not offset the corresponding decrease in the experienced agents' sales caused by their taking time out to help inexperienced agents. In contrast, the average tenure of the crew members in the sample of paper mill employees studied by Podsakoff et al. (1997)

was more than 18 years, and the average tenure of the pharmaceutical salespeople studied by MacKenzie et al. (1996) was about 8 years. In these two studies, the helping behavior provided by crew members or pharmaceutical sales team members probably paid off in terms of increased productivity.

Still another potential moderator of the relationship between helping behavior and the quantity of performance may be the technological requirements of the job. Thompson (1967) differentiates between jobs that require long-linked technologies (which require cooperative effort or mutual dependence among employees) and mediating technologies (which don't). One might expect OCBs to be more critical to organizational success when long-linked technologies, as opposed to mediating technologies, are employed. Unlike the mediating technologies used in the insurance industry sample, which require virtually no cooperative effort or mutual dependence among the agents, the long-linked technologies used in the paper industry require what Thompson (1967) calls "serial interdependence" among the crew members. This type of interdependence demands a considerable amount of cooperative effort by the work group to accomplish the task. Thus, differences in the relationship between helping behavior and work unit performance in the two studies may, in part, reflect differences in the nature of the dependency relationships required in the different types of jobs included in the studies.

In addition to the potential moderators of the relationship between helping behavior and the quantity of performance, the results summarized in Table 7.2 suggest that moderators of the relationship between civic virtue and the quantity of performance may exist. For example, the results show that civic virtue had a positive impact on performance for the two sales samples but not for the paper mill sample. This pattern of findings could result from the nature of the job included in the samples. Salespeople are boundary spanners—that is, they are primary points of contact between a company and its customers, competitors, and the environment in general. As such, they often possess critical information that others in the organization do not possess—regarding customers, the competitive environment, and/or business trends—that allows the organization to adapt to changes in its environment. Thus, when salespeople actively participate in meetings, provide constructive suggestions about how to improve the way in which the organization does its business, and are willing to risk disapproval to express their beliefs about what is best for the organization, they may enhance the organization's performance more than when non–boundary-spanning employees engage in these behaviors. Future research should explore this possibility.

Another potential cause of the differential impact of civic virtue on the quantity of performance across settings, noted by Podsakoff et al. (1997), is the differential quality of suggestions or the nature of participation by work group members. Sometimes, a person's suggestions are not helpful, or that participation does not result in useful discourse for some organizations. In such cases, high civic virtue would not translate into high organizational effectiveness.

This discussion suggests that future research examining the relationship between OCBs and organizational effectiveness could benefit from examining the moderating effects of organizational context (i.e., the level of turnover, the nature of the compensation system, and so forth) as well as task and technological requirements (i.e., the nature of the technology and/or tasks that employees perform, the amount of teamwork required across jobs, and so forth). In addition, future research might also investigate the potential moderating effects of individual differences such as ability, experience, training, and knowledge. It seems plausible that an OCB such as helping behavior might have different effects on performance depending on whether it was performed in units in which employees are high in ability, experience, training, or knowledge, or in units in which employees are low in these areas.

Need to Examine the Mechanisms Through Which OCB Influences Organizational Performance

Because the available empirical evidence indicates that OCBs influence unit performance, future research should examine the mechanisms through which this influence occurs. As we noted in our earlier discussion, the several reasons that OCBs may influence unit performance raise some interesting questions. For example, do OCBs influence unit performance *directly*, by reducing the need to devote scarce resources to purely maintenance functions, or *indirectly*, by enhancing coworker or managerial productivity? Alternatively, is the impact of OCBs on unit performance *immediate*, because they serve as an effective means of coordinating the day-to-day activities of team members and across work groups, or *delayed*, because OCBs enhance the organization's ability to attract and retain the best people? Finally, do OCBs enhance the effectiveness of organizations because they reduce the variability in the quality of performance or because they allow the organization to adapt more effectively to environmental changes? Obviously, these are fundamentally different mechanisms, and it is important to understand which of them underlie the effects of OCBs on unit and work-group performance.

What Is the Nature of the Relationship Between OCBs That Managers Value and OCBs That Lead to Organizational Success?

Another interesting direction for future research would be to study the extent to which managers weight the importance of OCBs when evaluating their subordinates. Motowidlo and Van Scotter (1994) and Conway (1999) argued that overall ratings of performance can be taken as measures of an individual's overall value to an organization. This suggests that the weights that managers give to OCBs when forming their evaluations correspond to the actual impact that these OCBs have on unit/organizational performance. Interestingly, the existing empirical evidence (e.g., Podsakoff & MacKenzie, 1994) is only partially supportive of this expectation. Podsakoff and MacKenzie (1994) contrasted the relative effects of OCBs on managerial evaluations with their relative effects on organizational effectiveness. They found that managers tended to overvalue helping behavior and undervalue civic virtue, not necessarily in proportion to these behaviors' actual effects on organizational success. Although the researchers' data did not permit them to determine why managers would tend to undervalue or overvalue different forms of OCB, there are several possibilities. Managers may have incorrect implicit theories about how important certain forms of OCB should be to organizational performance. For example, managers' implicit theories might lead them to believe that employee helping behavior should be more closely related to organizational effectiveness than civic virtue is. Another possibility is that managers give greater weight to some forms of OCBs because they have a greater impact on the managers' own personal performance, even though these behaviors do not have a substantial impact on the organization's success. In fact, OCBs specifically directed at helping the manager might be valued by him or her more than those directed at other people in the work setting—particularly if these behaviors help the manager perform other duties or responsibilities that he or she considers critical to the manager's success. Of course, this raises the possibility that employees may exhibit OCBs more for their managers' approval than to help the organization become more successful (which is a point we return to in the next sub-section). Finally, the finding that managers undervalue or overvalue some OCBs (when compared to these behaviors' actual impact on organizational success) could be a methodological artifact that results from the common practice of obtaining OCB ratings from managers rather than from peers or subordinates. Managers' ratings of OCBs could be a poor reflection of the extent to which OCBs actually are occurring in the workplace. Regardless of which of these explanations is correct, it would be unwise to extrapolate too far the results of one study. Therefore, a priority for future research should be to determine whether the same sorts of discrepancies occur in other environments.

OCB vs. Impression Management Behavior

Because OCBs have beneficial effects for those who exhibit them, including enhanced evaluations and receipt of promotions and raises, employees may be motivated to engage in these behaviors for the purpose of creating a favorable impression (Bolino, 1999; Fandt & Ferris, 1990; Ferris, Judge, Rowland, & Fitzgibbons, 1994; Schnake, 1991). Indeed, Bolino (1999) and Schnake (1991) argued that it is impossible to tell, on the basis of the behavior alone, whether an employee is exhibiting altruistic or impression-management behavior. Although the same can be said of almost any other behavior exhibited in the presence of others, including task performance, they argue that the motive behind the behavior is important "because motivation is likely to adversely affect the impact of OCBs on organizations/work group effectiveness" (Bolino, 1999, p. 96). According to Bolino, there are two reasons for this supposition. First, "when individuals undertake actions based on impression management concerns, they are less able to devote their full attention to the task at hand. Consequently . . . this concern frequently impairs their performance" (Bolino, 1999, p. 90). Second, when OCBs are motivated by impression management, "individuals may consciously invest less effort or expend less energy in carrying out the behavior" (Bolino, 1999, p. 90). In other words, the quality (not the quantity) of the OCB is lower when employees are motivated by self-interest than when they are not.

Bolino's (1999) first point is an interesting one. Indeed, by the same logic, one would have to expect that OCBs performed for any motive (even altruistic ones) would undermine in-role task performance.

Although the idea that extra-role behavior takes time away from in-role performance is intuitively plausible, the existing empirical evidence provides little support for it. For example, the average correlation between OCB and in-role task performance is r = .08 in the studies that obtained measures of OCB and in-role task performance from separate sources (Lowery & Krilowicz, 1994; MacKenzie et al., 1991; MacKenzie, Podsakoff, & Paine, 1999; Motowidlo & Van Scotter, 1994; Podsakoff & MacKenzie, 1994; Van Scotter & Motowidlo, 1996) and r = .50 in studies that obtained both measures from the same source (Allen & Rush, 1998; Bagozzi, Verbeke, & Gavino, 2003; Barksdale & Werner, 2001; Chen, Tsui, & Farh, 2002; Ferris, Witt, & Hochwarter, 2001; Hui, Law, & Chen, 1999; MacKenzie, Podsakoff, & Rich, 2001; Podsakoff, MacKenzie, & Fetter, 1993; Podsakoff, Niehoff, MacKenzie, & Williams, 1993; Randall, Cropanzano, Borman, & Birjulin, 1999; Rupp & Cropanzano, 2002; Settoon, Bennett, & Liden, 1996; Turnley, Bolino, Lester, & Bloodgood, 2003; Van Dyne & LePine, 1998; Williams & Anderson, 1991). This pattern of results suggests two things. First, when common method variance is not present, there is very little relationship between OCB and in-role task performance. Indeed, the average shared variance is less than 1%. Second, when common method variance is present, OCB and in-role task performance ratings are more strongly related—but in exactly the *opposite* direction from the one predicted by Bolino. That is, the higher an employee's OCB, the higher his/her task performance. Thus, a great deal of empirical evidence suggests that at the individual level, OCB is either unrelated to task performance or positively related to it.

Bolino's (1999) second point is that when individuals are motivated by impression-management motives, the quality of their OCB is lower than when they are motivated by altruistic motives. To our knowledge, no evidence in the literature exists to support this proposition. Indeed, this argument may not make sense, because it assumes that an employee can derive the image-enhancing benefits of engaging in OCB without actually fully participating in the behavior that he or she is being credited for. Bolino gives the following example:

> Compared with those motivated by traditional motives, employees who join a task force for impression management reasons will be more likely to simply show up for meetings and do the minimum required for them. In other words, those volunteering because they sincerely desire to contribute to the organization will be likely to contribute to a greater extent than those who volunteer for impression management reasons. (Bolino, 1999, pp. 90-91)

Bolino's argument is that the supervisor will be deceived into thinking that both of these types of employees participated in the meeting to the same extent. However, we do not think this is plausible. In our opinion, if this supervisor were asked to evaluate the extent to which an employee of each type "actively participated in the meeting," he or she would rate the former as having participated less than the latter. In other words, the impression manager would have been rated lower on this aspect of OCB. If so, the supervisor's overall evaluation of this employee's contribution to the organization would be lower, and the employee would receive fewer rewards.

Therefore, although several researchers have argued that the only reason that many employees engage in OCB is to create a good impression, and that in these instances the behavior either contributes little (because it is of poor quality) or undermines task performance (because it takes time away from more important tasks), the existing empirical evidence provides little support for this contention, and the logical arguments on which it is based are of questionable validity. Indeed, if this view was correct, it would be hard to explain the findings reviewed in this chapter. If OCB were primarily a form of impression management that was of no real benefit (and perhaps even a detriment) to the organization, why would units that exhibit higher overall levels of OCB have significantly higher levels of objective performance? If OCB was unrelated to unit performance (because OCB is all for show and is of no real value) or negatively related to unit performance (because OCB takes time away from important in-role tasks), it would support this argument. However, the fact that OCB is positively related to objective unit performance is *not* consistent with this argument.

Although we do not believe that impression management can account for the empirical evidence of the relationship between OCB and unit performance discussed in this chapter, we do believe that additional research directed at the extent to which impression-management motives influence the quality or quantity of OCB occurring in a work unit is warranted and may be an interesting avenue for future research.

What Other Organizational Outcomes Would OCB Be Expected to Influence?

With a few exceptions, the majority of research that has been conducted to date has focused on the effects of OCBs on organizational effectiveness as measured by some form of financial measure. However, as noted by Kaplan and Norton (1996), the effectiveness of an organization is more than its financial performance, as measured by return on investment (ROI), profitability, and/or growth. It also includes the following factors that are interrelated in a firm's value chain: customer criteria (e.g., customer satisfaction, customer retention, brand equity), improvements in business processes (e.g., innovativeness, best practices, speed to market, product and service quality), and employee criteria (e.g., employee performance, employee satisfaction, employee turnover/ retention, and job involvement). Thus, additional research is needed on the relationship between OCBs and these other indicators of organizational effectiveness. Although Walz and Niehoff (2000) took an important step in this direction by including measures of customer satisfaction, customer complaints, and customers' perceptions of performance quality along with financial measures in their study of limited-menu restaurants, we do not yet have a clear understanding of how OCBs might influence different links in a firm's value chain.

What Other Types of Extra-Role Behaviors Might Have Important Organizational Consequences?

Finally, future researchers should examine the effects of other types of extra-role behavior on organizational effectiveness. Up to this point, we have focused only on how extra-role behavior aimed at people within the organization affects organizational success. However, several types of extra-role behavior other than OCBs are of potential interest. For example, to our knowledge, research has not examined the relationships between *customer-oriented behaviors (COBs)* and organizational performance. COBs are extra-role behaviors aimed at the customer, including serving as an interface between the customer and others in the organization, providing referrals for products or services from other companies, and giving the customer information about the industry. We would expect that customer-oriented behaviors would enhance organizational performance based on the nature of the behaviors themselves and the fact that the effects of in-role behaviors directed at customers (e.g., sales/ service-oriented behaviors) have been shown to be positively related to organizational effectiveness (George & Bettenhausen, 1990; Kizilos & Cummings, 1996; Narver & Slater, 1990). In our view, future research needs to focus on identifying the dimensions of COB and more clearly articulate the difference between this type of behavior and sales/service-oriented behavior. Second, the impact of COBs on performance should be examined in the context of the effects of the other forms of extra-role behavior to gain a better understanding of their relative contribution to organizational success. Finally, future research should attempt to identify potential moderators of the relationship between COBs and organizational performance.

Yet another interesting direction for future research would be to examine the effects of extra-role behaviors that are detrimental to the organization. These might include anticitizenship behaviors, workplace deviance (cf. Bennett & Robinson, 2000; Dunlop & Lee, 2004), lack of sportsmanship (cf. Podsakoff & MacKenzie, 1994), and voluntary forms of counterproductive work behavior like unruliness, gossiping about coworkers, blaming coworkers for problems, and competing with coworkers nonbeneficially (cf. Kelloway, Loughlin, Barling, & Nault, 2002; Lau, Au, & Ho, 2003; Martinko, Gundlach, & Douglas, 2002; Miles, Borman, Spector, & Fox, 2002; Sackett, 2002; Spector & Fox, 2002). Indeed, the research reported by Dunlop and Lee (2004) discussed earlier in this chapter suggests that these types of behavior can have important effects on organizational performance, even in the context of OCBs. Similarly, Koh et al. (1995) found that negative forms of compliance also influenced organizational effectiveness. However, their study draws attention to the fact that some of the so-called counterproductive behaviors that have been examined in the literature—for example, negative compliance, work avoidance, unwarranted absenteeism, failure to follow safety regulations, selling proprietary company information, lying about hours worked, taking kickbacks from customers—may not actually be extra-role behaviors at all. Rather, they may be better categorized as negative forms of in-role behavior. Nevertheless, we believe that future research on the relationships between these types of negative extra-role behaviors and organizational performance should be conducted.

 **8**   Implications for
HR Practitioners and
OCB Researchers

The research we reviewed in this book demonstrates that OCBs enhance organizational effectiveness and that managers give them a considerable amount of weight when evaluating employees' overall contribution to the organization's success. The implications of this finding are twofold: (a) managers should do whatever they can to try to encourage OCBs, and (b) researchers should develop a deeper level of understanding of this phenomenon. Thus, in this chapter, we discuss what human resource (HR) practitioners can do to encourage OCBs without diminishing task performance, and we explore the conceptual and/or methodological issues that researchers need to address to further our understanding of this important organizational behavior.

Implications for HR Practitioners

In earlier chapters, we discussed some of the things that managers can do in terms of their own behavior, the structuring of subordinate tasks, and the shaping of the climate in which employees work to increase the probability of OCB. In this section, we shift our focus to those HR system practices that may also influence OCB. First, we discuss how recruiting and selection practices may be used to identify candidates with a propensity to exhibit OCBs in the workplace. Next, we examine how training and development procedures can be used to enhance the ability and motivation of employees to engage in OCBs. We also discuss the impact of different compensation systems and employee benefit programs on OCB. Finally, we explore the potential effects that characteristics of performance-appraisal procedures have on OCB.

Recruiting and Selection

The evidence we have reviewed in this book would suggest that OCBs are related to organizational effectiveness and success (e.g., refer to Table 7.2 in Chapter 7). This would imply that job candidates selected on the basis of their predisposition to exhibit OCB should help improve organizational effectiveness. At a minimum, this means that the selection criteria for employees should match the factors that determine success on the job. To do so, HR practitioners need to engage in comprehensive job analyses to identify OCBs that are critical to job success. Research suggests that current job analyses may not adequately recognize the impact of OCBs on job performance. Perhaps the first to call attention to this fact were Orr, Sackett, and Mercer (1989), who noted that OCBs were often neglected in job analyses even though most managers in their study assigned a dollar value to these behaviors as well as to task performance.

In addition to including the critical behaviors identified in job analyses, selection procedures also must weight these behaviors in a manner that corresponds to their importance in influencing job success. For example, if OCBs are as important to job success as task performance is, we would want them to be weighted equally in the selection process. Although some research indicates that the propensity of job candidates to exhibit OCB is one of the factors evaluated in interviews and used in making selection decisions (e.g., Gatewood & Feild, 1998; Seiss & Jackson, 1970; Werner, 2000), to our knowledge, there is little empirical evidence regarding the weight given to this information. However, research on promotability ratings reviewed in Chapter 6 (Shore et al., 1995; Van Scotter, Motowidlo, & Cross, 2000) may shed some light on this subject. This research suggests that OCBs are given a substantial amount of weight by managers when rating the promotability of their subordinates. It is not clear, however, whether the weight they give to OCBs is too much, too little, or about right. The answer would depend upon the actual impact of these behaviors on job success. This issue would be an interesting one for future research to investigate.

Assuming that an HR practitioner has identified the relevant OCBs and has decided what weights should be given to them, the next step would be to design selection procedures to assess a candidate's propensity to engage in these behaviors. A variety of procedures could be used for this purpose, including interviews, paper-and-pencil tests, job sampling, and/or assessment centers. In the case of paper-and-pencil tests, one might try to test for those traits or personality characteristics that have been shown to be predictors of OCB. For example, one might use measures of conscientiousness as predictors of OCB, because research suggests that this personality characteristic is associated with generalized compliance or job dedication. However, generally speaking (as noted in Chapter 4), the evidence regarding the relationship between personality traits and OCB is not very compelling.

Alternatively, one could also use the interview to predict OCB. Several researchers (e.g., Gatewood & Feild, 1998; Werner, 2000) have noted that the interview may be a particularly well-suited way to select people who exhibit OCB. Gatewood and Feild (1998) argued that interviews are particularly good for assessing two main types of characteristics: "personal relations, such as sociability and verbal fluency, and good citizenship, such as dependability, conscientiousness, stability and perseverance" (p. 482). As noted by Werner (2000), the traits described as good citizenship are similar to some forms of OCB. Research by Latham and Skarlicki (1995) suggests that the situational interview may be an effective way to assess the propensity to engage in OCB. In a study of 47 business school faculty members, they found that situational interviews significantly predicted faculty peer ratings of OCB toward the organization (r = .50) as well as toward individuals within it (r = .30).

In a follow-up study, Allen, Facteau, and Facteau (2004) found evidence that: (a) interview ratings for what they called "organizational support" significantly predicted (r = .36) peer ratings of the extent to which those interviewed engaged in OCBs aimed at supporting the organization (e.g., following organizational rules and policies, and endorsing, supporting, and defending the organization), and (b) the interview ratings for "conscientious initiative" (e.g., successful task completion and organizational initiative) significantly predicted (r = .50) peer ratings of the extent to which those interviewed exhibited organizational initiative, but (c) the interview score for "personal support" did not predict peer ratings of helping and cooperating with others. Moreover, their research demonstrated that this pattern of findings could not have been due to faking. This suggests that interviews may be an effective way of assessing the extent to which candidates are likely to engage in OCBs on the job. However, because the interview score for organizational support also predicted conscientious initiative and personal support, and the interview score for personal support predicted conscientious initiative, there are some questions about the discriminant validity of the interview scores.

The findings reported by Latham and Skarlicki (1995) and Allen et al. (2004) are encouraging in that they suggest that it may be possible to use interviews to assess a candidate's propensity to exhibit OCB. However, it is important to note that in both of these studies, the researchers developed specific questions to assess OCB propensities, and raters received special training on how to evaluate answers to these questions. Therefore, interviewers may require additional training to assess these behaviors in interview settings.

The fact that situational interview procedures are predictive of OCBs in work settings suggests that job samples or assessment centers activities might also be effective in predicting a job candidate's tendency to exhibit OCBs in the workplace. Although we are not aware of any research that has examined this issue, in principle, we believe that it should be possible to design activities that give people an opportunity to exhibit helpfulness, voice, sportsmanship, and so on. For example, to rate a job candidate's helping behavior, a researcher could design an activity in which an assessee who is busy working on a required task is asked to help a coworker (a confederate of the researcher or a member of the assessment team) who is experiencing difficulty with a task he or she is trying to complete. Or, to rate the candidate's organizational loyalty, one might ask the candidate to play the role of an employee in an organization and then observe how the candidate responds to criticisms of the organization by a coworker and/or an outsider.

Regardless of the specific selection procedure used to assess a candidate's tendency to engage in OCB, researchers need to make sure that the scores from the assessment procedures are valid predictors of job success.

Training and Development

Werner (2000) noted that most of the effort directed at encouraging OCBs has focused on selection rather than on training and development. However, there is no reason to assume that people cannot be trained to perform OCBs, just as they can be taught any other form of work behavior. Indeed, Kelly and Caplan (1993) provided evidence that suggests that average performers can be trained to be star performers if they are taught to go beyond the explicit requirements of their job and to exhibit greater initiative. People could be trained in a similar manner to perform OCBs.

In addition, to the extent that it is considered part of training, mentoring may also be used to increase OCB. Two studies (Donaldson,

Ensher, & Grant-Vallone, 2000; Tepper & Taylor, 2003) have examined the effects of workplace mentoring on OCB. In a longitudinal study, Donaldson et al. (2000) examined how variations in the quality of the mentoring received influenced organizational outcomes (organizational commitment and OCB). Building on the work of McManus and Russell (1997), these authors argued that, for the following reasons, mentoring should increase OCBs among those being mentored: Mentoring is often an OCB, mentors serve as role models of OCB by being good mentors, and good mentors provide support to their protégés. Their sample consisted of 157 ethnically diverse, nonprofessional employees who provided data in two waves collected 6 months apart. Each of the participants had the same mentor in both time periods. The quality of the mentoring relationship was categorized into three levels (high, moderate and low), based on the amount of instrumental and psychosocial support the protégés received from their mentors. In support of their hypotheses, Donaldson et al. (2000) reported that, in both time periods, protégés who reported high- and moderate-quality mentoring relationships also reported engaging in higher levels of altruism than protégés who reported low-quality mentoring relationships. However, in both time periods, peer reports of OCB did not support their hypotheses. Thus, common method biases might have influenced their findings.

Tepper and Taylor (2003) attempted to examine the mechanism through which mentoring behavior influences OCB. In a sample of military personnel, they found that mentoring by a leader influenced subordinate OCB indirectly (rather than directly) through its effects on subordinates' perceptions of procedural justice. In addition, because they obtained the ratings of mentoring behavior and OCB from different sources, common method biases pose less of a threat to the internal validity of this study than to Donaldson et al.'s (2000) study. Nevertheless, because only a few studies have empirically tested the effects of mentoring on OCB, additional research is needed before any conclusive statements regarding the relationship between mentoring and OCB can be made.

Individual Merit-Based Pay Systems

As we have discussed, the empirical evidence indicates that: (a) OCBs are related to organizational effectiveness, and (b) managers take them into account when evaluating an employee's performance. Therefore, one might reasonably conclude that employees ought to be explicitly compensated for them, especially because there is ample evidence that behaviors that are rewarded tend to increase in frequency. However, such compensation is difficult to implement due to two related problems that arise from the inherent difficulty of getting a complete picture of an employee's OCB. Recall that in Chapter 6 we noted that the main reason that raters (i.e., self, coworkers, and supervisors) often disagree in their ratings of the extent to which OCBs occur may be differences in their ability to observe these behaviors. Thus, the person allocating the rewards may not be able to observe all of the OCB that actually occurs, and therefore some (or even many) instances of OCB may not get rewarded. This weakens the behavior-reward contingency.

A second problem arises from the first. Because only the OCBs that are observed and rewarded will increase in frequency, the frequency of the most conspicuous, easy-to-observe forms of OCB will likely increase, but the forms of OCB that are more difficult for the person administering the rewards to observe will probably decrease. According to the Law of Relative Effect (Brown & Herrnstein, 1975), whenever we increase the rate of reward for some designated behavior, we automatically decrease the relative rate of reward for competing behaviors and cause them to decline in frequency. This suggests that forms of OCB that occur in the presence of the supervisor administering the rewards (e.g., sportsmanship or civic virtue) may increase in frequency, and forms of OCB that are not observable by the supervisor (e.g., altruism, courtesy, peacekeeping, cheerleading, and so on) may be extinguished. This may not result in the mix of OCBs that would maximize organizational effectiveness.

Another issue that may arise from explicitly linking rewards to OCB is the so-called overjustification effect (Deci, 1971, 1975; Lepper & Greene, 1978). In brief, studies of this phenomenon find that when salient extrinsic incentives—especially those involving some aspect of pay—are superimposed on a preexisting natural inclination to perform some behavior, the frequency of the behavior increases, but when the extrinsic incentive is removed, both the behavior and the apparent intrinsic attraction to it decline below original baseline levels. Several researchers have advanced competing explanations for this phenomenon, but the one that appears to meet with the most acceptance is some version of Deci's own "cognitive-evaluation" explanation. This theory suggests that salient extrinsic incentives may have the effect of causing us to revise our conception of the causes of our behavior. Absent any such incentive, a person's implicit inference is that the person does what he or she does for its own sake—that is, because I enjoy doing it, because it's the right thing to do, or because it's the kind of thing a person like me would do. However, given the introduction of an explicitly defined extrinsic contingency, whatever the incremental effect on the behavior targeted by the contingency, we may begin to attribute our action to the extrinsic incentive rather than to our natural inclination. The extrinsic incentive drives out the original motive, whatever that may have been. Thus, cognitive-evaluation theory predicts that the underlying motivational basis of OCB may change when salient contingencies for pay intrude in our cognitive field.

However, Deci (1975) himself noted that rewards made contingent upon task performance can convey two types of information. First, as previously described, rewards can draw attention to the inducement for the behavior and lead people to believe that it was the reward and not their interest in the activity that caused them to engage in the behavior. Under these circumstances, employees perceive rewards as instrumental to the behavior, and the frequency of the behavior will decrease if the rewards are withdrawn. Second, rewards can signal employees' meritorious accomplishment and inspire feelings of competence that are satisfying and that generalize to the task, thereby enhancing intrinsic motivation. Indeed, as Lepper and Greene (1976) observed, "To the extent that such information [from rewards] leads a person to believe that he has been successful and is personally responsible for his success, we expect that intrinsic motivation to engage in the task is enhanced" (p. 33).

Thus, the question is, which signal is the most salient: the inducement for the behavior or the signal of competence? Rosenfield, Folger, and Adelman (1980) achieved the following results in an experimental study they conducted to examine this issue:

> In the conditions in which subjects thought their rate of pay was based on their competence (the competency-feedback conditions) high pay led to greater willingness to work on the task in the future, greater liking for the task, and more free time spent . . . with the task than did low pay. In the other conditions, in which the rate of pay was determined randomly and did not reflect the subjects' ability, it was found that high pay led to less willingness to work on the task in the future, less liking for the task, and less free time spent on the task regardless of whether the pay was contingent. Thus the presence or absence of competency feedback seems to be a crucial determinant of intrinsic motivation. When greater rewards indicate greater competence, increases are associated with increases in intrinsic motivation. But when greater rewards do not mean greater competence, increases in rewards are associated with decreases in intrinsic motivation regardless of

whether the rewards are contingent. Thus contingency itself is not an important determinant of the effect of pay on intrinsic motivation.

Why should the presence or absence of competency feedback be critical in determining whether deficits in intrinsic motivation will occur as a result of contingent reward? In the absence of information about one's level of competence, being offered a high rate of pay is more likely to be viewed as an inducement to work on the task or to "take the job." Thus the attribution that "I did it for the money" is salient, and one's interest in the task is likely to be discounted as the reason for agreeing to undertake the task. The situation is different, however, when a person is offered a high rate of pay because he or she has demonstrated a high level of ability. Under these circumstances, the coercive aspect of rewards is less salient because the high level of payment offered reflects the person's high degree of competence rather than some special inducement. Thus, competency-based rewards are seen as tributes to one's skills rather than inducements to work on the task. Under these circumstances, one is less likely to make the attribution that "I did it for the money." Rather a person is more likely to experience the satisfying feelings associated with successful accomplishment and mastery of a task . . . , and such feelings are congruent with intrinsic motivation. (pp. 374–375)[1]

Interestingly, regardless of whether pay represents an extrinsic inducement or signals an employee's competence, the implications for the design of organizational pay systems to encourage OCBs are the same. If the pay system makes the inducement for engaging in OCBs salient, then intrinsic interest in OCB will decline, and the behavior will continue only as long as it is continuously rewarded. This would suggest that pay systems should be structured so that the inducement is less salient. This might be done by obscuring the contingency between pay and individual acts of OCB by using a variable ratio reinforcement schedule. Indeed, because pay decisions are made yearly in most organizations, the contingency between rewards and specific OCBs could never be very tight. On the other hand, for the pay system to be able to cause rewards to be viewed as a signal of competence, the rewards would have to be associated with achievements that are viewed as significant by the employee. However, because individual acts of OCB are likely to be fairly trivial in nature, OCB should probably be rewarded only in the aggregate over time—in other words, employers should use a ratio schedule of reinforcement in which the cumulative number of instances of OCB that is rewarded is large enough to be viewed as a significant accomplishment by the employee and a signal of his/her competence. Thus, a pay system that rewards OCB should increase the frequency of OCB as long as the contingency between pay and OCB is of the type described.

To our knowledge, there is no research that directly tests the effects of explicitly linking pay to OCB. However, in light of this discussion, this topic would be a fruitful direction for future research.

Although no research has investigated the effects of explicitly rewarding OCB, some researchers (Deckop, Mangel, & Cirka, 1999; Deckop, Merriman, & Blau, 2004) have studied the effects of explicitly rewarding task performance (narrowly defined) on OCB. In general, researchers hypothesized that pay-for-performance systems that narrowly define performance to include only task performance should decrease the frequency of OCB. The rationale articulated by Deckop, Mangel, and Cirka (1999, p. 421) is that pay-for-performance systems

> encourage employees to maximize their individual performance, or in-role effort. A possible by-product, however, may be a reduction in the effort devoted to OCB. By clearly specifying behaviors, and outputs that will be rewarded, organizations risk discouraging behaviors that will not be explicitly rewarded.

Deckop et al. (1999) tested this general proposition in a field study with a sample of 146 public utility employees in which they also hypothesized that employees' value alignment would moderate the strength of this effect. More specifically, they hypothesized that for employees whose values were not aligned very strongly with those of the organization, there would be a negative relationship between OCBs and the extent to which employees perceived their pay to be contingent upon task performance (narrowly defined). However, for employees whose values were highly aligned with the organization, they predicted that no relationship would exist between OCB and employees' perceptions that pay was linked tightly to task performance. Consistent with their expectations, in their sample of 146 public utility employees, they found that the perception that pay was linked to task performance had a negative impact on OCB for employees low on value alignment but that it had no impact on OCB for employees high on value alignment. In a follow-up study, Deckop, Merriman, and Blau (2004) found that the effects of pay-for-performance plans on OCB were also moderated by the risk preferences of employees. More specifically, they found that the relationship between OCB and the extent to which an employee is motivated to work hard because of the organization's merit pay system was negative when employees were risk averse but positive when employees had a high risk prefer-ence. Thus, some empirical evidence supports the proposition that pay-for-performance systems that narrowly define performance to include only task performance may decrease the frequency of OCB. However, the strength of this effect may be moderated by individual differences.

Profit-Sharing Plans

In addition to pay systems based on individual merit, another compensation approach that could be used to encourage OCBs takes the form of group- and organization-wide incentive schemes, such as the Scanlon Plan (Schuster, 1983). In such arrangements, individual merit is not at issue; instead, remuneration hinges on the total performance of the larger unit, with benefits allotted equally to members or in proportion to some other acceptable criterion, but not necessarily with respect to individual productivity. Insofar as motivational dynamics are concerned, the effects of such programs bear considerable similarity to the loosely contingent reward systems based on an individual's total contribution, because any one individual can hope but not know that a specific OCB has an ultimate or indirect link to personal gains. Individual productivity is, in effect, modestly encouraged, and at the very least, OCB is not discouraged. The additional virtue of Scanlon-type plans is that they do not require—although they permit—an explicit declaration or judgment of what a person's total contribution is, and thus they give employees little reason to perceive real or imagined inequities about such judgments.

To our knowledge, only one study has attempted to examine the effects of a gain-sharing plan on OCB. O'Bannon and Pearce (1999) argued that the linking of employee rewards through a group gain-sharing system causes employees to develop a vested interest in the outcomes of their fellow employees and, as a result, should foster OCB. Their rationale is that by " . . . helping coworkers, the self-interested employee is indirectly benefiting him or herself via improved group performance and subsequent group rewards" (O'Bannon & Pearce, 1999, p. 368). They attempted to test the effect of a gain-sharing plan on OCB, but unfortunately the design of their study did not permit a valid test to be conducted, because the companies differed in more aspects than simply whether they implemented a gain-sharing program, and little information was provided regarding how long the "treatments" had been in effect. Thus, although these researchers had a plausible hypothesis, it has yet to be rigorously tested.

Performance Appraisal

Because performance appraisals are directly related to pay, training, advancement opportunities, and career success, the fairness of the appraisals (distributive justice), and the manner by which they are derived (procedural justice), are of paramount interest to employees (cf. Cohen-Charash & Spector, 2001; Colquitt, 2001; Folger & Greenberg, 1985; Greenberg, 1987; Landy, Barnes, & Murphy, 1978; Landy, Barnes-Farrell, & Cleveland, 1980). Our review of the extant literature indicates that managers rely heavily on OCBs—either knowingly or unknowingly—when evaluating employees. As a result, unless they make sure their employees understand that these behaviors are important, they run the risk of undermining employee perceptions of the fairness of the evaluation process. If employees are confused about the relevant appraisal criteria or deem them unfair, these perceptions may undermine employees' job satisfaction and productivity (Kanfer, Sawyer, Earley, & Lind, 1987), and strain their relationship with their manager.

In addition, managers who fail to inform employees of the importance of OCBs in determining their evaluations may obscure employees' perceptions of the organization's reward contingencies. The use of OCBs as a performance evaluation criterion without the employee's awareness undermines the manager's effectiveness for two reasons. First, employees are unlikely to engage in OCBs as much as the manager might like, because the employees do not realize the importance their managers place on them. Second, employees may actually stop performing important in-role behaviors, because they might begin to think that the manager does not administer rewards on a contingent basis. Thus, if managers are going to set up effective reinforcement contingencies, they must make sure that their employees are aware that they value OCB.

In principle, this would suggest that managers need to clearly communicate to employees that OCBs are important to the organization and will influence the employees' performance appraisal. Managers also need to clarify the relative importance of OCB and task performance. Both are needed for the performance appraisal to be perceived as fair and for it to be effective in shaping the employee's behavior.

If managers fail to communicate the relative importance of OCBs in influencing employees' performance evaluation, the employees' perception of the fairness of the appraisal will depend upon whether the employee and the manager weight OCBs in a similar way. Thus, managers who give a substantial amount of weight to OCBs in their evaluations without telling their employees will be perceived as unfair by employees who feel that OCBs are not an important part of their job (because the OCBs are not part of their formal job description) but will be perceived as fair by employees who feel that OCBs are an important contribution to the success of the organization (regardless of whether OCBs are included in the formal job description). The potential discrepancy between the weights used by managers in appraising performance and weights employees feel are fair could be examined in a policy-capturing study. This type of study could be used to determine the extent to which individual managers include OCBs in their evaluations and the extent to which employees would include them if they were evaluating the performance of employees. Based on this information, researchers could then examine the correlation between employee perceptions of fairness and the similarity of the weights used by the manager and each employee.

Another factor that influences employees' perceptions of the fairness of the evaluation system is the potential gap between the nominal weights that managers say they assign to OCBs in their evaluations and the effective weights that they actually use. Our review of the empirical literature reported in Chapter 5 suggests that OCBs explain about as much variance in managerial evaluations of employee performance as does task performance. However, remember that these are the "effective" weights that reflect the relative contributions of OCBs and task performance, given the range of variation in these factors observed across these studies, not the "nominal" weights that reflect the managers' perceptions of how important these factors ought to be. In principle, perhaps the nominal weight that managers believe should be assigned to task performance should be three times more than the weight assigned to OCBs. However, if there is less variance in task performance than in OCBs, because task performance is considered by most employees to be a nondiscretionary part of their job that they must perform to retain employment, then OCBs may account for more variance in the evaluations even though they are less important than task performance. For example, if task performance varies only one third as much as OCBs, then the effective weights of the two in the manager's evaluation of the employee will be equal, even though the manager's nominal weight for task performance was three times higher than for OCB. Indeed, Murphy and Shiarella (1997) demonstrate that, generally speaking,

> Regardless of the organization's stated policy, if subjects actually differ more on one of the performance dimensions than on the other, the effective weight of each performance facet in defining overall job performance might be substantially different from the nominal weight. (p. 832).

Thus, even when managers are careful to communicate their nominal weights to employees, they need to be aware of the potential gap between the effective and nominal weights they assign to OCB in their evaluations of employees because of the effect that this gap has on employee perceptions of the fairness of the performance-appraisal process.

To our knowledge, no actual research in organizational settings has attempted to address the issues we have discussed in this section. However, some research has investigated how the characteristics of the performance-appraisal system/process influence OCBs. Findley, Giles, and Mossholder (2000) examined this issue using a sample of 199 teachers employed in two school systems in the Southeastern United States. The performance-appraisal system characteristics included the system openness (e.g., employees can file a protest if they feel their performance evaluation is wrong), system commitment (e.g., the company puts forth a great deal of effort to be sure that the appraisal system works well), system complexity (e.g., the appraisal system is too complex for the average employee to understand), and multiple inputs (e.g., my supervisor receives input from other managers when evaluating my performance). The performance-appraisal process characteristics included supervisor observation (e.g., my supervisor has adequately observed my performance during the past year), feedback/voice (e.g., in my appraisal-review session, my supervisor considered my views regarding my performance), and planning (e.g., in the appraisal-review session, my supervisor discussed plans and objectives to improve my performance). Findley et al. (2000) reported that supervisor observation and planning were the only performance-appraisal characteristics to influence OCBs. More specifically, employees' perceptions that their supervisor observed their behavior was positively related to OCBs, and their perception that their supervisor discussed plans and objectives for improving their performance was negatively related to this criterion variable. Findley et al. (2000) argued that the unexpected negative relationship between planning and OCB might be accounted for by the fact that the planning discussion may have focused on specific task behaviors, to the exclusion of OCB. Another possibility is that supervisors may have taken greater care to discuss plans and objectives for improving performance with employees who were low performers in the first place with respect to both in-role behavior and OCB.

All this research suggests that it is critical (although perhaps difficult) for managers to clearly communicate the relative importance of OCBs in the performance-appraisal process. Failure to do so will lead to decreased levels of OCB because it will undermine perceptions of the fairness of the appraisal system and confuse the reward contingencies in the organization. In addition, the study by Findley et al. (2000) suggests that it is essential for employees to perceive that their managers are actively observing and/or monitoring their job performance and for managers to take steps to include OCBs as well as task performance in developmental discussions with their employees.

Implications for OCB Researchers

In addition to having ramifications for HR practitioners, the research discussed in this book has important implications for those interested in conducting research on OCB. In this section, we highlight what we consider to be some of the more important issues in need of further investigation. First, we discuss issues that are primarily conceptual in nature. Next, we identify research issues that have both conceptual and methodological implications. Finally, we explore issues that are primarily methodological in nature.

Conceptual Issues

Nature and Types of OCB

A major unresolved issue is whether important additional forms of OCB that have not been recognized in the literature exist and whether those forms that have already been identified are really distinct from each other. In the appendix, we make an attempt to address the first of these issues. In our view, there are additional forms of OCB (e.g., self-development and individual initiative) that may prove worthwhile to examine. With respect to the question of the distinctiveness of the various forms of OCB, we believe this depends not only on whether the measures of the OCBs exhibit discrimimant validity but upon whether the types of OCBs are shown to have different antecedents and consequences.

Another conceptual issue that merits further investigation is whether other types of extra-role behavior exist that might have important consequences. To date, the literature has focused almost exclusively on the effect that extra-role behavior *aimed at people within the organization* has on organizational success. However, Podsakoff and MacKenzie (1997) and Podsakoff MacKenzie, Paine, & Bachrach (2000) suggested that it might also be worthwhile to examine the impact of extra-role behaviors *aimed at the customer* on organizational success. As noted in Chapter 7, one might expect that customer-oriented behaviors (COBs) like these would enhance organizational performance. Such a finding would not be surprising based on the nature of the behaviors and the fact that the effects of in-role behaviors directed at customers (e.g., sales/service oriented behaviors) have been found to be positively related to organizational effectiveness.

It would also be a good idea to examine the effects of extra-role behaviors that are detrimental to the organization, including anticitizenship behaviors, workplace deviance, poor sportsmanship, and voluntary forms of counterproductive work behavior (e.g., unruliness, gossiping about coworkers, blaming coworkers for problems, and competing with coworkers nonbeneficially). Although additional research on this issue is needed, the evidence gathered to date suggests that some of these behaviors have effects on performance over and above the effects of OCB. One specific issue that needs to be addressed is whether some of the so-called counterproductive extra-role behaviors that have been examined in the literature (e.g., work avoidance, unwarranted absenteeism, failure to follow safety regulations, and so on) are better thought of as negative forms of in-role behavior. Regardless of how this issue is resolved, examination of these behaviors—especially a comparison of their effects to the effects of OCB—would be a worthy course of further investigation.

Mediating Mechanisms

Turning our attention to the antecedents and consequences of OCB, our review of the literature suggests that greater attention should be directed at (a) the key mechanisms that leadership behaviors, task characteristics, group characteristics, organizational characteristics, and cultural context work through to influence OCBs; and (b) the mediating mechanisms that influence the effects of OCBs on individual and organizational outcomes.

In the case of the antecedents of OCBs, among the most prominent mediators that have been identified are trust in one's leader and the organization, satisfaction, a sense of obligation or a feeling of responsibility, a need to reciprocate, social norms/expectations, a sense of commitment, perceptions of fairness, and liking for the supervisor. In addition, we have suggested that task, group, and organizational characteristics— such as covenantal relationships, group efficacy/potency, group identity, and group cohesiveness—should also be examined as potential mediators. This is important, because we currently know much more about what influences OCBs than why these things influence it.

A similar state of affairs exists in terms of our knowledge about the mediators of the effects of OCBs on individual-level and organizational-level outcomes. At the individual level, we identified several potential reasons that managers may value OCBs and take them into account when evaluating employee performance (see Table 6.1 in Chapter 6). However, most of the studies that have been conducted at this level of analysis have not attempted to examine the reasons that managers include OCBs in their evaluations or reward-allocation decisions. At the organizational level, even less research has focused on the potential mechanisms through which OCBs influence effectiveness or success. As noted in Chapter 7, future research should examine whether OCBs influence organizational performance directly or indirectly through one or more of the mediators identified in Table 7.1 and whether these effects occur immediately or only after a delay.

In addition to investigating the mediating mechanisms themselves, future research should examine whether the cultural context influences the nature of the mechanisms giving rise to OCBs as well as those that determine their impact on important organizational outcomes. For example, is a mediator like the sense of obligation more important as a determinant of OCBs in collectivist cultures than in individualistic cultures? Is the perception of fairness more important in determining OCBs in individualistic cultures than in collectivist cultures? Do different forms of OCBs influence managerial evaluations through different mechanisms in different cultures? Is the importance of OCBs in determining organizational success, and are the mechanisms through which OCBs influence organizational success, different across cultures? These are important questions that have not been addressed adequately in the research literature.

Additional Consequences of OCB

Research indicates that OCBs have a number of important consequences for individuals, including the fact that they enhance managerial evaluations of overall performance, reward recommendations, awards, and promotions. However, as noted in Chapter 6, other possible consequences of OCBs should be examined in future research.

OCBs may decrease the probability of being laid off or terminated in the case of an organizational downsizing, increase the likelihood of being assigned to a high-profile job, increase opportunities for advanced training, lead to closer leader-member exchange relationships, result in the employee being given more autonomy in deciding how to perform his or her job, and/or enhance an employee's perceptions of his or her own self-efficacy or self-worth.

Future research also needs to examine additional consequences at the organizational level. Most prior research has focused on the effects that OCBs have on organizational effectiveness as measured by some form of financial measure. However, OCBs may also influence other important measures of organizational success, including customer satisfaction, customer retention, brand equity, innovativeness, best practices, speed to market, product and service quality, and employee turnover/retention. Thus, additional research is needed on the relationships between OCBs and these recognized indicators of organizational effectiveness.

Another future research avenue related to the consequences of OCBs would be to compare the impact of OCBs on managerial evaluations of individual-level performance to their aggregate effects on organizational success. This type of research is important because it is quite possible that the OCBs that managers value the most are not the same ones that make organizations effective. To our knowledge, only one study (Podsakoff & MacKenzie, 1994) has explored this topic. The researchers suggested that the weights that managers give to different forms of OCBs do not accurately reflect the impact of these behaviors on organizational performance. If future research upholds these findings, further studies should be conducted to investigate what accounts for this discrepancy.

Conceptual/Methodological Issues

Although there have been hundreds of empirical studies on OCBs, we still need better evidence of the causal priorities among OCBs and their presumed antecedents and consequences. Several times throughout this book, we have identified unresolved questions about the causal relationship between OCBs and other variables. For example, in Chapter 4, we called attention to the need to obtain better evidence of causality between OCB and presumed antecedents like employee attitudes; in Chapter 5, we noted the possibility that the relationship between leader behavior and OCB may be spurious (rather than causal) due to the fact that both are part of the leader-member exchange process, and discussed some unresolved questions regarding whether leadership behaviors and group process variables are better thought of as causes or consequences of OCB; and finally, in Chapter 7, we suggested that we needed better evidence of causality between OCB and some of its presumed consequences, such as organizational performance.

In all of these cases, additional controlled experimental research could disentangle these knots of causality. In our view, this should be a priority for future research. Obviously, one way to obtain better evidence of causality is to experimentally manipulate the presumed causal variable. In studies in which OCBs are presumed to be antecedents, this has been done through the use of written scenarios (e.g., Bachrach, Bendoly, & Podsakoff, 2001), policy-capturing methods (e.g., Orr et al., 1989; Rotundo & Sackett, 2002), or videotaped vignettes (e.g., Park, 1986). Researchers could also use interactive simulations (Fromkin & Streufert, 1983). However, when OCBs are the presumed consequence of other variables, causality may become more difficult to determine because the experimenter must somehow arrange for the opportunity for OCBs to occur in a particular place at a particular time without artificially constraining the nature or form of OCBs that the subjects in the study may choose to perform. In these cases, longitudinal designs might be used. Although these designs are obviously not as good as experiments at establishing temporal priority and controlling for confounding factors, they provide better evidence than purely cross-sectional designs. However, designing such a study would require some serious thought about the relevant time lags between variables.

Methodological Issues

Future research also needs to address issues that are more methodological in nature than the ones discussed in the previous sections. First, researchers need to think more carefully about the source of the OCB ratings. As noted in Chapter 6, the differences in rater knowledge and raters' motivation to communicate their knowledge without bias are potentially important. In other words, raters differ in both knowledge and trustworthiness, and both are needed for their ratings to be credible. In principle, one would want to choose the most knowledgeable and trustworthy source for the OCB ratings. However, in practice, one is forced to make a trade-off between these two factors because all rating sources do not have equivalent knowledge, and they may vary in their motivation to provide unbiased ratings. For example, although the person being rated has the greatest knowledge of his or her own OCB, that person may also be the one with the greatest motivation to distort (bias) the ratings so that he or she will appear in a favorable light. Alternatively, a supervisor may have little motivation to distort the ratings of a subordinate's OCBs but also little opportunity to observe some forms of these behaviors.

Thus far, the literature seems to favor selecting raters in a way that minimizes motivational biases in the reporting of OCB. However, we caution that this results in more credible ratings only if the source of the ratings actually has direct knowledge of the behavior being rated. In those cases in which no single source is both knowledgeable and unbiased, we recommend that researchers obtain ratings from multiple sources whose knowledge differences and motivational differences may compensate for each other. One way to do this might be to use a 360-degree OCB rating process requiring supervisors, peers, subordinates (if applicable), and the employee to all provide ratings. Although this will undoubtedly increase the amount of time and energy required to obtain OCB ratings, the extra effort might be worth it.

As a final note, we would like to emphasize the importance of controlling for common method variance in future OCB research. In Chapter 6, we noted the effects that method variance has had on the relationships between OCB and important consequences, like managerial evaluations. In addition, research reported by Podsakoff, MacKenzie, Moorman, and Fetter (1990) and MacKenzie, Podsakoff, and Rich (2001) suggests that method variance may also influence the relationships between OCBs and their antecedents. As noted by Podsakoff, MacKenzie, Lee, and Podsakoff (2003), method biases can be controlled in future research through the design of the study's procedures and/or statistical controls. Although perhaps the best way to control for method biases is through the design of the study, the most popular method of doing this (e.g., obtaining the measure of the predictor and criterion variables from different sources) could compromise the credibility of the ratings of some forms of OCB due to knowledge differences. As a result, we think that future research aimed at determining the best ways of controlling this form of bias is needed.

Conclusions

In this chapter, we focused on the implications of OCB research for HR practitioners and researchers interested in OCB. With respect to HR practitioners, the bottom line is that it is essential for all HR system elements (recruiting and selection, training and development, compensation, and performance appraisal) to be aligned to OCB. If they are not, they will undermine (a) the organization's ability to select, train, and motivate employee OCB, and (b) the likely effectiveness of the organization. With respect to OCB researchers, several fundamental conceptual and methodological issues still need to be resolved. These issues involve the nature and types of OCBs, mediating mechanisms, additional antecedents and consequences, the need for better evidence of causality, and the need to control for method biases without compromising the validity of the measures. Therefore, despite the fact that a considerable amount of research on OCB has been conducted, there is still much work to be done. We hope that this book has helped to identify some of the more fruitful areas for future research and that it will inspire readers to pursue these issues.

Note

1. Source of quote: Rosenfield, D., Folger, R. & Adelman, H. F. (1980). When rewards reflect competence: A qualification of the overjustification effect. *Journal of Personality and Social Psychology, 39,* 368–376. Copyright © by the American Psychological Association. Reprinted with permission.

Appendix

Issues in the Measurement and Conceptualization of OCB

Chapters 1 through 8 described OCB, its historical development, its antecedents and consequences, and the implications of this research for managers in organizational settings. This appendix is intended for researchers and serious practitioners who wish to explore the nature of OCB and its measurement in greater detail. Consequently, those who are not interested in these more technical issues can skip this material without losing the essence of what these types of behaviors are and why they are important in organizational settings.

In this appendix, we discuss the development of the most frequently used OCB/CP (organizational citizenship behavior/contextual performance) scales and evaluate their content validity and psychometric properties. Next, we attempt to clarify the conceptual similarities and differences among the various forms of OCB by briefly reviewing the literature on OCB and other related constructs. Finally, we end our discussion with some recommendations for future research in the conceptualization and measurement of OCB.

Review of OCB/Contextual Performance Measures

Researchers have used a variety of scales to measure OCB and CP. In the next section, we review several of the most frequently used measures. We discuss the conceptual definition of the constructs, the procedure used to develop the measures, the content validity of the items, and the psychometric properties of the scales.

Bateman and Organ (1983)

Conceptual Definition(s)

Bateman and Organ (1983) are credited with developing one of the first scales designed to measure OCB. According to these authors, organizational citizenship behaviors

> include any of those gestures (often taken for granted) that lubricate the social machinery of the organization but that do not directly inhere in the usual notion of task performance. Examples that come to mind include: helping co-workers with a job related problem; accepting orders without a fuss; tolerating temporary impositions without complaint; helping to keep the work area clean and uncluttered; making timely and constructive statements about the work unit or its head to outsiders; promoting a work climate that is tolerable and minimizes the distractions created by interpersonal conflict; and protecting and conserving organizational resources. For lack of a better term, the present authors shall refer to these acts as "citizenship" behaviors. (p. 588).

Scale Development Procedures

Bateman and Organ's (1983) 30-item OCB scale was developed as part of Bateman's (1980) doctoral dissertation, in which Bateman generated a set of 30 items that tapped a variety of types of OCB, such as cooperation, altruism, compliance, punctuality, housecleaning, protecting company property, conscientiously following company rules, and dependability. A small group of managers was asked to identify any ambiguities or irrelevancies in the items. After the items had been revised, they were used to rate a sample of 77 employees in a major university.

Bateman (1980) reported the first test of the factor structure of this 30-item scale. He found that that the scale was not unidimensional; it consisted of four factors with eigenvalues greater than unity. Unfortunately, the subdimensions had no clear theme—perhaps because, as noted by Organ (1988), the ratings were all so high that their variance was attenuated. Nevertheless, because many of the items had substantial loadings on the first factor, Bateman and Organ (1983) decided to treat the scale as a composite measure of OCB. They reported internal consistency reliability estimates of .92 at time 1 and .94 at time 2, and a test-retest reliability estimate was .80.

Scale Items

Respondents were asked to indicate their agreement or disagreement with each of the items listed here, using a 7-point scale ranging from −3 (disagree completely) through +3 (agree completely), with a midpoint labeled 0 (neither agree nor disagree). Reverse coded items are indicated by (R).

Comes up with new, original ideas for handling work.

Conscientiously follows organizational rules.

Trains or helps others to perform their jobs better.

Takes a personal interest in other employees.

Acts impulsively, on the spur of the moment. (R)

Has ups and downs in mood. (R)

Critically finds fault with other employees. (R)

Makes sure that things are neat, clean and orderly.

Tries to look busy doing nothing. (R)

Resists influence from others, including the boss. (R)

Acts cheerfully.

Expresses resentment at being given orders. (R)

Loses touch with things going on around him/her. (R)

Cooperates well with those around him/her.

Exhibits punctuality in arriving at work on time in the morning and after breaks.

Takes undeserved work breaks. (R)

Complains about insignificant things at work. (R)

Seeks others' help when he/she needs it.

Makes positive statements about his/her immediate supervisor.

Makes constructive statements about the department.

Purposefully interferes with someone else doing their job. (R)

Exhibits dependability in carrying out his/her responsibilities.

Has people go to him/her for assistance.

Goes out of his/her way to protect other employees.

Goes out of his/her way to protect organizational property.

Exhibits annoyance with others. (R)

Exhibits poor quality work. (R)

Starts arguments with other employees. (R)

Talks about wanting to quit his/her job. (R)

Wastes material or harms organizational property. (R)

Content Validity

Several of the items on this scale are of questionable content validity. For example, it is not clear how an item like "Seeks others' help when he/she needs it," which reflects the tendency to seek help rather than to provide it to others, helps to "lubricate the social machinery of the organization" (Bateman & Organ, 1983, p. 588). Indeed, Organ (1988) noted several other items that do not appear to fit the conceptual definition of the OCB construct:

> Looking back, one wonders at the source of inspiration for some of the items (e.g., "Acts impulsively, on the spur of the moment"; "has ups and downs in mood"). Also . . . several of the items would seem to constitute the rater's judgment of the satisfaction of the subordinate ("Acts cheerfully"; "Talks about wanting to quit his/her job"), and this property of the measure may artifactually contribute to its correlation with job satisfaction. (Organ, 1988, p. 115).

Psychometric Properties

To our knowledge, Turnipseed and Murkison (2000) are the only other researchers that have tested the factor structure of the Bateman and Organ (1983) 30-item scale. Their exploratory factor analysis indicated that a three-factor solution best accounted for the covariation among the items but that it was difficult to identify a clear conceptual theme for each of the three factors. According to Turnipseed and Murkison (2000), items with loadings greater than .40 on the first factor reflected constructive statements, cheerfulness, helpfulness, following rules, innovation, a positive attitude, and generally good interpersonal relations. Items with loadings greater than .40 on the second factor reflected a tendency to avoid resisting influence from others, complaining, arguing, or talking about quitting. And items like not acting impulsively, absence of mood swings, not expressing resentment at being given orders, and staying in touch with things going on in the workplace had loadings greater than .40 on the third factor. Two of the 30 items failed to have loadings greater than .40 on any factor. Turnipseed and Murkison (2000) did not report reliability estimates for the subdimensions. Thus, the existing empirical evidence suggests that the

30-item Bateman and Organ scale is not unidimensional, and its factor structure is not well understood.

Smith, Organ, and Near (1983)

Conceptual Definition(s)

In their paper on the nature of OCB in which they developed their 16-item scale, Smith, Organ, and Near (1983) argued that

> Citizenship behaviors comprise a dimension of individual and group functioning that Roethlisberger and Dickson (1964) seemed to have in mind when they used the term "cooperation." . . . cooperation refers to something other than productivity. The latter was regarded as a function of the formal organization (the authority structure, role specifications, technology) and the "logic of facts." Cooperation, on the other hand, referred to acts that served more of a maintenance purpose, to "maintain internal equilibrium." Cooperation thus included the day-to-day spontaneous prosocial gestures of individual accommodation to the work needs of others (e.g., coworkers, supervisor, clients in other departments), whereas productivity (or efficiency) was determined by the formal or economic structure of the organization. (Smith et al., 1983, p. 653)

Scale Development Procedures

Smith et al. (1983) developed the OCB scale via a series of stages. In the first stage, several people with supervisory duties in manufacturing organizations were interviewed using a semistructured interview format. The managers were asked to describe those subordinate actions that they appreciated but that they could not demand, enforce, or directly reward. The researchers developed a 20-item scale using the interview protocol as a guide to selecting and rewording items in the Bateman and Organ (1983) measure. The measure was pretested by administering it to a group of 67 students who were either managers at the time or had in the past exercised supervisory responsibilities. They were asked to think of an employee who was presently working for them, or had at some time worked for them, and they were instructed to describe that person's work behavior and their responses to the scale. The data were factor analyzed and after dropping four items, two interpretable factors emerged.

Smith et al. (1983) then used the resulting 16-item scale. The sample for this study was 422 employees working in 58 departments in two banks in the Midwestern United States. The data were analyzed with an exploratory factor analysis that revealed two factors that were similar to the ones found in the pretest. According to Smith et al. (1983),

Factor 1 . . . appears to capture behavior that is directly and intentionally aimed at helping a specific person in face-to-face situations (e.g., orienting new people, assisting someone with heavy workload). The eliciting stimulus, in other words, is someone needing aid, as in the fashion of social psychological studies of altruism. Thus, this dimension is referred to as *Altruism* . . . Factor 2 . . . , by contrast, pertains to a more impersonal form of conscientiousness that does not provide immediate aid to any one specific person, but rather is indirectly helpful to others involved in the system. The behavior (e.g., punctuality, not wasting time) seems to represent something akin to compliance with internalized norms defining what a "good employee ought to do." This factor is referred to as *Generalized Compliance.* (Smith et al., 1983, p. 657)

Of the 16 items in the scale, 6 had loadings greater than .50 on the altruism factor, and 8 items had loadings greater than .50 on the generalized compliance factor. Two items failed to load on either factor. In addition, Smith et al. (1983) reported that the intercorrelation between the altruism and generalized compliance dimensions was .44, suggesting that these OCB dimensions were relatively distinct from each other.

Scale Items

Respondents were asked to indicate how characteristic the behaviors listed here are of the employee using a 5-point scale ranging from "very characteristic" to "not at all characteristic," with a separate column for "does not apply." Items indicated with an asterisk did not meet the minimum loading criterion of .50, and reverse coded items are indicated by (R).

Altruism

Helps others who have been absent.

Volunteers for things that are not required.

Orients new people even though it is not required.

Helps others who have heavy work loads.

Assists supervisor with his or her work.

Makes innovative suggestions to improve department.

*Attends functions not required but that help company image.

Generalized Compliance

Punctuality.

Takes undeserved breaks. (R)

Attendance at work is above the norm.

*Coasts towards the end of the day. (R)

Gives advance notice if unable to come to work.

Great deal of time spent with personal phone conversations. (R)

Does not take unnecessary time off work.

Does not take extra breaks.

Does not spend time in idle conversation.

Content Validity

Although generally speaking, the items for altruism capture behavior that is directly and intentionally aimed at helping a specific person in face-to-face situations, three of the items ("Volunteers for things that are not required," "Makes innovative suggestions to improve department," and "Attends functions not required but that help company image") do not necessarily suggest face-to-face interactions stimulated by a specific individual needing aid. However, in our opinion, the items for generalized compliance all seem to reflect compliance with internalized norms defining what a good employee ought to do. Thus, with the exception of the altruism items noted above, the overall content validity of the scale is reasonably good.

Psychometric Properties

Several studies (e.g., Barksdale & Werner, 2001; Dalton & Cosier, 1988; Farh, Podsakoff, & Organ, 1990; Goodman & Svyantek, 1999; Koh, Steers, & Terborg, 1995; Organ & Konovsky, 1989; Podsakoff, Niehoff, MacKenzie, & Williams, 1993; Smith et al., 1983) have examined the psychometric properties of the complete 16-item scale developed by Smith et al. (1983). The factor structure of the scale was tested using exploratory factor analyses by all of these researchers, with the exception of Barksdale and Werner (2001), who used confirmatory factor analysis. Three of these studies (Barksdale & Werner, 2001; Farh et al., 1990; Goodman & Svyantek, 1999) found support for the two-factor structure (altruism and generalized compliance) identified by Smith et al. (1983). However, three of these studies (Koh et al. 1995; Organ & Konovsky, 1989; Podsakoff, Niehoff et al., 1993) reported that a three-factor solution best fit the data. Generally speaking, in these three studies, the altruism items identified by Smith et al. (1983) loaded consistently on their intended factor. However, the compliance items split into two factors in a variety of ways across these studies. Organ and Konovsky (1989) reported that all of the reverse-scored compliance items loaded on one factor, and items consisting of negative statements with positive connotations loaded on another factor. Podsakoff, Niehoff et al. (1993) found that the compliance items related to conscientiousness loaded on one factor, and the items related to attendance loaded on another factor. Koh et al. (1995) observed that the negatively worded compliance items loaded on one factor, and the positively worded items loaded on another factor. Finally, Dalton and Cosier (1989) reported that a four-factor solution fit the data. In contrast to all of the other studies, these authors reported that three of the altruism items failed to load on any of their factors at the .50 cutoff level they used in their study. In addition, they found that the compliance items loaded on three factors. However, the lack of experience of their sample, which consisted of undergraduate students who are unlikely to have had much experience in supervising employees, may have affected their findings.

Thus, the overall pattern of results suggests that the altruism factor in the Smith et al. (1983) scale has received a substantial amount of support, but the underlying structure of compliance measures is unclear. The latter is especially disappointing in view of the fact that all but one of these studies used an exploratory factor analysis, which is a weak way to test a hypothesized factor structure.

Estimates of internal consistency reliability for the altruism scale across the seven studies that reported coefficient alpha ranged from a low of .72 to a high of .91, with an average of .85. Estimates of internal consistency reliability (alpha) for the four studies that reported a generalized compliance factor ranged from a low of .81 to a high of .91, with an average of .85. Finally, estimates of alpha for the more specific subdimensions of compliance ranged from a low of .80 to a high of .88, with an average of .82.

Podsakoff, MacKenzie, Moorman, and Fetter (1990)

Conceptual Definition(s)

Building on the conceptual work of Organ (1988), Podsakoff, MacKenzie, Moorman, and Fetter (1990) identified the following five major categories of organizational citizenship behavior:

- *Altruism:* Discretionary behaviors on the part of employees that have the effect of helping a specific other with an organizationally relevant problem.

- *Conscientiousness:* Discretionary behaviors on the part of the employee that go well beyond the minimum role requirements of the organization in the areas of attendance, obeying rules and regulations, taking breaks, and so forth.

- *Sportsmanship:* Willingness of the employee to tolerate less than ideal circumstances without complaining—to "avoid complaining, petty grievances, railing against real or imagined slights, and making federal cases out of small potatoes" (Organ, 1988, p.11).

- *Courtesy:* Discretionary behavior on the part of an individual aimed at preventing work-related problems with others from occurring.

- *Civic virtue:* Behavior on the part of an individual that indicates that he/she responsibly participates in, is involved in, or is concerned about the life of the company. (Podsakoff et al., 1990, p. 115)

Scale Development Procedures

Podsakoff et al. (1990) used a 24-item scale they developed through a series of stages following the recommendations of Schwab (1980) and Churchill (1979). In the first stage, Podsakoff et al. generated items for each of the five constructs previously defined in the "Conceptual Definition" section. These items were then given to a group of 10 colleagues, who were asked to conduct a Q-sort of the items. These colleagues were provided with definitions of the five OCB dimensions and were asked to sort each item into the most appropriate OCB category, or a sixth category—"other"—for any item which, in their judgment, did not fit any of the conceptual definitions. The final scale consisted of only those items on which at least 80% of the judges agreed on the item's coding.

Podsakoff et al. (1990) administered the scale in a sample of 988 exempt employees working for a diversified petrochemical company with divisions throughout the United States, Canada, and Europe.

Eighty percent of the sample had a college degree. The hypothesized five-factor structure was tested using confirmatory factor analysis. Overall, the hypothesized measurement model fit the data well (Tucker Lewis Index = .94), all of the items loaded on the factors they were intended to represent, and the internal consistency reliabilities (alphas) averaged .81 (altruism = .85; courtesy = .85; sportsmanship = .85; conscientiousness = .82, and civic virtue = .70). In addition, tests of discriminant validity indicated that all of the constructs were empirically distinct, although altruism shared about two thirds of its variance with conscientiousness and courtesy.

Scale Items

Respondents were asked to indicate their agreement or disagreement with each of the items listed here, using a 7-point scale ranging from "strongly disagree" through "strongly agree," with a midpoint labeled "neither agree nor disagree." Reverse coded items are indicated by (R).

Altruism

Helps others who have been absent.

Helps others who have heavy work loads.

Helps orient new people even though it is not required.

Willingly helps others who have work related problems.

Is always ready to lend a helping hand to those around him/her.

Conscientiousness

Attendance at work is above the norm.

Does not take extra breaks.

Obeys company rules and regulations even when no one is watching.

Is one of my most conscientious employees.

Believes in giving an honest day's work for an honest day's pay.

Sportsmanship

Consumes a lot of time complaining about trivial matters. (R)

Always focuses on what's wrong, rather than the positive side. (R)

Tends to make "mountains out of molehills." (R)

Always finds fault with what the organization is doing. (R)

Is the classic "squeaky wheel" that always needs greasing. (R)

Courtesy

Takes steps to try to prevent problems with other workers.

Is mindful of how his/her behavior affects other people's jobs.

Does not abuse the rights of others.

Tries to avoid creating problems for coworkers.

Considers the impact of his/her actions on coworkers.

Civic Virtue

Attends meetings that are not mandatory, but are considered important.

Attends functions that are not required, but help the company image.

Keeps abreast of changes in the organization.

Reads and keeps up with organization announcements, memos, and so on.

Content Validity

Generally speaking, it appears that most of the items tap relevant aspects of the domain of the construct they were intended to represent. However, there are a few exceptions to this generalization. For example, two of the items in the conscientiousness scale ("Obeys company rules and regulations even when no one is watching," and "Believes in giving an honest day's work for an honest day's pay") do not explicitly indicate that the employee's behavior goes "well beyond the minimum role requirements of the organization." In addition, note that all of the sportsmanship items are negatively worded (i.e., they all reflect examples of poor sportsmanship); there are no positively worded examples of sportsmanship behavior. Thus, although the content validity of the scale is generally pretty good, there are a few potentially problematic items.

Psychometric Evidence

A number of studies (e.g. Bell & Menguc, 2002; Goodwin, Wofford, & Whittington, 2001; Hui, Lee, & Rousseau, 2004; Lam, Hui, & Law, 1999;

Pillai, Schriesheim, & Williams, 1999; Podsakoff et al., 1990) have examined the psychometric properties of the complete 24-item scale developed by Podsakoff et al. (1990), or a slightly modified version of the scale (Moorman, 1991, 1993; Moorman, Niehoff, & Organ, 1993; Niehoff & Moorman, 1993; Podsakoff, MacKenzie, & Fetter, 1993). All but three of these studies (Goodwin et al., 2001; Moorman, 1993; Pillai et al., 1999) used confirmatory factor analysis to examine the factor structure of the scales. Ten of the studies (Bell & Menguc, 2002; Hui et al., 2004; Lam et al., 1999; Moorman, 1991, 1993; Moorman et al., 1993; Niehoff & Moorman, 1993; Pillai et al., 1999; Podsakoff et al., 1990; Podsakoff, MacKenzie, & Fetter, 1993) found general support for the five-factor structure of the OCB scale, although Pillai et al. (1999) reported that in their two samples, a few items loaded on factors other than the ones hypothesized. Particularly interesting among this set of studies are the ones conducted by Lam et al. (1999) and Hui et al. (2004). Lam et al. (1999) examined the factor structure of the 24-item scale in four cultural settings (United States, Australia, Japan, and Hong Kong) using confirmatory factor analysis. They found that the five-factor solution fit the data across all four of the subsamples. Similar support for the five-factor structure of the scale was also reported by Hui et al. (2004) in their sample of employees working for a Chinese steel conglomerate.

However, a few studies have reported a lack of support for the five-factor structure of the Podsakoff et al. (1990) scale. Goodwin et al. (2001) reported that their slightly modified version of the 24-item scale did not meet the response distribution assumptions of confirmatory factor analysis (i.e., the responses were not normally distributed) and that their subsequent exploratory factor analysis yielded only one factor with an eigenvalue greater than unity. Therefore, they collapsed the five subscales into one overall OCB dimension. Rioux and Penner (2001) conducted a study in which they obtained ratings of OCB from employees, their peers, and their supervisors. The researchers concluded that "the best fitting model indicated moderate convergent validity across the rating sources, but a relative lack of discriminant validity of the OCB subscales within rating sources." (p. 1309). The data they reported for peer ratings suggest that altruism and courtesy had slightly more than half of their variance in common (53%).

Taken as a whole, the majority of studies support the five-factor structure of the Podsakoff et al. (1990) OCB measures. This is significant because the majority of the tests of this scale have used confirmatory factor analysis, which is a more rigorous test of the hypothesized factor structure than the exploratory factor analysis technique used to test some of the other scales. However, several studies have reported that the altruism and courtesy constructs are relatively highly correlated with each other and thus may not be empirically distinct.

Estimates of internal consistency reliability for the five OCB dimensions averaged across the 12 samples reported by Podsakoff et al. (1990); Moorman (1991, 1993); Podsakoff, MacKenzie, & Fetter (1993); Moorman et al. (1993); Niehoff and Moorman (1993); Lam et al. (1999); Pillai et al. (1999); and Bell and Menguc (2002) were as follows: altruism (.88), courtesy (.87), conscientiousness (.85), sportsmanship (.88), and civic virtue (.84). Thus, overall, empirical research indicates the scales are fairly reliable.

Williams and Anderson (1991)

Conceptual Definition(s)

Williams and Anderson (1991) identified two broad categories of OCB: "(a) OCBO–behaviors that benefit the organization in general (e.g., gives advance notice when unable to come to work, adheres to informal rules devised to maintain order), and (b) OCBI—behaviors that immediately benefit specific individuals and indirectly through this means contribute to the organization (e.g., helps others who have been absent, takes a personal interest in other employees)" (pp. 601–602).

Scale Development Procedures

Williams and Anderson's (1991) seven-item OCBO and seven-item OCBI scales were developed as part of Williams's (1988) doctoral dissertation at Indiana University. Wiliams took most of the measures representing these constructs from previous research by Bateman and Organ (1983), Graham (1986a), Organ (1988), and Smith et al. (1983). In addition, he developed some new items based on the conceptual definitions. Moreover, to establish the discriminant validity of his OCBO and OCBI scales, Williams also developed a scale to measure employee in-role behavior (IRB).

Williams and Anderson (1991) tested the hypothesized three-factor structure using exploratory factor analysis among a sample of 127 full-time employees, their peers, and their supervisors. The employees worked for various organizations and were all attending evening MBA classes. These authors found that "in all cases the items had their highest loading on the appropriate factor and this loading met the .35 criterion, with the exception of ['... conserves and protects organizational property']" (pp. 609–610). In addition, they report that the OCBO and OCBI factors were correlated .43, the OCBO and IRB factors were correlated .47, and the OCBI and IRB factors were correlated .48, suggesting that these factors are relatively distinct forms of behavior. Finally, they reported that the internal consistency reliability of the OCBI scale was .88, and the internal consistency reliability of the OCBO scale was .75.

A more stringent test of this factor structure was reported by Williams (1988), who analyzed the same data in his dissertation. Williams (1988) conducted a three-factor confirmatory factor analysis and found that: (a) all of the items loaded on their hypothesized factors, (b) the construct intercorrelations ranged from .38 to .47 (after correcting for measurement error), (c) the three-factor model fit significantly better than a two-factor model or a one-factor model, but unfortunately (d) the three-factor model did not fit very well in an absolute sense (normed fit index = .70; root mean square residual = .098). Thus, although the exploratory factor analysis results provide some support for the hypothesized factor structure of the scale, the confirmatory factor analysis results suggest that the factor structure may be more complicated than Williams and Anderson (1991) hypothesized.

Scale Items

Respondents were asked to indicate their agreement or disagreement with each of the items listed below, using a 7-point scale ranging from "strongly disagree" through "strongly agree," with a midpoint labeled "neither agree nor disagree." Reverse coded items are indicated by (R).

OCBI

Helps others who have been absent.

Helps others who have heavy work loads.

Assists supervisor with his/her work (when not asked).

Takes time to listen to co-workers' problems and worries.

Goes out of way to help new employees.

Takes a personal interest in other employees.

Passes along information to co-workers.

OCBO

Attendance at work is above the norm.

Gives advance notice when unable to come to work.

Takes undeserved work breaks. (R)

Great deal of time spent with personal phone conversations. (R)

Complains about insignificant things at work. (R)

Conserves and protects organizational property.

Adheres to informal rules devised to maintain order.

IRB

Adequately completes assigned duties.

Fulfills responsibilities specified in job description.

Performs tasks that are expected of him/her.

Meets formal performance requirements of the job.

Engages in activities that will directly affect his/her performance evaluation.

Neglects aspects of the job he/she is obligated to perform. (R)

Fails to perform essential duties. (R)

Content Validity

With a few exceptions, the items on the OCBI and OCBO scales generally appear to reflect their underlying constructs. For example, although the item "takes a personal interest in other employees" reflects OCBI in the sense that it involves other individuals, it is not clear that this behavior immediately benefits those individuals or indirectly benefits the organization because the item is too vague with respect to the form that this "personal interest" might take. In addition, the item "passes along information to co-workers" is potentially problematic because it fails to specify whether this behavior is required or discretionary, and thus it may overlap with in-role behavior to some extent.

Psychometric Properties

Only two studies (Randall, Cropanzano, Borman, & Birjulin, 1999; Turnley, Bolino, Lester, & Bloodgood, 2003) have tested the three-factor structure of Williams and Anderson's (1991) scale. Randall et al. (1999) reported:

> Factor analysis recovered three correlated but distinct behavior factors. Seven items measure the first factor, job performance . . . Seven items measure the second factor, OCB that benefits a specific individual (OCBI). . . . The third and final factor was OCB that benefits the organization as a whole (OCBO). This dimension is assessed by six items . . . (p. 165).

Turnley et al. (2003) reported a confirmatory factor analysis of Williams and Anderson's (1991) OCBO, OCBI, and IRB scales, with one OCBI item missing ("Assists supervisor with his/her work when not asked") and one IRB item missing. They reported that the hypothesized three-factor model fit the data reasonably well and that each item loaded on its specified factor.

Estimates of internal consistency reliability for the OCBI scale averaged .85 across the studies conducted by Williams and Anderson (1991), Turnley et al. (2003), and Randall et al. (1999), ranging from a low of .80 to a high of .88. The internal consistency reliability estimates for OCBO in these studies averaged .76, ranging from a low of .70 to a high of .83. Thus, overall, the scale appears to be reasonably reliable.

Motowidlo and Van Scotter (1994)

Conceptual Definition(s)

In a book chapter published in the early 1990s, Borman and Motowidlo (1993) made a conceptual distinction between task performance and contextual performance. A year later, Motowidlo and Van Scotter (1994) reported the first study designed to empirically test the merits of this distinction. According to these authors, unlike task performance, which relates either to transforming raw materials into goods and services that the organization produces or to activities that service and maintain the technical core of the organization, contextual performance behaviors

> do not support the technical core itself as much as they support the broader organizational, social, and psychological environment in which the technical core must function. Drawing on theoretical and empirical work in organizational citizenship behavior (Organ, 1988), prosocial organizational behavior (Brief & Motowidlo, 1986), models of soldier effectiveness (Borman, Motowidlo, & Hanser, 1983; Campbell, 1990), and models of management effectiveness (Borman & Brush, 1993), Borman and Motowidlo (1993) identified five

categories of contextual performance. The categories are (a) volunteering to carry out task activities that are not formally part of the job; (b) persisting with extra enthusiasm when necessary to complete own task activities successfully; (c) helping and cooperating with others; (d) following organizational rules and procedures even when it is personally inconvenient; and (e) endorsing, supporting, and defending organizational objectives . . . Contextual performance captures many of the helping and co-operating elements of organizational citizenship behavior (Organ, 1988), prosocial organizational behavior (Brief & Motowidlo, 1986), and organizational spontaneity (George & Brief, 1992), but task performance does not. (Motowidlo & Van Scotter, 1994, p. 476).

Scale Development Procedures

The sample in Motowidlo and Van Scotter's (1994) study was 715 Air Force mechanics. For each mechanic, the researchers assigned one supervisor to rate the mechanic's task performance, another to rate the mechanic's contextual performance, and a third to rate the mechanic's overall performance. Unfortunately, Motowidlo and Van Scotter (1994) provided little information about how they developed their measure of contextual performance other than to say that the 16-item scale was "developed for this study to tap dimensions of contextual performance identified by Borman and Motowidlo (1993)" (p. 477). Factor analysis was not conducted on the scale, but the authors did report that Cronbach's alpha for the 16-item scale was .95, suggesting that the scale did possess a relatively high internal consistency reliability. In addition, they also provided evidence that contextual performance was: (a) not highly correlated with task performance ($r = .20$), (b) more strongly correlated with several personality characteristics than was task performance, and (c) more weakly related to experience than was task performance. Taken together, this evidence suggests that contextual performance and task performance are distinct constructs.

Scale Items

Supervisors were asked to indicate on a 5-point scale ranging from 1 (not at all likely) to 5 (extremely likely) how likely each person would be to engage in the behaviors listed here while performing his or her job.

Comply with instructions even when supervisors are not present?

Cooperate with others in the team?

Persist in overcoming obstacles to complete a task?

Display proper military appearance and bearing?

Volunteer for additional duty?

Follow proper procedures and avoid unauthorized shortcuts?

Look for a challenging assignment?

Offer to help others accomplish their work?

Pay close attention to important details?

Defend the supervisor's decisions?

Render proper military courtesy?

Support and encourage a coworker with a problem?

Take the initiative to solve a work problem?

Exercise personal discipline and self-control?

Tackle a difficult work assignment enthusiastically?

Voluntarily do more than the job requires to help others or contribute to unit effectiveness?

Content Validity

Generally speaking, two of the subdimensions of the contextual performance domain that Motowidlo and Van Scotter (1994) identified (helping and cooperating with others, and volunteering to carry out tasks that are not formally part of the job) are adequately tapped by the items included in their scale. For example, at least three items ("Cooperate with others in the team?" "Offer to help others accomplish their work?" and "Support and encourage a coworker with a problem?") appear to measure helping and cooperating with others, and at least three other items ("Volunteer for additional duty?" "Voluntarily do more than the job requires to help others or contribute to unit effectiveness?" and "Look for a challenging assignment?") appear to measure volunteering to carry out task activities that are not formally part of the job (although the last item is ambiguous in that it does not adequately specify whether the challenging assignment is part of the job or not).

However, it is difficult to determine whether some of the other subdimensions are measured adequately or not, or which specific subdimension some of the items are intended to measure. For example, it is not completely clear whether some items (e.g., "Exercise personal discipline and self-control?" "Render proper military courtesy?" "Comply with instructions even when supervisors are not present?" and "Display proper military appearance and bearing?") are designed to be measures of the "following procedures even when inconvenient" subdimension or the "endorsing, supporting, and defending organizational objectives" subdimension. These items do not seem to be particularly strong examples of the latter subdimension because they do not explicitly refer to endorsing and/or supporting organizational objectives. However, they would appear to be deficient measures of the "following procedures even when inconvenient" subdimension, because none of these items indicate that the behaviors described are exhibited in the face of inconvenience.

Similar problems exist for the item "Take the initiative to solve a work problem?" We assume that this item was designed either to tap into the persistence or volunteerism subdimension of the contextual performance domain. However, this item does not appear to be a particularly good measure of the volunteerism subdimension, because the problem being addressed is work-related (and, thus, could be considered a formal part of the job). Nor does it appear to be a particularly good measure of the persistence subdimension, because it does not indicate that the initiative is taken with "extra enthusiasm," as required by the conceptual definition of this subdimension. A related problem is that the item "Persist in overcoming obstacles to complete a task?" is also intended to measure the "persistence" subdimension, but it also lacks the "enthusiasm" aspect of this dimension.

Finally, it is not clear which subdimension the item "Pay close attention to important details?" is intended to measure. It may be intended to capture "following organizational rules," but it lacks the notion of "even when it is personally inconvenient." Or, it could be intended to measure the persistence subdimension, but it lacks the idea of doing this with "extra enthusiasm."

Psychometric Properties

Little is known about the factor structure of the Motowidlo and Van Scotter (1994) scale. These authors did not report a factor analysis of the scale in their original study, and even though items from the scale have been used in other studies (e.g., Hogan, Rybicki, Motowidlo, & Borman, 1998), none of these studies have reported a factor analysis of the full 16-item scale. This is important because the fact that the scale has been shown to have high internal consistency reliability is not evidence of unidimensionality (Cortina, 1993; Nunnally & Bernstein, 1994).

In addition, within a few years of the publication of this scale, Van Scotter and Motowidlo (1996) argued that the contextual performance domain was better conceptualized as being composed of two separate dimensions—job dedication and interpersonal facilitation. (We discuss this study later in this appendix.) Thus, although this scale represents the first attempt to develop a measure of the contextual performance domain, little is known about its psychometric properties.

Podsakoff and MacKenzie (1994)

Conceptual Definition(s)

In 1990, Organ (1990b) expanded the domain of the construct by identifying two new forms of OCB—peacekeeping and cheerleading. In an effort to incorporate these two new forms of behavior, Podsakoff and MacKenzie (1994) developed a more comprehensive and somewhat refined OCB scale. In their view, peacekeeping and cheerleading (along with altruism and courtesy) are subdimensions of a higher-order, more general construct called *helping behavior*. More specifically, they argued that in a sales setting, which was the focus of their study,

> Organizational citizenship behaviors (OCBs) are discretionary behaviors on the part of a salesperson that are believed to directly promote the effective functioning of an organization, without necessarily influencing a salesperson's objective sales productivity. There are a variety of forms of OCB: Sportsmanship is a willingness on the part of a salesperson to tolerate less than ideal circumstances without "complaining . . . railing against real or imagined slights, and making federal cases out of small potatoes" (Organ, 1988; p. 11); civic virtue is behavior that indicates that the salesperson responsibly participates in and is concerned about the life of the company (e.g., attending meetings/functions that are not required but that help the company, keeping up with changes in the organization, taking the initiative to recommend how company operations or procedures can be improved); and helping behavior is a composite of several types of citizenship behavior—altruism, courtesy, peacekeeping, and cheerleading—identified by Organ (1988, 1990a, 1990b), all of which share the theme of helping coworkers to solve or avoid work-related problems. Altruism consists of those voluntary actions that help another person with a work-related problem (e.g., sharing sales strategies, voluntarily helping to orient new salespeople); courtesy consists of actions that help prevent work-related problems with others from occurring (e.g., touching base with the manufacturing plant before finalizing a large sale); peacemaking consists of actions that help prevent, resolve, or mitigate unconstructive interpersonal conflict (e.g., acting as a stabilizing influence in the organization when others have disagreements over commissions, prospects, territories); and cheerleading is defined as encouraging and reinforcing coworkers' accomplishments and professional development, which can be viewed as helping behavior when a salesperson

encourages a coworker who is discouraged about his or her accomplishments or professional development (e.g., encourages other salespeople when they are down or in a sales slump). (Podsakoff and MacKenzie, 1994, pp. 351-352)

Note that unlike their earlier scale (Podsakoff et al., 1990), Podsakoff and MacKenzie (1994) did not include one of Organ's original constructs (conscientiousness). This construct was dropped because it: (a) was not viewed as a discretionary form of behavior in many work settings (e.g., the managers in their sales sample viewed conscientiousness as a form of in-role rather than extra-role behavior) and (b) differs from in-role behavior only in terms of degree rather than kind. The latter point has been made by Organ (1988) himself, who noted that, unlike the other OCB dimensions, which are qualitatively different from in-role behavior, the conscientiousness dimension is different from in-role behavior only in the sense that it involves going beyond the normative or enforceable levels of the behaviors in question.

Scale Development Procedures

Podsakoff and MacKenzie (1994) developed the measures of helping, sportsmanship, and civic virtue using the scale development procedures recommended by Schwab (1980), Churchill (1979), and Nunnally (1978). Briefly, the scale development progressed through four stages. In the first stage, the authors developed items to tap into the OCB construct domains. In the second stage, they asked several colleagues to classify the randomly ordered items into categories based on the construct definitions, and the researchers retained those items that were assigned to the proper a priori category at least 80% of the time. In the third stage, the construct definitions and items were discussed with company representatives to confirm their applicability to the insurance sales context in which the researchers were conducting their study. In the final stage, Podsakoff and MacKenzie administered the remaining items to a sample of insurance sales managers (from the same company as those participating in the study), conducted confirmatory factor analyses and item reliability analyses, and used the results to further refine the scales.

In their discussions with company representatives, Podsakoff and MacKenzie (1994) took several steps to ensure that the OCB items faithfully represented Organ's (1988, 1990b) OCB constructs and did not tap aspects of the in-role performance of insurance sales personnel. First, vice presidents, general managers, unit managers, and sales marketing training personnel were asked whether they believed that Organ's OCB dimensions were indeed discretionary forms of behavior that were not explicitly recognized by the formal reward structure in their company. Next, they were asked to indicate whether the specific items used to operationalize the instances of OCB were appropriate examples of OCB in an insurance sales context. As a result of these discussions, some of the items were reworded for the insurance sales context.

According to Organ's (1988) definition, OCB must not be explicitly recognized by the formal organizational reward system. Consistent with this requirement, the financial compensation of agents in the Podsakoff and MacKenzie (1994) study was not influenced in any way by the performance of OCB. Agents were paid solely on the basis of their objective sales productivity. Moreover, conversations with the vice presidents, general managers, and other sales personnel indicated that agents were not explicitly punished for failing to exhibit OCB; they received no training in how to perform OCB (even though they received extensive training in techniques designed to improve sales effectiveness); and job descriptions made no mention of OCB-like behaviors. These were all consistent with Organ's requirement that OCBs must be discretionary forms of behavior that are not directly or explicitly recognized by the formal reward system of the organization.

For the purposes of their research, Podsakoff and MacKenzie (1994) gathered managerial ratings of the OCB of 987 full-time insurance agents working for a major insurance company in the United States. In the first study of the two that they reported in their 1994 paper, they examined the effects of the three dimensions of OCB (helping, sportsmanship, and civic virtue) on managers' overall evaluations of the agents' performance. In their second study, Podsakoff and MacKenzie (1994) aggregated the ratings of these agents at the agency level (N = 116) to determine the effect that unit-level OCB had on agency effectiveness (as measured by an objective effectiveness index obtained from company records).

Podsakoff and MacKenzie (1994) tested the hypothesized factor structure of their OCB scales in both studies using confirmatory factor analysis. Consistent with their conceptual definitions, helping behavior was modeled as a second-order latent factor consisting of Organ's (1988, 1990b) altruism, courtesy, peacekeeping, and some aspects of his cheerleading constructs; whereas civic virtue and sportsmanship were modeled as first-order constructs. The results of their first study (agents' sample) indicated that: (a) the hypothesized factor structure fit the data well (Tucker-Lewis Index = .96; CFI = .97), (b) all of the items loaded significantly on their intended factors, (c) the internal consistencies for the scales were relatively good (helping = .89, civic virtue = .82, and sportsmanship = .84), and (d) tests of the discriminant validity of the scales indicated that the constructs' intercorrelations were significantly (p < .05) less than 1.00, and the variance shared among any two of the OCB constructs was always less than the average variance in the items that was explained by the construct that they were intended to measure (cf. Fornell & Larcker, 1981). However, even though all of the constructs were distinct, the helping and civic virtue constructs had slightly more than half (53%) of their variance in common.

The results reported for the confirmatory factor analysis of the aggregated (agency level) data in the second study were generally quite similar. More specifically, as in the first study, Podsakoff and MacKenzie (1994) found that: (a) the hypothesized factor structure fit the data well (Tucker-Lewis Index = .96; CFI = .97), (b) all of the items loaded significantly on their intended factors, and (c) the internal consistencies for the scales were relatively good (helping = .90, civic virtue = .80, and sportsmanship = .83). With one exception, the tests of discriminant validity indicated that all of the construct intercorrelations were significantly (p < .05) less than 1.00 and that the square of the correlation between any two of the OCB latent constructs was always less than the average variance in the items that was explained by the construct that they were intended to measure. The one partial exception to this was that the square of the correlation between helping and civic virtue (.61) was somewhat smaller than the average variance in the items explained by the helping construct (.69) and somewhat higher than the average variance in the items explained by the civic virtue construct (.57). However, it is important to note that the intercorrelations among the constructs have been corrected for attenuation caused by measurement error and are therefore larger than the uncorrected factor correlations reported in many other studies.

Taken together, the results reported by Podsakoff and MacKenzie (1994) indicated that at both the individual and unit level: (a) all of the items loaded significantly on their intended factors, (b) the hypothesized factor structure for the scale was confirmed, (c) the internal consistency reliability estimates were all greater than .80, (d) the construct reliability indices were all greater than .80, (e) the average variance accounted for in the items by their latent constructs were all greater than .52, (f) all of the construct intercorrelations were significantly less than 1.00, and (g) with one partial exception, the constructs all passed Fornell and Larcker's (1981) test of discriminant validity. Despite this strong support for the scale, it is important to note that the helping and civic virtue dimensions had 50% to 60% of their variance in common.

Scale Items

Respondents were asked to indicate their agreement or disagreement with each of the items listed below, using a 7-point scale ranging from "strongly disagree" through "strongly agree," with a midpoint labeled "neither agree nor disagree." Reverse coded items are indicated by (R).

Helping Behavior

Altruism

Willingly gives of his or her time to help other agents who have work-related problems.

Is willing to take time out of his or her own busy schedule to help with recruiting or training new [employees].

Courtesy

"Touches base" with others before initiating actions that might affect them.

Takes steps to try to prevent problems with other agents and/or other personnel in the agency.

Cheerleading

Encourages other agents when they are down.

Peacekeeping

Acts as a "peacemaker" when others in the agency have disagreements.

Is a stabilizing influence in the agency when dissention occurs.

Civic Virtue

Attends functions that are not required but help the agency/company image.

Attends training/information sessions that agents are encouraged but not required to attend.

Attends and actively participates in agency meetings.

Sportsmanship

Consumes a lot of time complaining about trivial matters. (R)

Always finds fault with what the agency/company is doing. (R)

Tends to make "mountains out of molehills" (makes problems bigger than they are). (R)

Always focuses on what is wrong with his or her situation rather than the positive side of it. (R)

Content Validity

As noted earlier, Podsakoff and MacKenzie (1994) define helping behavior as a "composite of several types of citizenship behavior—altruism, courtesy, peacekeeping, and cheerleading . . . all of which share the theme of helping coworkers to solve or avoid work-related problems" (p. 351). This suggests that the measures of helping behavior should include items tapping each of these subdimensions. In this respect, we think that the scale developed by Podsakoff and MacKenzie (1994) does a good job in representing all four of these subdimensions of helping. With the exception of cheerleading, each of the subdimensions is represented by more than one item, and these items appear to be consistent with the conceptual definitions provided by the authors. However, the cheerleading measure may be deficient. Podsakoff and MacKenzie (1994) argued that only certain aspects of cheerleading can be viewed as helping behavior, such as "when a salesperson encourages a coworker who is discouraged about his or her accomplishments or professional development" (p. 352). Although the item they use to measure cheerleading is consistent with this conceptual definition, it refers broadly to encouraging coworkers when they are down rather than more specifically to encouraging coworkers when they are down *about their accomplishments or professional development.* Although this may or may not have been implied by the context of their questionnaire, it should have been explicitly mentioned.

Turning our attention to civic virtue, Podsakoff and MacKenzie (1994) defined this construct as "behavior that indicates that the salesperson responsibly participates in and is concerned about the life of the company" (p. 351) and then provided several examples of this behavior (e.g., "attending meetings/functions that are not required but that help the company, keeping up with changes in the organization, taking the initiative to recommend how company operations or procedures can be improved" (p. 351). Although the items used to measure this construct are consistent with the examples, they do not fully capture the range of behaviors specified in the examples they provide. There is no item that measures "keeping up with changes in the organization" or that explicitly speaks of "taking the initiative to recommend how company operations or procedures can be improved." Thus, the items used to measure civic virtue appear to be deficient.

Finally, although all four of the items used to measure sportsmanship appear to be generally consistent with the conceptual definition of this construct, they are all negatively worded. As we argued earlier in this appendix, we believe that the conceptual definition of sportsmanship is narrower than its label would imply and should be broadened to include the idea of maintaining a positive attitude even when things do not go your way, not being offended when others do not follow your suggestions, being willing to sacrifice your personal self-interest for the good of the work group, and not taking the rejection of your ideas personally. Strictly speaking, this is more a criticism of the conceptual definition than it is a criticism of the content validity of Podsakoff and MacKenzie's (1994) sportsmanship items. However, we believe that this is an important issue that needs to be addressed in future research.

Psychometric Properties

Two studies (Bachrach, Bendoly, & Podsakoff, 2001; MacKenzie, Podsakoff, & Paine, 1999, Sample 2) have examined the psychometric properties of the complete 14-item scale developed by Podsakoff and MacKenzie (1994) or a slightly modified version of the scale. Both of these studies used confirmatory factor analysis to examine the factor structure of the scales. MacKenzie et al. (1999, Sample 2) reported that all of the items had significant loadings ($p < .05$) on their intended factors, the hypothesized factor structure fit the data adequately (CFI = .95; NFI = .90; GFI = .89), the alphas ranged from .75 to .92, the construct reliability indices ranged from .75 to .92, average variance accounted for in the items by their constructs ranged from .47 to .45, the construct intercorrelations were significantly ($p < .05$) less than 1.00, and the variance shared among any two of the OCB constructs was always less than the average variance in the items that was explained by the constructs, with one partial exception. The square of the correlation between the helping and civic virtue latent constructs was .64, which was larger than the average variance in the items accounted for by the civic virtue construct (.47) but smaller than the average variance in the items accounted for by the helping construct (.75). Once again, it is important to remember that the intercorrelations among the constructs have been corrected for attenuation caused by measurement error and thus are larger than the uncorrected correlations often reported in other studies.

Bachrach et al. (2001) provided similar support for the hypothesized measurement model. The researchers reported that all of the items loaded significantly ($p < .05$) on their intended factors, the hypothesized factor structure fit the data adequately (CFI = .99; NFI = .97, GFI = .98), and the internal consistency reliabilities were acceptable (alpha's > .74). They reported that the intercorrelation between helping and civic virtue latent variables (corrected for attenuation) was .82, which suggests that these two constructs shared about two thirds of their variance.

Van Dyne, Graham, and Dienesch (1994)

Conceptual Definition(s)

Van Dyne, Graham, and Dienesch (1994) based their conceptualization of OCB on the work of Graham (1991), who conceived of OCB as a global concept composed of several correlated substantive categories modeled after the notion of civic citizenship in the political science literature. Graham (1991) defines the fundamental categories as follows:

> Organizational obedience reflects acceptance of the necessity and desirability of rational rules and regulations governing organizational structure, job descriptions, and personnel policies. Obedience can be demonstrated by respect for rules and instructions, punctuality in attendance and task completion, and stewardship of organizational resources. Organizational loyalty is identification with and allegiance to an organization's leaders and the organization as a whole, transcending the parochial interests of individuals, work groups, and departments. Representative behaviors include defending the organization against threats, contributing to its good reputation, and cooperating with others to serve the interests of the whole. Organizational participation is interest in organizational affairs guided by ideal standards of virtue, validated by an individual's keeping informed, and expressed through full and responsible involvement in organizational governance. Representative activities include attending nonrequired meetings, sharing informed opinions and new ideas with others, and being willing to deliver bad news or support an unpopular view to combat 'groupthink' (Janis, 1982). (Graham, 1991, p. 255)

Scale Development Procedures

Van Dyne et al. (1994) developed a 34-item scale to measure the three categories of OCB (i.e., obedience, loyalty, and participation) suggested by Graham (1991). The initial OCB questionnaire contained 54 items that were ultimately reduced to 34 on the basis of research in a primary and a cross-validation sample. The obedience construct was originally measured with 16 items that, according to the authors, were adapted and expanded from Smith et al.'s (1983) conscientiousness dimension. The loyalty (16 items) and participation (22 items) constructs were originally measured with items generated by focus group interviews conducted with employees from a variety of job levels at three research sites.

The primary sample used by Van Dyne et al. (1994) consisted of a total of 538 respondents from five settings (90 employees from a professional accounting firm, 131 employees from a savings and loan organization, 40 employees from a social service agency, 145 employees from a construction products firm, and 132 evening MBA students). Contrary to the authors' expectations, self-report responses obtained from these employees to the original 54-item scale indicated that a five-factor solution fit the data the best after 17 items with multiple loadings were eliminated.

In this 37-item scale, the first factor, loyalty, consisted of 7 items that Van Dyne et al. (1994) felt "represented allegiance to an organization and promotion of its interests" (p. 780). The second factor, obedience, consisted of 10 items that measured "respect for the rules and policies of an organization and willingness to expend appropriate effort on its behalf" (p. 780). As indicated in our summary of the scale items presented in the next section, the items that loaded on these two factors were consistent with their a priori assignment by the authors, which according to Van Dyne et al. (1994, p. 780), provided "strong empirical support for the substantive categories of loyalty and obedience."

However, the empirical findings for the third theoretical category of OCB, participation, were more complex than they hypothesized. Indeed, although Van Dyne et al. (1994) argued that all three of the remaining factors reflected participation, two of the three factors included items that were originally intended to measure loyalty or obedience. For example, the third factor comprised two items that were expected to load on a participation factor, two items that were expected to load on a loyalty factor, and one item that was expected to load on an obedience factor. Van Dyne et al. (1994) labeled this third factor "social participation" because they felt that

> All of these items . . . can be interpreted as concerning forms of participation that are noncontroversial and that involve interaction with other individuals. Examples include attending meetings, engaging in positive communications with others, and involvement in other affiliative group activities. In other words, these items describe participation in the form of interpersonal and social contact. (p. 780)

In the 37-item scale, the fourth factor, termed "advocacy participation" by Van Dyne et al. (1994), contained 8 items (later trimmed to 7) that were all originally hypothesized by the authors to measure participation according to the following reasoning:

> They describe innovation, maintaining high standards, challenging others, and making suggestions for change—behaviors targeted at other members of an organization and reflecting a willingness to be controversial. . . . In organizational settings, these behaviors are typical of an internal change agent. (pp. 780, 783)

The fifth factor, which they called "functional participation," included four behaviors that were originally intended to measure participation and three that were initially intended to measure loyalty (later trimmed to five total items). The authors felt that the underlying theme that held these behaviors together was that each one of them described

> a form of participatory contribution in which individuals focus on themselves rather than others in their organizations but yet contribute to organizational effectiveness. These personally focused behaviors include participation through performing additional work activities, self-development, and volunteering for special assignments. . . . In an organizational context, these behaviors are typical of a dedicated individual contributor whose commitment, self-development, and participation add value to the functioning of the organization." (p. 783).

Van Dyne et al. (1994) attempted to cross-validate the factor structure of the scale by asking 85 supervisors working for 48 organizations to rate the OCB of 412 of their subordinates. These data were utilized by the authors as a check on the dimensionality and internal consistency reliability of the OCB questionnaire. In addition, because 47 of the original supervisors completed a second questionnaire on 233 subordinates 4 weeks after the first questionnaire was administered, this sample also allowed for an assessment of the test-retest reliability of the OCB measures.

Confirmatory factor analysis was used to test the hypothesized five-factor structure of the OCB measure in the cross-validation sample. The initial test on the 37-item scale produced a chi-square of 2,337 ($df = 619$) and a goodness-of-fit index (GFI) of .76. Based on the modification indices the authors dropped three of the items, indicating that this reduced 34-item scale fit the five-factor model better (chi-square = 1,803, $df = 517$; GFI = .80; ratio of chi-square/df = 3.48) and that the five-factor model produced a significantly better fit than a more traditional one-factor model (chi-square = 1,777, $df = 112$). However, it is important to note that the fit of the final model reported by Van Dyne et al. (1994) did not meet conventional standards for any of the goodness-of-fit indices they reported in their paper (Hu & Bentler, 1999). Thus, the hypothesized five-factor structure was not consistent with the cross-validation data.

Estimates of the internal consistency reliability of the scales in the original (cross-validation) sample were .88 (.83) for obedience, .84 (.79) for loyalty, .68 (.68) for social participation, .86 (.84) for advocacy participation, and .75 (.75) for functional participation. The test-retest results in the cross-validation sample were .81 for obedience, .88 for loyalty, .76 for social participation, .83 for advocacy participation, and .83 for functional participation.

Scale Items

Respondents were asked to rate each of the items listed below, using a 7-point scale. Labels in parentheses indicate the authors' a priori expectation of the specific dimension the item would load on. (R) indicates reverse coded items.

Loyalty

Represents organization favorably to outsiders. (Loyalty)

Does not go out of way to defend organization against outside threats. (R) (Loyalty)

Does not tell outsiders this is a good place to work. (R) (Loyalty)

Does not defend organization when employees criticize it. (R) (Loyalty)

Actively promotes organization's products and services. (Loyalty)

Would accept job at competing organizations for more money. (R) (Loyalty)

Would not urge coworkers to invest money in organization. (R) (Loyalty)

Obedience

Rarely wastes time while at work. (Obedience)

Produces as much as capable of at all times. (Obedience)

Always comes to work on time. (Obedience)

Regardless of circumstances, produces highest quality work. (Obedience)

Does not meet all deadlines set by organization. (R) (Obedience)

Is mentally alert and ready to work when arrives at work. (Obedience)

Follows work rules and instructions with extreme care. (Obedience)

Sometimes wastes organizational resources. (R) (Obedience)

Keeps work area clean and neat. (Obedience)

Sometimes misses work for no good reason. (R) (Obedience)

Social Participation

Only attends work-related meetings if required by job. (R) (Participation)

Shares ideas for new projects or improvements widely. (Participation)

Keeps informed about products and services and tells others. (Loyalty)

Works so personal appearance is attractive and appropriate. (Obedience)

Is not involved in outside groups for benefit of organization. (R) (Loyalty)

Advocacy Participation

Frequently makes creative suggestions to coworkers. (Participation)

Uses professional judgment to assess right/wrong for organization. (Participation)

Encourages management to keep knowledge/skills current. (Participation)

Encourages others to speak up at meetings. (Participation)

Helps coworkers think for themselves. (Participation)

Keeps well-informed where opinion might benefit organization. (Participation)

Does not push superiors to perform to higher standards. (R) (Participation)

Functional Participation

Does not pursue additional training to improve performance. (R) (Participation)

Avoids extra duties and responsibilities at work. (R) (Loyalty)

Does not work beyond what is required. (R) (Loyalty)

Volunteers for overtime work when needed. (Loyalty)

Has difficulty cooperating with others on projects. (R) (Participation)

Content Validity

The employee loyalty items of the Van Dyne et al. (1994) scale generally appear to measure their intended underlying construct. The one possible exception may be the item "Would not urge coworkers to invest money in [the] organization," because it is not clear that the failure to engage in this behavior would necessarily be a sign of disloyalty in many organizations. For example, many organizations are privately held, and employee investments are not possible. And other organizations may not stress the importance of investing in the organization or expect employees to do so.

With respect to the obedience items, it is worth noting that although all of the items are generally consistent with the authors' conceptual definition of obedience, the items do not appear to be *adapted and expanded* from Smith et al.'s (1983) measures of conscientiousness as claimed by the authors.

The participation items are partially deficient because they fail to capture the notion of "being willing to deliver bad news" or the idea of "support[ing] an unpopular view to combat 'groupthink'" that are essential parts of the definition of participation—especially as originally articulated by Graham (1991). In addition, the item "Has difficulty cooperating with others on projects" may reflect a person's difficulty in cooperating as much as it reflects a person's lack of cooperation. The latter would be consistent with the conceptual definition of participation, but the former would not be.

Three of the five items for the social participation construct were not originally intended to measure participation, and it is difficult to see how some of them represent unconfounded measures of this construct. For example, "Keeps informed about products and services and tells others" is a compound item including the idea of "keeping informed" and the issue of "telling others." The former reflects participation as defined by Van Dyne et al. (1994), but the latter reflects loyalty and is quite similar to one of the other loyalty items ("Actively promotes organization's products and services"). This may explain why this item loaded on one of the participation factors instead of on the loyalty factor as originally hypothesized. In addition, it is not clear how "Works so personal appearance is attractive and appropriate" (an item originally intended to measure obedience) is an example of socially participating in the organization. One could engage in this behavior without ever interacting with anyone else. In fact, other people would not normally be involved in this activity. Finally, how is the fact that a person "Is not involved in outside groups for benefit of organization" a reflection of their failure to socially participate in the organization on noncontroversial issues? Indeed, one could imagine that this behavior might be a means of focusing greater efforts on participation within the organization. Thus, a majority of the items for the social participation construct do not seem to be consistent with its conceptual theme and were originally intended to reflect the content domain of one of the other constructs.

Similar problems exist for the functional participation construct, which Van Dyne et al. defined as, "a form of participatory contribution in which individuals focus on themselves rather than others in their organizations but yet contribute to organizational effectiveness." (p. 783). Although all of the items appear to be generally consistent with this definition, there are several problems with this scale. First, based on the conceptual definition, virtually all of the obedience items would qualify as measures of functional participation, because they are all self-focused and contribute to the effectiveness of the organization. Second, the majority (three of five) of the items that loaded on this factor were originally intended to load on the loyalty dimension, because they reflect an individual's "allegiance to an organization's leaders and the organization as a whole, transcending the parochial interests of individuals, work groups, and departments" (p. 767). For example, "volunteer[ing] for overtime work when needed" is an example of a person showing allegiance by putting the interest of the organization ahead of his or her self-interest. Being unwilling to "work beyond what is required" and "avoid[ing] extra duties and responsibilities at work" would seem to be examples of a person's unwillingness to transcend his or her parochial self-interest for the good of the organization. Thus, at least at the item level and perhaps at the conceptual level, the functional participation construct overlaps with the obedience and loyalty constructs.

Finally, there are also some problems with the content validity of the advocacy participation items. The key distinction between social participation and advocacy participation is that advocacy participation is defined as "behaviors targeted at members of the organization and reflecting a willingness to be controversial" for the good of the organization, and social participation encompasses behaviors that are targeted at other members of the organization but that are noncontroversial (Van Dyne et al., 1994, p. 780). The problem is that not all of the items used to measure advocacy participation reflect a willingness to be controversial for the good of the organization. For example, in most organizations, it is not controversial to "make creative suggestions to coworkers," "encourage others to speak up at meetings," "help coworkers think for themselves," or to "keep well informed where opinion might benefit the organization." Thus, although these items loaded together and with a few others on one factor, it is not clear what this factor represents conceptually.

In sum, our discussion suggests that there are some major problems with the content validity of the 34-item OCB scale developed by Van Dyne et al. (1994). The most serious problems involve the three participation constructs. Perhaps this is not surprising, because these three factors were not anticipated in the authors' original conceptualization. Thus, despite the fact that Van Dyne et al. (1994) have demonstrated that these scales have good internal consistency and test-retest reliability, their validity is in question.

Psychometric Properties

To our knowledge, only one study (Turnipseed, 2002) has attempted to replicate the five-factor structure found by Van Dyne et al. (1994) and to examine the psychometric properties of their scale. This study provides only modest support for the validity of Van Dyne et al.'s (1994) OCB scale. Turnipseed (2002) asked a sample of 106 employees of a large company in the financial industry to rate their own OCB using Van Dyne et al.'s (1994) 34-item scale. As in Van Dyne et al.'s (1994) initial evaluation of the scale, Turnipseed analyzed his data using exploratory factor analysis with oblique rotation. However, unlike Van Dyne et al. (1994), he found support for only four factors. He called these factors *loyalty, obedience, social advocacy,* and *functional participation.* A comparison of his factor structure with that of Van Dyne et al. (1994) indicates that there were several inconsistencies in the factor solutions obtained in these studies.

First, the reason for the difference in the total number of factors found is that most of the social participation and advocacy participation items loaded on a single factor that Turnipseed (2002) called *social advocacy.* Only two items from either of these scales failed to load on the social advocacy factor. One of these items ("Only attends work-related meetings if required by job") failed to meet the minimum .35 loading on any factor. The other item ("Uses professional judgment to assess right/wrong for organization") loaded on both the obedience and loyalty factors. Second, two of Van Dyne et al.'s (1994) seven loyalty items did not load on the loyalty factor. One ("Would accept job at competing organizations for more money") failed to load above .35 on any factor. The other ("Would not urge coworkers to invest money in organization") loaded on the functional participation factor. Third, two of Van Dyne et al.'s obedience items ("Does not meet all deadlines set by organization," and "Keeps work area clean and neat") also loaded on the functional participation factor. Finally, two of Van Dyne et al.'s functional participation items failed to load above .35 on the functional participation factor. One ("Volunteers for overtime work when needed") did not load on any of the factors, and the other ("Has difficulty cooperating with others on projects") loaded on the loyalty factor. Turnipseed (2002) did not provide estimates of reliability for the scales.

Thus, Turnipseed's (2002) study raises some doubts about the factor structure of Van Dyne et al.'s (1994) scale. However, given the small sample size that he used in his study, additional work designed to examine the psychometric properties of these scales needs to be conducted before any definitive conclusions can be drawn about its factor structure.

Moorman and Blakely (1995)

Conceptual Definition(s)

As was the case for Van Dyne et al.'s (1994) scale, the theoretical foundation for Moorman and Blakely's (1995) OCB scale was Graham's (1989) conceptualization based on the notion of civic citizenship in the political science literature. Thus, it is somewhat surprising that the four dimensions of OCB measured by Moorman and Blakely are different from the dimensions developed by Van Dyne et al. (1994). According to Moorman and Blakely (1995),

> Graham (1989) has proposed a four-dimension model of OCB and she suggested that there may be different causes for different dimensions. Her four dimensions of OCB are: (1) interpersonal helping, which focuses on helping co-workers in their jobs when such help is needed, (2) individual initiative, which describes communications to others in the workplace to improve individual and group performance, (3) personal industry, which describes the performance of specific tasks above and beyond the call of duty, and (4) loyal boosterism, which describes the promotion of the organizational image to outsiders. (p. 130)

Scale Development Procedures

Moorman and Blakely (1995) developed their 19-item OCB scale in several stages. In the first stage, the authors identified 49 items measuring the four OCB dimensions (interpersonal helping, individual initiative, personal industry, and loyal boosterism) and asked 14 colleagues to Q-sort these items into one of these four OCB categories. Items that were placed into categories other than their hypothesized dimension were either modified or replaced by the authors. Following this stage, the 49 refined items were pretested by administering them to 111 students in undergraduate and graduate business classes. The results of a factor analysis of this pretest data were used to refine the scale to 20 items, which loaded significantly on their hypothesized factors. Following their preliminary scale development, Moorman and Blakely (1995) obtained self-reported ratings on the 20-item OCB scale in a sample of 155 employees of a southeastern financial services organization. They used confirmatory factor analysis to assess the fit of their data to the hypothesized four-factor structure. Based on their analysis, they retained 19 of the original 20 items. According to the authors, "The 19 items were chosen because the data for these items fit the model well, they all had significant loadings on their hypothesized factor, and had no significant cross-loadings" (p. 131). The authors reported that Bentler's (1990) confirmatory fit index (CFI) for the 19-item scale was .91 and that the Tucker-Lewis Index (TLI) was .90. Although the authors may have slightly overstated the goodness of fit because their fit indices are below the currently recommended level of .95 (Hu & Bentler, 1999), overall the fit appears to have been adequate. However, several of their items may not have loaded very highly on their intended factors. Indeed, four of the five interpersonal helping items, and all four of the personal industry items, loaded below .50 on their intended factors. If these were what LISREL calls completely standardized loadings, this would suggest that the item reliabilities were low. However, it is not clear from the authors' description whether the "completely standardized" or just "standardized" loadings were reported.

Moorman and Blakely (1995) reported that the internal consistency reliability for the personal industry scale (.61) was below the minimum value of .70 recommended by Nunnally and Bernstein (1994) for newly developed scales. However, the reliabilities for the interpersonal helping (.74) and individual initiative (.76) dimensions were adequate, and the reliability for the loyal boosterism scale (.86) was good. Finally, Moorman and Blakely (1995) reported that the OCB dimensions were relatively independent, with none of the dimensions sharing more than 24% of their variance with each other.

Scale Items

Respondents were asked to indicate their agreement or disagreement with each of the items listed here, using a 7-point scale ranging from 1 ("strongly disagree") through 7 ("strongly agree").

Interpersonal Helping

Goes out of his/her way to help co-workers with work-related problems.

Voluntarily helps new employees settle into the job.

Frequently adjusts his/her work schedule to accommodate other employees' requests for time-off.

Always goes out of the way to make newer employees feel welcome in the work group.

Shows genuine concern and courtesy toward co-workers, even under the most trying business or personal situations.

Individual Initiative

For issues that may have serious consequences, expresses opinions honestly even when others may disagree.

Often motivates others to express their ideas and opinions.

Encourages others to try new and more effective ways of doing their job.

Encourages hesitant or quiet co-workers to voice their opinions when they otherwise might not speak-up.

Frequently communicates to co-workers suggestions on how the group can improve.

Personal Industry

Rarely misses work even when he/she has a legitimate reason for doing so.

Performs his/her duties with unusually few errors.

Performs his/her job duties with extra-special care.

Always meets or beats deadlines for completing work.

Loyal Boosterism

Defends the organization when other employees criticize it.

Encourages friends and family to utilize organization products.

Defends the organization when outsiders criticize it.

Shows pride when representing the organization in public.

Actively promotes the organization's products and services to potential users.

Content Validity

Generally speaking, the items developed by Moorman and Blakely (1995) appear to do a reasonably good job of representing the conceptual domains of the four OCB dimensions. However, there are several exceptions. For example, the conceptual definition of interpersonal helping requires that the behaviors focus on "helping co-workers *in their jobs* when such help is needed" (p. 130; emphasis added). This focus on helping with work-related problems is not apparent in the item "Always goes out of the way to make newer employees feel welcome in the work group," because making people feel welcome is not really helping others with work-related problems when they need it. Similarly, the item "Shows genuine concern and courtesy toward co-workers, even under the most trying business or personal situations" may also be problematic because it is not clear that showing concern or courtesy is a form of helping behavior and because this behavior may be a response to personal problems rather than work-related problems. In addition, the standardized loadings for four of the five items for this factor seem to be low, which suggests low item reliability.

The conceptual definition for individual initiative involves communications to others in the workplace that "improve individual and group performance" (Moorman and Blakely, 1995, p. 130). However, two of the five items ("Often motivates others to express their ideas and opinions," "Encourages hesitant or quiet co-workers to voice their opinions when they otherwise might not speak-up") do not necessarily refer to communications that would lead to improved performance. Merely getting others to express their opinions will not necessarily lead to improved performance, and the items do not clearly specify that the opinions/ideas are about how to improve work performance.

The personal industry items should all describe the performance of tasks "above and beyond the call of duty" (Moorman and Blakely, 1995, p. 130). Although all four of the items generally meet this requirement, this is less clear for one of the items ("Always meets or beats deadlines for completing work"), because the item does not indicate that this behavior goes beyond normal expectations. We would think that generally it is expected that employees would meet deadlines for completing their work. A potentially bigger problem with this factor is that the item loadings were all fairly low, which suggests either low reliability or perhaps that the measures are formative, rather than reflective, in nature (cf. Bollen & Lennox, 1991; Jarvis, MacKenzie, & Podsakoff, 2003).

With the exception of possibly one item ("Defends the organization when other employees criticize it"), the five items designed to measure loyal boosterism appear to be consistent with the construct definition. This item is inconsistent with the definition because it does not involve "the promotion of the organization image *to outsiders*" (Moorman and Blakeley, 1995, p. 130; emphasis added).

Psychometric Properties

Other than Moorman and Blakely (1995), only one study (Blakely, Andrews, & Fuller, 2003) has examined the factorial structure of this OCB scale. In their study, Blakely et al. (2003) asked supervisors at a federal government research facility to rate 203 of their subordinates using a modified 21-item version of Moorman and Blakely's (1995) 19-item scale. Although these authors did not report a list of all of the items or their factor loadings in the paper, the results of their confirmatory factor analysis suggested that: (a) their four-factor model fit the data adequately (CFI = .92; RMSEA = .085), (b) all of their items loaded significantly on their intended factors with no significant cross-loadings, and (c) all of the dimensions had acceptable internal consistency reliabilities (Cronbach's alpha was .91 for interpersonal helping, .90 for individual initiative, .89 for loyal boosterism, and .87 for personal industry).

In summary, the available evidence from two confirmatory factor analyses generally supports the hypothesized four-factor structure for Moorman and Blakely's (1995) OCB scale. However, the factor loadings for two of the factors (interpersonal helping and personal industry) seem to be low in the original Moorman and Blakely (1995) study and are not reported in the Blakely et al. (2003) study. There are several possible reasons for these low loadings. First, the items might have had low reliabilities. Second, because the items had high social desirability content and were self-reported in the Moorman and Blakely (1995) study, the variance of the items may have been attenuated due to a ceiling effect. Indeed, the interpersonal helping and personal industry factors had the highest means (6.2 and 6.0, respectively, on a 7-point scale) and lowest standard deviations (.50 and .57, respectively) of any of the variables examined in their study. Third, the loadings may have been low because the items should have been modeled as determinants of these dimensions rather than as reflections of them (Bollen & Lennox, 1991; Jarvis et al., 2003). Therefore, it may be beneficial to obtain additional confirmation of the psychometric properties of this scale before it is more widely used as a measure of OCB.

Van Scotter and Motowidlo (1996)

Conceptual Definition(s)

Although the study reported by Motowidlo and Van Scotter (1994) provided some support for viewing task performance and contextual performance as distinct elements of job performance, Van Scotter and Motowidlo (1996) felt that further refinement of the contextual performance construct was warranted, because it included "both interpersonal elements, such as maintaining good working relationships and cooperating with others, and volitional or motivational elements, such as persisting in the face of adversity and volunteering to perform additional tasks" (p. 526). They used the label "interpersonal facilitation" to refer to the former category of interpersonally oriented behaviors and the label "job dedication" to refer to the latter category of behaviors that demonstrated persistence and effort. They defined these behaviors in the following manner:

> Interpersonal facilitation consists of interpersonally oriented behaviors that contribute to organizational goal accomplishment. It differs from job-specific task performance. In addition to the spontaneous helping behaviors that Smith et al. (1983) called altruism, and George and Brief (1992) labeled helping coworkers, interpersonal facilitation encompasses deliberate acts that improve morale, encourage cooperation, remove barriers to performance, or help coworkers perform their task-oriented job activities. Thus, interpersonal facilitation encompasses a range of interpersonal acts that help maintain the interpersonal and social context needed to support effective task performance in an organizational setting.
>
> Job dedication centers on self-disciplined behaviors such as following rules, working hard, and taking the initiative to solve a problem at work. It encompasses Smith et al.'s (1983) generalized compliance dimension, as well as the "will do" factors identified in recent personnel selection research conducted for the U.S. Army in Project A (Campbell et al., 1990). Job dedication is the motivational foundation for job performance that drives people to act with the deliberate intention of promoting the organization's best interests. (Van Scotter & Motowidlo, 1996, p. 526)

Scale Development Procedures

Van Scotter and Motowidlo (1996) did not provide much information regarding how they developed their measures of job dedication and interpersonal facilitation in their original paper, other than to say that: (a) they initially developed 13 items for each of these constructs and factor analyzed them using data from an independent sample, (b) the refined interpersonal facilitation scale consisted of seven items that possessed an internal consistency reliability of .93 in their scale development sample and .89 in the primary sample of their study, and (c) their refined job dedication measure consisted of eight items that possessed an internal consistency reliability of .95 in their scale development sample and .94 in the primary sample of their study. However, two subsequent papers (Van Scotter, 2000; Van Scotter, Motowidlo, & Cross, 2000) provide a more detailed discussion of the scale development procedures that Van Scotter and Motowidlo (1996) used to develop their scales. Therefore, we relied on these accounts to describe the process more completely.

Van Scotter et al. (2000) indicate that although the majority of the 13 items used initially to measure interpersonal facilitation in the Van Scotter and Motowidlo (1996) study were gleaned from the literature, most of the 13 items used to measure job dedication were adapted from Motowidlo and Van Scotter's (1994) earlier measure of contextual performance. Van Scotter (1994) conducted a pilot study as part of his dissertation to investigate the reliability and convergent validity of these items. For the purposes of this study, Van Scotter (1994) had two supervisors independently rate Air Force mechanics on their task performance, job dedication, or interpersonal facilitation behaviors. Two of the supervisors rated the task performance of 192 mechanics (for a total of 384 individual ratings on this dimension), two supervisors rated the interpersonal facilitation of 147 subordinates (for a total of 294 individual ratings on this dimension), and two supervisors rated the job dedication of 168 subordinates (for a total of 336 individual ratings on this dimension). One of the pairs of supervisors rating each of the three performance categories (task performance, job dedication, and interpersonal facilitation) was randomly assigned to Group A, and the other was assigned to Group B.

An iterative process using maximum likelihood factor analysis was conducted to refine the scales with supervisors in Group A. As a first step in this process, the researchers chose 4 of the 13 items in each scale as anchors because they represented the central theme of each of the performance dimensions. Then, for each of the three dimensions, they fit a two-factor solution to the data and identified items with loadings greater than or equal to |.30|. Next, they removed the nonanchor item with the largest loading on the second factor and tested the fit of a one-factor model to the remaining data. They repeated this step until the chi-square goodness-of-fit index for the one-factor model became nonsignificant or no items loaded on the second factor in a two-factor model greater than or equal to I.30I. This process resulted in a refined measure of task performance, job dedication, and interpersonal facilitation that consisted of 6 items, 8 items, and 7 items, respectively.

After completing the exploratory factor analyses with supervisors in Group A, the researchers conducted confirmatory factor analyses on the data from the Group B supervisors. Van Scotter et al. (2000) reported that the CFIs from these analyses were .97 for task performance, .98 for job dedication, and .94 for interpersonal facilitation. Van Scotter et al. also reported a subsequent confirmatory factor analysis on a set of cases that could not be used for the Motowidlo and Van Scotter (1996) study, because these cases lacked supervisory ratings on at least one of the performance dimensions. The CFIs (and sample sizes) from these confirmatory factor analyses were .98 (N = 168) for task performance, .95 (N = 147) for interpersonal facilitation, and .94 (N = 123) for job dedication.

Finally, Van Scotter and Motowidlo (1996) found that none of the three performance dimensions (task performance, job dedication, and interpersonal facilitation) shared more than 24% of their variance. Thus, these findings suggest that these performance dimensions are relatively distinct from each other.

Scale Items

Supervisors were asked to indicate on a 5-point scale ranging from 1 (not at all likely) to 5 (extremely likely) how likely each person would be to engage in the behaviors listed here while performing his or her job.

Interpersonal Facilitation

Praise co-workers when they are successful.

Support or encourage a co-worker with a personal problem.

Talk to other workers before taking actions that might affect them.

Say things to make people feel good about themselves or the work group.

Encourage others to overcome their differences and get along.

Treat others fairly.

Help someone without being asked.

Job Dedication

Put in extra hours to get work done on time.

Pay close attention to important details.

Work harder than necessary.

Ask for a challenging work assignment.

Exercise personal discipline and self-control.

Take the initiative to solve a work problem.

Persist in overcoming obstacles to complete a task.

Tackle a difficult work assignment enthusiastically.

Content Validity

Generally speaking, the items designed to measure interpersonal facilitation appear to capture their intended content domain. However, it does not appear that any of these items adequately measures behaviors that are aimed at "remov[ing] barriers to performance" (Van Scotter & Motowidlo, 1996, p. 526), except perhaps in the most general sense. Similarly, none of the items designed to measure job dedication adequately taps the "following rules" component of the conceptual definition of this construct. Thus, to the extent that these elements are considered important components of these constructs, the measures are probably somewhat deficient.

Finally, the item "Exercise personal discipline and self-control" is somewhat ambiguous with respect to how it is connected to *job* dedication and the motivation to "act with the deliberate intention of promoting the organization's best interests" (Van Scotter & Motowidlo, 1996, p. 526). The fact that this item explicitly refers to *personal* discipline and self-control, rather than discipline and self-control in work settings, introduces some ambiguity. It may be possible to be very disciplined and self-controlled in one's personal life but not be disciplined and self-controlled on the job.

Psychometric Properties

Although two studies (Van Scotter, 2000; Van Scotter et al., 2000) reported using the job dedication and interpersonal facilitation measures from Van Scotter and Motowidlo (1996), both of these studies appear to have used samples that were composed primarily of the same samples reported in Van Scotter and Motowidlo (1996). Therefore, although these studies report that the job dedication and interpersonal facilitation measures possess high internal consistency reliabilities and are relatively distinct from each other and from the task performance dimension, additional research using these scales in other samples that are independent from the ones reported by Van Scotter and Motowidlo (1996), Van Scotter (2000), and Van Scotter et al. (2000) should be conducted.

Farh, Earley, and Lin (1997)

Conceptual Definition(s)

Noting that most of the research on OCB had been conducted in Western cultures and that little was known about it in a global context, Farh, Earley, and Lin (1997) were interested in exploring whether OCB "has an etic (universal) meaning in cultures in which expectations for employees differ drastically" (p. 421). For the purposes of their research, they developed a Chinese OCB scale. Based on a series of studies, they identified five OCB dimensions. They noted that two of these dimensions (altruism toward colleagues and conscientiousness) were virtually identical to the altruism and conscientiousness dimensions identified by Organ (1988) and measured by Podsakoff et al. (1990). In addition, they identified another dimension, which they labeled "identification with the company," that was very similar conceptually to the civic virtue dimension measured by Podsakoff et al. (1990) but that included a few additional items that emphasized the willingness on the part of employees to spread positive company news to outsiders, defend the company's reputation, and make suggestions for improvements. Despite these minor differences, Farh et al. (1997) concluded that their altruism, conscientiousness, and identification with company dimensions were relatively universal (etic) in nature. They defined these three dimensions in the following manner:

> Altruism toward colleagues—Discretionary behavior that has the effect of helping others around him or her (mostly peers, clients, supervisors), with an organizationally relevant task or problem.
>
> Conscientiousness—Discretionary behaviors on the part of the employee that go well beyond the minimum role requirements of the organization in the areas of attendance, obeying rules and regulations, taking breaks, working hard, and so forth.

> Identification with company—Discretionary behavior that indicates that one responsibly participates in, is involved in, or is concerned about the life of the organization, e.g., attending important but nonmandatory meetings; keeping abreast of changes in the organization, reading company memos and announcements and performing functions that help company image . . . willingness . . . to spread positive company news to outsiders, defend the company's reputation, and make suggestions for improvements. (Farh et al., 1997, p. 429)

However, Farh et al. (1997) did not have dimensions comparable to either the sportsmanship or courtesy dimensions reported by Podsakoff et al. (1990). Rather, they reported two new dimensions (interpersonal harmony and protecting company resources) that emerged from their research, suggesting that these two dimensions were emic (or more particularlistic) in nature. They noted that the presence of these two dimensions in the Chinese citizenship behavior scale

> can be attributed to their cultural roots. As noted by many writers (e.g., Bond and Hwang, 1987; Yang, 1993), one of the most distinctive features of Chinese societies is their family orientation. The influence of the family is so strong in Chinese society that it has an undeniable predominance over its members in almost all domains of life. The submerging of one's self or individuality into his or her family is a special type of in-group collectivism called familistic collectivism, which can be distinguished from universal collectivism (Schwartz, 1990). One of the natural consequences of familistic collectivism is in-group favoritism, which may manifest itself in organizational life in the form of using one's position to benefit oneself or one's family members (e.g., nepotism). This is especially true when an employee is working in a business that is not related to his or her family. Because such abuses by employees interfere with economic efficiency, it is a common challenge for Chinese organizations to devise strategies to guard against such behavior. The emergence of protecting company resources as a major form of citizenship behavior in Chinese societies is a manifestation of such concern. The cultural root of interpersonal harmony in the Chinese citizenship behavior scale is a cherished cultural value of interpersonal harmony found in Chinese societies (Yang, 1993). For example, it is common practice in traditional Chinese societies for anyone who first violates interpersonal harmony, for whatever reason, to take a much larger share of the blame, no matter whether his or her behavior is justifiable. Interpersonal harmony is so stressed by Chinese people that it appears to outsiders that they pursue harmony for harmony's sake. (Farh et al. 1997, pp. 429–430)

Farh et al. (1997) went on to define these two new dimensions in the following manner:

> Interpersonal harmony—Discretionary behavior by an employee to avoid pursuing personal power and gain with detrimental effects on others in the organization.

Protecting company resources—Discretionary behavior by an employee to avoid negative behaviors that abuse company policies and resources for personal use. (p. 429)

Scale Development Procedures

Farh et al. (1997) used three samples to develop their 20-item Chinese OCB scale. The first sample was 109 Chinese students and employees enrolled in an MBA program or in management courses at the National Chengchi University in Taiwan. For the purposes of this study, Farh et al. (1997) presented these participants with a broad definition of OCB along with several examples. However, the researchers were careful not to inform these participants of the five dimensions of OCB identified by Organ (1988). They asked each participant to draw on his or her work experience to list 10 to 20 examples of OCB. Farh et al. (1997) obtained more than 1,500 statements regarding citizenship behaviors, which they transcribed onto cards to accomplish a three-stage sorting process. In the first stage, the authors sorted the cards into 115 categories. Following this step, they had three assistants independently decide how the categories could be combined. These assistants reached consensus on collapsing the 115 categories into 60 more general categories. Finally, the authors selected a representative statement from each of the 60 categories to develop the original version of their scale.

Farh et al. (1997) tested their 60-item scale in a sample of 75 managers drawn from 10 organizations from a variety of industries, including machinery, electronics, chemical and food products firms, financial institutions, management consultants, and government agencies. Based on an examination of the item-to-total score correlations, they eliminated four of the items and then conducted a series of factor analyses on the remaining 56 items. These analyses resulted in a five-factor solution with from 6 to 19 items loading on each dimension. However, to make the scale more manageable, the authors constructed a reduced 22-item OCB scale by selecting 4 to 6 items with the highest loadings on each factor.

In the final stage of their scale development process, Farh et al. (1997) administered their 22-item scale to 227 supervisors in their primary study sample and used confirmatory factor analysis to test if the five-factor structure was consistent in this sample. After dropping 2 items, they reported that all of the remaining 20 items loaded significantly on their intended factors and that the fit of the five-factor solution was adequate (TLI = .91; GFI = .87; CFI = .92). Cronbach's alpha was .87 for identification with the company, .87 for altruism toward colleagues, .82 for conscientiousness, .86 for interpersonal harmony, and .81 for protecting company resources, suggesting that all five of the subdimensions possessed reasonably good internal consistency reliability. In addition, the highest correlation between any of the scales was .58 (harmony and protecting company resources), suggesting that the dimensions were relatively distinct from each other.

Scale Items

Respondents were asked to indicate their agreement or disagreement with each of the items listed here, using a 7-point scale ranging from "strongly disagree" through "strongly agree," with a midpoint labeled "neither agree nor disagree." Reverse coded items are indicated by (R).

Identification with the company

Willing to stand up to protect the reputation of the company.

Eager to tell outsiders good news about the company and clarify their misunderstandings.

Makes constructive suggestions that can improve the operation of the company.

Actively attends company meetings.

Altruism toward colleagues

Willing to assist new colleagues to adjust to the work environment.

Willing to help colleagues solve work-related problems.

Willing to cover work assignments for colleagues when needed.

Willing to coordinate and communicate with colleagues.

Conscientiousness

Complies with company rules and procedures even when nobody watches and no evidence can be traced.

Takes one's job seriously and rarely makes mistakes.

Does not mind taking on new or challenging assignments.

Tries hard to self-study to increase the quality of work outputs.

Often arrives early and starts to work immediately.

Interpersonal harmony

Uses illicit tactics to seek personal influence and gain with harmful effect on interpersonal harmony in the organization. (R)

Uses position power to pursue selfish personal gain. (R)

Takes credits, avoids blames, and fights fiercely for personal gain. (R)

Often speaks ill of the supervisor or colleagues behind their backs. (R)

Protecting company resources

Conducts personal business on company time (e.g., trading stocks, shopping, going to barber shops). (R)

Uses company resources to do personal business (e.g., company phones, copy machines, computers, and cars). (R)

Views sick leave as benefit and makes excuse for taking sick leave. (R)

Content Validity

Generally speaking, most of the items on the altruism toward colleagues, interpersonal harmony and protecting company resources scales reflect the underlying constructs they were intended to measure. Despite this, there are a few points worth noting about these measures. First, the altruism item "Willing to coordinate and communicate with colleagues" appears to be somewhat general and does not explicitly indicate that the coordination or communication relates to an "organizationally relevant task or problem" (Farh et al., 1997, p. 429). Second, all of the items included on the interpersonal harmony and protecting company resources scales are negatively worded, raising the possibility these factors resulted from response biases rather than to their particularistic (emic) meaning in the Chinese culture. However, Farh et al. (1997) felt that this was an unlikely explanation of their findings for two reasons:

> First, it is common in the Chinese language for positive attributes to be expressed using a negation of a negative. For example, someone who performs "well" is said to perform "bu cuo," or literally, "did not do the wrong things," and someone who performs "extremely well" is said to perform "hen bu cuo," or literally, "did not do the wrong things at all," which is consistent with a culture stressing personal modesty. The use of negative phrasing is connotatively different in Chinese than it is in English in many cases. It is therefore not surprising that when subjects were asked to describe citizenship behaviors, instead of identifying all positive behaviors, they

also identified negative behaviors that one should not do to represent good behavior. The fact that negative items were heavily used to describe harmony and resources suggests that they are indeed emic. Second, if the factor analyses were shaped by a negative rather than a positive wording, we would not expect to see two independent "negative" dimensions produced. Rather, these two dimensions should have loaded on a common factor reflecting a "negative" wording. Based on these analyses and our tracing of these two dimensions to Chinese culture, we think that these two dimensions are emic dimensions and not simply a methodological artifact. (Farh et al., 1997; p. 430).

With respect to the identification with the company dimension, it is probably fair to say that, although the items that are included in the scale reflect their underlying construct fairly well, none of the items on the scale appears to measure those parts of the conceptual definition that relate to "keeping abreast of changes in the organization" or "reading company memos and announcements" (Farh et al., 1997, p. 429). Thus, if these types of activities are really considered an important part of the construct, the measures may be somewhat deficient.

Psychometric Properties

We are not aware of any study other than the one published by Farh et al. (1997) that has examined the factor structure of their full 20-item scale. However, Hui, Law, and Chen (1999) conducted research using a modified 15-item version of the scale in a sample of 386 supervisor-subordinate dyads working in a Sino–Hong Kong joint venture. Their revised scale consisted of 3 items taken from each of the five OCB dimensions in the original Farh et al. (1997) scale. Hui et al. (1999) tested the hypothesized five-factor structure using confirmatory factor analysis. They reported that their results generally supported the five-factor measurement model (CFI = .90; RMR = .066) and that, with the exception of the protecting company resources dimension (alpha = .69), all of the other OCB subdimensions had adequate internal consistency reliabilities (.79 for altruism, .72 for conscientiousness, .74 for identification with the company, and .83 for interpersonal harmony). Thus, although additional research clearly needs to be conducted with the full 20-item version of Farh et al.'s (1997) OCB scale, the first two studies using this measure in Chinese samples would suggest that the psychometric properties of the scale are acceptable.

However, it is not clear whether the Farh et al. (1997) scale affords a decided psychometric advantage over other scales in a Chinese context or whether the two OCB dimensions (courtesy and sportsmanship) from Organ's (1988) conceptual domain that Farh et al. omitted in their study are indeed inappropriate in this context. As noted earlier in this appendix, Lam et al. (1999) reported support for the dimensional struc-ture of Podsakoff et al.'s (1990) five-factor OCB measure (which includes the sportsmanship and courtesy dimensions) in four cultural contexts (including Hong Kong), and Hui et al. (2004) reported sup-port for this same measurement model in their study of Chinese steel workers. Thus, it seems that either of these scales can be used in a Chinese context, and researchers may want to give some thought to the one that they believe is the most appropriate in their research.

Van Dyne and LePine (1998)

Conceptual Definitions

Building on the conceptual framework of Van Dyne, Cummings, and McLean-Parks (1995), Van Dyne and LePine (1998) developed measures of helping behavior and voice behavior, and differentiated these extra-role behaviors from in-role behavior in their study:

> We defined helping as promotive behavior that emphasizes small acts of consid-eration. Helping is cooperative behavior that is noncontroversial. It is directly and obviously affiliative; it builds and preserves relationships; and it emphasizes inter-personal harmony. We defined voice as promotive behavior that emphasizes expression of constructive challenge intended to improve rather than merely crit-icize. Voice is making innovative suggestions for change and recommending mod-ifications to standard procedures even when others disagree. Helping is important to organizations when roles are interdependent and employee cooperation facili-tates overall performance. Voice is important when an organization's environment is dynamic and new ideas facilitate continuous improvement (Nemeth & Staw, 1989). We note that helping and voice are not always extra-role behaviors. Some care-giving jobs (such as nursing) require helping, and some change-agent/ control jobs (such as auditor and devil's advocate) require voice. These cases of helping and voice are in-role and not extra-role and differ from the behaviors that our research focuses on: helping and voice that are not required as part of a job. (Van Dyne & LePine, 1998, p.109)

Scale Development Procedures

Van Dyne and LePine's (1998) helping and voice behavior scales were developed by drawing on previous measures of these constructs. They measured helping behavior with seven items adapted from Organ and Konovsky (1989) and Smith et al. (1983). They measured voice behavior with six items based on the work of Van Dyne et al. (1994) and

Whithey and Cooper (1989). In addition, to establish the discriminant validity of these measures from measures of in-role behavior, they also included four items developed by Williams and Anderson (1991) to measure in-role behavior.

Van Dyne and LePine (1998) conducted two pilot studies of their scales. In the first, they asked 48 evening MBA students to rate themselves on the OCB dimensions at a 2-week interval. They reported that Cronbach's alpha was .85 for helping, .89 for voice, and .89 for in-role behavior and that the test-retest reliabilities for these scales over the 2-week interval were .81, .78, and .75, respectively. In their second pilot study, they obtained supervisor ratings of 321 subordinates from 36 organizations. They reported that exploratory factor analysis in this sample supported a three-factor solution, with the items loading on the helping, voice, and in-role behavior factors.

Following the pilot tests, Van Dyne and LePine (1998) gathered data from their primary sample. The sample consisted of 597 employees, their work group peers (N = 597), and their supervisors (N = 97), all of whom were working in one of 95 intact work teams located in 21 manufacturing and nonmanufacturing organizations throughout the Midwestern United States. They obtained self, peer, and supervisor ratings of both the in-role and extra-role measures of performance at two different time periods separated by 6 months. Van Dyne and LePine (1998) tested the hypothesized three-factor structure using a series of nested confirmatory factor analysis models for each of the three sources (self, peer, and supervisor) from which they had obtained ratings. In addition, they conducted a two-group multigroup analysis to cross-validate their results and to determine whether their hypothesized three-factor solution fit the data equally well at time 1 and time 2. They also conducted a three-group multigroup analysis to determine whether the factor structure for their scales was invariant across the three rating sources.

Van Dyne and LePine (1998) reported that: (a) all of the items loaded significantly on their intended latent constructs; (b) the three-factor model fit the data better than either a two-factor measurement model in which the two extra-role behaviors were constrained to load together onto one factor, or a one-factor measurement model in which all of the in-role and extra-role measures were constrained to load on one factor; (c) this pattern of results held across the three rating groups for both time 1 and time 2; and (d) with the exception of the peer ratings in time 1 and time 2, the three-factor solution fit the data reasonably well in an absolute sense (average GFI = .92, average CFI = .95, average RMSEA = .06, excluding the fit indices for peer ratings in time 1 and time 2).

In addition, they reported that their multigroup assessment of the three-factor measurement model over time indicated that the factor loadings for the helping, voice, and in-role dimensions were stable over time, and their multigroup assessment across raters indicated that the factor loadings were *not* equivalent across rating sources. Finally, Van Dyne and LePine reported that: (a) the internal consistency reliability (alpha) for the helping behavior measure averaged across the three raters was .94 in time 1 and .93 in time 2; (b) the alpha for the voice behavior measure averaged across the three raters was .92 in time 1 and .93 in time 2; (c) the test-retest reliabilities for helping behavior were .61 for self-ratings, .55 for peer ratings, and .66 for supervisor ratings; and (d) the test-retest reliabilities for voice behavior were .64 for self-ratings, .65 for peer ratings, and .72 for supervisor ratings.

Thus, the results reported by Van Dyne and LePine (1998) suggest that their helping and voice behavior measures have good internal consistency and test-retest reliabilities over time and across all three rating sources. In addition, the helping and voice behavior measures are factorially sound, except for the peer ratings. In the peer rating data, the hypothesized three-factor structure was significantly better than either a two-factor or a one-factor structure, but it did not fit the data well in an absolute sense, thus suggesting that a more complex factor structure might have been indicated for this sample only. Finally, although the nested model comparisons indicated that the helping and voice constructs were less than perfectly correlated, according to the results presented in Table 2 of their paper, the average intercorrelation among these dimensions (.74) taken from the same sources at the same points in time suggests that these measures share a fairly substantial amount of variance (55%) with each other.

Scale Items

Respondents were asked to indicate their agreement or disagreement with each of the items listed below, using a 7-point scale ranging from "strongly disagree" through "strongly agree."

Helping

This particular co-worker volunteers to do things for this work group.

This particular co-worker helps orient new employees in this group.

This particular co-worker attends functions that help this work group.

This particular co-worker assists others in this group with their work for the benefit of the group.

This particular co-worker gets involved to benefit this work group.

This particular co-worker helps others in this group learn about the work.

This particular co-worker helps others in this group with their work responsibilities.

Voice

This particular co-worker develops and makes recommendations concerning issues that affect this work group.

This particular co-worker speaks up and encourages others in this group to get involved in issues that affect the group.

This particular co-worker communicates his/her opinions about work issues to others in this group even if his/her opinion is different and others in the group disagree with him/her.

This particular co-worker keeps well informed about issues where his/her opinion might be useful to this work group.

This particular co-worker gets involved in issues that affect the quality of work life here in this group.

This particular co-worker speaks up in this group with ideas for new projects or changes in procedures.

In-Role Behavior (from Williams & Anderson, 1991)

This particular co-worker fulfills the responsibilities specified in his/her job description.

This particular co-worker performs the tasks that are expected as part of the job.

This particular co-worker meets performance expectations.

This particular co-worker adequately completes responsibilities.

Content Validity

With two possible exceptions, the helping behavior measures seem to be consistent with their conceptual definition of helping. Given their definition, the item "This particular co-worker attends functions that help this work group" would not seem to fit, because it does not appear to fit into the category "acts of consideration," and it is not clear how this behavior "emphasizes interpersonal harmony" or "builds and preserves relationships" (Van Dyne & LePine, 1998, p.109). In addition, their item "This particular co-worker gets involved to benefit this work group" may be questionable because getting involved is a pretty general statement that may not involve behaviors that are directly and obviously acts of consideration or that promote interpersonal harmony.

As noted earlier, Van Dyne and LePine (1998) define voice behavior as "making innovative suggestions for change and recommending modifications to standard procedures even when others disagree" (p. 109). Generally speaking, the items developed to measure this construct are framed more broadly than the conceptual definition would seem to permit. For example, four of the six items used to measure this construct ("This particular co-worker develops and makes recommendations concerning issues that affect this work group," "This particular co-worker speaks up and encourages others in this group to get involved in issues that affect the group," "This particular co-worker keeps well informed about issues where his/her opinion might be useful to this work group," "This particular co-worker gets involved in issues that affect the quality of work life here in this group"), appear to be fairly general and do not specifically reflect "making innovative suggestions for change and recommending modifications to standard procedures." In addition, two of these items vaguely speak of "getting involved" in issues that affect the group or the quality of work life, but such involvement does not necessarily take the form of "making innovative suggestions for change and recommending modifications to standard procedures." People can be involved in the group (e.g. showing up for all group meetings, listening intently to what other group members say, implementing actions agreed to by the group as a whole, and so forth) without exhibiting voice behavior. Finally, the conceptual definition appears to emphasize that voice has an element of speaking about action (e.g., making suggestions or recommendations) as opposed to taking action. However, at least two of the items ("This particular co-worker keeps well informed about issues where his/her opinion might be useful to this work group," "This particular co-worker gets involved in issues that affect the quality of work life here in this group") seem to focus on taking action rather than speaking about taking it. Thus, despite the favorable psychometric properties of these scales reported by Van Dyne and LePine (1998), there do appear to be some questions regarding their content validity, particularly of the voice behavior measures. This is an issue that should be addressed in future research.

Psychometric Properties

To our knowledge, Van Dyne and LePine (1998) is the only study to have examined the factor structure of the complete complement of helping behavior and voice behavior items. Across six samples of data (obtained from three sources at two points in time), they report that the helping and voice scales were found to have high internal consistency reliabilities, high test-retest reliabilities, and were relatively distinct from each other. However, because this is the only study that has provided evidence of discriminant validity and the psychometric properties of the full scale, additional empirical research is needed.

Types of OCB

From our discussion thus far in this appendix, it is obvious that many different forms of OCB/CP have been identified and measured in the literature. Indeed, Podsakoff, MacKenzie, Paine, & Bachrach (2000) identified nearly 30 potentially different forms of OCB in the literature, and LePine, Erez, and Johnson (2002) identified more than 40 measures of behaviors that scholars have referred to as OCB or something similar. In this section, we discuss the similarities and differences among these constructs to identify the fundamental dimensions of OCB. Table A.1 provides our integration of the various OCB/CP constructs by organizing them into seven common themes or dimensions:

1. Helping
2. Sportsmanship
3. Organizational Loyalty
4. Organizational Compliance
5. Individual Initiative
6. Civic Virtue
7. Self-Development

Helping has been identified as an important form of citizenship behavior by virtually everyone who has worked in this area (e.g., Borman & Motowidlo, 1993, 1997; George & Brief, 1992; George & Jones, 1997; Graham, 1989; MacKenzie et al., 1999; MacKenzie et al., 2001; Organ, 1988, 1990a, 1990b; Podsakoff & MacKenzie, 1994; Smith,

Table A.1 Summary of Employee In-Role and Extra-Role Work Performance Dimensions

Author(s)	Helping	Sportsmanship	Organizational Loyalty	Organizational Compliance	Individual Initiative	Self-Development
Smith, Organ, & Near (1983)	**Altruism**—". . . capture(s) behavior that is directly and intentionally aimed at helping a specific person in face-to-face situations (e.g., orienting new people, assisting someone with a heavy workload) . . ." (p. 657).			**Generalized compliance**—". . . pertains to a more impersonal form of conscientiousness that does not provide immediate aid to any one specific person, but rather is indirectly helpful to others involved in the system. The behavior (e.g., punctuality, not wasting time) seems to represent something akin to compliance with internalized norms defining what a 'good employee ought to do'" (p. 657).		
Organ (1988, 1990b, 1990c)	**Altruism**—"Voluntary actions that help another person with a work problem—instructing a new hire on how to use equipment, helping a co-worker catch up with a backlog of work, fetching materials that a colleague needs and cannot procure on his own." (Organ, 1990c, p. 96).	**Sportsmanship**—"A citizen-like posture of tolerating the inevitable inconveniences and impositions of work without whining and grievances . . ." (Organ, 1990c, p. 96).			**Civic virtue**—"is responsible, constructive involvement in the political process of the organization, . . . expressing opinions" (Organ, 1990c, p. 96).	

Author(s)	Helping	Sportsmanship	Organizational Loyalty	Organizational Compliance	Individual Initiative	Self-Development
	Courtesy—"Subsumes all of those foresightful gestures that help someone else prevent a problem—touching base with people before committing to actions that will affect them, providing advance notice to someone who needs to know to schedule work" (Organ, 1990c, p. 96). **Peacemaking**—"actions that help to prevent, resolve, or mitigate unconstructive interpersonal conflict" (p. 96). **Cheerleading**—"The words and gestures of encouragement and reinforcement of coworkers' accomplishments and professional development" (Organ, 1990c, p. 96).					

(Continued)

Author(s)	Helping	Sportsmanship	Organizational Loyalty	Organizational Compliance	Individual Initiative	Self-Development
Graham (1989) and Moorman & Blakely (1995)	**Interpersonal helping**—"focuses on helping coworkers in their jobs when such help was needed" (Moorman & Blakely, p. 130).		**Loyal boosterism**—"the promotion of the organizational image to outsiders" (Moorman & Blakely, p. 130).		**Individual initiative**—"Communications to others in the workplace to improve individual and group performance" (Moorman & Blakely, p. 130).	
Graham (1991) and Van Dyne, et al. (1994)			**Organizational loyalty**—"Identification with and allegiance to organizational leaders and the organization as a whole, transcending the parochial interests of individuals, work groups, and departments. Representative behaviors include defending the organization against threats; contributing	**Organizational obedience**—"An orientation toward organizational structure, job descriptions, and personnel policies that recognizes and accepts the necessity and desirability of a rational structure of rules and regulations. Obedience may be demonstrated by a respect for rules and instructions, punctuality in attendance and task completion, and stewardship of organizational resources" (Graham, 1991, p. 255).	**Organizational participation**—"Acts of responsible participation in the governance of the organization, when they include . . . sharing informed opinions and new ideas with others, and being willing to deliver bad news and support an unpopular view to combat	

Author(s)	Helping	Sportsmanship	Organizational Loyalty	Organizational Compliance	Individual Initiative	Self-Development
			to its good reputation; and cooperating with others to serve the interests of the whole" (Graham, 1991, p. 255).		groupthink" (Graham, 1991, p. 255).	
Williams & Anderson (1991)	OCBI—"Behaviors that immediately benefit specific individuals and indirectly through this means contribute to the organization (e.g., helps others who have been absent, takes a personal interest in other employees) ... Prior research has labeled the OCBI dimension as altruism ..." (p. 602).			OCBO—"Behaviors that benefit the organization in general (e.g, gives advance notice when unable to come to work, adheres to informal rules devised to maintain order) ... Prior research has labeled ... the OCBO dimension as generalized compliance" (pp. 601–602).		
George & Brief (1992) and George & Jones (1997)	Helping coworkers—"includes all voluntary forms of assistance that organizational members provide each other to facilitate the accomplishment of tasks and attainment of goals.		Spreading goodwill—"Is the means by which organizational members voluntarily contribute to organizational effectiveness through efforts to represent		Making constructive suggestions—"Includes all voluntary acts of creativity and innovation in organizations. Such suggestions	Developing oneself—"Includes all the steps that workers take to voluntarily improve their knowledge, skills, and abilities so as to be better able to contribute to their organizations. Seeking

(Continued)

Table A.1 (Continued)

Author(s)	Helping	Sportsmanship	Organizational Loyalty	Organizational Compliance	Individual Initiative	Self-Development
	"Helping coworkers includes behaviors ranging from helping a coworker with a heavy workload and sharing resources, to calling attention to errors and omissions and providing instruction in the use of new technology when one is not required to do so" (George & Jones, p. 154).		"their organizations to wider communities in a beneficial light whether it be describing one's organization as supportive and caring or describing an organization's goods and services as being high quality and responsive to customers' needs, instances of spreading goodwill contribute to organizational effectiveness by insuring that organizations obtain needed resources from various stakeholder groups." (George & Jones, p. 155).		"can range from the relatively mundane (a more efficient way to handle paperwork) to the more monumental (reorganization of an entire unit to better serve a changing customer base) ... workers who engage in this form of organizational spontaneity ... actively try to find ways to improve individual, group, or organizational functioning" (George & Jones, p. 155).	out and taking advantage of advanced training courses, keeping abreast of the latest developments in one's field and area, or even learning a new set of skills so as to expand the range of one's contributions to an organization ..." (George & Jones, p. 155).

Author(s)	Helping	Sportsmanship	Organizational Loyalty	Organizational Compliance	Individual Initiative	Self-Development
Borman & Motowidlo (1993, 1997)	**Helping and cooperating with others**—"[Including] assisting/helping coworkers . . . assisting/helping customers . . . [and] altruism" (Borman & Motowidlo, 1993, p. 82).	**Helping and cooperating with others**— "[Including] organizational courtesy and not complaining . . ." (Borman & Motowidlo, 1993, p. 82).	**Endorsing, supporting, and defending organizational objectives**— "[Including] organizational loyalty . . . concern for unit objectives . . . staying with the organization during hard times and representing the organization favorably to outsiders" (Borman & Motowidlo, 1993, p. 82).	Following organizational rules and procedures— "[Including] following orders and regulations and respect for authority . . . complying with organizational values and policies . . . conscientiousness . . . meeting deadlines . . ." (Borman & Motowidlo, 1993, p. 82).	**Volunteering to carry out task activities**—"when it includes suggesting organizational improvements" (Borman & Motowidlo, 1993, p. 82).	
Van Scotter & Motowidlo (1996)	**Interpersonal facilitation**—"Consists of interpersonally oriented behaviors that contribute to organizational goal accomplishment . . . In addition to the spontaneous helping behaviors that Smith et al. (1983) called altruism, and George and Brief (1992)			**Job dedication**—"Centers on self-disciplined behaviors such as following rules . . . It encompasses Smith et al.'s (1983) generalized compliance dimension . . ." (p. 526).		

(Continued)

Author(s)	Helping	Sportsmanship	Organizational Loyalty	Organizational Compliance	Individual Initiative	Self-Development
	labeled helping coworkers, interpersonal facilitation encompasses deliberate acts that improve morale, encourage cooperation, remove barriers to performance, or help coworkers perform their task-oriented job activities. Thus, interpersonal facilitation encompasses a range of interpersonal acts that help maintain the interpersonal and social context needed to support effective task performance in an organizational setting" (p. 526).					
Van Dyne & LePine (1998) and LePine & Van Dyne (1998)	Helping—"promotive behavior that emphasizes small acts of consideration. Helping is cooperative behavior that is noncontroversial. It is directly and obviously affiliative; it builds and preserves relationships; and it emphasizes				Voice—"speaking out and challenging the status quo with the intent of improving the situation . . . voice is particularly important today given the emphasis	

Author(s)	Helping	Sportsmanship	Organizational Loyalty	Organizational Compliance	Individual Initiative	Self-Development
	interpersonal harmony" (Van Dyne & LePine, p. 109).				on flexibility, innovation, and continuous improvement.... One example of voice as we define it is when a group member makes an innovative suggestion for change to a standard operating procedure in order to improve work flow, even when such a suggestion might upset others" (LePine & Van Dyne, pp. 853–854).	
Podsakoff, MacKenzie, Paine, & Bachrach (2000)	**Helping**—"Conceptually, helping behavior involves voluntarily helping others with, or preventing the occurrence of work related problems" (p. 516).	**Sportsmanship**—"Organ (1990b [Organ 1990c]: 96) has defined sportsmanship as a willingness to tolerate the inevitable	**Organizational loyalty**—"Essentially, organizational loyalty entails promoting the organization to outsiders, protecting		**Individual initiative**—"Such behaviors include voluntary acts of creativity and innovation designed to improve one's task	**Self-development**—"includes voluntary behaviors employees engage in to improve their knowledge, skills, and abilities. According to George and Brief (1992: 155)

(Continued)

Table A.1 (Continued)

Author(s)	Helping	Sportsmanship	Organizational Loyalty	Organizational Compliance	Individual Initiative	Self-Development
		inconveniences and impositions of work without complaining." However, his definition seems somewhat narrower than the label of this construct would imply. For example, in our opinion "good sports" are people who not only do not complain when they are inconvenienced by others, but also maintain a positive attitude even when things do not go their way, are not offended when others do not follow their suggestions, are willing to sacrifice their personal	and defending it against external threats, and remaining committed to it even under adverse conditions" (p. 517).		or the organization's performance ... and encouraging others in the organization to do the same" (p. 524).	this might include "seeking out and taking advantage of advanced training courses, keeping abreast of the latest developments in one's field and area, or even learning a new set of skills so as to expand the range of one's contributions to an organization'" (p. 525).

Author(s)	Helping	Sportsmanship	Organizational Loyalty	Organizational Compliance	Individual Initiative	Self-Development
		interest for the good of the work group, and do not take the rejection of their ideas personally" (p. 517).				
Farh et al. (2004)	**Helping coworkers**—"refers to helping colleagues in work-related matters or nonwork matters, and is similar to altruism . . . or helping" (p. 246).	**Keeping the workplace clean and neat** (p. 247).	**Promoting company image**—"is similar to loyalty and loyal boosterism" (p. 247).		**Voice**—"making constructive suggestions or speaking up to prohibit harmful behavior to the firm" (p. 246).	**Self-training**—"Refers to improving one's own knowledge or working skills" (p. 247).
	Interpersonal harmony—"Refers to employee actions aimed at facilitating and preserving harmonious relations in the workplace . . ." (p. 247).					

NOTE: All excerpts reprinted with permission.

Organ, & Near, 1983; Van Scotter & Motowidlo, 1996; Williams & Anderson, 1991). Conceptually, helping behavior involves voluntarily helping others with, or preventing the occurrence of, work-related problems. The first part of this definition (helping others with work-related problems) includes Organ's (1988, 1990b) altruism, peace-making, and cheerleading dimensions; Graham's (1989) interpersonal helping; Williams and Anderson's (1991) OCBI; Van Scotter and Motowidlo's (1996) interpersonal facilitation; Van Dyne and LePine's (1998) helping behavior; George and Brief (1992) and George and Jones's (1997) helping others; and the helping coworkers and interpersonal harmony constructs of Farh et al. (1997) and Farh, Zhong, and Organ (2004). The second part of the definition captures Organ's (1988, 1990b) notion of helping others by taking steps to prevent the creation of problems for coworkers. Empirical research (Bachrach et al., 2001; MacKenzie et al., 1999; MacKenzie et al., 2001; Podsakoff, Ahearne, & MacKenzie, 1997; Podsakoff & MacKenzie, 1994) has generally confirmed the fact that all of these forms of helping behavior load on a single factor.

Sportsmanship is a form of citizenship behavior that has received much less attention in the literature. Organ (1990b) defined sportsmanship as "a willingness to tolerate the inevitable inconveniences and impositions of work without complaining." (p. 96). However, his definition seems somewhat narrower than the label of this construct would imply. For example, in our opinion, "good sports" are people who not only do not complain when they are inconvenienced by others but also who maintain a positive attitude even when things do not go their way, are not offended when others do not follow their suggestions, are willing to sacrifice their personal interest for the good of the work group, and do not take the rejection of their ideas personally. Empirical research (e.g., Bachrach et al., 2001; MacKenzie, Podsakoff, & Fetter, 1991, 1993; MacKenzie, et al., 1999; MacKenzie et al., 2001; Podsakoff et al., 1997; Podsakoff & MacKenzie, 1994) that has included this construct in the context of other forms of OCB has shown it to be distinct from them and to have somewhat different antecedents (cf. Podsakoff et al., 1990; Podsakoff et al., 1996b) and consequences (Podsakoff et al., 1997; Podsakoff & MacKenzie, 1994; Walz & Niehoff, 2000).

Organizational loyalty consists of the loyal boosterism and organizational loyalty constructs (Graham, 1989, 1991); loyalty (Van Dyne et al., 1994); spreading goodwill and protecting the organization (George & Brief, 1992; George & Jones, 1997); promoting the company's image

(Farh et al., 2004); and some aspects of Borman and Motowidlo's (1993, 1997) endorsing, supporting, and defending organizational objectives construct. Essentially, organizational loyalty entails promoting the organization to outsiders, protecting and defending it against external threats, and remaining committed to it even under adverse conditions. Research by Moorman and Blakely (1995) and Blakely, Andrews, and Fuller (2003) has indicated that this dimension is distinct from several other forms of OCB, although a confirmatory factor analysis conducted by Moorman, Blakely, and Niehoff (1998) failed to confirm this. Thus, additional work on these scales appears to be warranted.

As indicated in Table A.1, *organizational compliance* has a long tradition of research in the citizenship behavior area. This dimension has been called "generalized compliance" by Smith et al. (1983), "organizational obedience" by Graham (Graham, 1991; Van Dyne et al., 1994), OCBO by Williams and Anderson (1991), following organizational rules and procedures by Borman and Motowidlo (1993), and contains some aspects of Van Scotter and Motowidlo's (1996) job dedication construct. This dimension appears to capture a person's internalization and acceptance of the organization's rules, regulations, and procedures, which results in a scrupulous adherence to them, even when no one observes or monitors compliance. The reason that this behavior is regarded as a form of OCB is that even though everyone is expected to obey company regulations, rules, and procedures at all times, many employees simply do not. Therefore, an employee who religiously obeys all rules and regulations, even when no one is watching, is regarded as an especially "good citizen."

Another dimension that several researchers have identified as a form of OCB is *individual initiative*. This type of OCB is extra-role only in the sense that it involves engaging in task-related behaviors at a level that is so far beyond minimally required or generally expected levels that it takes on a voluntary flavor. Such behaviors include voluntary acts of creativity and innovation designed to improve one's task or the organization's performance, persisting with extra enthusiasm and effort to accomplish one's job, volunteering to take on extra responsibilities, and encouraging others in the organization to do the same. All of these behaviors share the idea that the employee is going above and beyond the call of duty. This dimension is similar to Organ's conscientiousness construct (Organ, 1988), Graham's (1989) and Moorman and Blakely's (1995) personal industry and individual initiative constructs, George's

(George & Brief, 1992; George & Jones, 1997) making constructive suggestions construct, Borman and Motowidlo's (1993, 1997) constructs of persisting with enthusiasm and volunteering to carry out task activities, Morrison and Phelps' 1999) taking charge at work construct, Farh et al.'s (2004) taking initiative construct, and some aspects of Van Scotter and Motowidlo's job dedication construct (Van Scotter & Motowidlo, 1996). Organ (1988) indicated that this form of behavior is among the most difficult to distinguish from in-role behavior, because it differs more in degree than in kind. Therefore, it is not surprising that some researchers have not included the individual initiative dimension in their studies of OCB (e.g., MacKenzie et al. 1991, 1993; Podsakoff & MacKenzie, 1994) or have found that this behavior is difficult to distinguish empirically from in-role or task performance (e.g., Van Scotter & Motowidlo, 1996).

The next dimension is derived from Graham's (1991) discussion of the responsibilities that employees have as "citizens" of an organization. *Civic virtue* represents a macro-level interest in, or commitment to, the organization as a whole. This mindset is shown by a willingness to participate actively in its governance (e.g., to attend meetings, engage in policy debates, express one's opinion about what strategy the organization ought to follow, and so on), to monitor its environment for threats and opportunities (e.g., to keep up with changes in the industry that might affect the organization), and to look out for its best interests (e.g., to report fire hazards or suspicious activities, lock doors, and so on) even at great personal cost. These behaviors reflect a person's recognition of being part of a larger whole and accepting the responsibilities that such membership entails, in the same way that citizens are members of a country. This dimension has been referred to as "civic virtue" by Organ (1988, 1990b), "organizational participation" by Graham (1989), and "protecting the organization" by George and Brief (1992).

The final dimension is *self-development*. Based on the work of Katz (1964), George and Brief (1992) identified developing oneself as a key dimension of OCB. Self-development includes voluntary behaviors employees engage in to improve their knowledge, skills, and abilities. According to George and Jones (1997), this might include "seeking out and taking advantage of advanced training courses, keeping abreast of the latest developments in one's field and area, or even learning a new set of skills so as to expand the range of one's contributions to an organization" (p. 155). Interestingly, self-development has not received any empirical confirmation in the OCB literature. However, it does appear to be a discretionary form of employee behavior that is conceptually distinct from the other OCB dimensions, and thus might be expected to improve organizational effectiveness through somewhat different mechanisms than the other forms of citizenship behavior.

Thus, when one examines the different types of citizenshiplike behavior that have been identified in the literature, they seem to fall into one of the previously discussed seven categories. Because almost all of the OCB research was influenced by Katz (1964), perhaps it is not surprising that these underlying dimensions bear a strong resemblance to the dimensions of "innovative and spontaneous" behavior that he identified, including (a) cooperating with others, (b) protecting the organization, (c) volunteering constructive ideas, (d) self-training, and (e) maintaining a favorable attitude toward the company. For example, cooperating with others is reflected in the helping and sportsmanship dimensions, protecting the organization is reflected in the civic virtue and organizational loyalty dimensions, volunteering constructive ideas is reflected in the individual initiative dimension, self training is reflected in the self-development dimension, and maintaining a favorable attitude toward the company is reflected in the organizational loyalty and, perhaps, sportsmanship dimensions. Thus, in a sense, the roots of almost every form of OCB can be traced back to Katz's (1964) seminal framework.

Implications for Future Research

How Many OCB Dimensions?

Our review of the conceptualization of OCB at the end of this appendix (summarized in Table A.1) identified a considerable number—i.e., seven—of OCB dimensions. One consequence of the proliferation of OCB constructs is that it is difficult to determine which ones are the most important to consider or how finely grained the distinctions between types of OCB dimensions should be. Empirical evidence can be quite helpful in making this determination but should not drive the conceptualization. Rather, there should be interplay between conceptual and empirical considerations. If the focus is only on conceptual similarities and differences between various types of OCB, researchers may tend to make finer distinctions than raters would recognize on their own. If the focus is driven by the empirical evidence alone (especially exploratory factor analysis), the meanings of the factors may be difficult to determine because it may be hard to identify a clear theme that the items are measuring, and/or the OCB factors may be sample specific and difficult to generalize to other research settings. So, the question is, how many OCB dimensions should be distinguished?

One way to answer this question is by examining which forms of OCB have independent effects on organizational effectiveness or which have different antecedents. In other words, if some forms of OCB do not have unique effects on organizational effectiveness and do not have unique antecedents, they are essentially redundant constructs, even though they might be conceptually distinguishable from other forms of OCB. On the other hand, if they have unique effects on organizational effectiveness, either because they increase the proportion of variance accounted for in this criterion variable or because they influence different aspects of organizational effectiveness than other forms of OCB do, they are important to understand. Similarly, if the causes (antecedents) of some forms of OCB are different, they are important to understand, because this fact suggests that there are multiple mechanisms through which organizational success can be achieved.

Therefore, we would argue that the distinction between these forms of behavior is useful to the field only to the extent that these behaviors have different antecedents and/or consequences. This suggests that we need additional theory development that identifies the potentially unique antecedents and consequences of the different forms of OCB. Van Dyne et al. (1995) took an important step in this direction when they provided an overview of the antecedents and consequences of four types of extra-role behavior (i.e., affiliative/promotive, affiliative/prohibitive, challenging/prohibitive, and challenging/promotive). However, their forms of extra-role behavior were conceptualized at a fairly aggregate level, and it would be more instructive to develop theories at the individual citizenship behavior construct level. In addition, we need empirical studies that include multiple forms of OCB, and those studies need to statistically test for differences in the strength of the effects on various criterion measures to determine whether individual citizenship behaviors have unique effects.

Are OCB/CP Indicators the Cause or the Effect of Their Constructs?

Another issue that researchers should consider is the nature of the relationship between the measures and the OCB subdimensions (altruism, courtesy, peacemaking, sportsmanship, civic virtue, and so on) and between the OCB subdimensions and a more general higher-order OCB construct. Several researchers (e.g., Bollen & Lennox, 1991; Jarvis et al., 2003; Law, Wong, & Mobley, 1998; MacKenzie, Podsakoff, & Jarvis, in press) have stressed the importance of thinking carefully about measurement model specification. Nearly all of the research (e.g., Bollen, 1989; Nunnally & Bernstein, 1994) examining the factor structure of the OCB measures described in this appendix has assumed a reflective indicator model, in which each measure is viewed as an imperfect *reflection* of the underlying latent construct. Although this type of measurement model is conceptually appropriate in many instances, Bollen and Lennox (1991) noted that it does not make sense for all constructs. Indeed, they argued that measures do not always reflect underlying latent constructs; instead, sometimes they combine to *form* them. This idea is consistent with the views of several other researchers (e.g., Blalock, 1964; Bollen, 1984, 1989; MacCallum & Browne, 1993; Law & Wong, 1999), who argue that for some latent constructs, it makes more sense to view meaning as emanating from the measures to the construct in a definitional sense, rather than vice versa. This perspective is important because researchers have suggested that some of the OCB/CP constructs should be modeled as having formative, rather than reflective, indicators. For example, Jarvis et al. (2003) provided a set of conceptual criteria that can be used to determine the appropriate measurement model and applied it to the OCB domain. Based on these criteria, the researchers suggested that altruism, courtesy, peacemaking, and cheerleading should be modeled as formative indicators of a helping behavior construct. Similarly, Motowidlo (2000) argued that job dedication and interpersonal facilitation should be modeled as formative indicators of contextual performance.

This issue is more than simply an abstract theoretical concern, because empirical research indicates that measurement model misspecification biases estimates of the relationships between constructs (Jarvis et al. 2003; Law & Wong, 1999; MacKenzie et al., in press). Monte Carlo simulations by Jarvis et al. (2003) demonstrated that when a construct that should have formative indicators is incorrectly modeled as if the indicators were reflective, the estimates of the relationships between the misspecified construct and its antecedents are biased downward by about 90%, and the estimates of the relationships between the misspecified construct and its consequences are biased upward by 300% to 500%. That is a strong enough bias to lead to a significant number of Type I and

Type II errors of inference. Therefore, researchers need to think more carefully about the measurement relationships in future OCB/CP research.

Need for Additional Validation of the OCB Scales

We also believe that additional research needs to be directed at the validation of many of the OCB/CP scales. Schwab (1980) noted the problems encountered when the substantive validity of constructs is examined before the construct validity of their measures has been established. For example, it may be necessary to discard some of the knowledge that has been acquired if the scales turn out to misrepresent the construct. In light of this, our own review of research in the OCB domain indicates several disturbing trends. First, many studies use scales that are idiosyncratic to that study. For example, when conducting their meta-analysis, LePine et al. (2002) observed,

> In conducting this study, it became clear to us that there are several characteristics of OCB research that hinder the systematic accumulation of knowledge. Perhaps most important, scholars have introduced many new OCB (or OCB-like) constructs and measures without adequate construct validity support. In the pool of 133 studies, we found more than 40 different measures of behavior that scholars have referred to as OCB or something very similar (e.g., contextual performance, extra-role behavior). Almost without exception, however, the authors of these studies did not empirically evaluate the extent to which the OCB constructs they introduced were different than or similar to others that already existed. This shortcoming, together with the fact that full scales were rarely reported, made it impossible to use relationships with these newer dimensions in our meta-analysis. (p. 62).

Another disturbing trend that hinders research in this area is the tendency for researchers to include items adapted from several other scales without reporting any information at all about the specific items used or the construct validity of the scales. This makes it impossible to assess the extent to which the measure faithfully captures the content domain of the construct or to replicate the findings of the research.

Yet another problem is that some scales that have been shown to have poor psychometric properties or whose factor structures cannot be replicated by other researchers continue to be used without taking steps to improve them. Indeed, some of the scales that were reviewed earlier in this appendix continue to be used even though the empirical evidence suggests that they have poor psychometric properties and/or that their factor structures do not replicate. Instead of continuing to use these scales, future researchers should attempt to improve them by modifying or deleting unreliable items or by generating new items that better capture the content domain of the factors that they are intended to measure.

Additional Attention Should Be Given to the Source of the OCB Measures

Additional consideration also needs to be given to the source from which the OCB/CP measures are obtained. In most studies, the source of the OCB/CP ratings has been determined by either convenience or a desire to separate the source of the predictor and criterion variables. One reason that this issue merits more careful consideration is that different sources do not have the same knowledge of OCB or the same motivational biases that might affect their ratings of these behaviors. For example, some types of OCB are more likely to be directed at and therefore observed by peers (e.g., helping behavior), others are more likely to be directed at and therefore observed by supervisors (e.g., sportsmanship), and still others may be behaviors that the individual himself or herself has the most complete knowledge of (e.g., complying with organizational rules, even when no one else is around). However, the tendency to distort self-ratings of compliance or conscientiousness may be greater than the tendency for peers or supervisors to distort ratings of these behaviors. This suggests that researchers need to think more carefully about which source is able and willing to provide the most accurate information about OCB/CP behavior.

However, we generally would caution against the use of self-reported measures of OCB (or self-reported measures of a person's intention to exhibit these behaviors) for several reasons. First, there is a considerable amount of evidence (e.g., Allen, Barnard, Rush, & Russell, 2000; Beehr, Ivanitskaya, Hansen, Erofeev, & Gudanowski, 2001; Donaldson, Ensher, & Grant-Vallone, 2000; Van Dyne & LePine, 1998) that self-reports of OCB-like behavior do not tend to correlate very highly with peer, supervisor, and/or subordinate reports of the same behavior and that when a discrepancy exists between sources of OCB ratings, the biggest discrepancy exists between self and other rating sources. This is important because some research suggests that when the predictor and criterion variables come from different sources, self-ratings may not be as strongly related to criterion variables as peer and supervisory ratings. For example, Van Dyne and LePine (1998) reported that self-ratings of helping, voice, and in-role performance correlated with supervisory ratings of performance .13, .07, .13 at time 1 and .09, .08, .20 at time 2. In contrast, peer ratings of helping, voice, and in-role performance correlated with supervisory ratings of performance .38, .33, .41 at time 1 and .36, .31, and .41 at time 2. Thus, peer ratings of OCB accounted for about 14 times more variance in this criterion measure than self-report ratings did. One reason for this difference is that when individuals are rating themselves, they may have a tendency to report their intentions as well as their actual behavior. We are aware of only one study (Becker, Randall, & Riegel, 1995) that has examined the relationships between OCB intentions and OCBs. In this study, Becker et al. (1995) examined the relationships between respondents' intent to exhibit altruism and intent to exhibit punctuality, and the respondents' altruism and tardiness behavior. In addition, they also measured respondents' subjective norms regarding both altruism and punctuality and their attitudes about these behaviors. They found that the average correlation between employees' self-reported altruism intent, subjective norms regarding altruism, and attitudes about altruism and supervisory ratings of altruism behavior was .16, and the average correlation between employees' self-reported punctuality intent, subjective norms regarding punctuality, and attitudes about punctuality and actual employee tardiness was .03. Thus, we do not think that intentions to exhibit OCB are compelling as surrogates of OCBs, and we would not generally recommend the use of self-report measures of OCBs or OCB intentions without a considerable amount of justification.

References

Adams, J. S. (1965). Inequity in social exchange. In L. Berkowitz (Ed.), *Advances in experimental psychology* (Vol. 2, pp. 267–299). New York: Academic Press.

Ahearne, M. A., MacKenzie, S. B., & Podsakoff, P. M. (2004). *Determinants of sales team success: An empirical examination of the indirect effects of leadership empowerment behaviors on sales team performance.* Unpublished working paper, Indiana University, Bloomington.

Allen, T. D., Barnard, S., Rush, M. C., & Russell, J. E. A. (2000). Ratings of organizational citizenship behavior: Does the source make a difference? *Human Resource Management Review, 10*(1), 97–114.

Allen, T. D., Facteau, J. D., & Facteau, C. L. (2004). Structured interviewing for OCB: Construct validity, faking, and the effects of question type. *Human Performance, 17*(1), 1–24.

Allen, T. D., & Rush, M. C. (1998). The effects of organizational citizenship behavior on performance judgments: A field study and a laboratory experiment. *Journal of Applied Psychology, 83,* 247–260.

Allen, T. D., & Rush, M. C. (2001). The influence of ratee gender on ratings of organizational citizenship behavior. *Journal of Applied Social Psychology, 31*(12), 2561–2587.

Allport, G. W. (1954). *The nature of prejudice.* Cambridge, MA: Addison-Wesley.

Almond, G. A., & Verba, S. (1963). *The civic culture: Political attitudes and democracy in five nations.* Princeton, NJ: Princeton University Press.

Antonakis, J., & Atwater, L. (2002). Leader distance: A review and a proposed theory. *The Leadership Quarterly, 13*(6), 673–704.

Arvey, R. D., Bouchard, T. J., Segal, N. L., & Abraham, L. M. (1989). Job satisfaction: Environmental and genetic components. *Journal of Applied Psychology, 74,* 187–192.

Arvey, R. D., & Campion, J. E. (1982). The employment interview: A summary and review of recent research. *Personnel Psychology, 35,* 281–322.

Arvey, R. D., & Faley, R. H. (1988). *Fairness in selecting employees* (2nd ed.). Reading, MA: Addison-Wesley.

Austin, J. T., Humphreys, L. G., & Hulin, C. L. (1989). Another view of dynamic criteria: A critical reanalysis of Barrett, Caldwell, and Alexander. *Personnel Psychology, 42,* 597–612.

Avila, R. A., Fern, E. F., & Mann, O. K. (1988). Unraveling criteria for assessing the performance of salespeople: A causal analysis. *Journal of Personal Selling and Sales Management, 8,* 45–54.

Bachrach, D. G., Bendoly, E., & Podsakoff, P. M. (2001). Attributions of the "causes" of group performance as an alternative explanation of the relationship between organizational citizenship behavior and organizational performance. *Journal of Applied Psychology, 86*(6), 1285–1293.

Bagozzi, R. P., Yi, Y., & Phillips, L. W. (1991). Assessing construct validity in organizational research. *Administrative Science Quarterly, 36,* 421–458.

Bagozzi, R. P., Verbeke, W., & Gavino, J. C., Jr. (2003). Culture moderates the self-regulation of shame and its effects on performance: The case of salespersons in the Netherlands and the Philippines. *Journal of Applied Psychology, 88,* 219–233.

Barksdale, K., & Werner, J. M. (2001). Managerial ratings of in-role behaviors, organizational citizenship behaviors, and overall performance: testing different models of their relationship. *Journal of Business Research, 51*(2), 145–155.

Barnard, C. I. (1938). *The functions of the executive.* Cambridge, MA: Harvard University Press.

Bass, B. M. (1962). Further evidence on the dynamic character of the criteria. *Personnel Psychology, 15,* 93–97.

Bass, B. M. (1985). *Leadership and performance beyond expectations.* New York: Free Press.

Bass, B. M., & Avolio, B. J. (1993). Transformational leadership: A response to critiques. In M. M. Chemers & R. Ayman (Eds.), *Leadership theory and research: Perspectives and directions.* San Diego, CA: Academic Press.

Bateman, T. S. (1980). *A longitudinal investigation of role overload and its relationships with work behaviors and job satisfaction.* Unpublished doctoral dissertation, Indiana University, Bloomington.

Bateman, T. S., & Organ, D. W. (1983). Job satisfaction and the good soldier: The relationship between affect and employee "citizenship." *Academy of Management Journal, 26,* 587–595.

Becker, T. E., Randall, D. M., & Riegel, C. D. (1995). The multidimensional view of commitment and the theory of reasoned action: A comparative evaluation. *Journal of Management, 21,* 617–638.

Beehr, T. A., Ivanitskaya, L., Hansen, C. P., Erofeev, D., & Gudanowski, D. M. (2001). Evaluation of 360 degree feedback ratings: Relationships with each other and with performance and selection predictors. *Journal of Organizational Behavior, 22*(7), 775–788.

Bell, S. J., & Menguc, B. (2002). The employee-organization relationship, organizational citizenship behaviors, and superior service quality. *Journal of Retailing, 78,* 131–146.

Bennett, R. J., & Robinson, S. L. (2000). Development of a measure of workplace deviance. *Journal of Applied Psychology, 85,* 349–360.

Bennis, W., & Nanus, B. (1985). *Leaders: The strategies for taking charge.* New York: Harper & Row.

Bentler, P. M. (1990). Comparative fit indices in structural models. *Psychological Bulletin, 107,* 238–246.

Berman, J. S., & Kenny, D. A. (1976). Correlational bias in observer ratings. *Journal of Personality and Social Psychology, 34,* 263–273.

Berscheid, E., & Walster, E. (1978). *Interpersonal attraction.* Reading, MA: Addison-Wesley.

Bies, R. J., Martin, C. L., & Brockner, J. (1993). Just laid off, but still a "good citizen?" Only if the process is fair. *Employee Responsibilities and Rights Journal, 6,* 227–238.

Bishop, J. W., Scott, K. D., & Burroughs, S. M. (2000). Support, commitment, and employee outcomes in a team environment. *Journal of Management, 26,* 1113–1132.

Blakely, G. L., Andrews, M. C., & Fuller, J. (2003). Are chameleons good citizens? A longitudinal study of the relationship between self-monitoring and organizational citizenship behavior. *Journal of Business and Psychology, 18,* 131–144.

Blalock, H. M., Jr. (1964). *Causal inferences in nonexperimental research.* New York: W. W. Norton.

Blau, G. (1994). Developing and testing a taxonomy of lateness behavior. *Journal of Applied Psychology, 79,* 959–970.

Blau, P. M. (1964). *Exchange and power in social life.* New York: Wiley.

Bolino, M. C. (1999). Citizenship and impression management: Good soldiers or good actors? *Academy of Management Review, 24,* 82–98.

Bolino, M. C., Turnley, W. H., & Bloodgood, J. M. (2002). Citizenship behavior and the creation of social capital in organizations. *Academy of Management Review, 27*(4), 505–522.

Bollen, K. A. (1984). Multiple indicators: Internal consistency or no necessary relationship? *Quality and Quantity, 18,* 377–385.

Bollen, K. A. (1989). *Structural equations with latent variables.* New York: Wiley.

Bollen, K. A., & Lennox, R. (1991). Conventional wisdom on measurement: A structural equation perspective. *Psychological Bulletin, 110,* 305–331.

Bommer, W. H., Miles, E. W., & Grover, S. L. (2003). Does one good turn deserve another? Coworker influences on employee citizenship. *Journal of Organizational Behavior, 24*(2), 181–196.

Bond, M. H., & Hwang, K. K., (1987). In M. H. Bond (Ed.), *The social psychology of Chinese people in "The psychology of the Chinese people"* (pp. 213–266). Hong Kong: Oxford University Press.

Borman, W. C. (1983). Implications of personality theory and research for the rating of work performance in organizations. In F. Landy, S. Zedeck, & J. Cleveland (Eds.), *Performance measurement and theory*. Hillsdale, NJ: Lawrence Erlbaum.

Borman, W. C. (1987). Personal constructs, performance schemata, and "folk theories" of subordinate effectiveness: Explorations in an Army officer sample. *Organizational Behavior and Human Decision Processes, 40,* 307–322.

Borman, W. C., & Brush, D. H. (1993). More progress toward a taxonomy of managerial performance requirements. *Human Performance, 6,* 1–21.

Borman, W. C., & Motowidlo, S. J. (1993). Expanding the criterion domain to include elements of contextual performance. In N. Schmitt, W. C. Borman, and Associates (Eds.), *Personnel selection in organizations* (pp. 71–98). San Francisco: Jossey-Bass.

Borman, W. C., & Motowidlo, S. J. (1997). Task performance and contextual performance: The meaning for personnel selection research. *Human Performance, 10,* 99–109.

Borman, W. C., Motowidlo, S. J., & Hanser, L. M. (1983, August). A model of individual performance effectiveness: Thoughts about expanding the criterion space. In N. K. Eaton & J. P. Campbell (Chairs), *Integrated criterion measurement for large-scale computerized selection and classification*. Symposium conducted at the 91st Annual Convention of the American Psychological Association, Anaheim, CA.

Borman, W. C., Penner, L. A., Allen, T. D., & Motowidlo, S. J. (2001). Personality predictors of citizenship performance. *International Journal of Selection and Assessment, 9*(1–2), 52–69.

Borman, W. C., White, L. A., & Dorsey, D. W. (1995). Effects of ratee task-performance and interpersonal factors on supervisor and peer performance ratings. *Journal of Applied Psychology, 80*(1), 168–177.

Bossidy, L., & Charan, R. (2002). *Execution: The discipline of getting things done.* New York: Random House.

Brayfield, A. H., & Crockett, W. H. (1955). Employee attitudes and employee performance. *Psychological Bulletin, 52,* 396–424.

Brickman, P., Folger, R., Goode, E., & Schul, Y. (1981). Microjustice and macrojustice. In Lerner, M. J., & Lerner, S. C. (Eds.), *The justice motive in social behavior* (pp. 173–204). New York: Plenum Press.

Brief, A. P., & Motowidlo, S. J. (1986). Prosocial organizational behaviors. *Academy of Management Review, 11,* 710–725.

Brockner, J. (2003). Unpacking country effects: On the need to operationalize the psychological determinants of cross-national differences. In R. Kramer & B. Staw (Eds.), *Research in organizational behavior* (Vol. 25, pp. 366–367). Greenwich, CT: JAI Press.

Bromley, D., & Busching, B. (1988). Understanding the structure of contractual and covenantal social relations: Implications for the sociology of religion. *Sociological Analysis, 49,* 15–32.

Brown, R., & Herrnstein, R. J. (1975). *Psychology.* New York: Free Press.

Bruner, J. S., & Tagiuri, R. (1954). The perception of people. In G. Lindzey (Ed.), *Handbook of social psychology.* Reading, MA: Addison-Wesley.

Bryman, A. (1992). *Charisma and leadership in organizations.* London: Sage.

Burns, J. M. (1978). *Leadership.* New York: Harper & Row.

Byrne, D. (1971). *The attraction paradigm.* New York: Academic Press.

Byrne, D., & Clore, G. L. (1970). A reinforcement model of evaluative responses. *Personality: An International Journal, 1,* 103–128.

Campbell, J. P. (1990). An overview of the Army Selection and Classification Project (Project A). *Personnel Psychology, 43,* 231–239.

Campbell, J. P. (1994). Alternative models of job performance and their implications for selection and classification. In Rumsey, M. G., Walker, C. B., & Harris, J. H. (Eds.), *Personnel selection and classification* (pp. 33–52). Hillsdale, NJ: Lawrence Erlbaum.

Campbell, J. P., McHenry, J. J., & Wise, L. L. (1990). Analyses of criterion measures: The modeling of performance. *Personnel Psychology, 43*, 313–343.

Cardona, P., Lawrence, B. S., & Bentler, P. M. (2004). The influence of social and work exchange relationships on organizational citizenship behavior. *Group and Organization Management, 29*, 219–247.

Cardy, R. L., & Dobbins, G. H. (1986). Affect and appraisal accuracy: Liking as an integral dimension in evaluating performance. *Journal of Applied Psychology, 71*, 672–678.

Chapman, L. J. (1967). Illusory correlation in observational reports. *Journal of Verbal Learning and Verbal Behavior, 6*, 151–155.

Chapman, L. J., & Chapman, J. P. (1967). Genesis of popular but erroneous psychodiagnostic observations. *Journal of Abnormal Psychology, 72*, 193–204.

Chapman, L. J., & Chapman, J. P. (1969). Illusory correlation as an obstacle to the use of valid psychodiagnostic signs. *Journal of Abnormal Psychology, 74*, 271–280.

Chapman, L. J., & Chapman, J. P. (1971). Test results are what you think they are. *Psychology Today, 5*(6), 18–22, 106–110.

Chen, Z. X., Tsui, A. S., & Farh, J. L. (2002). Loyalty to supervisor vs. organizational commitment: Relationships to employee performance in China. *Journal of Occupational and Organizational Psychology, 75*, 339–356.

Cherrington, D. L., Reitz, H. J., & Scott, W. E., Jr. (1971). Effects of reward and contingent reinforcement on satisfaction and task performance. *Journal of Applied Psychology, 55*, 531–536.

Churchill, G. A., Jr. (1979). A paradigm for developing better measures of marketing constructs. *Journal of Marketing Research, 16*, 64–73.

Cialdini, R. B., & Kenrick, D. T. (1976). Altruism as hedonism: A social development perspective on the relationship of negative mood and helping. *Journal of Personality and Social Psychology, 34*, 907–914.

Cohen, S. (1980). Aftereffects of stress on human performance and social behavior: A review of research and theory. *Psychological Bulletin, 88*, 82–108.

Cohen-Charash, Y., & Spector, P. E. (2001). The role of justice in organizations: A meta-analysis. *Organizational Behavior and Human Decision Processes, 86*(2), 278–321.

Colquitt, J. A. (2001). On the dimensionality of organizational justice: A construct validation of a measure. *Journal of Applied Psychology, 86*(3), 386–400.

Conger, J., & Kanungo, R. N. (1988). The empowerment process: Integrating theory and practice. *Academy of Management Review, 13*, 471–482.

Conway, J. M. (1999). Distinguishing contextual performance from task performance for managerial jobs. *Journal of Applied Psychology, 84*(1), 3–13.

Cooper, W. H. (1981). Ubiquitous halo. *Psychological Bulletin, 90*, 218–244.

Cortina, J. M. (1993). What is coefficient alpha? An examination of theory and applications. *Journal of Applied Psychology, 78*, 98–104.

Cote, J. A. & Buckley, R. (1988). Measurement error and theory testing in consumer research: An illustration of the importance of construct validation. *Journal of Consumer Research, 14*, 579–582.

Cowherd, D. M., & Levine, D. I. (1992). Product quality and pay equity between lower-level employees and top management: An investigation of distributive justice theory. *Administrative Science Quarterly, 37*, 302–320.

Dalton, D. R., & Cosier, R. A. (1988). Psychometric properties of the organizational citizenship behavior scale. *Educational and Psychological Measurement, 48*, 479–482.

Dansereau, F. D., Jr., Graen, G., & Haga, W. J. (1975). A Vertical dyad linkage approach to leadership within formal organizations: A longitudinal investigation of the rolemaking process. *Organizational Behavior and Human Performance, 13*, 46–78.

Darley, J. M., & Batson, C. D. (1973). From Jerusalem to Jericho: A study of situational and dispositional variables in helping behavior. *Journal of Personality and Social Psychology, 27,* 100–108.

Deadrick, D. L., & Madigan, R. M. (1990). Dynamic criteria revisited: A longitudinal study of performance stability and predictive validity. *Personnel Psychology, 43,* 717–744.

Deci, E. L. (1971). Effects of externally mediated rewards on intrinsic motivation. *Journal of Personality and Social Psychology, 18,* 105–115.

Deci, E. L. (1975). *Intrinsic motivation.* New York: Plenum Press.

Deckop, J. R., Cirka, C. C., & Andersson, L. M. (2003). Doing unto others: The reciprocity of helping behavior in organizations. *Journal of Business Ethics, 47,* 101–113.

Deckop, J. R., Mangel, R., & Cirka, C. C. (1999). Getting more than you pay for: Organizational citizenship behavior and pay-for-performance plans. *Academy of Management Journal, 42*(4), 420–428.

Deckop, J. R., Merriman, K. K., & Blau, G. (2004). Impact of variable risk preferences on effectiveness of control by pay. *Journal of Occupational and Organizational Psychology, 77,* 63–80.

Deluga, R. J. (1998). Leader-member exchange quality and effectiveness ratings: The role of subordinate-supervisor conscientiousness similarity. *Group and Organization Management, 23*(2), 189–216.

DeNisi, A. S., Cafferty, T. P., & Meglino, B. M. (1984), A cognitive view of the performance appraisal process: A model and research propositions. *Organizational Behavior and Human Performance, 33,* 360–96.

DeNisi, A. S., & Williams, K. J. (1988). A cognitive approach to performance appraisal. In K. Rowland & G. Ferris (Eds.), *Research in personnel and human resources management* (Vol. 6, pp. 109–156). Greenwich, CT: JAI Press.

Dennis, W. (1954). Predicting scientific productivity in later maturity from records of earlier decades. *Journal of Gerontology, 9,* 465–467.

Dennis, W. (1956). Age and productivity among scientists. *Science, 123,* 724–725.

DePree, M. (1989). *Leadership is an art.* New York: Dell.

Donaldson, S. I., Ensher, E. A., & Grant-Vallone, E. J. (2000). Longitudinal examination of mentoring relationships on organizational commitment and citizenship behavior. *Journal of Career Development, 26,* 233–249.

Dougherty, W. T., Ebert, R. J., & Callender, J. C. (1986). Policy capturing in the employment interview. *Journal of Applied Psychology, 71*(1), 9–15.

Dreher, G. F., Ash, R. A., & Hancock, P. (1988). The role of traditional research design in underestimating the validity of the employment interview. *Personnel Psychology, 4*(2), 315–327.

Dunham, R. B. (1979). Job design and redesign. In S. Kerr (Ed.), *Organizational behavior* (pp. 335–354). Columbus, OH: Grid.

Dunlop, P. D., & Lee, K. (2004). Workplace deviance, organizational citizenship behavior, and business unit performance: The bad apples do spoil the whole barrel. *Journal of Organizational Behavior, 25,* 67–80.

Dunnette, M. D., Arvey, R. D., & Arnold, J. A. (1971). *Validity study results for jobs relevant to the petroleum refining industry.* Minneapolis, MN: Personnel Decisions.

Ehrhart, M. G. (2004). Leadership and procedural justice climate as antecedents of unit-level organizational citizenship behavior. *Personnel Psychology, 57,* 61–94.

Eisenberger, R., Armeli, S., Rexwinkel, B., Lynch, P. D., & Rhoades, L.A. (2001). Reciprocation of perceived organizational support. *Journal of Applied Psychology, 86*(1), 42–51.

Eisenberger, R., Fasolo, P., & Davis-LaMastro, V. (1990). Perceived organizational support and employee diligence, commitment, and innovation. *Journal of Applied Psychology, 75,* 107–116.

Eisenberger, R., Huntington, R., Hutchison, S., & Sowa, D. (1986). Perceived organizational support. *Journal of Applied Psychology, 71,* 500–507.

Elazar, D. J. (1980). The political theory of covenant: Biblical origins and modern developments. *Publius, 10,* 3–30.

Epstein, S. (1980). The stability of behavior: II. Implications for psychological research. *American Psychologist, 35,* 790–806.

Fandt, P. M., & Ferris, G. R. (1990). The management of information and impressions: When employees behave opportunistically. *Organizational Behavior and Human Decision Processes, 45,* 140–158.

Farh, J. L., Earley, P. C., & Lin, S. C. (1997). Impetus for action: A cultural analysis of justice and organizational citizenship behavior in Chinese society. *Administrative Science Quarterly, 42*(3), 421–444.

Farh, J. L., Podsakoff, P. M., & Organ, D. W. (1990). Accounting for organizational citizenship behavior: Leader fairness and task scope versus satisfaction. *Journal of Management, 16*(4), 705–721.

Farh, J. L., Zhong, C. B., & Organ, D. W. (2002). An inductive analysis of the construct domain of organizational citizenship behavior. In A. S. Tsui & C. M. Lau (Eds.), *The management of enterprises in the People's Republic of China* (pp. 445–470). Boston: Kluwer Academic.

Farh, J. L., Zhong, C. B., & Organ, D. W. (2004). Organizational citizenship behavior in the People's Republic of China. *Organization Science, 15,* 241–253.

Farris, G. F., & Lim, F. G., Jr. (1969). Effects of performance on leadership, cohesiveness, influence, satisfaction, and subsequent performance. *Journal of Applied Psychology, 53,* 490–497.

Ferris, G. R., Judge, T. A., Rowland, K. M., & Fitzgibbons, D. E. (1994). Subordinate influence and the performance evaluation process: Test of a model. *Organizational Behavior and Human Decision Processes, 58,* 101–135.

Ferris, G. R., Witt, L. A., & Hochwarter, W. A. (2001). Interaction of social skill and general mental ability on job performance and salary. *Journal of Applied Psychology, 86*(6), 1075–1082.

Findlay, P., McKinlay, A., Marks, A., & Thompson, P. (2000). In search of perfect people: Teamwork and team players in the Scottish spirits industry. *Human Relations, 53*(12), 1549–1574.

Findley, H. M., Giles, W. F., & Mossholder, K. W. (2000). Performance appraisal process and system facets: Relationships with contextual performance. *Journal of Applied Psychology, 85,* 634–640.

Fiske, S. T. (1981). Social cognition and affect. In J. Harvey (Ed.), *Cognition, social behavior, and the environment.* Reading MA: Addison-Wesley.

Fiske, S. T. (1982). Schema-triggered affect: Applications to social perception. In M. Clark and S.T. Fiske (Eds.), *Affect and cognition: The 17th annual Carnegie symposium on cognition.* Hillsdale, NJ: Lawrence Erlbaum.

Fiske, S. T., & Pavelchak, M. (1986). Category-based versus piecemeal-based affective responses: Developments in schema-triggered affect. In R. M. Sorrentino & E. T. Higgens (Eds.), *The handbook of motivation and cognition: Foundations of social behavior.* New York: Guilford, 167–203.

Fleishman, E. A., & Fruchter, B. (1960). Factor structure and predictability of successive stages of learning Morse code. *Journal of Applied Psychology, 44,* 97–101.

Foa, E. B., & Foa, U. G. (1980). Resource theory: Interpersonal behavior in exchange. In K. J. Gergen, M. S. Greenberg, & R. H. Willis (Eds.), *Social exchange: Advances in theory and research* (pp. 77–94). New York: Plenum Press.

Folger, R., & Greenberg, J. (1985). Procedural justice: An interpretive analysis of personnel systems. In K. M. Rowland & G. R. Ferris (Eds.), *Research in personnel and human resources management* (Vol. 3, pp. 141–183). Greenwich, CT: JAI Press.

Fornell, C., & Larcker, D. F. (1981). Evaluating structural equation models with unobservable variables and measurement error. *Journal of Marketing Research, 18,* 39–50.

Freeman, R. E. (1984). *Strategic management: A stakeholder approach.* London: Pitman.

Fromkin, H. L., & Streufert, S. (1983). Laboratory experimentation. In M. D. Dunnette (Ed.), *Handbook of industrial and organizational psychology* (pp. 415–465). New York: Wiley.

Gannon, M. J., & Noon, J. P. (1971). Management's critical deficiency. *Business Horizons, 14,* 49–56.

Gatewood, R. D. & Feild, H. S. (1998). *Human resource selection* (4th ed.). Fort Worth, TX: Dryden Press.

George, J. M. (1990). Personality, affect, and behavior in groups. *Journal of Applied Psychology, 75,* 107–116.

George, J. M., & Bettenhausen, K. (1990). Understanding prosocial behavior, sales performance, and turnover: A group-level analysis in a service context. *Journal of Applied Psychology, 75,* 698–709.

George, J. M., & Brief, A. P. (1992). Feeling good doing good: A conceptual analysis of the mood at work—organizational spontaneity relationship. *Psychological Bulletin, 112*(2), 310–329.

George, J. M., & Jones, G. R. (1997). Organizational spontaneity in context. *Human Performance, 10,* 153–170.

Ghiselli, E. E. (1956). Dimensional problems of criteria. *Journal of Applied Psychology, 40,* 1–4.

Ghiselli, E. E. (1966). *The validity of occupational aptitude tests.* New York: Wiley.

Ghiselli, E. E., & Haire, M. (1960). The validation of selection tests in the light of dynamic character of criteria. *Personnel Psychology, 13,* 225–231.

Goodman, P. S., Ravlin, E., & Schminke, M. (1990). Understanding groups in organizations. In L. L. Cummings & B. M. Staw (Eds.), *Leadership, participation, and group behavior* (pp. 333–385). Greenwich, CT: JAI Press.

Goodman, S. A., & Svyantek, D. J. (1999). Person-organization fit and contextual performance: Do shared values matter? *Journal of Vocational Behavior, 55,* 254–275.

Goodwin, V. L., Wofford, J. C., & Whittington, J. L. (2001). A theoretical and empirical extension to the transformational leadership construct. *Journal of Organizational Behavior, 22*(7), 759–774.

Gouldner, A. W. (1960). The norm of reciprocity: A preliminary statement. *American Sociological Review, 25,* 161–178.

Graen, G. B., & Uhl-Bien, M. (1995). Development of LMX theory of leadership over 25 years: Applying a multi-level-multi-domain perspective. *Leadership Quarterly, 6,* 210–247.

Graham, J. W. (1986a). Organizational citizenship informed by political theory. Paper presented at the meeting of the Academy of Management, Chicago.

Graham, J. W. (1986b). Principled organizational dissent: A theoretical essay. In B. M. Staw & L. L. Cummings (Eds.), *Research in organizational behavior* (Vol. 8, pp. 1–52). Greenwich, CT: JAI Press.

Graham, J. W. (1989). Organizational citizenship behavior: Construct redefinition, operationalization, and validation. Unpublished working paper, Loyola University of Chicago.

Graham, J. W. (1991). An essay on organizational citizenship behavior. *Employee Responsibilities and Rights Journal, 4,* 249–270.

Graham, J. W., & Organ, D. W. (1993). Commitment and the covenantal organization. *Journal of Managerial Issues, 5,* 483–502.

Greenberg, J. (1987). Approaching equity and avoiding inequity in groups and organizations. In Greenberg, J., & R. L. Cohen (Eds.), *Equity and justice in social behavior.* New York: Academic Press.

Greene, C. N. (1975). The reciprocal nature of influence between leader and subordinate. *Journal of Applied Psychology, 60,* 187–193.

Greenleaf, R. K. (1970). *The servant as leader.* Newton Center, MA: Robert K. Greenleaf Center.

Greenleaf, R. K. (1973). *The servant as leader* (Rev. ed.). Newton Center, MA: Robert K. Greenleaf Center.

Greenleaf, R. K. (1997). *Servant leadership: A journey into the nature of legitimate power and greatness.* New York: Paulist Press.

Griffin, R. W. (1982). *Task design: An integrative approach.* Glenview, IL: Scott, Foresman.

Grover, N. L. 1982. Contracts, covenants, and creative interchange. In J. A. Brayer & W. S. Minor (Eds.), *Creative interchange* (pp. 291–306). Carbondale: Southern Illinois University Press.

Guion, R. M., & Gottier, R. F. (1965). Validity of personality measures in personnel selection. *Personnel Psychology, 18,* 135–164.

Guzzo, R. A., Yost, P. R., Campbell, R. J., & Shea, G. P. (1993). Potency in groups: Articulating a construct. *British Journal of Social Psychology, 32,* 87–106.

Hackman, J. R., & Lawler, E. (1971). Employee reactions to job characteristics. *Journal of Applied Psychology, 55,* 259–286.

Hackman, J. R., & Oldham, G. (1975). Development of the job diagnostic survey. *Journal of Applied Psychology, 60,* 159–170.

Hackman, J. R., & Oldham, G. (1976). Motivation through the design of work: Test of a theory. *Organizational Behavior and Human Performance, 16,* 250–279.

Hall, R. H. (1991). *Organizations: Structures, processes, and outcomes* (5th ed.). Englewood Cliffs, NJ: Prentice Hall.

Hamilton, D. L. (1981). Illusory correlation as a basis for stereotyping. In D. L. Hamilton (Ed.), *Cognitive processes in stereotyping and intergroup behavior* (pp. 115–144). Hillsdale, NJ: Lawrence Erlbaum.

Harris, M. M., & Schaubroeck, J. (1988). A meta-analysis of self-supervisor, self-peer, and peer-supervisor ratings. *Personnel Psychology, 41,* 43–62.

Harvey, J. H., & Weary, G. (1981). *Perspectives on attributional processes.* Dubuque, IA: William C. Brown.

Henry, R. A., & Hulin, C. L. (1987). Stability of skilled performance across time: Some generalizations and limitations on utilities. *Journal of Applied Psychology, 72,* 457–462.

Hofstede, G. H. (1984). *Culture's consequences: International differences in work-related values (Abridged edition).* Beverly Hills, CA: Sage.

Hogan, J., & Hogan, R. (1989). How to measure reliability. *Journal of Applied Psychology, 69,* 273–279.

Hogan, J., Rybicki, S. L., Motowidlo, S. J., & Borman, W. C. (1998). Relations between contextual performance, personality, and occupational advancement. *Human Performance, 11*(2–3), 189–207.

Homans, G. (1961). *Social behavior: Its elementary forms.* New York: Harcourt Brace.

House, R. J. (1971). A path-goal theory of leader effectiveness. *Administrative Science Quarterly, 16,* 321–339.

House, R. J. (1977). A 1976 theory of charismatic leadership. In J. G. Hunt & L. L. Larson (Eds.), *Leadership: The cutting edge.* Carbondale: Southern Illinois University Press.

House, R. J., & Dessler, G. (1974). The path-goal theory of leadership: Some post hoc and priori tests. In J. G. Hunt & L. L. Larson (Eds.), *Contingency approaches to leadership* (pp. 29–55). Carbondale, IL: Southern Illinois University Press.

House, R. J., & Mitchell, T. R. (1974). Path-goal theory of leadership. *Contemporary Business, 3,* 81–98.

Hu, L. T., & Bentler, P. M. (1999). Cutoff criteria for fit indexes in covariance structure analysis: Conventional criteria versus new alternatives. *Structural Equation Modeling, 6,* 1–55.

Hui, C. (1994). *Effects of leadership empowerment behaviors and followers' personal control, voice, and self-efficacy on in-role and extra-role performance: An extension and empirical test of Conger and Kanungo's empowerment process model.* Unpublished doctoral dissertation, Indiana University, Bloomington.

Hui, C., Law, K. S., & Chen, Z. X. (1999). A structural equation model of the effects of negative affectivity, leader-member exchange, and perceived job mobility on in-role and extra-role performance: A Chinese case. *Organizational Behavior and Human Decision Processes, 77,* 3–21.

Hui, C., Lee, C., & Rousseau, D. M. (2004). Psychological contract and organizational citizenship behavior in China: Investigating generalizability and instrumentality. *Journal of Applied Psychology, 89,* 311–321.

Hunt, J. B. (1991). *Leadership: A new synthesis.* London: Sage.

Hunter, J. E., & Hunter, R. F. (1984). Validity and utility of alternative predictors of job performance. *Psychological Bulletin, 96,* 72–98.

Iaffaldano, M. T., & Muchinsky, P. M. (1985). Job satisfaction and job performance: A meta-analysis. *Psychological Bulletin, 97,* 251–273.

Jackson, D. W., Keith, J. E., & Schlacter, J. L. (1983). Evaluation of selling performance: A study of current practices. *Journal of Personal Selling and Sales Management, 3,* 42–51.

James, L. A., & James, L. R. (1989). Integrating work environment perceptions: Explorations into the measurement of meaning. *Journal of Applied Psychology, 74,* 739–751.

Janis, I. (1982) *Groupthink: Psychological studies of policy decisions and fiascoes.* Boston: Houghton Mifflin.

Jarvis, C. B., MacKenzie, S. B., Podsakoff, P. M. (2003). A critical review of construct indicators and measurement model misspecification in marketing and consumer research. *Journal of Consumer Research, 30*(3), 199–218.

Jex, S. M., Adams, G. A., Bachrach, D. G., Sorenson, S. (2003). The impact of situational constraints, role stressors, and commitment on employee altruism. *Journal of Occupational Health Psychology, 8*(3), 171–180.

Jex, S. M., & Thomas, J. L. (2003). Relations between stressors and group perceptions: Main and mediating effects. *Work and Stress, 17,* 158–169.

Johnson, D. E., Erez, A., Kiker, D. S., & Motowidlo, S. J. (2002). Liking and attributions of motives as mediators of the relationships between individuals' reputations, helpful behaviors, and raters' reward decisions. *Journal of Applied Psychology, 87*(4), 808–815.

Johnson, J. W. (2001). The relative importance of task and contextual performance dimensions to supervisor judgments of overall performance. *Journal of Applied Psychology, 86*(5), 984–996.

Jones, E. E., & Nisbett, R. E. (1972). The actor and the observer: Divergent perceptions of the causes of behavior. in E. E. Jones, D. E. Kanouse, H. H. Kelly, R. E. Nisbett, S. Valins, & B. Weiner (Eds.), *Attribution: Perceiving the causes of behavior* (pp. 79–94). Morristown, NJ: General Learning Press.

Jordan, M. H., Feild, H. S., & Armenakis, A. A. (2002). The relationship of group process variables and team performance: A team-level analysis in a field setting. *Small Group Research, 33,* 121–150.

Judge, T. A., Bono, J. E., & Locke, E. A. (2000). Personality and job satisfaction: The mediating role of job characteristics. *Journal of Applied Psychology, 85,* 237–249.

Judge, T. A., Thoresen, C. J., Bono, J. E., & Patton, G. K. (2001). The job satisfaction-job performance relationship: A qualitative and quantitative review. *Psychological Bulletin, 127*(3), 376–407.

Kamp, J. O., & Hough, L. M. (1988). Utility of temperament for predicting job performance. In L. M. Hough (Ed.), *Literature review: Utility of temperament, biodata, and interest assessment for predicting job performance* (ARI Research Note 88–02). Alexandria, VA: U.S. Army Research Institute for the Behavioral and Social Sciences.

Kanfer, R., Sawyer, J. Earley, P. & Lind, E. (1987). Fairness and participation in evaluation procedures: Effects on task attitudes and performance. *Social Justice Research, 1,* 235–249.

Kanter, R. M. (1968). Commitment and social organization: A study of commitment mechanisms in utopian communities. *American Sociological Review, 33,* 499–517.

Kaplan, A. (1964). *The conduct of inquiry: Methodology for behavioral science.* San Francisco: Chandler.

Kaplan, R. S., & D. P. Norton. (1996). The balanced scorecard: Translating strategy into action. Boston: Harvard Business School Press.

Karambayya, R. (1990). *Contexts for organizational citizenship behavior: Do high performing and satisfying units have better "citizens"?* Unpublished working paper, York University, Toronto, Ontario.

Katz, D. (1960). The functional approach to the study of attitudes. *Public Opinion Quarterly, 24,* 163–204.

Katz, D. (1964). The motivational basis of organizational behavior. *Behavioral Science, 9,* 131–146.

Katz, D., & Kahn, R. L. (1966). *The social psychology of organizations.* New York: Wiley.

Katz, D., & Kahn, R. L. (1978). *The social psychology of organizations* (2nd ed.). New York: Wiley.

Katzell, R. A., & Yankelovich, D. (1975). *Work, productivity, and job satisfaction.* New York: The Psychological Corporation.

Kelloway, K., Loughlin, C., Barling, J., & Nault, A.(2002). Counterproductive and organizational citizenship behaviours; separate but related constructs. *International Journal of Selection and Assessment, 10*(1–2), 143–151.

Kelly, R. & Caplan, J. (1993). How Bell Labs creates star performers. *Harvard Business Review, 128–139.*

Kerr, S., & Jermier, J. M. (1978). Substitutes for leadership: Their meaning and measurement. *Organizational Behavior and Human Performance, 22,* 375–403.

Kidwell, R. E., Jr., Mossholder, K. W., & Bennett, N. (1997). Cohesiveness and organizational citizenship behavior: A multilevel analysis using work groups and individuals. *Journal of Management, 23,* 775–793.

Kiker, D. S., & Motowidlo, S. J. (1999). Main and interaction effects of task and contextual performance on supervisory reward decisions. *Journal of Applied Psychology, 84*(4), 602–609.

Kirkman, B., & Rosen, B. (1997). A model of work team empowerment. In R. Woodman & W. Pasmore (Eds.), *Research in organizational change and development* (Vol. 10, pp. 131–167). Greenwich, CT: JAI Press.

Kirkman, B., & Rosen, B. (1999). Beyond self-management: Antecedents and consequences of team empowerment. *Academy of Management Journal, 42,* 58–74.

Kishor, N. (1995). The effect of implicit theories on raters' inference in performance judgement: Consequences for the validity of student ratings of instruction. *Research in Higher Education, 36*(2), 177–195.

Kizilos, M. A., & Cummings, T. G. (1996). *Employee involvement, prosocial organizational behavior, and organization performance.* Unpublished working paper, University of Alberta, Edmonton, Canada.

Koh, W. L., Steers, R. M., & Terborg, J. R. (1995). The effects of transformational leadership on teacher attitudes and student performance in Singapore. *Journal of Organizational Behavior, 16*(4), 319–333.

Konovsky, M. A., Elliot, J., & Pugh, S. D. (1995). *Citizenship behavior and its determinants in Mexico.* Paper presented at the meeting of the National Academy of Management, Vancouver, British Columbia, Canada.

Konovsky, M. A., & Organ, D. W. (1996). Dispositional and contextual determinants of organizational citizenship behavior. *Journal of Organizational Behavior, 17*(3), 253–266.

Konovsky, M. A., & Pugh, S. D. (1994). Citizenship behavior and social exchange. *Academy of Management Journal, 37*(3), 656–669.

Kornhauser, A. W., & Sharp, A. A. (1932). Employee attitudes: Suggestions from a study in a factory. *Personnel Journal, 10,* 393–404.

Koys, D. J. (2001). The effects of employee satisfaction, organizational citizenship behavior, and turnover on organizational effectiveness: A unit-level, longitudinal study. *Personnel Psychology, 54*(1), 101–114.

Krebs, D. L. (1970). Altruism: An examination of the concept and a review of the literature. *Psychological Bulletin, 73,* 258–302.

Krzystofiak, F., Cardy, R., & Newman, J. (1988). Implicit personality and performance appraisal: The influence of trait inferences on evaluations of behaviors. *Journal of Applied Psychology, 73,* 515–521.

Kuhnert, K. W., & Lewis, P. (1987). Transactional and transformational leadership: A constructive/developmental analysis. *Academy of Management Review, 12,* 648–657.

Lam, S. S., Hui, C., & Law, K. S. (1999). Organizational citizenship behavior: Comparing perspectives of supervisors and subordinates across four international samples. *Journal of Applied Psychology, 84*(4), 594–601.

Lambert, S. J. (2000). Added benefits: The link between work-life benefits and organizational citizenship behavior. *Academy of Management Journal, 43*, 801–815.

Landy, F. J., Barnes, J. L., & Murphy, K. R. (1978). Correlates of perceived fairness and accuracy of performance evaluation. *Journal of Applied Psychology, 63*, 751–754.

Landy, F. J., Barnes-Farell, J. L., & Cleveland, J. N. (1980). Perceived fairness and accuracy of performance evaluation: A follow-up. *Journal of Applied Psychology, 65*, 355–56.

Landy, F. J., & Becker, W. S. (1987). Motivation theory reconsidered. In L. L. Cummings and B. M. Staw (Eds.), *Research in organizational behavior* (Vol. 9, pp. 1–38). Greenwich, CT: JAI Press.

Landy, F. J., & Farr, J. L. (1980). Performance rating. *Psychological Bulletin, 87*, 72–107.

Langer, E. J. (1983). *The psychology of control.* Beverly Hills, CA: Sage.

Latham, G. P., & Skarlicki, D. P. (1995). Criterion-related validity of the situational and patterned behavior interviews with organizational citizenship behavior. *Human Performance, 8*(2), 67–80.

Lau, V. C. S, Au, W. T., & Ho, J. M. C. (2003). A qualitative and quantitative review of antecedents of counterproductive behavior in organizations. *Journal of Business & Psychology, 18*, 73–99.

Law, K., & Wong, C. S. (1999). Multidimensional constructs in structural equation analysis: An illustration using the job perception and job satisfaction constructs. *Journal of Management, 25*, 143–160.

Law, K. S., Wong, C. S., & Mobley, W. H. (1998). Toward a taxonomy of multidimensional constructs. *Academy of Management Review, 23*, 741–755.

Lawler, E. E., III, & Porter, L. W. (1967). Perceptions regarding management compensation. *Industrial Relations, 3*, 41–49.

Lee, C., Ashford, S. J., & Bobko, P. (1990). Interactive effects of "type A" behavior and perceived control on worker performance, job satisfaction, and somatic complaints. *Academy of Management Journal, 33*, 870–881.

Lefkowitz, J. (2000). The role of interpersonal affective regard in supervisory performance ratings: A literature review and proposed causal model. *Journal of Occupational and Organizational Psychology, 7*, 67–85.

LePine, J. A., Erez, A., & Johnson, D. E. (2002). The nature and dimensionality of organizational citizenship behavior: A critical review and meta-analysis. *Journal of Applied Psychology, 87*, 52–65.

LePine, J. A., & Van Dyne, L. (1998). Predicting voice behavior in work groups. *Journal of Applied Psychology, 83*, 853–868.

Lepper, M., & Greene, D. (1976). On understanding "overjustification": A reply to Reiss and Sushinsky. *Journal of Personality and Social Psychology, 33*, 25–35.

Lepper, M., & Greene, D. (1978). *The hidden costs of reward.* Hillsdale, NJ: Lawrence Erlbaum.

Lerner, M. J. (1980). *The belief in a just world: A fundamental delusion.* New York: Plenum Press.

Leventhal, G. S. (1980). What should be done with equity theory? New approaches to the study of fairness in social relationships. In K. G. Gergen, M. S. Greenberg, & R. H. Willis (Eds.), *Social exchange: Advances in theory and research* (pp. 27–55). New York: Plenum Press.

Liden, R. C., & Graen, G. (1980). Generalizability of the vertical dyad linkage model of leadership. *Academy of Management Journal, 23*, 451–465.

Liden, R. C., Wayne, S. J., Kraimer, M. L., & Sparrowe, R. (2003). The dual commitments of contingent workers: An examination of contingents' commitment to the agency and the organization. *Journal of Organizational Behavior, 24*, 609–625.

Liden, R. C., Wayne, S. J., & Sparrowe, R. T. (2000). An examination of the mediating role of psychological empowerment on the relations between the job, interpersonal relationships, and work outcomes. *Journal of Applied Psychology, 85*(3), 407–416.

Lin, P., & Humphreys, L. G. (1977). Predictions of academic performance in graduate and professional schools. *Applied Psychological Measurement, 1,* 249–257.

Lott, A. J., & Lott, B. E. (1974). The role of reward in the formation of positive interpersonal attitudes. In T. L. Huston (Ed.), *Foundations of interpersonal attraction* (pp. 171–189). New York: Academic Press.

Lovell, S. E., Kahn, A. S., Anton, J., Davidson, A., Dowling, E., Post, D., & Mason, C. (1999). Does gender affect the link between organizational citizenship behavior and performance evaluations? *Sex Roles, 41,* 469–478.

Lowery, C. M., & Krilowicz, T. J. (1994). Relationships among nontask behaviors, rated performance, and objective performance measures. *Psychological Reports, 74,* 571–578.

Lowin, A., & Craig, J. R. (1968). The influence of level of performance on managerial style: An experimental object lesson in the ambiguity of correlational data. *Organizational Behavior and Human Performance, 3,* 440–458.

Mabe, P. A., & West, S. G. (1982). Validity of self-evaluation of ability: A review and meta-analysis. *Journal of Applied Psychology, 67,* 280–296.

Macaulay, J. (1970). A skill for charity. In J. Macaulay & L. Berkowitz (Eds.), *Altruism and helping behavior: Social psychological studies of some antecedents and consequences.* New York: Academic Press.

MacCallum, R. C., & Browne, M. W. (1993). The use of causal indicators in covariance structure models: Some practical issues. *Psychological Bulletin, 114,* 533–541.

MacKenzie, S. B., Podsakoff, P. M., & Ahearne, M. (1996). *Effects of OCB on sales team effectiveness.* Unpublished data analysis, Indiana University School of Business, Bloomington.

MacKenzie, S. B., Podsakoff, P. M., & Fetter, R. (1991). Organizational citizenship behavior and objective productivity as determinants of managerial evaluations of salespersons' performance. *Organizational Behavior and Human Decision Processes, 50*(1), 123–150.

MacKenzie, S. B., Podsakoff, P. M., & Fetter, R. (1993). The impact of organizational citizenship behavior on evaluations of salesperson performance. *Journal of Marketing, 57*(1), 70–80.

MacKenzie, S. B., Podsakoff, P. M., & Jarvis, C. (in press). The problem of measurement model misspecification in behavioral and organizational research and some recommended solutions. *Journal of Applied Psychology.*

MacKenzie, S. B., Podsakoff, P. M., & Paine, J. B. (1999). Do citizenship behaviors matter more for managers than for salespeople? *Journal of the Academy of Marketing Science, 27*(4), 396–410.

MacKenzie, S. B., Podsakoff, P. M., & Rich, G. A. (2001). Transformational and transactional leadership and salesperson performance. *Journal of the Academy of Marketing Science, 29*(2), 115–134.

Macneil, I. R. (1985). Relational contracts: What we do and do not know. *Wisconsin Law Review,* 483–525.

Many companies now base workers' raises on their productivity. (1985, November 15). *Wall Street Journal,* p. 1.

Martinko, M. J., Gundlach, M. J., & Douglas, S. C. (2002). Toward an integrative theory of counterproductive workplace behavior: A causal reasoning perspective. *International Journal of Selection and Assessment, 10,* 36–50.

Massie, J. L. (1965). Management theory. In J. G. March (Ed.), *Handbook of organizations.* Chicago: Rand-McNally.

Masterson, S. S., Lewis, K., Goldman, B. M., & Taylor, M. S. (2000). Integrating justice and social exchange: The differing effects of fair procedures and treatment on work relationships. *Academy of Management Journal, 43,* 738–748.

Mayfield, E. C. (1964). The selection interview: A reevaluation of published research. *Personnel Psychology, 17,* 239–260.

McCrae, R. R., & Costa, P. T., Jr. (1987). Validation of the five-factor model of personality across instruments and observers. *Journal of Personality and Social Psychology, 52,* 81–90.

McManus, S. E., & Russell, J. E. A. (1997). New directions in mentoring research: An examination of related constructs. *Journal of Vocational Behavior, 51,* 145–161.

Miles, D. E., Borman, W. E., Spector, P. E., & Fox, S. (2002). Building an integrative model of extra role work behaviors: A comparison of counterproductive work behavior with organizational citizenship behavior. *International Journal of Selection and Assessment, 10*(1–2), 51–57.

Mischel, W. (1973). Toward a cognitive social learning reconceptualization of personality. *Psychological Review, 80,* 252–283.

Mischel, W. (1977). The interaction of person and situation. In D. Magnusson & N. S. Endler (Eds.), *Personality at the crossroads: Current issues in interactional psychology.* Hillsdale, NJ: Lawrence Erlbaum.

Monson, T. C., Hesley, J. W., & Chernick, L. (1982). Specifying when personality traits can and cannot predict behavior: An alternative to abandoning the attempt to predict single act criteria. *Journal of Personality and Social Psychology, 32,* 385–399.

Moorman, R. H. (1991). Relationship between organizational justice and organizational citizenship behaviors: Do fairness perceptions influence employee citizenship? *Journal of Applied Psychology, 76,* 845–855.

Moorman, R. H. (1993). The influence of cognitive and affective based job-satisfaction measures on the relationship between satisfaction and organizational citizenship behavior. *Human Relations, 46*(6), 759–776.

Moorman, R. H., & Blakely, G. L. (1995). Individualism-collectivism as an individual difference predictor of organizational citizenship behavior. *Journal of Organizational Behavior, 16*(2), 127–142.

Moorman, R. H., Blakely, G. L., & Niehoff, B. P. (1998). Does perceived organizational support mediate the relationship between procedural justice and organizational citizenship behavior? *Academy of Management Journal, 41*(3), 351–357.

Moorman, R. H, Niehoff, B. P., & Organ, D. W. (1993). Treating employees fairly and organizational citizenship behavior: Sorting the effects of job satisfaction, organizational commitment, and procedural justice. *Employee Responsibilities and Rights Journal, 6,* 209–225.

Morrison, E. W. (1994). Role definitions and organizational citizenship behavior: The importance of the employee's perspective. *Academy of Management Journal, 37*(6), 1543–1567.

Morrison, E. W., & Phelps, C. C. (1999). Taking charge at work: Extrarole efforts to initiate workplace change. *Academy of Management Journal, 42*(4), 403–419.

Motowidlo, S. J. (2000). Some basic issues related to contextual performance and organizational citizenship behavior in human behavior. *Human Resource Management Review, 10,* 115–126.

Motowidlo, S. J., & Van Scotter, J. R. (1994). Evidence that task-performance should be distinguished from contextual performance. *Journal of Applied Psychology, 79*(4), 475–480.

Mount, M. K., Barrick, M. R., & Strauss, J. P. (1994). Validity of observer ratings of the big five personality factors. *Journal of Applied Psychology, 79,* 272–280.

Murphy, K., & DeShon, R. (2000). Inter-rater correlations do not estimate the reliability of job performance ratings. *Personnel Psychology, 53,* 873–900.

Murphy, K. R., & Shiarella, A. H. (1997). Implications of the multidimensional nature of job performance for the validity of selection tests: Multivariate frameworks for studying test validity. *Personnel Psychology, 50*(4), 823–854.

Napier, B. J., & Ferris, G. R. (1993). Distance in organizations. *Human Resource Management Review, 3,* 321–357.

Narver, J. C. & Slater, S. F. (1990). The effect of a market orientation on business profitability. *Journal of Marketing, 54*(4), 20–34.

Near, J. P., & Miceli, M. P. (1987). Whistle-blowers in organizations: Dissidents or reformers? In L. L. Cummings & B. M. Staw (Eds.), *Research in organizational behavior* (Vol. 9, pp. 321–368). Greenwich, CT: JAI Press.

Nemeth, C. J., & Staw, B. M. (1989). The tradeoffs of social control and innovation within groups and organizations. In L. Berkowitz (Ed.), *Advances in experimental social psychology* (Vol. 22, pp. 175–210). New York: Academic Press.

Niehoff, B. P., & Moorman, R. H. (1993). Justice as a mediator of the relationship between methods of monitoring and organizational citizenship behavior. *Academy of Management Journal, 36*(3), 527–556.

Nisbett, R., & Ross, L. (1980). *Human inference: Strategies and shortcomings of social judgment.* Englewood Cliffs, NJ: Prentice Hall.

Nunnally, J. C. (1978). *Psychometric theory* (2nd ed.). New York: McGraw-Hill.

Nunnally, J. C., & Bernstein, I. H. (1994). *Psychometric theory* (3rd ed.). New York: McGraw-Hill.

O'Bannon, D. P., & Pearce, C. L. (1999). An exploratory examination of gainsharing in service organizations: Implications for organizational citizenship behavior and pay satisfaction. *Journal of Management Issues, 11,* 363–378.

Organ, D. W. (1977). A reappraisal and reinterpretation of the satisfaction-causes-performance hypothesis. *Academy of Management Review, 2,* 46–53.

Organ, D. W. (1988). *Organizational citizenship behavior: The good soldier syndrome.* Lexington, MA: Lexington Books.

Organ, D. W. (1990a). Fairness, productivity, and organizational citizenship behavior: Tradeoffs in student and manager pay decisions. Paper presented at the meeting of the Academy of Management meetings, San Francisco.

Organ, D. W. (1990b). The motivational basis of organizational citizenship behavior. In B. M. Staw and L. L. Cummings (Eds.), *Research in organizational behavior* (Vol. 12, pp. 43–72). Greenwich, CT: JAI Press.

Organ, D. W. (1990c). The subtle significance of job satisfaction. *Clinical Laboratory Management Review, 4,* 94–98.

Organ, D. W. (1997a). Organizational citizenship behavior: It's construct clean-up time. *Human Performance, 10*(2), 85–97.

Organ, D. W. (1997b). Toward an explication of "morale": In search of the *m* factor. In C. I. Cooper & S. E. Jackson (Eds.), *Creating tomorrow's organizations* (pp. 493–503). London: John Wiley & Sons.

Organ, D. W., & Konovsky, M. (1989). Cognitive versus affective determinants of organizational citizenship behavior. *Journal of Applied Psychology, 74*(1), 157–164.

Organ, D. W., & McFall, J. B. (2004). Personality and citizenship behavior in organizations. In B. Schneider & D. B. Smith (Eds.), *Personality and organizations* (pp. 291–316). Mahwah, NJ: Lawrence Erlbaum.

Organ, D. W., & Paine, J. B. (1999). "A new kind of performance" for industrial and organizational psychology: Recent contributions to the study of organizational citizenship behavior. *International Review of Industrial and Organizational Psychology, 14,* 337–368.

Organ, D. W., & Ryan, K. (1995). A meta-analytic review of attitudinal and dispositional predictors of organizational citizenship behavior. *Personnel Psychology, 48*(4), 775–802.

Orr, J. M., Sackett, P. R., & Mercer, M. (1989). The role of prescribed and nonprescribed behaviors in estimating the dollar value of performance. *Journal of Applied Psychology, 74,* 34–40.

Osborn, S. M., Hubert, S. F., & Veres, J. G. (1998). Introversion-extraversion, self-monitoring, and applicant performance in a situational panel interview: A field study. *Journal of Business and Psychology, 13,* 143–156.

Ouchi, W. G. (1980). Markets, bureaucracies, and clans. *Administrative Science Quarterly, 25,* 129–141.

Paine, J. B., & Organ, D. W. (2000). The cultural matrix of organizational citizenship behavior: Some preliminary conceptual and empirical observances. *Human Resource Management Review, 10*(1), 45–59.

Park, O. S. (1986). *Beyond cognition in leadership: Prosocial behavior and affect in managerial judgment.* Unpublished doctoral dissertation, Pennsylvania State University, State College.

Pearce, J. L., & Gregersen, H. B. (1991). Task interdependence and extra-role behavior: A test of the mediating effects of felt responsibility. *Journal of Applied Psychology, 76,* 838–844.

Peters, L. H., & O'Connor, E. J. (1980). Situational constraints and work outcomes: The influences of a frequently overlooked construct. *Academy of Management Review, 5,* 391–397.

Pfeffer, J., & Langton, N. (1993). The effect of wage dispersion on satisfaction, productivity, and working collaboratively: Evidence from college and university faculty. *Administrative Science Quarterly, 38,* 382–407.

Pillai, R., Schriesheim, C. A., & Williams, E. S. (1999). Fairness perceptions and trust as mediators for transformational and transactional leadership: A two-sample study. *Journal of Management, 25*(6), 897–933.

Podsakoff, P. M., Ahearne, M., & MacKenzie, S. B. (1997). Organizational citizenship behavior and the quantity and quality of work group performance. *Journal of Applied Psychology, 82*(2), 262–270.

Podsakoff, P. M., Bommer, W. H., Podsakoff, N. P., & MacKenzie, S. B. (2004). *Relationships between leader reward and punishment behavior and subordinate attitudes, perceptions and behaviors: A meta-analytic review of existing and new research.* Unpublished working paper, Indiana University, Bloomington.

Podsakoff, P. M., & MacKenzie, S. B. (1993). Citizenship behavior and fairness in organizations: Issues and directions for future research. *Employee Responsibilities and Rights Journal, 6,* 257–269.

Podsakoff, P. M., & MacKenzie, S. B. (1994). Organizational citizenship behaviors and sales unit effectiveness. *Journal of Marketing Research, 31,* 351–363.

Podsakoff, P. M., & MacKenzie, S. B. (1997). Impact of organizational citizenship behavior on organizational performance: A review and suggestions for future research. *Human Performance, 10*(2), 133–151.

Podsakoff, P. M., MacKenzie, S. B., & Bommer, W. H. (1996a). A meta-analysis of the relationships between Kerr and Jermier's substitutes for leadership and employee job attitudes, role perceptions, and performance. *Journal of Applied Psychology, 81,* 380–399.

Podsakoff, P. M., MacKenzie, S. B., & Bommer, W. H. (1996b). Transformational leader behaviors and substitutes for leadership as determinants of employee satisfaction, commitment, trust, and Organizational Citizenship Behaviors. *Journal of Management, 22,* 259–298.

Podsakoff, P. M., MacKenzie, S. B., & Fetter, R. (1993). Substitutes for leadership and the management of professionals. *Leadership Quarterly, 4,* 1–44.

Podsakoff, P. M., MacKenzie, S. B., & Hui, C. (1993). Organizational citizenship behaviors and managerial evaluations of employee performance: A review and suggestions for future research. In G. R. Ferris & K. M. Rowland (Eds.), *Research in personnel and human resources management* (Vol. 11, pp. 1–40). Greenwich, CT: JAI Press.

Podsakoff, P. M., MacKenzie, S. B., Lee, J. Y., & Podsakoff, N. P. (2003). Common method biases in behavioral research: A critical review of the literature and recommended remedies. *Journal of Applied Psychology, 88,* 879–903.

Podsakoff, P. M., MacKenzie, S. B., Moorman, R. H., & Fetter, R. (1990). Transformational leader behaviors and their effects on followers' trust in leader, satisfaction, and organizational citizenship behaviors. *Leadership Quarterly, 1,* 107–142.

Podsakoff, P. M., MacKenzie, S. B., Paine, J. B., & Bachrach, D. G. (2000). Organizational citizenship behaviors: A critical review of the theoretical and empirical literature and suggestions for future research. *Journal of Management, 26*(3), 513–563.

Podsakoff, P. M., Niehoff, B. P., MacKenzie, S. B., & Williams, M. L. (1993). Do substitutes for leadership really substitute for leadership? An empirical examination of Kerr and Jermier's situational leadership model. *Organizational Behavior and Human Decision Processes, 54,* 1–44.

Podsakoff, P. M., & Organ, D. W. (1986). Self-reports in organizational research: Problems and prospects. *Journal of Management, 12,* 69–82.

Pond, S. B., Nacoste, R. W., Mohr, M. F., & Rodriguez, C. M. (1997). The measurement of organizational citizenship behavior: Are we assuming too much? *Journal of Applied Social Psychology, 27*(17), 1527–1544.

Puffer, S. M. (1987). Prosocial behavior, noncompliant behavior, and work performance among commission salespeople. *Journal of Applied Psychology, 72,* 615–621.

Pulakos, E. D., Borman, W. C., & Hough, L. M. (1988). Test validation for scientific understanding: Two demonstrations of an approach to studying predictor-criterion linkages. *Personnel Psychology, 41,* 703–716.

Quine, W. V. (1953). *From a logical point of view.* Cambridge, MA: Harvard University Press.

Randall, M. L., Cropanzano, R., Borman, C. A., & Birjulin, A. (1999). Organizational politics and organizational support as predictors of work attitudes, job performance, and organizational citizenship behavior. *Journal of Organizational Behavior, 20,* 159–174.

Rhoades, L., & Eisenberger, R. (2002). Perceived organizational support: A review of the literature. *Journal of Applied Psychology, 87*(4), 698–714.

Rioux, S. M., & Penner, L. A. (2001). The causes of organizational citizenship behavior: A motivational analysis. *Journal of Applied Psychology, 86*(6), 1306–1314.

Roethlisberger, F. J., & Dickson, W. J. (1939). *Management and the worker.* Cambridge, MA: Harvard University Press.

Rosenfield, D., Folger, R. & Adelman, H. F. (1980). When rewards reflect competence: A qualification of the overjustification effect. *Journal of Personality and Social Psychology, 39,* 368–376.

Rotundo, M., & Sackett, P. R. (2002). The relative importance of task, citizenship, and counterproductive performance to global ratings of job performance: A policy-capturing approach. *Journal of Applied Psychology, 87*(1), 66–80.

Rousseau, D. M. (2001). The idiosyncratic deal: Flexibility versus fairness? *Organizational Dynamics, 29,* 260–273.

Rousseau, D. M., & Parks, J. M. (1993). The contracts of individuals and organizations. In L. L. Cummings & B. M. Staw (Eds.), *Research in organizational behavior* (Vol. 15, pp. 1–43). Greenwich, CT: JAI Press.

Rowley, H. H. (1962). How to read the Bible with understanding: The diversity and unity of the scriptures. In H. G. May & B. M. Metzger (Eds.), *The Oxford annotated Bible: Revised standard version* (pp. 1513–1516). New York: Oxford University Press.

Rupp, D. E., & Cropanzano, R. (2002). The mediating effects of social exchange relationships in predicting workplace outcomes from multifoci organizational justice. *Organizational Behavior and Human Decision Processes, 89,* 925–946.

Sackett, P. R. (2002). The structure of counterproductive work behaviors: Dimensionality and relationships with facets of job performance. *International Journal of Selection and Assessment, 10*(1–2), 5–11.

Sashkin, M. (1988). The visionary leader. In J. A. Conger & R. A. Kanugo (Eds.), *Charismatic leadership: The elusive factor in organizational effectiveness* (pp. 122–160). San Francisco: Jossey-Bass.

Schmitt, N. (1976). Social and situational determinants of interview decisions: implications for the employment interview. *Personnel Psychology, 29,* 79–101.

Schnake, M. (1991). Organizational citizenship: A review, proposed model, and research agenda. *Human Relations, 44,* 735–759.

Schnake, M., Cochran, D. S., & Dumler, M. P. (1995). Encouraging organizational citizenship: The effects of job satisfaction, perceived equity and leadership. *Journal of Managerial Issues, 7,* 209–221.

Schnake, M., Dumler, M. P., & Cochran, D. S. (1993). The relationship between traditional leadership, super leadership, and organizational citizenship behavior. *Group and Organization Management, 18*(3), 352–365.

Schneider, B. (1987). The people make the place. *Personnel Psychology, 40,* 437–454.

Schneider, B., Smith, D. B., Taylor, S., & Fleenor, J. (1998). Personality and organizations: A test of the homogeneity of personality hypothesis. *Journal of Applied Psychology, 83,* 464–470.

Schuster, M. (1983). Forty years of Scanlon plan research: A review of the descriptive and empirical literature. In C. Crouch & F. A. Heller (Eds.), *Organizational democracy and political processes* (Vol. 1, pp. 53–71). New York: Wiley.

Schwab, D. P. (1980). Construct validity in organizational behavior. In B. M Staw & L. L. Cummings (Eds.), *Research in organizational behavior* (Vol. 2, pp. 3–43). Greenwich, CT: JAI Press.

Schwartz, S. H. (1990). Individualism-collectivism: Critique and proposed refinements. *Journal of Cross-Cultural Psychology, 21,* 139–157

Seers, A. (1989). Team-member exchange quality: A new construct for role-making research. *Organizational Behavior and Human Decision Processes, 43,* 118–135.

Seiss, T. F., & Jackson, D. N. (1970). Vocational interests and personality: An empirical integration. *Journal of Counseling Psychology, 17,* 27–35.

Seligman, M. E. P. (1975). *Helplessness: On depression, development and death.* San Francisco: Freeman.

Seltzer, J., & Bass, B. M. (1990). Transformational leadership: Beyond initiation and consideration. *Journal of Management, 16,* 693–703.

Settoon, R. P., Bennett, N., & Liden, R. C. (1996). Social exchange in organizations: Perceived organizational support, leader-member exchange, and employee reciprocity. *Journal of Applied Psychology, 81,* 219–227.

Shaw, M. E. (1981). *Group dynamics: The psychology of small group behavior.* New York: McGraw-Hill.

Shore, L. M., Barksdale, K., & Shore, T. H. (1995). Managerial perceptions of employee commitment to the organization. *Academy of Management Journal, 38*(6), 1593–1615.

Sims, H. P., Szilagyi, A. D. (1976). Job characteristic relationships: Individual and structural moderators. *Organizational Behavior and Human Performance, 17,* 211–30.

Smith, C. A., Organ, D. W., & Near, J. P. (1983). Organizational citizenship behavior: Its nature and antecedents. *Journal of Applied Psychology, 68,* 653–663.

Snyder, M., & Cantor, N. (1980). Thinking about ourselves and others: Self-monitoring and social knowledge. *Journal of Personality and Social Psychology, 39,* 222–234.

Spector, P. E., & Fox, S. (2002). An emotion-centered model of voluntary work behavior: Some parallels between counterproductive work behavior and organizational citizenship behavior. *Human Resource Management Review, 12,* 269–292.

Spiro, R. L., Stanton, W. J. & Rich, G. A. (2002). *Management of a sales force.* Chicago: McGraw-Hill/Irwin.

Spreitzer, G. M. (1995). Psychological empowerment in the workplace: Dimensions, measurement, and validation. *Academy of Management Journal, 38*(5), 1442–1465.

Staw, B. M. (1975). Attribution of the "causes" of performance: A general alternative interpretation of cross-sectional research on organizations. *Organizational Behavior and Human Decision Processes, 13*(3), 414–432.

Staw, B. M., Bell, N. E., & Clausen, J. A. (1986). The dispositional approach to job attitudes. *Administrative Science Quarterly, 31,* 56–77.

St. Clair, L., & Quinn, R. E. (1997). Progress without precision: The value of ambiguity as a tool for learning about organizational phenomena. In W. A. Pasmore & R. W. Woodman (Eds.), *Research in organizational change and development* (Vol. 10, pp. 105–129). Greenwich, CT: JAI Press.

Steel, R. P., & Rentsch, J. R. (1997). The dispositional model of job attitudes revisited: Findings of a ten-year study. *Journal of Applied Psychology, 82,* 873–879.

Tansky, J. W. (1993). Justice and organizational citizenship behavior: What is the relationship? *Employees Responsibilities and Rights Journal, 6,* 195–207.

Taylor, S. E., & Crocker, J. (1981). Schematic bases of social information processing. In E. T. Higgins, C. P. Herman, & M. P. Zanna (Eds.), *Social cognition: The Ontario symposium.* (Vol. 1, pp. 89–134). Hillsdale, NJ: Lawrence Erlbaum.

Tedeschi, J. T., & Lindskold, S. (1976). *Social psychology.* New York: Wiley.

Tepper, B. J., Duffy, M. K., Hoobler, J., & Ensley, M. D. (2004). Moderators of the relationship between coworkers' organizational citizenship behavior and fellow employees' attitudes. *Journal of Applied Psychology, 89,* 455–465.

Tepper, B. J., & Taylor, E. C. (2003). Relationships among supervisors' and subordinates' procedural justice perceptions and organizational citizenship behaviors. *Academy of Management Journal, 46,* 97–105.

Thompson, J. D. (1967). *Organizations in action.* New York: McGraw-Hill.

Thornton, G. C. (1980). Psychological properties of self-appraisals of job performance. *Personnel Psychology, 33,* 267–271.

Trice, H. M., & Beyer, J. M. (1986). Charisma and its routinization in two social movement organizations. In B. M. Staw & L. L. Cummings (Eds.), *Research in organizational behavior* (Vol. 8, pp. 113–164). Greenwich, CT: JAI Press.

Turner A. N., & Lawrence, P. R. (1965). *Industrial jobs and the worker,* Boston: Harvard Graduate School of Business Administration.

Turnipseed, D. (2002). Are good soldiers good? Exploring the link between organization citizenship behavior and personal ethics. *Journal of Business Research, 55*(1), 1–15.

Turnipseed, D., & Murkison, G. (2000). Good soldiers and their syndrome: Organizational citizenship behavior and the work environment. *North American Journal of Psychology, 2,* 281–302.

Turnley, W. H., Bolino, M. C., Lester, S. W., & Bloodgood, J. M. (2003). The impact of psychological contract fulfillment on the performance of in-role and organizational citizenship behaviors. *Journal of Management, 29,* 187–206.

Uhl-Bien, M., & Maslyn, J. M. (2003). Reciprocity in manager-subordinate relationships: Components, configurations, and outcomes. *Journal of Management, 29*(4), 511–532.

Ulrich, L., & Trumbo, D. (1965). The selection interview since 1949. *Psychological Bulletin, 63,* 100–116.

Van der Vegt, G. S., Van de Vliert, E. & Oosterhof, A. (2003). Informational dissimilarity and organizational citizenship behavior: The role of interteam interdependence and team identification. *Academy of Management Journal, 46,* 715–727.

Van Dyne, L., Cummings, L. L., & McLean-Parks, J. M. (1995). Extra-role behaviors: In pursuit of construct and definitional clarity (a bridge over muddied waters). In L. L. Cummings & B. M. Staw (Eds.), *Research in organizational behavior* (Vol. 17, pp. 215–285). Greenwich, CT: JAI Press.

Van Dyne, L., Graham, J. W., & Dienesch, R. M. (1994). Organizational citizenship behavior: Construct redefinition, measurement and validation. *Academy of Management Journal, 37,* 765–802.

Van Dyne, L., & LePine, J. A. (1998). Helping and voice extra-role behaviors: Evidence of construct and predictive validity. *Academy of Management Journal, 41*(1), 108–119.

Van Scotter, J. R. (1994). *Evidence for the usefulness of task performance, job dedication, and interpersonal facilitation as components of performance.* Unpublished doctoral dissertation, University of Florida, Gainesville.

Van Scotter, J. R. (2000). Relationships of task performance with turnover, job satisfaction, and affective commitment. *Human Resource Management Review, 10*(1), 79–95.

Van Scotter, J. R., & Motowidlo, S. J. (1996). Interpersonal facilitation and job dedication as separate facets of contextual performance. *Journal of Applied Psychology, 81,* 525–531.

Van Scotter, J. R., Motowidlo, S. J., & Cross, T. C. (2000). Effects of task performance and contextual performance on systemic rewards. *Journal of Applied Psychology, 85*(4), 526–535.

Verba, S., & Nie, N. H. (1972). *Participation in America: Social equality and political democracy.* New York: Harper & Row.

Vroom, V. H. (1964). *Work and motivation.* New York: Wiley.

Wagner, R. (1949). The employment interview: A critical summary. *Personnel Psychology, 2,* 17–46.

Walz, S. M., & Niehoff, B. P. (2000). Organizational citizenship behaviors: Their relationship to organizational effectiveness. *Journal of Hospitality and Tourism Research, 24,* 301–319.

Watson, D., & Tellegen, A. (1985). Toward a consensual structure of mood. *Psychological Bulletin, 98,* 219–235.

Wayne, S. J., & Green, S. A. (1993). The effects of leader-member exchange on employee citizenship and impression management behavior. *Human Relations, 46,* 1431–1440.

Wayne, S. J., Shore, L. M., Bommer, W. H., & Tetrick, L. E. (2002). The role of fair treatment and rewards in perceptions of organizational support and leader-member exchange. *Journal of Applied Psychology, 87*(3), 590–598.

Wayne, S. J., Shore, L. M., & Liden, R. C. (1997). Perceived organizational support and leader-member exchange: A social exchange perspective. *Academy of Management Journal, 40,* 82–111.

Weiss, H. M., & Adler, S. (1990). Personality and organizational behavior. In B. M. Staw & L. L. Cummings (Eds.), *Personality and organizational influence* (pp. 1–50). Greenwich, CT: JAI Press.

Werner, J. M. (1994). Dimensions that make a difference: Examining the impact of in-role and extrarole behaviors on supervisory ratings. *Journal of Applied Psychology, 79*(1), 98–107.

Werner, J. M. (2000). Implications of OCB and contextual performance for human resource management. *Human Resource Management Review, 10*(1), 3–24.

Whithey, M. J., & Cooper, W. H. (1989). Predicting exit, voice, loyalty and neglect. *Administrative Science Quarterly, 34,* 521–539.

Williams, L. J. (1988). *Affective and nonaffective components of job satisfaction and organizational commitment as determinants of organizational citizenship and in-role behaviors.* Unpublished doctoral dissertation, Indiana University, Bloomington.

Williams, L. J., & Anderson, S. E. (1991). Job satisfaction and organizational commitment as predictors of organizational citizenship and in-role behaviors. *Journal of Management, 17,* 601–617.

Williams, L. J., & Brown, B. K. (1994). Method variance in organizational behavior and human resources research: Effects on correlations, path coefficients, and hypothesis testing. *Organizational Behavior and Human Decision Processes, 57,* 185–209.

Williamson, O. E. (1975). *Markets and hierarchies.* New York: Free Press.

Witt, L. A. (1991). Exchange ideology as a moderator of job attitudes: Organizational citizenship behavior relationships. *Journal of Applied Social Psychology, 21,* 1490–1501.

Wright, O. R. (1969). Summary of research on the selection interview since 1964. *Personnel Psychology, 22,* 391–413.

Wright, P. M., George, J. M., Farnsworth, S. R., & McMahan, G. C. (1993). Productivity and extrarole behavior: The effects of goals and incentives on spontaneous helping. *Journal of Applied Psychology, 78,* 374–381.

Yang, K. S. (1993). Chinese social orientation: An integrative analysis. In L. Y. Cheng, F. M. C. Cheung, and Char-Nie Chen (Eds.), *Psychotherapy for Chinese: Selected papers from the first international conference* (pp. 19–56). Hong Kong: Chinese University of Hong Kong.

Zedeck, S., Tziner, A., & Middlestadt, S. E. (1983). An individual analysis approach. *Personnel Psychology, 36,* 355–370.

Index

About the Authors

Dennis W. Organ (PhD, University of North Carolina) is Professor of Management at the Kelley School of Business, Indiana University. He is a Fellow of the American Psychological Association and the Society for Industrial and Organizational Psychology. He has taught organizational behavior at the undergraduate, MBA, doctoral, and executive education levels at Indiana as well as during a Visiting Professor appointment at the Babcock Graduate School of Management at Wake Forest University. Previous books include four editions of a textbook, *Organizational Behavior: An Applied Psychological Approach;* four editions of a companion edited book of readings, *The Applied Psychology of Work Behavior;* and a monograph, *Organizational Citizenship: The Good Soldier Syndrome.* He served as Editor of *Business Horizons* from 1994 to 2004. Since 1988, he has authored or coauthored more than 20 journal articles and book chapters on the topic of organizational citizenship behavior. Organ lives in Bloomington, Indiana, where he enjoys bicycling, softball, photography, ballroom dancing, and monitoring the performance of the Atlanta Braves.

Philip M. Podsakoff (DBA, Indiana University) is Professor of Organizational Behavior and Human Resource Management, and holder of the John F. Mee Chair of Management at the Kelley School of Business at Indiana University. He received his doctoral degree in 1980 from Indiana University and joined the faculty of the School of Business in 1982, after teaching for two years on the faculty at Ohio State University. He is a member of the Society of Industrial/Organizational Psychologists and the National Academy of Management, and he is a past Chair of the Academy Research Methods Group. He is the author of more than 70 articles that have appeared in a variety of journals, including the *Journal of Applied Psychology, Psychological Bulletin, Organizational Behavior and Human Decision Processes, Personnel Administrator, Personnel Psychology, Research in Organizational Behavior, Research in Personnel and Human Resources Management, Academy of*

Management Journal, Journal of Management, Journal of Marketing Research, Journal of Marketing, and *Leadership Quarterly.* More than 20 of the articles he has published relate to some aspect of organizational citizenship behavior. Professor Podsakoff, a former recipient of the William A. Owens Scholarly Achievement Award sponsored by the Society for Industrial and Organizational Psychology, currently serves as an Associate Editor of the *Journal of Applied Psychology* and is on the editorial boards of *Leadership Quarterly* and *Organizational Behavior and Human Decision Processes.* He lives with his wife, Vernie, in Bloomington, Indiana.

Scott B. MacKenzie (PhD, UCLA) is the Neal Gilliatt Chair and Professor of Marketing at the Kelley School of Business at Indiana University. He is the author or coauthor of more than 50 articles on organizational citizenship behavior, leadership, advertising, and research methodology that have appeared in *Journal of Applied Psychology, Organizational Behavior and Human Decision Processes, Personnel Psychology, Journal of Management, Leadership Quarterly, Journal of Marketing Research, Journal of Marketing, Journal of Consumer Research,* and *Journal of the Academy of Marketing Science.* He is a member of the American Marketing Association, the Association for Consumer Research, and the Society for Consumer Psychology. Dr. MacKenzie is a former winner of the Harold H. Maynard Award sponsored by the *Journal of Marketing* and the William A. Owens Scholarly Achievement Award sponsored by the Society for Industrial and Organizational Psychology. He has served on the editorial boards of the *Journal of Marketing Research, Journal of Marketing, Journal of Consumer Research, International Journal of Research in Marketing, Journal of the Academy of Marketing Science,* and *Journal of Consumer Psychology.* He lives with his wife, Jane, and their five children in Bloomington, Indiana.